Game Play

Game Play

Therapeutic Use of Childhood Games

Second Edition

Edited by

Charles Schaefer

and

Steven E. Reid

John Wiley & Sons, Inc.

New York • Chichester • Weinheim • Brisbane • Singapore • Toronto

Library of Congress Cataloging-in-Publication Data:

Game play : therapeutic use of childhood games / edited by Charles Schaefer and Steven E. Reid.—2nd ed.
    p.   cm.
    Includes bibliographical references and index.
    ISBN 0-471-36256-5 (cloth : alk. paper)
    1. Play therapy. 2. Child psychotherapy. 3. Games—Therapeutic use. I. Schaefer, Charles E. II. Reid, Steven E.
    RJ505.P6 G36 2001
    618.92′891653—dc21

                                                          00-042293

Printed in the United States of America.

10 9 8 7 6 5 4 3 2 1

Contributors

Jill C. Archer, MSW
Social Worker
Tucson, Arizona

April K. Bay-Hinitz, PhD
Clinical Psychologist
Reno, Nevada

Irving N. Berlin, MD
Medical Director
Villa Santa Maria Residential
    Treatment Center
Albuquerque, New Mexico

James N. Bow, PhD
Director of Psychology
Hawthorn Center
Northville, Michigan

Rebecca Bridges, PhD

Harold F. Burks, PhD
Writer and Lecturer in Clinical
    Psychology
Big Bear Lake, California

Bethany E. Casarjian, PhD
Psychology Fellow
The Children's Village
Dobbs Ferry, New York

Billie F. Corder, PhD
Codirector, Psychological Services
Child Psychiatry Training Program
Dorothea Dix Hospital
Raleigh, North Carolina

Elyce A. Cron, PhD
Assistant Professor
Department of Counseling
Oakland University
Rochester, Michigan

Yakov M. Epstein, PhD
Professor of Psychology
Director, Center for Mathematics,
    Science, and Computer
    Education
Rutgers–The State University of
    New Jersey
Piscataway, New Jersey

Richard A. Gardner, MD
Clinical Professor of Child
    Psychiatry
Columbia University
College of Physicians and
    Surgeons
New York City

v

Rollin Gilman, MA
Psychological Intern
Henry Mayo Newhall Memorial
  Hospital
Santa Clarita, California
Resource Associate
Center for Study of Young People
  in Groups
Teen Line
Cedar Sinai Hospital
Los Angeles, California

Heidi G. Kaduson, PhD
Clinical Psychologist
Private Practice
East Windsor, New Jersey

Richard Kagan, PhD
Director of Psychological Services
Parsons Child and Family Center
Albany, New York

Craig Winston LeCroy, PhD
Professor
Arizona State University
School of Social Work
Tucson, Arizona

Marjorie Mitlin, SW
School Adjustment Counselor
North Attleboro High School
Private Practice
Sharon, Massachusetts

Eva M. Netel-Gilman, PsyD
Staff Psychologist
Hillside Home for Children
Pasadena, California

Francella A. Quinnell, MS
Doctoral Student at The
  University of Wisconsin-
  Milwaukee
Milwaukee, Wisconsin

Steven E. Reid, PhD
Private Practice
Massapequa Park, New York

Helane S. Rosenberg, PhD
Associate Professor of Education
Graduate School of Education
Rutgers–The State University of
  New Jersey
Piscataway, New Jersey

Charles E. Schaefer, PhD
Professor of Psychology
Director, Center for Psychological
  Services
Fairleigh Dickinson University
Teaneck, New Jersey

Susan Corkins Siegner, MS
Marriage and Family Therapist
Private Practice
Torrance, California

**Isabelle C. Streng, C PSYCHOL.
  AFBPsS**
Child and Adolescent Psychologist
Sophia Children's Hospital
Erasmus University
Rotterdam, The Netherlands

Arthur J. Swanson, PhD
Chief Psychologist
St. Barnabas Hospital
Bronx, New York

Preface

Historically, games have provided people enjoyment and diversion, but they also have played a significant role in the growing child's understanding and acceptance of societal rules. This dual nature of games is uniquely suited for child psychotherapy. The inherent enjoyment of games helps resistant children engage with therapists and enhances therapeutic communication between therapist and client. The rules and structural components of games provide a natural medium for children to learn how to be civilized and well-adjusted. Game play offers an important extension of play therapy techniques for use with older children, opening up the field for work with school-age children, adolescents, and adults.

The interest in using games as a specialized therapeutic medium continues to grow. When the first edition of this book was published in 1986, the field of game play was a relatively new branch of play therapy. Games were being used frequently in child psychotherapy—as suggested by the considerable space occupied by games in therapists' offices—yet, there was no game play handbook and few published guidelines on using games in child psychotherapy. The first edition of this book was devoted to providing a guide for mental health professionals by elucidating the psychological meanings of game play, identifying its therapeutic elements, and providing case illustrations on game therapy techniques. A new classification scheme for games was developed in an effort to bring order and coherence to the field of game therapy. Games were categorized based on how they are used in therapy to further the child's emotional growth, as follows: communication games, problem-solving games, ego-enhancing games, and socialization games.

The upsurge in interest and use of games in child therapy over the past 10 years has been dominated by specialization and the burgeoning of therapeutic board games. Games have been developed specifically to help children suffering from the aftermath of divorce, sexual abuse, the death of a parent, and domestic violence. Therapeutic games developed for specific populations continue to proliferate. There are therapeutic games available for children with ADHD, depression, self-control deficits, and socialization deficits, among several others.

This volume reflects the growing specialization of game play therapy, allowing for an increasingly prescriptive approach to treatment. Experts in the field were asked to write original chapters describing their approaches to game play to help children with specific, often debilitating psychological problems. These contributions were grouped in sections on games for children in psychological crisis, game play for ADHD children, and games for children with socialization deficits. What is apparent in these works is the almost limitless flexibility of games to be adapted to suit the unique needs of the child and further the therapeutic process. By "making a game of it," the most difficult and painful subjects can be brought to the surface and discussed in a nonthreatening and supportive atmosphere. Using a game approach can effectively help children learn new behaviors, become better problem solvers, and gain insight into their difficulties.

The more traditional approach of using games as adjuncts to the therapy process has not been lost or forgotten. The initial two sections of this book contain chapters describing the use of games within the adjunctive framework, which views games as a stepping stone to the real therapeutic work of interpretation and insight. These authors show how games can be used to enhance the therapeutic alliance, elicit fantasy expression, and provide important diagnostic information regarding the child's ego functioning and personality integration.

This book should be of interest to students and more advanced mental health practitioners who work with children, including clinical, counseling, and school psychologists, social workers, psychiatrists, psychiatric nurses, child care workers, and child-life specialists.

Charles E. Schaefer
Steven E. Reid

Contents

The Psychology of
Play and Games

STEVEN E. REID

The purpose of this chapter is to give a brief overview of the psychology of play and games. Concepts with particular relevance to therapeutic work with children are emphasized.

DEFINITIONS

The terms *play* and *games* have different meanings in the play therapy literature. Play is seen as a pleasurable, naturally occurring behavior found in human and animal life. A voluntary, spontaneous activity that has no particular endpoint or goal (Beach, 1945; Plant, 1979), play is thought to be intrinsically motivated by desire for fun (Garvey, 1977). Play is also a driving force in human development. In infancy and early childhood, play has a key role in promoting exploration and mastery, exercising muscles and the mind, and relating to other people. Play in early childhood often involves pretense, a symbolization of reality allowing for manipulation and mastery of psychic desires (Erickson, 1950). Child therapists have long understood the power of pretend play as a vehicle for the expression of painful psychic material that would ordinarily be difficult for a child to express consciously. In therapy with children, play is at times a substitute for verbalization, fantasy expression, or free association.

1

Typically found in a play therapy room are toys and play materials that can be played within a variety of ways and have high symbolic value. These are the tools of symbolic play; dolls, dollhouses, puppets, miniature human and animal figures, toy vehicles, art supplies, molding clay, and water.

Game playing is a form of play and is, thereby, a form of amusement and source of enjoyment to the participants. Game playing has been traced back to prehistoric times and is thought to play a significant role in adaptation to the environment (Sutton-Smith, 1961). Games invoke behavior that is more goal-directed and carries a greater sense of seriousness than play. Most games have rules that define players' roles, set limits and expectations for behavior, and describe how the game works. As a result, the range and scope of game behavior is limited in comparison to unstructured play, and imagination and pretending become secondary to more concrete objectives. This altered focus is apparent in the games used in child therapy, which typically include board games, card games, street games, computer games, and fine and gross motor games. Not all types of games are adaptable to therapy; organized sports, recreational games, and arcade games, for example, are generally not utilized in child psychotherapy.

Games also usually involve some sort of competition. In contrast to the open-ended nature of early childhood play, the outcome of game play is very important to its participants, who are competing, often against each other, to win. Sutton-Smith (1971) terms games "models of power" in that they provide a context for socially acceptable aggression and competition. Game play has become a central metaphor and a research tool for the study of social conflict. The competition in games provides a useful analogy for the conflicts of interest that recur in business, political, and interpersonal interactions (Schlenker & Bonoma, 1978).

Whereas free play taps the id, game play invokes ego processes. Even the simplest of games requires greater cognitive ability than does play. To play hopscotch or the card game war, one must be able to count in sequence, recognize written primary numbers, and understand the concept of greater/lesser. On the other hand, the cognitive and linguistic requirements of playing with water or molding clay are negligible. Children playing a game must also have enough frustration tolerance and reality testing to accept limits on their behavior, take turns, follow rules, and accept losing. A certain amount of attention and persistence is necessary to follow a game to its conclusion. Further, game playing involves a personal challenge to apply one's skills to win a contest.

The final defining characteristic of games is their requirement for interpersonal interaction. Throughout history, games have been developed as social activities to be engaged in by two or more people. In most games, the actions of the participants are interdependent, meaning that the outcome of the game depends on the interactions of the players, not on one player's actions alone. In contrast, unstructured play can be carried on by two or more children with little interaction between them.

HISTORICAL PERSPECTIVE

Games have been a part of human societies since prehistoric times. Archaeological and cross-cultural studies have found that civilizations throughout history developed a remarkably vast number and variety of games. Hundreds of dice games, guessing games, card games, board games, hoop-and-stick games, counting games, party games, hide-and-seek games, chase games, indoor athletic games, outdoor athletic games, singing/rhyming/dancing games, and others have been catalogued. The Aborigines of North America, for example, played over 1,400 games (Wood & Goddard, 1940).

Early game playing appears to have had a direct correlation to adaptation and survival. Physical agility and strength were invaluable in prehistoric times. Prehistoric people played the earliest known form of ball play by throwing sticks, bones, and stones. These objects were shaped and rounded for rolling and ease of catching. As early as 2050 B.C., people playing ball were depicted on Egyptian hieroglyphics. Ball playing has been found to be a universal activity in virtually all societies studied (Sutton-Smith, 1961). The Eskimos made balls of leather filled with moss. Tribes living on remote islands in the Indian Ocean were found playing ball by early explorers. Ancient Romans produced balls made from pigskin and inflated with air. Ball playing can be linked to several adaptive behaviors that have critical survival value. Games that involve repeated exchanging of meaningless objects among players require practicing the act of sharing real valued objects and resources, which serves to reinforce the values of cooperation and group belonging. Throwing games also served as practice for accurate and coordinated throwing of weapons for the killing of prey. Today, the ball is the central object found in organized sports, which are ubiquitous in modern civilizations.

Games also evolved from spiritual beliefs and rituals. The game of tag was born of the ancient superstition that touching objects made of wood or stone would ward off evil spirits or break spells. This ritual then led to a belief that one could pass on or contract evil spirits by touching another human being. Today, the fundamental aspect of tag remains, where one touch from a finger spreads the evil of being "it" from one person to another.

Blindman's bluff was derived from prehistoric rites of human sacrifice. In ancient Greece, approximately 1,000 B.C., the game was called muinda, or brazen fly, and was played among boys. One boy was blindfolded while the others whipped him with papyrus husks. During Elizabethan times, blindman's bluff was popular in England, and it retained the sado-masochistic qualities rooted in earlier sacrificial rites. In the updated version, the blindfolded person was gently hit with a knotted rope. The game became notorious as fondling replaced hitting, and blindman's bluff became very popular for foreplay and jest in the English Court. This highly sensuous version was ceremoniously prohibited by the Victorians as society changed dramatically in England. Today, the game is devoid of violent or sexual overtones and has lost much of its popularity.

Modern-day games also have their roots in the earlier codification and organization of aggression. Chess, checkers, and backgammon all have direct correlates to war and battle strategy. Playing cards originated in ancient Asian cultures for the purpose of teaching military strategies to young nobles. Cards have two different red "armies" and two different black "armies," allowing for more intricate military maneuvers and a greater number of participants in the game. In their beginning forms, playing card sets portrayed a variety of symbols and personifications, including natural forces (wind, fire, air, water), military resources, and soldiers and officers of differing military ranks. In medieval times, cards became identified with the royal Court of England; the face of King Henry VII is preserved on all four kings in the traditional deck of cards. Card playing proliferated and identification with military strategies was replaced by concepts of monetary power and worth. Again, the foundational meanings have evaporated, and card playing today has no direct purpose other than for the enjoyment of intellectual challenge and competition.

Throughout history, different types of games have been found to be prevalent in different cultures. Games of a particular culture reflect the prevailing societal concerns, pressures, and conflicts of its members and of the societal group as a whole. Ring-around-the-rosy, which in modernity is known only as a whimsical social game usually learned and played in early childhood, has its roots in a poem from the Middle Ages.

> Ring, A Ring, A Rosey;
> A pocketful of posies;
> Achoo, Achoo;
> We all fall down.

The verse describes the round red blotches that first appeared on those stricken with the Black Plague, followed by the practice of stuffing the victim's pocket with flowers to cover up the smell of both the illness and death because a quick burial often was not possible. The "Achoos" refer to the respiratory illness that caused the victim to fall down and die.

Sutton-Smith's (1971) cross-cultural research found that games of chance predominate in cultures subjected to a high degree of environmental uncertainty and unpredictability, those in which food supplies, climate, and migratory patterns are highly variable. The lack of human control over environmental forces is reflected in games in which chance, not ability or strategy, decides the outcome. Games such as tag, hide-and-seek, and red rover (central-person games), on the other hand, represent anxiety about exercising social independence. Research has shown that in cultures in which central-person games are prominent, there exists a significantly greater collective concern with establishing early independence of adolescents (Sutton-Smith, 1971).

One can see that many of our present-day games have roots in ancient cultures. The prevalence of games throughout history, as well as their multiplicity, suggests their enduring importance in the human experience. The section below on theories of game playing helps identify the enduring appeal of games.

THEORETICAL FOUNDATIONS

Early game playing appears to have been instrumental in providing members of society with opportunities to practice and master prevailing cultural concerns and psychological needs (e.g., sharing resources, killing prey, warding off evil spirits). Abstracting these concerns in the form of a game made it possible to exert control and mastery over situations that, in the real world, were unpredictable and threatening. Early play theorists employed biological and genetic concepts to explain the human interest in games. Groos (1898) developed the instinct-practice theory, in which game play is viewed as instinctive and instrumental in the practice of essential behavioral patterns later in life. His theory was based on observations of the play of both animals and humans, and focused on the similarity between play behavior and real-life activities of humans and the development of survival skills of animals. All game play, according to Groos, is an offshoot of a human instinct to practice survival skills endemic to the species.

Whereas game playing subsequently failed to fit the definition of instinct, the "practicing" notion has remained prevalent in theoretical formulations on game playing. Piaget (1962) and Avedon and Sutton-Smith (1971) suggest that game playing has a unique role in the socialization of children. Game playing is inherently social and involves learning and following rules, problem solving, self-discipline, and emotional control, and adoption of leader and follower roles, all of which are essential components of socialization (Serok & Blum, 1983).

A particular aspect of socialization, control of aggression, has received considerable attention in the game literature. Games afford opportunities to express aggression in socially acceptable ways. Milberg (1976) theorizes that play and games were created by humans to provide acceptable outlets for anger and hostility, which are derivatives of the fight response. Fighting is a natural human response to threatening stimuli, but as society developed, the need for control of aggression increased.

Redl (1958) argues that aggression, power, and dominance/submission exist in all games. Nearly all games involve some sort of contest, which by itself is a symbolic expression of aggression. Symbolic aggression is inherent in games such as chess and checkers, in which one opponent attacks another by capturing or neutralizing the opponent's piece. Games become a vehicle for learning socially acceptable ways to succeed over others. Many games establish a hierarchy of dominance, such as follow-the-leader and Simon says. Game theory has been used to study the evolution of territoriality and mate selection in mammals as well as cooperation and conflict in humans (Maynard-Smith, 1984).

Freud (Strachey, 1962) emphasizes the concept of catharsis as being central in play. Catharsis involves discharge of pent-up emotional and psychic energy. Freud theorized that the fundamental process of personality development is the inhibition and repression of basic drives, a process that results in built-up tension that needs to be discharged in socially acceptable ways. One way to release this energy is through game playing. The cathartic theory of game play offers an interpretation of blindman's bluff as it was played long ago as a release and displacement of aggressive and sexual drives. Peller (1954) elaborates on a psychoanalytic view of game play as involving not only the discharge of pent-up impulses (primary process), but also the mastery of anxiety (secondary process). She viewed game play as a vehicle for sublimation of basic impulses. The rules and structure inherent in games represent the superego's role in successfully repressing and sublimating socially unacceptable impulses. Game play thus becomes particularly important for the resolution of the aggressive feelings characteristic of the oedipal period.

Mitchell and Masson (1948) present a similar conceptualization of game play, the surplus-energy theory, but one that focused on the release of excess physical energy as opposed to psychic energy. This theory suggests that game play is random and noninstrumental, a form of pleasure and amusement and nothing more. Although this view is not popular, others have postulated that the main "purpose" of play and games is to provide pleasure and relaxation to the participants. Wood and Goddard (1940), for example, postulate that ball playing, one of the most ancient of games, emerged because the rhythm and repetition involved in throwing and catching have a relaxing and calming effect on the players. While the discharge of energy tension provides a relief, it also increases energy that has been lost through physical exertion or other forms of work (Milberg, 1976).

DEVELOPMENTAL PERSPECTIVE

Game playing occupies a central place late in the developmental stages of play. Research on cooperation in play has found that it emerges as early as 22 months (Ross & Kay, 1980) but does not become a critical ingredient in play until middle childhood (Stoll, Inber, & James, 1968; Zigler & Child, 1956). Theoretical formulations of play development are remarkably similar in placing the emergence of game playing in early latency, somewhere between 5 and 8 years of age. Game playing for latency-age children reflects their readiness and interest in exploring more realistic and complex forms of play. The school-age child's characteristics and capacities, especially in relation to game play, along the lines of cognitive, social, emotional, and identity development are discussed below.

COGNITIVE

Piaget (1962) identifies three stages of cognitive development in play: sensory motor play (2 months to 2 years), fantasy play (2 to 7 years), and games with rules (7 to 11 years). Earliest forms of play in infants and toddlers are dominated by sensorimotor actions of the child. These egocentric body movements reflect the emergence of a primitive sense of self and the narcissism characteristic of the first stage of psychological development. In the preschool years, children's play is imbued with fantasy and symbolization. Children begin playing roles and imitating adult behaviors as well as real-life events. Strong feelings and magical thinking predominate in symbolic play. Psychological concerns reflected in play are frequently centered on children's relationship with significant adult figures. As children enter the elementary school years, play becomes increasingly realistic and complex, involving interpersonal interactions and situations that gradually approximate real-life social phenomena.

Children age 7 to 11 years are in the stage of "concrete operations," which involves the ability to conserve, classify, and order (Piaget, 1952, 1967). Children develop the capacity to compare and contrast information and to make their perceptions more consistent with reality. Cognitive processes can be used to determine what is correct and real and to override sensory and experiential impressions. Organizing and classifying information becomes important to children in this stage. Thus, the organization, rules, and procedures of formal games become appealing to children's sense of order and realism at this stage of development.

EMOTIONAL

In her psychoanalytic theory of play, Peller (1954) links the preference for playing games to the reduction of oedipal preoccupations. Oedipal play is marked by idiosyncratic fantasy and magical thinking focusing on the basic psychosexual triangle (Freud, 1923). Through dramatic play, children can fantasize about putting themselves in the place of envied adults. Resolution of oedipal strivings is achieved through identification with an adult figure and is reflected in the shift in interest from fantasy play to games that parallel life in the adult world. Game playing also facilitates identification with peers of the same sex, which helps loosen oedipal ties. The shift away from oedipal preoccupations is the first step toward the formation of autonomous personality functioning within the confines of prescribed social roles.

SOCIAL

Social theorists argue that game playing reflects the young child's readiness to band together with equals, not only for friendship and camaraderie, but for help in facing the authority of the adult world. Mead (1934) was among the first to recognize the importance of games in the socialization process, particularly for the emergence of awareness of one's place in society. Through participation in games, the child learns to differentiate self from others. Mead stresses that by following rules constraining game behavior, the child learns about the power of society as the "generalized other" and that social behavior is seldom removed from public view and sanction. Redl (1958) calls games "models of power," highlighting the concepts of power and control in games. He argues that subjecting oneself to control and command by others is a central aspect of most games. Many games require that a leader is chosen and that the other players follow the leader. The process is analogous to learning to deal with others in the real world who are more powerful than oneself. The opposite is also true, in that leader roles in games provide opportunities to accept responsibility, influence others, and learn to wield power fairly.

Many writers have stressed the importance of games in the socialization process. Serok and Blum (1983) describe games as mini–life situations in which the basic elements of socialization—rule conformity, acceptance of norms of the group, and control of aggression—are integral components of the process of play. Game play provides opportunities to acquire new information, experiment with new roles and behaviors, and adapt to the demands of the game and norms of the collective. Games provide an opportunity for children to deal with competitive and aggressive urges in socially acceptable ways. Dealing with rules becomes a particularly meaningful process. Children often argue the interpretation of the rules and the "fairness" of the contest, gaining practice in the process of negotiation and compromise. Further socialization experiences arise when rules are violated. Peer pressure may be felt for the first time. Rule violators are often stigmatized or must offer an apology to remain in the game. Children are sensitized to the aversive consequences of rule-violating behavior.

IDENTITY

Game playing, particularly the adoption of roles within games, has been linked to development of identity and self-esteem in children. Baumeister (1986, 1987) postulates that children's identities develop and expand over time through three self-definition processes. The simplest form of self-definition, Type I, involves the passive acquisition of stable features of identity. Beginning recognition of self as having a certain gender, belonging to a particular family, and having specific physical characteristics are examples of early self-definition. These identity features are passively acquired; the individual does nothing to acquire them. Type II self-definition, called single transformational, involves a discrete change in identity based on meeting a certain set of criteria. Although these components are not passively acquired, many are universal milestones in a child's development that are not self-selected. Learning to walk or ride a bike and entering school are examples of single transformational changes. Type II self-definition occurs throughout the life span as people acquire new aspects of identity, such as by joining a social organization, becoming a physician, or becoming a parent. In Type II self-definitional processes, the identity is stable until the transformation takes place, and is stable afterward. Type III self-definition is labeled hierarchical and involves identity acquisition based on external, quantifiable, hierarchal dimensions. Aspects of Type III self-definition are heavily based on an individual's competence, are continually subject to change, and often involve multiple dimensions. Seeing oneself as wealthy, intelligent, successful, well-liked, or important among peers are examples of Type III self-definitions.

Baumeister suggests that the role structures in children's games reflect the progression of identity development from more stable, passively acquired roles to those that are externally defined, self-selected, and unstable. In a 1988 study by Baumeister and Senders, 339 children, ranging in age from 2.5 to 15 years, were asked to identify their favorite games from a list of games that were identified on the basis of their role structure, as follows: (1) Type I games, consisting of Simon says, house, Mother may I, *Candyland*, doctor, and others in which a player adopts a single, stable role throughout the game; (2) Type II games, consisting of dodgeball, hide-and-seek, blindman's bluff, and others in which players change roles as part of the game; and (3) Type III games, consisting of basketball, *Monopoly*, baseball, chess, and others in which players change or identify with several roles or adopt subroles. In many Type III games, each player takes and holds one continuous role and simultaneously switches among subroles. In baseball, for example, a player's team membership remains constant, but the player rotates among several subroles: batter, fielder, runner, and so forth.

Findings of the study indicate that children in the symbolic-play stage of development preferred noncompetitive games involving the single enactment of preassigned, stable roles. Theoretically, these games help affirm the preschooler's growing awareness of stable features of his or her identity. Children in the early latency stage preferred games that involve role switching among a few roles that are more complex and less directly representative of important people in a child's social world. Preadolescent and adolescent children preferred competitive games based on competence that allow for more variation in role structure.

The developmental progression from noncompetitive to competitive games involves a transitional step in which competitive games are played but in which the demand and threat of the contest are diluted by reliance on luck to decide the outcome. Chance-based competitive games are preferred by children 5 to 8 years (Type II age range), as found in the study by Baumeister and Senders (1988). Such games enable children to experiment with new and different roles without requiring them to cope strategically and skillfully with opposition. In this stage of development, children's identities are in flux, as they are just beginning to make comparisons against their peers as a basis for self-definition (Ruble, 1983). It is not until late childhood that identity and self-definition come to focus on issues of competence and measurement against peers, in which the self becomes increasingly equated with performance (Erikson, 1968).

THERAPEUTIC ELEMENTS OF GAME PLAY

Game playing occupies an important place in the psychological and social world of childhood. The versatility of games has been exploited by clinicians in helping children resolve psychological conflicts and further their emotional growth. Playing a game can promote the emotional growth of children in direct and indirect ways. The experiential process of play brings pleasure, catharsis, and relaxation. The ongoing game play process can promote socialization, reality testing, and mastery of anxiety. Playing a game can help strengthen the therapeutic alliance and provide a metaphorical stage for the expression and resolution of conflict.

THERAPEUTIC ALLIANCE

Because games usually evoke positive associations for children, even the most resistant child will be drawn to game play in the therapy context. The therapist becomes a game participant, which has the effect of relaxing the adult-child boundary and rendering the therapist more accessible to the child. By joining in play, the adult moves into the child's world. This subtle shift can be of utmost importance to children, many of whom do not enter into the therapy situation of their own volition.

PLEASURE

Game playing even without therapeutic intervention is understood to often be emotionally fulfilling. Play is thought to be the antithesis of work. Erikson (1950) states that play is "free from the compulsions of a conscience and impulsions of irrationality" (p. 214). Play, then, has special significance for withdrawn or autistic children, who might have difficulty experiencing pleasure. The concept of enjoyment is reciprocal, relating not only to nurturing oneself but to nurturing others. The child's experience of sharing enjoyment with an adult through game play enhances the therapeutic relationship and helps the child feel needed and useful.

DIAGNOSIS

The structure and rules of games, in addition to their inherently competitive makeup, are particularly useful for eliciting behavior reflective of a child's ego strength. The sense of challenge is heightened because in the therapy setting the child is playing against someone who is superior in intellect and experience. As a result, feelings of self-worth, aggressiveness, trust, and helplessness in relation to adults are often revealed in the child's style of play. A child's ego processes, including impulse control, intellectual strengths and weaknesses, locus of control, and concentration, are readily observable.

Because games invoke ego processes, they may be more valuable for examining a child's ego functioning than for uncovering unconscious conflicts. At the same time, games, like unstructured play, bring a sense of safety and permissiveness, opening doors for expression. Games mimic real life to some extent and thus provide a metaphor for projection of unconscious material. Many board games involve moving from a home base to an endpoint elsewhere on the board, which could symbolize a variety of issues and experiences related to separation, attachment and individuation, parental abandonment, and social isolation. Therapeutic board games such as the *Imagine!* game (Burks, 1978) and *Our Game* (Vlosky, 1986) have been developed for the specific purpose of eliciting fantasy expression.

Therapeutic game play provides a window into the child's personality structure, defense mechanisms, and psychopathological symptoms. O'Connor (1991) notes that the play of emotionally troubled children in therapy is often compulsive, impulsive, and irrational, a far cry from what one would consider enjoyable. Children with obsessional/compulsive tendencies might become fixated on rules or minor aspects of the game and therefore lose sight of the overall goal. A borderline child might overreact with rage or utter dejection to minor setbacks or attach inordinate importance to battles won. A child with antisocial tendencies or conduct problems might lose self-control quickly in the face of adversity.

COMMUNICATION

Although some may view the rules and goal striving of game play as impediments to self-expression, these structural elements actually promote communication between players. The social aspect of game play makes it dependent on a certain level of cooperation and mutuality of purpose among participants. Practical discussion of rules and attentiveness toward the actions of other players are natural accompaniments of game play.

A game, by definition, is separate from reality, thereby inviting the relaxation of defenses that would normally inhibit expression of feelings, thoughts, and attitudes in normal social discourse. Thus, one often sees a high level of affective involvement in game play. A certain type of expression, catharsis, is often elicited through game play. Strong feelings of anger, resentment, frustration, and jealousy can be discharged within the safe confines of the game. Negative feelings a child might have about parents or other adults are especially amenable for expression during game play.

As children relax and involve themselves in the game, they often begin to talk about feelings and ideas that are important to them. An important concept of game play is "points of departure" (Frey, 1986; Gardner, 1986), in which players "leave" the game to discuss psychological issues expressed during game play. For the therapist, a key aspect of game play therapy is managing and guiding discussion back and forth between the safety of the game and the realistic discussion of issues through points of departure.

INSIGHT

Game play not only reveals disturbed behavioral patterns, it can provide a vehicle for a child to observe and understand these patterns. Because the therapist is usually a player in the game, he or she can model responses that set the tone for self-examination, such as "Oh, I keep choosing the wrong turn!" A negative self-evaluation of game behavior is less threatening to the child than any such appraisal of real-life behavior. The task of the therapist is to help the child gradually become aware of negative behavioral patterns that generalize from the game context to the child's larger world.

SUBLIMATION

Compared to free play, game play provides more opportunities for sublimation of instinctual and forbidden urges due to their higher degree of role definition and structure. For instance, a child's sexual and aggressive urges might be channeled into increased competitiveness and effort to win. In many therapeutic board games, a variety of adaptive responses and solutions to conflict are readily available for the child to consider. These outcomes might not otherwise have been within the child's awareness. This educational aspect of board games draws on their history of application of learning and behavior problems in the classroom (Nickerson & O'Laughlin, 1980). Children are more likely to try out new ways of thinking and acting in the context of a game than if an adult directly offers such suggestions.

EGO ENHANCEMENT

Playing a game tends to enhance ego strength because it requires a certain amount of concentration and impulse control. The experiential processes of learning how to play a game and striving to improve performance challenge and promote organization, mastery of anxiety, and self-esteem. Reid (1993) describes the disorganized, frenetic game behavior in the beginning stages of game therapy of a hyperactive, aggressive 6-year-old boy. This child had suffered the crises of attachment failure and repeated foster placements. Initially in therapy he related to the therapist in an extremely defensive, angry, and provocative manner. He played exclusively with fine-motor games (e.g., ball toss) with few defining rules, and his play was ego-centric, devoid of turn-taking and cooperation. He would throw three balls, one after another, at the target hanging on the wall and then move closer and closer to the target to ensure success. Slowly, the child accepted the therapist's input on structuring the activity to make it a real game that included turn-taking, rules, a small degree of competition, and an ultimate endpoint or goal. By the tenth session, the child began to take turns spontaneously, to pay attention to the therapist's game playing, and to interact with the therapist in a less emotional and impulse-ridden manner. The process of game play set the stage for deeper therapeutic intervention in subsequent sessions.

REALITY TESTING

Games are realistic forms of play that contain rules that normally are not subject to change by a child's imagination or will. Games are usually played by at least two people, necessitating a certain amount of shared objective perception of reality. To participate, players implicitly reach a consensus on the rules and procedural aspects of play. Within this structure, distortion of reality is seen in the form of cheating, denial of events, and idiosyncratic interpretation of the rules. These deviations become the fodder for therapeutic intervention, part of which involves recurring reinforcement of more adaptive and realistic response during game play.

RATIONAL THINKING

Intellectual challenge is a key ingredient in countless games. Games call on cognitive skills such as memory, concentration, anticipation of consequences, logical thinking, and creative problem solving. Learning new behaviors, self-reflection, and self-understanding are cognitive processes that are essential to emotional development in and out of the therapeutic relationship.

Rational thinking is a critical element of many theoretical approaches to understanding and correcting emotional problems in childhood. Conversely, irrational thought processes are believed by some to be the foundation of psychopathology (Ellis, 1962). Games are especially useful in therapy for the practice of realistically appraising situations in the context of the game, which often mirror real-life phenomena. Many games invite risk taking, requiring the child to analyze the potential outcomes of different choices. For example, in the *Wizard of Oz* board game, players must decide which of two paths to take in the middle of the journey. One path is much shorter to the end, but contains pitfalls that, if landed on, send the player back to the beginning. By promoting discussion of this situation, the therapist can help the child learn to think about the future and about consequences of actions.

SOCIALIZATION

Games are the dominant play activity for latency-age children, whose primary developmental task is to develop social relationships with peers. Game play is an inherently social activity, requiring cooperation and communication among the participants. The process of game playing often contains positive peer pressure for socialized behavior. Concepts of fair play and sportsmanship apply to game play. Often, unspoken group norms exist that define how winners and losers should behave in relation to one another. Conversely, unacceptable group behavior exhibited during game play is often punished in some way, providing opportunities for children to learn consequences of socially unacceptable behavior. In naturalistic childhood game play, rule violators are generally stigmatized and are forced to atone for the transgression, or at least apologize, to remain in the game. In this way, children become sensitized to the aversive consequences of "antisocial" behaviors.

While games demand cooperative behavior, they also often require controlled expression of aggressive urges. The competitive nature of games requires that players attempt to defeat others in order to win. Rules provide boundaries within which children must compete and assert themselves without losing self-control.

Games offer opportunities to experience depersonalized sources of authority in the form and rules and procedures that define the games. In this sense, the game itself represents adult authority, and game players are required to subject themselves to the control or command of the rules and procedures of the game. This process is analogous to learning to deal with others in the real world who are more powerful than oneself.

TYPES OF GAMES

The broadest classification of games separates commercial games (i.e., traditional childhood and adult games) from those developed specifically for use in therapy or counseling. Commercial games such as checkers (Gardner, 1986), *Monopoly* (Crocker & Wroblewski, 1975), and card games (Reid, 1986) are often used in child therapy. The classification scheme developed by Sutton-Smith and Roberts (1971) applies to the vast number of traditional, historical, and commercial games catalogued across various societies. The scheme has relevance to game play therapy as well. These authors distinguish three types of games based on what determines who wins: (1) games of physical skill, in which the outcome is determined by the players' motor abilities; (2) games of strategy, in which cognitive skill determines the winner; and (3) games of chance, in which the outcome is random and accidental.

PHYSICAL SKILL

Games of physical skill can be further divided into gross and fine motor games. Gross motor games include tag, simple ball games, and relay races. Active movement games may seem unsuitable for therapy because of space limitations and because they may cause children to become overactive or overexcited. Further, intense physical movement is usually incompatible with verbalization and discussion of feelings and emotions. However, games that involve a significant amount of gross motor movement have been found to help hyperactive and impulsive children develop greater self-control through the codification and structure of movements through game play. Reid (1993) describes how a game of soft darts actually helped a hyperactive, defensive child become more organized and controlled in the beginning stage of treatment. Others (Kendall & Braswell, 1985; Shapiro, 1981) have used active movement games to treat children with deficits in self-control.

Schachter (1974, 1984, 1986) has developed a series of physical interactive games, which he calls kinetic psychotherapy, to treat a range of psychological disturbances in children, particularly depression. Schachter posits that the creative movement games of kinetic psychotherapy facilitate the expression of certain emotional reactions that are otherwise difficult to elicit without the release function of movement.

Fine motor games include tiddlywinks, *Pic-Up Stix*, *Perfection*, *Operation*, darts, penny hockey, and so forth. These games are usually highly competitive, have easily explained rules, and are particularly valuable for assessing a child's impulse control and general level of personality integration (Bow & Goldberg, 1986).

STRATEGY

The outcome of strategy games depends primarily on the cognitive abilities of the participants. Many strategy games have been brought into the therapy room, including *Connect Four*, chess, checkers, *Uno*, card games, and *Trouble*. Advantages of strategy games include: (1) they can be played by two people in an office, (2) they provide opportunities to observe the child's intellectual strengths and weakness, and (3) they permit the expression of aggression symbolically without the physiological arousal associated with physical games. Strategy games activate ego processes including intellectual effort, concentration, and self-control. Depending on one's theoretical orientation, these ego processes may enhance or detract from the therapy process. It is clear, however, that more complex strategy games, such as chess and Stratego, require extended expenditure of intellectual effort that serves to suspend and sidetrack real therapeutic work.

CHANCE

Games of chance include bingo, roulette, the *Candyland* and *Chutes and Ladders* board games, and a few card games (e.g., war). Childhood games that depend on pure chance for winning tend to be on a simple level and are therefore useful as an introduction to game playing. Chance games have value in therapy because they neutralize the adult's superiority in intellect, experience, and ability. However, children quickly become inured to games that do not require use of strategy or skill, primarily because the competitive aspects have been removed. Triumph in chance games is victory over odds, not another opponent. It has been observed that when real competition is removed, participants are less motivated and derive less enjoyment from the game (Holmes, 1964; Rapoport, 1966; Steele & Tedeschi, 1967).

A number of classification schemes have been developed for therapeutic games. Games have been categorized on the basis of the number of rules (Rabin, 1983), type of game activity, either behavioral or cognitive (Varenhorst, 1973), and the underlying theoretical orientation of the game (Shapiro, 1993).

The primary method in promoting change has also been used as a basis for classifying therapeutic board games. Schaefer and Reid (1986) identified four categories of games: communication games, problem-solving games, ego-enhancing games, and socialization games. Communication games typically de-emphasize competition to encourage self-expression. These types of games usually are less structured than other therapeutic games and are designed to promote a nonthreatening, permissive atmosphere. Problem-solving games, on the other hand, are often highly structured activities that offer opportunities to discuss specific problems and practice solutions to the problems. Problem-solving games usually have a behavioral theoretical orientation. Ego-enhancing games challenge players to outperform each other; the focus here is on competition and strategy. Older children often gravitate toward ego-enhancing games because they mirror issues in the adolescent's development of identity, in which increasingly specific comparisons of skills and attributes among peers help shape the child's sense of self (Baumeister & Senders, 1988). Socialization games are generally used in group therapy and are geared toward practicing prosocial interactions and increasing sensitivity to the dynamics that underlie social discourse.

Therapeutic games have also been classified based on their theoretical orientation. Shapiro (1993) categorized each of 81 psychotherapeutic games according to theoretical emphasis. The most common classifications were psychoeducational (26%), client-centered (17%), values clarification (15%), psychodynamic (12%), and cognitive-behavioral (11%). The authors cautioned that users of therapeutic games should be familiar with the major theory underlying the games to use them effectively. The section below elaborates on the various clinical applications of game play.

CLINICAL APPLICATIONS

Earliest clinical applications of game play in child psychotherapy focused on their projective value. Games were seen as tools to promote projection of unconscious material, but were not regarded as being directly therapeutic. Loomis's (1957) article on the use of checkers in therapy marked the first serious discussion of the therapeutic value of board games. Loomis viewed the game as a projective template, particularly valuable for the expression of resistance to therapy. Meeks (1970) further espoused the projective value of game playing in terms of the relationship between the players involved. Components of the working relationship between therapist and child, including resistance, transference, and countertransference, are more readily expressed within the confines of game play than in conscious discourse between therapist and child.

Gardner (1969) cautions that formal games have less intrinsic projective value than traditional play media. Instead of promoting relaxation of ego controls, games activate the ego by challenging participants to apply their skills to win the game. Levinson (1976) emphasizes that games tend to elicit only certain types of projection of unconscious material, namely, those associated with the child's relationships with significant adults. Bettelheim (1972) and Berlin (1986) discuss games in terms of their value in eliciting conflicts regarding helplessness, power, and aggression. In therapy, a child is faced with playing against an adult who is superior in intelligence and experience. It is little wonder that underlying feelings of aggressiveness, trust, and helplessness are projected by the child into the game play.

Beginning in the 1970s, there appeared signs of greater appreciation of the value of board games for promoting self-expression and communication. Games began to be viewed as a nonthreatening activity through which therapist and child could communicate. The first therapeutic board games appeared, including the *Ungame* (Zakich, 1975) and the *Talking, Feeling, and Doing Game* (Gardner, 1973). To foster an open, accepting atmosphere in the therapy situation, therapeutic board games were designed with a reduced emphasis on competition, skill, and strategy, concomitant with an increased focus on cooperation as well as reward for self-expression. Thus, players advance along a path or receive tokens or chips for just expressing their thoughts or feelings. The correctness of responses is typically not evaluated or directly rewarded in therapeutic board games.

Over the past 30 years, there has been an explosion in development of board games specifically for use in counseling and therapy. Therapeutic board games have become increasingly specialized and sophisticated, encouraging self-expression on different levels, ranging from projection to fantasy material to statements of beliefs and moral judgments. Most therapeutic games are designed with a high amount of flexibility of rules and endpoints, allowing the therapist to steer the game play to ensure the child's continued involvement along the way. Therapeutic board games also usually encourage actual expression of feelings or behaviors rather than just talking about feelings or behaviors. For example, in a game of Social Security, one may draw a card with the instruction to make a sad face or to jump up and shout. The purpose of these game features is to relax defenses and encourage actual expression of thoughts and feelings.

Kritzberg (1975) and Frey (1986) discuss the communicative value of games in terms of their pretend, "as if" quality. The metaphorical "world" within the game becomes a safe place to open up and express uncomfortable feelings, wishes, and thoughts. Game pieces become the blank projective stimuli onto which psychic material is displaced. Channeling thoughts and feelings through a "third person" is much less threatening and anxiety-provoking than overt conscious discussion. The task of the therapist is to connect metaphorical expression with reality. In game play therapy, therapeutic discourse repeatedly shifts back and forth between the safety of the game to the more challenging arena of face-to-face discussion.

The creation of therapeutic board games for use with specific populations continues to proliferate. There are games available for use with specific populations, such as abused children (e.g., *Breakaway, Let's Talk about Touching*), children with learning disabilities (e.g., *Guess Who?*), children of divorce (e.g., *My Two Homes, Could This Happen*), children who have experienced loss of a love one (e.g., *The Good Mourning Game*), angry and aggressive children (e.g., *The Anger Control Game, Angry Animals*), and children who have experienced domestic violence (e.g., *The Peace Path*), to name only a handful. The flexibility inherent in game playing also has enabled game developers to create computerized versions of therapeutic board games (Olsen-Rando, 1994; Resnick, 1986).

The burgeoning use of therapeutic board games has not replaced traditional competitive games in child therapy. Both types of games are typically part of the child therapist's arsenal. Use of competitive games evolved from early specific applications to reduce resistance. More recently, commercial games have been used to promote expression of specific psychic material and to work through conflicts. Thorne (1982) describes her use of the game *Clue* to help a 9-year-old boy cope with the grief stemming from the loss of his grandfather, an important person in his life. The child used the game, with its descriptive vocabulary for violence and death, to talk symbolically about the act of dying. He switched back and forth between the metaphor of the game and real-life discussion of his feelings and sense of responsibility for his grandfather's death.

The use of traditional competitive games is particularly helpful for enhancing the ego functioning of children. Feelings of competence or self-doubt, impulse control, reality testing, intellectual skills, and self-image are among the ego functions that are revealed during competitive game play. Increasing specialization has seen the use of games expand to help children improve their self-control (Bow & Goldberg, 1986; Swanson, 1986), reduce aggression (Bay-Hinitz, Peterson, & Quilitch, 1994), and improve basic cognitive skills relevant to academic learning (Reid, 1986).

RESEARCH FOUNDATIONS

It is clear that today the use of games in child psychotherapy is widespread. Empirical research on the therapeutic efficacy of game play has not caught up to the clinical lore that espouses the usefulness of games. However, efficacy research has begun, as seen in the sections below which provide a sampling of recent developments in game play therapy in which some evaluative research has been conducted.

DIVORCE

Epstein (1986) developed two games for children of divorce, the *Children's Feedback Game* and the *Could This Happen Game*. These games have been used as part of structured three-month group therapy programs for children who have experienced the breakup of their parents' marriage. In the *Children's Feedback Game,* children learn to take the role of peers, give and receive feedback, share and take turns. This game is primarily designed to introduce children to the processes of game playing and positive group interaction, including listening to peers and talking about feelings. The second game, the *Could This Happen Game,* is then introduced, in which children are asked to consider the probabilities of events in hypothetical stories occurring in real life. Children are divided into two teams that compete with each other. The stories are innocuous to begin with, then gradually approximate situations, events, and conflicts relating to divorce and its effects on children. Teams win points for realistic guessing and for discussion of feelings related to the story. Positive outcomes for children on measures of social competence and self-esteem have been found for children who have played these games.

Berg (1982, 1986) describes using the *Changing Family Game* to help children improve their problem-solving skills regarding divorce-related issues. This board game incorporates cognitive-behavioral principles to help children cope with divorce. The game involves moving from start to finish by answering questions on cards. The questions cover a range of divorce-related concerns, including peer ridicule and avoidance, paternal and maternal blame, self-blame, fear of abandonment, hopes of reunification, and conflicts related to visitation and communication with parents. An efficacy study on the *Changing Family Game* found that adequacy of solutions children offer to problems improved over game-playing sessions (Berg, Hickey, & Snyder, 1985). A subsequent study (Berg et al., 1985) found that scores on the Children's Separation Inventory (Berg, 1986) correlated highly with the adequacy of children's responses to the game cards. The Children's Separation Inventory is included in the *Changing Family Game* and has been found to be a valid and reliable measure of children's attitudes toward divorce-related problems (Berg, 1979, 1980). To assess improvement, the subjects' attitudes were measured on the scale before and after playing the game. Children whose responses on the scale reflected the fewest problems gave the most adequate responses to the game cards. Further, the adequacy of solutions children offer to problems improved over game-playing sessions.

SOCIAL SKILLS

The *Good Behavior Game,* developed by Barrish and colleagues (Barrish, Saunders, & Wolf, 1969), has been found to be effective in reducing impulsive and disruptive behaviors of students in the classroom (Barrish et al., 1969; Harris & Sherman, 1973; Medland & Stacknick, 1972). The play of the *Good Behavior Game* begins with dividing the class into teams based on the inappropriate behavior they exhibited most frequently during baseline recording sessions. Each inappropriate behavior displayed by a team member is recorded by a mark on the blackboard in the team's designated area. If the team's total marks at the end of the play session do not exceed the criterion specified by the teacher, the team receives the agreed-on reinforcement. Positive peer pressure is created by grouping children into teams and serves as additional incentive for children to control their inappropriate behavior. A study by Salend and colleagues (Salend, Reynolds, & Coyle, 1989) found the *Good Behavior Game* to be effective in reducing inappropriate behaviors of emotionally disturbed children in a special education class.

Clarke and Schoech (1994) describe the development of computer games to help adolescents learn impulse control. The rapid branching and looping capabilities of computer programming, as well as the immediate feedback provided by microchip technology, are thought by the authors to be particularly appealing to children with self-control deficit. The process of repetitive play, immediate feedback, and support and guidance from the therapist enables children to master their impulses in at least one setting with one set of materials. An initial efficacy study described by the authors indicated that computer game play was effective in improving cooperation in therapy and enthusiasm for behavioral change.

LeCroy's (1987) research demonstrated the effectiveness of the *Social Skills Game* in promoting assertive prosocial behavior. The *Social Skills Game* is a therapeutic board game focusing on improving skills in four areas: making friends, responding positively to peers, cooperating with peers, and communicating needs. LeCroy divided 11 children into two groups: a social skills game group, in which children played the *Social Skills Game* without structured training, and a social skills group that received structured training in social skills but did not play the game. Results indicate that children in both groups exhibited a significantly greater number of prosocial behaviors following intervention. The board game was as effective as the social skills training group in promoting assertive prosocial behavior.

Games, and other activities involving more active interaction between therapist and child, have also been found to be more effective than traditional cognitive and behavioral interventions in impacting on severe behavioral disturbances such as chronic aggression (Bugental, Whalen, & Henker, 1977; Sprafkin & Rubenstein, 1982). Dubow and colleagues (Dubow, Huesmann, & Eron, 1987) found that a control condition consisting of game play with cards and traditional board games, directed by an adult leader, was more effective in reducing aggression than cognitive and behavioral interventions. The authors attributed this unexpected finding to the intrinsic motivating factor of winning a game against a peer, a goal seen as being more immediate and real than the rewards offered by the structured interventions.

SOCIAL ISOLATION/INHIBITION

Much has been written about the benefits of game play for teaching social skills, not only for preschool children emerging from the parental orbit to explore peer interaction (e.g., Ross, 1982), but also for typical older children and adolescents, juvenile delinquents, and retarded adults (e.g., Foxx, McMorrow, & Schloss, 1983). Research developments in this area include studies involving action-oriented games, nontherapeutic board games, and cooperative games.

Favelle (1998) investigated the effects of systematic creative movements games on the social communication of hypoactive, socially withdrawn elementary school students age 7 to 10 years. Children helped design the games that included a reward component for unusual or challenging movements, leading to an eventual winner for the player who accumulated the most reward points. After four months of game play, subjects were found to be significantly more active, as measured on the Hypoactive Behavior Scale, than other students in the no-game control group. Significantly improved ratings on the Cooperation and Assertion Scales of the Social Skills Rating System were also found.

The game of *Trivial Pursuit* was adapted for use with adolescents and adults with developmental disabilities by Nochajski and Gordon (1987). Game questions were revised to tap knowledge regarding basic components of socialization and daily living skills for mentally retarded individuals in supported living residences. Game play was found to improve overall community living skills and social approach and greeting behaviors.

A study by Johnson and colleagues (Johnson, Goetz, Baer, & Green, 1981) found that repeated play of a cooperative game by two children, one identified as a social isolate, dramatically increased the number of social interactions initiated by the inhibited child. Group entry behaviors also increased. The isolated child tended to approach and interact selectively more with children with whom she played the cooperative game.

FEAR OF MEDICAL PROCEDURES

Over the past 35 years, hospital-based play programs have been developed to prepare children for medical interventions, including hospitalizations, surgery, diagnostic testing, and painful medical procedures (Arzanoff, 1986). Play has been used to help children suffering from acute medical crises, including cancer (Goodman, 1991; Wotjtasik & Sanborn, 1991). Several studies have validated the effectiveness of play in reducing anxiety and promoting positive psychosocial outcomes (e.g., Chan, 1980; Ferguson, 1986; Thomson, 1985). The traditional play materials used to prepare children for medical intervention, particularly dolls and puppets, may not be suitable for older children. Henkens-Matzke and Abbott (1990) developed the game *Hospital Windows,* a medically oriented game activity designed to educate young children and decrease anxiety about common health care practices and procedures. The game contains real photographs of medical procedures and provides opportunities to handle real medical equipment. An initial study found favorable results in terms of reducing fears and increasing knowledge about medical procedures.

THE PROCESS OF GAME PLAY THERAPY

Game play therapy is a psychotherapeutic method that utilizes a variety of game forms to help relieve the emotional distress of children. Game play therapy is not associated with any one theoretical position, nor is it defined by a specific set of procedures or applications. Clearly, however, therapists select and use games differently depending on their theoretical orientation. A psychoanalytic clinician might use games designed to elicit fantasy and wish expression; a behaviorist would be more likely to use games that provide opportunities to experiment with and teach new behaviors.

The emphasis that therapists place on games is often a reflection of how much they believe games can have a direct impact on therapeutic outcome. Playing itself, without verbal processing or interpretation, is thought to have value in terms of providing a direct "corrective experience" (O'Connor, 1991, p. 254). This concept reflects the traditional, nondirective play therapy approach, where the ultimate goal of therapy is to reestablish the child's ability to engage in play behavior as it is classically defined: fun, intrinsically complete, and characterized by natural flow. With this approach, the child's game behavior represents a direct projection of feelings and conflicts that are played out, rather than talked out, over the course of intervention. Although interpretation and verbal discussion are utilized whenever possible in this framework, they are not considered indispensable to the therapeutic process.

At the other end of the spectrum, some view games only as an adjunct to the real work of the therapy (e.g., Gardner, 1986; Nickerson & O'Laughlin, 1980). This orientation views game play as a vehicle to help a child feel comfortable with therapy and as a stimulus for expression of otherwise unattainable information. Verbal processing and interpretation can be done within the metaphor of play, but ultimately the goal of therapy is to bring the conflicts and psychological issues expressed within the context of the game into the arena of conscious awareness and verbal expression (Ekstein & Caruth, 1966). Within this theoretical orientation, game play is viewed as having potential to actually impede the therapeutic process. Matorin and McNamara (1996) contend that game play can be a medium for avoidance for children in therapy. By providing a structured and comfortable way to interact with an adult, games may allow children to avoid developing a deeper bond with the therapist and thereby avoid confronting uncomfortable issues. Gardner (1986) believes games should not be the only therapeutic modality because eventually they will deprive the therapist of deeper unconscious material that can be obtained more readily through other modalities, such as storytelling.

Regardless of theoretical orientation or stance regarding the role of play in child therapy, all game play therapists share the common goal of helping the child move systematically toward mental health. Games may have a central or adjunctive role in the process. The game play therapist is a highly trained clinician who integrates his or her given theoretical positions with a cluster of game materials to help improve the psychological functioning of children.

TRANSFERENCE AND COUNTERTRANSFERENCE

Game playing in therapy can quickly become a conduit for countertransference because the normal boundaries between client and therapist are blurred somewhat when both are engaged as players. The normal stance of the therapist, at least in the psychoanalytic sense, of being "distant" and objective, a reflective mirror of the client's associations, is compromised once game play begins. The therapist is more susceptible to losing perspective and self-awareness while playing a game, particularly because game playing elicits attendant emotions and needs—for example, competitive desires, feelings of self-worth, and a desire for fair play—for the therapist as well as the child. Games undoubtedly have some historical meaning and emotional association for the therapist, given their archetypal nature and their ubiquitousness in the historical and developmental landscapes. Therefore, game play may create a magnet that pulls for the therapist's unconscious emotions, thoughts, and behaviors reflective of the clinician's history and life experiences. Therapists must manage countertransference in game play therapy by vigilantly maintaining a level of self-awareness that prevents needs and wishes from filtering into the therapeutic process.

The blurring of adult-child boundaries that occurs in game play therapy also has implications for the child's engagement in transference. Frequently, children develop parental transferences in child therapy in which the therapist is seen as either the good parent or the bad parent. Transference reactions in which the child views the therapist as omniscient and all-powerful are also common. Transference reactions occur more readily when the therapist is uninvolved and neutral, a "blank space" that can be filled up with the child's unconscious emotions and thoughts. However, when playing a game, therapists tend to naturally reveal more of themselves in the course of play. This state of affairs could disrupt transference reactions because aspects of the therapist's personality may be incompatible with the child's parental transferences.

Game play also has the potential for eliciting immediate and powerful transference reactions because the competitive nature of games may reinforce the child's feelings of helplessness in the face of playing against an adult. The concept of the omniscient and powerful adult may become readily accessible to the child during the early stages of game play. Hence, the therapist's approach to dealing with the imbalance of power in the game play situation becomes an important part of managing the therapy process. This issue is discussed below.

CHEATING AND HANDICAPPING

Cheating usually arises as an issue in game play therapy. Cheating is almost always a reflection of the child's feelings of inadequacy, and most children in therapy are struggling on some level with their sense of self. For young latency-age children, cheating is often related to the transition from magical wish fulfillment to concrete-operational thinking. For these children, cheating might reflect the struggle between attempting to compete realistically and the lingering desire for omnipotent control. For older latency-age children, cheating is often a more serious matter, representing avoidance and inability to cope with reality (Meeks, 1970).

Most play theorists agree that by allowing cheating, the therapist is enabling and reinforcing weakened reality testing (Beiser, 1979; Cooper & Wanerman, 1977; Meeks, 1970; O'Connor, 1991). Others (e.g., Berlin, 1986) contend that some cheating should be allowed if the therapist acknowledges the child's need to win. Reid (1993) emphasizes that, generally, cheating should not be allowed to occur unchecked, but nor should it be viewed as a problem that needs to be eliminated. By ignoring cheating, the therapist perpetuates the child's feelings that underlie it: I am inadequate and cannot win without playing outside of the rules. Yet, to unilaterally prohibit cheating is to ignore its psychological meaning for the child. The therapist must remember that the focus of therapy must be the process of game play rather than the outcome of the game. Reid (1993) suggests that cheating should be brought out in the open and discussed and that the therapist be creative in managing cheating. For example, for the child whose need to cheat is strong, the therapist can suggest that cheating can be done by both players.

Although cheating often reflects a neurotic process, it may also be a situational response to the unusual circumstances of a child's playing a competitive game against an adult. There is an inherent unfairness to this situation, given the adult's superior intellect, authority, and experience, that violates one of the basic tenet of games and game play: fair play. The enjoyment of playing a competitive game evaporates when there is no chance of winning. Because children may feel they are being "cheated" out of a chance to win before the game even begins, they may feel that cheating during the game is subtly expected or allowed. Further, without the sense of fair play, children might feel compelled to cheat strategically, for the entirely rational reason that they cannot otherwise win against adults who play straight up.

Faced with the inequity in ability and intellect in the game play therapy situation, many therapists might be tempted to let the child win. Berlin (1986) has argued that letting a child win a game on even terms, without handicapping the therapist, can help the child's self-esteem and sense of mastery. Others (e.g., Cooper & Wanerman, 1977; O'Connor,

1991) contend that letting children win damages self-esteem because the children understand the message that they cannot win on their own. Allowing a child to win is a covert process that sets the tone for secrecy and mistrust; most children catch on when an adult plays a game at less than capacity.

Handicapping the therapist is thought by many to be a more effective way to balance the inequity of intellect and experience between the child and adult in game play therapy (Reid, 1993; Schaefer & Reid, 1986). There are as many ways to handicap the therapist as there are games. Many board games, for instance, involve moving one or more pieces from a home base to an endpoint. These games may be set up so that the therapist has twice as many pieces to get home as the child, thereby leveling the playing field in terms of ability to win. Or the child and therapist can agree that the therapist should have to go around the board twice to win.

Another technique to balance the playing field in game therapy is to choose a game of chance or, if possible, to modify the chosen game so that chance is a major factor in winning. Chance games neutralize the adult's superiority and losing chance games causes less stress for the child. Young game players especially might feel intimidated by the prospect of engaging in a symbolic contest that pits therapist and child against one another. Attributing losing to chance factors is much less challenging to one's self-esteem. The therapist and child can work together to "win," thereby maintaining the goal-orientation and competitive aspects of a traditional game.

SELECTION AND EVALUATION OF GAMES

The following guidelines are offered for evaluating and selecting games for game play therapy:

1. Consider the age of the child and the developmental preferences for certain types of games, particularly along the continua of adoption of roles and chance versus skill factors in winning. Younger children, for example, prefer chance-based games with stable, easily recognizable roles that also have some competitive aspects. Older children may be drawn to games that are more challenging and complex.
2. Consider a variety of games with different complexities to allow for regression or progression, as the child may need.

3. Identify the purpose for using a game or set of games in relation to the child's presenting problems, the goals of therapy, and the theoretical orientation of the therapist. The increasing specialization of therapeutic games allows for a prescriptive approach to selecting games to address specific psychological problems.

4. Identify the potential therapeutic ingredients and methods of change contained in the game (i.e., communication, problem solving, diagnosis, catharsis, rational thinking, socialization). Which process does the game pull for? Is the game associated with a specific theoretical position? (e.g., the *Transactional Awareness Game*).

5. Set the ground rules for game play at the beginning of therapy. How the therapist portrays the game to the child will depend on several factors, including the therapist's theoretical views on the potential for corrective experience through play. For example, if the therapist's goals for game play are limited to decreasing resistance and strengthening the therapeutic alliance, then the session may be structured so that game-playing time is limited to only part of the therapy session. Other clinicians might allow the child free access to a wide variety of games and allow the play to proceed naturalistically, following the child's interests. This approach would follow from the theoretical view emphasizing the projective and emotionally corrective elements of unencumbered play.

6. Assess the face value of the game from the child's perspective, especially for new clients. Many therapeutic board games may be seen by children as "tricks" to open up and talk about uncomfortable topics. A child with a history of aggressive acting-out behavior may not be ready to play the *Angry Control Game* at the outset of treatment. "Safer," less threatening games (e.g., familiar games such as *Candyland*) should be made available at the beginning of treatment.

7. Choose games that can be played several times within the therapy hour. Playing a game several times within the hour allows for immediate application of what was learned from the previous play.

REFERENCES

Arzanoff, P. (1986). Preparation with medically-oriented play. In *Medically-oriented play for children in health care: The issues* (pp. 221–240). Santa Monica, CA: Pediatric Projects.

Avedon, E. M., & Sutton-Smith, B. (1971). *The study of games.* New York: Wiley.

Barrish, H.H., Saunders, M., & Wolf, M.M. (1969). Good behavior game: Effects of individual contingencies for group consequences on disruptive behavior in a classroom. *Journal of Applied Behavior Analysis, 2,* 119–124.

Baumeister, R.F. (1986). *Identity: Cultural change and the struggle for self.* New York: Oxford University Press.

Baumeister, R.F. (1987). How the self became a problem: A psychological review of historical research. *Journal of Personality and Social Psychology, 52,* 163–176.

Baumeister, R.F., & Senders, P.S. (1988). Identity development and the role structure of children's games. *Journal of Genetic Psychology, 150,* 19–37.

Bay-Hinitz, A.K., Peterson, R.F., & Quilitch, H.R. (1994). Cooperative games: A way to modify aggressive and cooperative behaviors in young children. *Journal of Applied Behavior Analysis, 27,* 435–466.

Beach, F. (1945). Current concepts of play in animals. *American Naturalist, 79,* 523–541.

Beiser, H.R. (1979). Formal games in diagnosis and therapy. *Journal of Child Psychiatry, 18,* 480–490.

Berg, B. (1979). *Children's attitudes toward parental separation inventory.* Dayton, OH: University of Dayton Press.

Berg, B. (1980). *Children's attitudes toward parental separation inventory: Reliability and validity.* Paper presented at the Midwestern Psychological Association, St. Louis, MO.

Berg, B. (1982). *The changing family game.* Dayton, OH: Cognitive-Behavioral Resources.

Berg, B. (1986). The changing-family game: Cognitive-behavioral intervention for children of divorce. In C. Schaefer & S. Reid (Eds.), *Game play: Therapeutic uses of childhood games* (pp. 111–128). New York: Wiley.

Berg, B., Hickey, N., & Snyder, L. (1985). *The changing family game: Efficacy of cognitive behavioral intervention for children of divorce.* Paper presented at the meeting of the Midwestern Psychological Association, Chicago, IL.

Berlin, I.N. (1986). The use of competitive games in play therapy. In C. Schaefer & S. Reid (Eds.), *Game play: Therapeutic uses of childhood games* (pp. 197–214). New York: Wiley.

Bettelheim, B. (1972). Play and education. *School Review, 81,* 1–13.

Bow, J.N., & Goldberg, T.E. (1986). Therapeutic use of games with a fine motor component. In C. Schaefer & S. Reid (Eds.), *Game play: Therapeutic uses of childhood games* (pp. 243–256). New York: Wiley.

Bugental, D.B., Whalen, C.K., & Henker, D.B. (1977). Causal attributions of hyperactive children and motivational assumptions of two behavior change approaches: Evidence for an interactionist position. *Child Development, 48,* 874–884.

Burks, H.F. (1978). *Psychological meanings of the Imagine! game.* Huntington Beach, CA: Arden.

Chan, J. (1980). Preparation for procedures and survey through play. *Pediatrician, 9*, 210–219.

Clarke, B., & Schoech, D. (1994). A computer-assisted therapeutic model for children and adolescents: Initial development and comments. *Computers in Human Services, 11*(1–2), 121–140.

Cooper, S., & Wanerman, L. (1977). *Children in treatment: A primer for beginning psychotherapists.* New York: Brunner/Mazel.

Crocker, J.W., & Wroblewski, M. (1975). Using recreational games in counseling. *Personnel and Guidance Journal, 53*, 453–458.

Dubow, E.F., Huesmann, L.R., & Eron, L.D. (1987). Mitigating aggression and promoting prosocial behavior in aggressive elementary schoolboys. *Behavioral Research Therapy, 25*, 527–531.

Ekstein, R., & Caruth, E. (1966). Interpretation within the metaphor: Further considerations. In R. Ekstein (Ed.), *Children of time and space, of action and impulse* (pp. 158–166). New York: Appleton-Century-Crofts.

Ellis, A. (1962). *Reason and emotion in psychotherapy.* New York: Lyle Stuart.

Epstein, Y.M. (1986). Feedback and Could This Happen: Two therapeutic games for children of divorce. In C. Schaefer & S. Reid (Eds.), *Game play: Therapeutic uses of childhood games* (pp. 159–186). New York: Wiley.

Erikson, E. (1950). *Childhood and society.* New York: Norton.

Erikson, E. (1968). *Identity: Youth and crisis.* New York: Norton.

Favelle, G.K. (1998). Therapeutic applications of commercially available computer software. *Computers in Human Services, 11*(1–2), 151–158.

Ferguson, R.V. (1986). Medically-oriented play: The need for research. In P. Azarnoff (Ed.), *Medically-oriented play for children in health care: The issues* (pp. 292–317). Santa Monica, CA: Pediatric Projects.

Foxx, R.M., McMorrow, M.J., & Schloss, C.N. (1983). Stacking the deck: Teaching social skills to retarded adults with a modified table game. *Journal of Applied Behavior Analysis, 16*, 167–170.

Freud, S. (1923). *The ego and the id.* London: Hogarth Press.

Frey, D. (1986). Communication boardgames with children. In C. Schaefer & S. Reid (Eds.), *Game play: Therapeutic uses of childhood games* (pp. 21–40). New York: Wiley.

Gardner, R.A. (1969). The game of checkers as a diagnostic and therapeutic tool in child psychotherapy. *Acta Paedopsychiatrica, 36*, 142–152.

Gardner, R.A. (1973). *The talking, feeling and doing game.* Cresskill, NJ: Creative Therapeutics.

Gardner, R.A. (1986). The game of checkers in child therapy. In C. Schaefer & S. Reid (Eds.), *Game play: Therapeutic uses of childhood games* (pp. 215–232). New York: Wiley.

Garvey, C. (1977). *Play.* Cambridge, MA: Harvard University Press.

Goodman, R.F. (1991). The diagnosis of childhood cancer. In N.B. Webb (Ed.), *Play therapy for children in crisis: A casebook for practitioners* (pp. 310–332). New York: Guilford Press.

Groos, K. (1898). *The play of animals* (E. Balkwin, Trans.). New York: Appleton.

Harris, V.W., & Sherman, J.A. (1973). Use and analysis of the "Good Behavior Game" to reduce disruptive classroom behavior. *Journal of Applied Behavior Analysis, 6*, 405–417.

Henkens-Matzke, A., & Abbott, D.A. (1990). Game playing: A method for reducing young children's fear of medical procedures. *Early Childhood Research Quarterly, 5*, 19–26.

Holmes, D.J. (1964). *The adolescent in psychotherapy.* Boston: Little, Brown.

Johnson, T.J., Goetz, E.M., Baer, D.M., & Green, D.R. (1981). The effects of an experimental game on the classroom cooperative play of a preschool isolate. *Revista Mexicana de Analisis de la Conducta, 1*, 37–48.

Kendall, P.C., & Braswell, L. (1985). *Cognitive-behavioral therapy for impulsive children.* New York: Guilford Press.

Kritsberg, N. (1975). *The structured therapeutic game method of child analytic psychotherapy.* Hicksville, NY: Exposition.

LeCroy, C.W. (1987). Teaching children social skills: A game format. *Social Work, 32*, 440–442.

Levinson, B.M. (1976). The use of checkers in therapy. In C. Schaefer (Ed.), *The therapeutic uses of child's play* (pp. 383–390). New York: Aronson.

Loomis, E.A. (1957). The use of checkers in handling certain resistances in child therapy and child analysis. *Journal of the American Psychoanalytic Association, 5*, 130–135.

Matorin, A.I., & McNamara, J.R. (1996). Using board games in therapy with children. *International Journal of Play Therapy, 5*(2), 3–16.

Maynard-Smith, J. (1984). Game theory and the evolution of behaviour. *Behavioral and Brain Sciences, 7*, 95–125.

Mead, G.H. (1934). *Mind, self and society.* Chicago: University of Chicago Press.

Medland, M.B., & Stacknick, T.J. (1972). Good Behavior Game: A replication and systematic analysis. *Journal of Applied Behavior Analysis, 5*, 45–51.

Meeks, J. (1970). Children who cheat at games. *Journal of Child Psychiatry, 9*, 157–174.

Milberg, A. (1976). *Street games.* New York: McGraw-Hill.

Mitchell, E. D., & Masson, B. S. (1948). *The theory of play.* New York: Burns.

Nickerson, E.T., & O'Laughlin, K.B. (1980). It's fun—but will it work? The use of games as a therapeutic medium for children and adolescents. *Journal of Clinical Child Psychology, 9*, 78–81.

Nochajski, S.B., & Gordon, C.Y. (1987). The use of Trivial Pursuit in teaching community and independent living skills to adults with developmental disabilities. *American Journal of Occupational Therapy, 41*, 10–15.

O'Connor, K.J. (1991). *The play therapy primer: An integration of theories and techniques.* New York: Wiley.

Olsen-Rando, R.A. (1994). Proposal for development of a computerized version of the Talking, Feeling, and Doing Game. *Computers in Human Services, 11*, 69–80.

Peller, L.E. (1954). Libidinal development as reflected in play. *Psychoanalysis, 3,* 3–11.

Piaget, J. (1952). *The origins of intelligence in children.* New York: International Universities Press.

Piaget, J. (1962). *Play, dreams and imitation in childhood.* New York: Norton.

Piaget, J. (1967). *Six psychological studies.* New York: Vintage.

Plant, E. (1979). Play and adaptation. *Psychoanalytic Study of the Child, 4,* 217–232.

Rabin, C. (1983). *Towards the use and development of games for social work practice.* Unpublished manuscript.

Rapoport, A. (1966). *Two-person game theory: The essential ideas.* Ann Arbor: University of Michigan Press.

Redl, F. (1958). The impact of game ingredients on childrens' play behavior. *Proceedings of the Fourth Conference on Group Processes, 4,* 33–81.

Reid, S.E. (1986). Therapeutic use of card games with learning-disabled children. In C. Schaefer & S. Reid (Eds.), *Game play: Therapeutic uses of childhood games* (pp. 257–276). New York: Wiley.

Reid, S.E. (1993). It's all in the game: Game play therapy. In T. Kottman & C. Schaefer (Eds.), *Play therapy in action: A casebook for practitioners* (pp. 527–560). New York: Aronson.

Resnick, H. (1986). Electronic technology and rehabilitation: A computerized simulation game for youthful offenders. *Simulation and Games, 17,* 460–466.

Ross, H.S. (1982). The establishment of social games among toddlers. *Developmental Psychology, 18,* 509–518.

Ross, H.S., & Kay, D.A. (1980). The origins of social games. In K. Rubin (Ed.), *Children's play* (pp. 29–53). San Francisco: Jossey-Bass.

Ruble, D. (1983). The development of social comparison processes and their role in achievement-related self-socialization. In E.T. Higgins, D. Ruble, & W. Hartup (Eds.), *Social cognition and social behavior: Developmental perspectives* (pp. 162–188). New York: Cambridge University Press.

Salend, S.J., Reynolds, C.J., & Coyle, E.M. (1989). Individualizing the Good Behavior Game across type and frequency of behavior with emotionally disturbed children. *Behavior Modification, 13,* 108–126.

Schachter, R.S. (1974). Kinetic psychotherapy in treatment of children. *American Journal of Psychotherapy, 28,* 430–437.

Schachter, R.S. (1984). Kinetic psychotherapy in the treatment of depression in latency age children. *International Journal of Group Psychotherapy, 34,* 83–91.

Schachter, R.S. (1986). Techniques of kinetic psychotherapy. In C. Schaefer & S. Reid (Eds.), *Game play: Therapeutic uses of childhood games* (pp. 95–107). New York: Wiley.

Schaefer, C., & Reid, S. E. (Eds.). (1986). *Game play: Therapeutic uses of childhood games.* New York: Wiley.

Schlenker, B.R., & Bonoma, T.V. (1978). Fun and games: The validity of games for the study of conflict. *Journal of Conflict Resolution, 22,* 7–38.

Serok, S., & Blum, A. (1983). Therapeutic uses of games. *Residential Group Care and Treatment, 1,* 3–14.

Shapiro, L.E. (1981). *Games to grow on.* Englewood Cliffs, NJ: Prentice-Hall.

Shapiro, L.E. (1993). *The book of psychotherapeutic games.* King of Prussia, PA: Center for Applied Psychology.

Sprafkin, J., & Rubenstein, E.A. (1982). Using television to improve the social behavior of institutionalized children. In J. Sprafkin, C. Swift, & R.H. Ross (Eds.), *Prevention in human services: Rx television: Enhancing the preventive impact of TV* (pp. 200–221). New York: Haworth.

Steele, M.W., & Tedeschi, J.T. (1967). Matrix indices and strategy choices in mixed-motive games. *Journal of Conflict Resolution, 11,* 198–205.

Stoll, C.T., Inber, M., & James, S.F. (1968). *Game experiences and socialization: An exploration of sex differences.* Baltimore: Johns Hopkins University Press.

Strachey, J. (Ed.). (1962). *The standard edition of the psychological works of Sigmund Freud* (Vol. 1.) London: Hogarth.

Sutton-Smith, B. (1961). Cross-cultural study of children's games. *American Philosophical Society Yearbook, 426–429.*

Sutton-Smith, B. (1971). Play, games and controls. In J.P. Scott (Ed.), *Social control* (pp. 84–100). Chicago: University of Chicago Press.

Sutton-Smith, B., & Roberts, J.M. (1971). The cross-cultural and psychological study of games. *International Review of Sport Sociology, 6,* 79–87.

Swanson, A.J. (1986). Using games to improve self-control deficits in children. In C. Schaefer & S. Reid (Eds.), *Game play: Therapeutic uses of childhood games* (pp. 233–242). New York: Wiley.

Thomson, R.H. (1985). *Psychosocial research on pediatric hospitalization and health care: A review of the literature.* Springfield, IL: Thomas.

Thorne, E.M. (1982). The child's use of a game to do grief work. In E.T. Nickerson & K. O'Laughlin (Eds.), *Helping through action: Action-oriented therapies* (pp. 202–205). Amherst, MA: Human Resource Development Press.

Varenhorst, B.B. (1973). Game theory, simulations, and group counseling. *Educational Technology, 13,* 40–43.

Vlosky, M. (1986). *Our game.* Broomfield, CO: Transitional Dynamics.

Wood, C., & Goddard, G. (1940). *The complete book of games.* Garden City, NY: Garden City Press.

Wotjtasik, S., & Sanborn, S. (1991). The crisis of acute hospitalization. In N.B. Webb (Ed.), *Play therapy for children in crisis* (pp. 295–309). New York: Guilford Press.

Zakich, R. (1975). *The Ungame.* Anaheim, CA: Ungame Company.

Zigler, E., & Child, I.L. (1956). Socialization. In G. Lindzey & E. Aronson (Eds.), *Handbook of social psychology* (pp. 210–248). Reading, MA: Addison-Wesley.

PART ONE

GAMES TO ELICIT COMMUNICATION AND FANTASY EXPRESSION

CHAPTER ONE

Using the *Imagine* Game as a Projective Technique

HAROLD F. BURKS

The *Imagine* game is constructed to be a psychological tool whose functions are based on the projective analysis and interpretation of verbal and nonverbal observations stimulated by fairy tale symbols together with an investigation of the related affinity given these mythological motifs.

Why concentrate on fairy tale symbols as a basis for acquiring significant projective content?

To begin, fairy tales apparently are faithful and amazing chronicles of imperative psychological stages occurring in human development (Bettelheim, 1976). Further, they seem to arouse more emotional responses than do other kinds of stimuli. While it is true that humans are compulsive anthropomorphizers (Budiansky, 1999)—always on the lookout for behaviors (animate and inanimate) that imitate, even superficially, human social phenomena, such as bravery, loyalty, reciprocal love, anger, and jealousy—some types of stimulation elicit more projective material than others do. It has occurred to me that placing a game setting in an old western pioneer town would supply players with opportunities to relate to many characters of that period: cowboy, Indian, saloon keeper, sheriff, mayor, and so on. But it is my impression that stories of the Old West are learned later in development and do not carry the emotional significance attributed to fairy tales and myths, which are related to children at early and impressionable stages of living. The symbols in fairy stories (human and otherwise) excite keen interest because listeners intuitively understand inherent mythological meanings. For instance, small children recognize the signification behind the story of the three pigs. Age brings smarts. The littlest pig is stupid—making a house out of straw that can be blown away at the first sign of stress. The next pig, being older, is brighter; he builds his (psychological) defenses more sturdily. The most mature pig, because he erects the strongest defenses, is the one who will survive when things get rough.

Are fairy tales shared unconscious fantasies? Some researchers (Bettelheim, 1976; Heuscher, 1974) believe they are. Beneath the shimmer of castles, kings and queens, trolls and elves, fairy tales carry the accumulated wisdom of the ages and teach solutions to the deepest turmoils of the human spirit. Further, the themes in the stories symbolize universal concerns humans find hard to face in isolation. Sharing troubling preoccupations is comforting. The *Imagine* game takes fairy tale symbols, uses them to activate and nourish imagination, promote creative thinking, and increase opportunities to resolve difficulties, all in the company of others.

The *Imagine* game employs several procedures to elicit projective responses. These techniques include:

Verbal methods. Players can be asked questions (either oral or written) about the meaning of game board symbols. Of course, verbal techniques presuppose that subjects possess adequate language skills and can hear or read words. Users of *Imagine* will find the projective queries quick and easy to administer.

Visual methods. Much like the Rorschach test (Rorschach, 1949) and the Thematic Apperception Test (Murray, 1943), the *Imagine* game employs two-dimensional visual stimuli requiring verbal responses. The interpretation of the replies depends, naturally, on the theoretical orientation of the clinician and on the purpose of the investigation. No normative studies or scoring systems have been established. Clinicians must intuitively analyze contents for understanding moods, attitudes, and conflicts.

Other methods. The astute diagnostician should be aware that projective material can be derived from *Imagine* game play through techniques other than verbal or visual. Some youngsters express themselves by drawing. They wish to copy the game board figures and are encouraged to do so. The drawn figures can provide additional projective data. Other children will reveal themselves best through physical movement (which is also encouraged). Finally, when youngsters write down stories the clinician will seek meanings not available in previously outlined methods.

Just like any other projective technique, the *Imagine* game, as an adjunct diagnostic and therapeutic device, is not suitable for use with all subjects.

GAME DESCRIPTION

The *Imagine* game is composed of a large game board (17.5 × 29 inches) with 40 dispersed figures (human and otherwise) from fairy tales and mythology. The board and images are in color. A game trail or path shaped like a four-leaf clover is printed on the board. Players begin the game by placing colored plastic markers in the middle of the board, on top of the Wise Wizard. Participants employ the path to advance or go back in any direction by counting out the number of spaces indicated on a thrown dice. Wherever a player lands, instructions on the space tell the person either to do something directly, such as "Use the Amazing Telephone to talk to anyone on the game board," or to draw a card from the Imagination or Pretend deck of cards. These cards have printed directions that instruct the players to do something such as "Tell a story about the Flying Horse."

Players follow the directions on the board or on the cards only if they choose to. A player who does not wish to participate simply says "I pass." If other members decide they would like to share in the question turned down by the original player, they ask that individual for permission to do so. Even if the original player has obeyed the board request, he or she may want to grant permission to others to talk about the subject of the board request. When a player has completed his or her turn, another participant may inquire, "May I ask a question about your answer?" The original player may accept or decline the request, but even when the question is accepted, the first player is not required to answer.

Players are urged to talk but are cautioned not to interrupt each other.

Directions for participating in the game are outlined on the inside of the box cover. In general, these instructions permit great scope in player actions (only answer as you desire, come and go as you wish, move about as you like, etc.).

The *Imagine* game was constructed with a number of psychological and educational beliefs in mind (Burks, 1993, 1999), all designed to encourage player participation and creative thinking. Participants are asked to:

Understand that "winning" or "losing" is not possible.
Fantasize at will.
Refrain from negative monitoring.
Listen carefully to story output of others.
Applaud the efforts of others.
Play or not play the game as desired.
Leave or come back to the game as desired.
Search imagination.
Play in a spirit of fun.
Use humor whenever possible.
Help one another.
Look over a large number of possible answers.
Act out stories physically, if desired.
Draw game board figures, if inclined.
Write down stories, if wished.

HISTORICAL BACKGROUND AND RATIONALE

In tracing the background and rationale for the *Imagine* game (Burks, 1993), I feel it proper to give credit for its early construction to a small 8-year-old boy named Sammy. Sammy was a patient under my treatment. When I first saw him he was residing in his fourth foster placement home; the first three foster families had given up because of his behavior difficulties and the present foster parents were about ready to call it quits, too.

Sammy and I quickly became good friends. During office visits he thought it only right he tidy up the room, set out the refreshments I provided, and help in any way he could. I often felt as though he had adopted me. My part of the bargain was to go to bat for him by instructing the foster parents and school personnel about the nature of his emotional problems and how I thought they could be handled better. Whenever he got into trouble at school, Sammy and I would sit down with the teacher to discuss problems and misunderstandings. The teacher was happy to co-operate. I think she, too, had a soft spot in her heart for Sammy.

Sammy was intensely interested in a game I was trying to devise using fairy tale symbols.

In a corner of my office I placed the cut-out symbols (figures and objects) of the most famous fairy tales (Cinderella, Little Red Riding Hood, Jack and the Beanstalk, etc.) on a table. As children came in for conferences I would ask them to recall the stories and to improve on them, if possible, or to try to continue the stories beyond their usual endings and to formulate different conclusions to the tales. None of these attempts, in my opinion, produced satisfactory results.

It was Sammy who taught me what needed to be done. When he studied the symbols he was distressed to find no mother figure he could use in a story he was trying to make up (he was always trying to find out about my own mother and whether she looked after me), so he reached over and preempted the queen emblem used in another tale and put her in his tale. He did the same with a figure of a giant, incorporating it in his story as a manifestation of a threatening father. To symbolize a dangerous child (Sammy was afraid of the children at school), he utilized the angry troll.

I got the point. The mythological symbols should be scattered about a game board to be employed whenever needed in story fabrications. Each figure, hopefully, should be designed to represent a particular feeling, attitude, or need, and game participants should be encouraged to use disparate symbols as required for stories.

As soon as Sammy caught on to possible projective meanings of fairy tale symbols, he became even more creative. He insisted that a child figure be included that showed someone "scared" (as he put it). I suggested we put in frightened-looking boy peering over a wall. He agreed, saying that the wall (psychological defense?) could protect the boy. For some reason that now escapes me, the wall was to be called the Lonely Wall. We discussed children who could be lost, and so, on the game board, a small boy and girl are shown wandering down a path. The king and queen figures especially intrigued Sammy. He insisted they be shown next to each other. "Mothers and fathers should stay together," he said emphatically. The house (castle) should be near children of the royal pair so they could "talk to the mother and father whenever they needed to." Sammy was conflicted about the Candy House. He wasn't sure whether or not a person should try to eat as much of the house as possible when coming on the dwelling in a forest because, as he put it, "If you don't, you may not find the house again when you leave it and then you would go hungry."

Symbol Placement

Should the fairy tale representations be placed haphazardly on the game board? In some cases, I thought not. For instance, the prince and princess, representing a more immature level of sexual development (i.e., they had not yet established completely, at this adolescent period, the ideal melding of feminine and masculine characteristics), should probably be separated. If players wanted to bring them together, they could do so. The king and queen, having attained a more exalted state of sexual union, should, as Sammy indicated, be placed next to each other. The Talking Tree (guiding father) could have a childlike, irresponsible monkey hanging from a branch that possibly needed training or discipline. The Enchanted Lake, a calm transitional area, could be placed next to the Dark Forest, another transitional locale but possibly more threatening in nature. Someone who has experienced danger in the woods might want to relax and be reborn in the waters of the lake (water being both a feminine symbol and a representation of the unconscious). The threatening Giant (dangerous father?) could be placed over the Puzzling Cave (feminine sexual symbol?) as a possible representation of the Oedipus complex. The Little Mouse (helpless child) should be placed next to the Interesting House (mother figure) because a house is a natural habitat of mice and because maternal representations should be in close proximity to child symbols. It seemed natural to put the Wise Wizard (perhaps the only adult attribute depicted in the game) in the middle of the board at the crossroads of the paths, as he was the one most likely to be consulted about perplexities brought up in stories. In short, he could be readily available to players for advice, consolation, or reassurance.

Many of the remaining symbols bear little obvious relationship to one another and are placed haphazardly on the board.

Some Mythological Meanings of Game Board Figures

Although it is true that (1) images and motifs from fairy stories carry special meanings for different people, and (2) the figures take their significance from the context of the tales in which they are used, and (3) it is an unrealizable task to try to comprehend the ultimate meanings of any story theme, it is still possible to assume that the game board images carry rich meanings to the players that may or may not be communicated to others. The images are not simple metaphors; they do not correspond to physical persons or objects in the concrete world. The correspondence to dreams or hallucinations seems slight. Nevertheless, I go along with the idea that projective analyses of responses to game board figures (even though their validity is difficult to prove) can be superior to formalized personality tests because the participants are less guarded and less likely to give controlled responses thought to please test givers.

We cannot, of course, assume that the use of a game board figure implies the storyteller is employing it for profound psychological reasons. It may be put in the story for superficial, satirical, moralizing, or entertainment purposes.

The deeper, unconscious possible meanings of the game board fairy tale figures have been categorized by Burks (1993) and Heuscher (1974) and are classified according to the possible and essential differences listed below.

BEINGS THAT FUSE HUMAN AND INFRAHUMAN CHARACTERISTICS

Characters in this classification are understood to have peculiar powers (both good and evil). Fairies, trolls, witches, elves, and sirens are such creatures. Game board characters under this heading include the Elf (primitive, childlike impulses); the Genie ("bottled-up" feelings, male sexual impulses, out-of-control feelings); the Giant (fear of father, oedipal tension); the Old Witch (bad mother, angry feelings, regressed stage of life, depression-oriented tendencies); the Troll (chronic anger, poor manners, overbearing conscience, meanness); the Wise Wizard (adult part of the personality, higher mental faculties, deliberate reasoning powers).

REPRESENTATIVES OF PROFESSIONS AND ROLES

Entities in this classification are not assumed to have paranormal powers. Instead, the roles they play reflect the deepest qualities of their basic condition (i.e., ego purposes dealing with reality as opposed to beings in the previous section, who display superego determinations, and characters in the next section, who reflect instinctual or id qualities). To illustrate ego functions, we may say that a shoemaker could be the trade of someone who reaches for the proper balance between material essence (the ground) and spirituality (the human's erect and agreeable walk through life).

Beings fitting this category include the Handsome Prince and Beautiful Princess (the adolescent personality with some immature impulses, the coming union of masculine and feminine personality aspects, the coming solution to the oedipal conflict); the King and Queen (good mother and father, higher functions of the personality, protective figures); the Lost Children (stage where child is trying to separate from parents, feelings of loneliness, sibling rivalry); the Tin Soldier (the good child who obeys rules, the handicapped individual, or a person with flaws).

ANIMAL PORTRAYALS

Animals appear to us to embody the primitive, instinctual qualities that exist in humans. For that reason, animals have become important symbols in fables. We use expressions all the time that validate the use of animals for this purpose ("stubborn as a mule," "sneaky as a weasel," "blind as a bat," "greedy as a pig," etc.). Although some of the figures illustrate obvious meanings, others do not. A horse, for instance, can be seen as both helpful or aggressive and dangerous. The little pig is stupid but not threatening, the mouse clever but weak.

Storytellers who turn to animals as assisting, helpful beings may tend to have had good "mothering" in early years. They see the world in optimistic ways. Those who concentrate on dangerous, threatening animals perhaps did not experience this kind of nurturing experience (of course, feeling threatened by animals could have other causations, sexual or otherwise). The individual who focuses on wild and untamed animals as admired subjects may possess impulses not subject to superego control.

Animals on the game board that fit this classification include the Flying Horse (friendly helper, masculine sexual force, id impulses under control, higher cortex functions, rescuer); the Frog (nonassertive, untamable impulses; represents the fluid, psychic realm of water and the firm, physical world of land; messenger with prophetic sexual knowledge); the Gossipy Parrot (nonaggressive and tamable, not free because tied to perch, not bright, difficult to teach, lacks judgment, uncaring but friendly); the Little Mouse (nonassertive, untamable, helpless, unseen, uses wits to survive, inhabits dark and dirty corners—all characteristics of small children); the Little Pig (nonaggressive, tamable, helpless, greedy and oral without proper ego restraints, messy, lives for pleasure, uncaring); Mickey the Monkey (complete child: carefree, cute, fun loving, mischievous, lovable, impulsive, shows ability to act naturally, if bothered can be aggressive, possesses little superego); the Prickly Porcupine (primitive instinctual personality, "burned child," arouses sympathy because misunderstood); Stinky Skunk (independent but not aggressive but can be dangerous if pushed; avoided for unpleasant characteristics, arouses sympathy because ostracized); the Three Bears (aggressive but tamable, evoke image of solid family with mutual concerns, intelligent and resourceful with strong ego); Wiley Wolf (sexually aggressive, dangerous, untamable, strong, quick, cunning, no superego, orally greedy, hostile).

DWELLINGS

From an unconscious point of view, dwellings (caves, houses, castles) may be observed as structures that house the human spirit (much as the body of a person does), or they can be seen as the representations of development learned in relation to the mother figure. Various expressions ("bats in the belfry," "feeling at home," "he or she lacks a good foundation") all point to the fact that a house can represent aspects of a human's personality.

Childhood experiences in the home give the house a concentrated and intense association to family relationships and home life. Responses to game board dwellings indicating the participant in alienated from structures may lead the clinician to believe the individual is alienated from his or her private self or body.

The following game board structures fit this category: the Candy House (regressed stage of development, the "good" or "bad" mother, indication of oral stage of development); the Interesting House (the mother figure, the body or self of the player, reflection of how rules and regulations were introjected); the Puzzling Cave (the primitive mother, sexual symbol, place to reflect, indication of depression); the Stone Castle (restrictive parent, the "armored" personality, great psychic strength).

MANUFACTURED OBJECTS

Any article made by humans represents something of worth, separating humans from the animal kingdom and giving us the ability to make life easier and to acquire more power over nature. Objects serve many purposes; all are useful in wish fulfillment.

The following game objects fit this classification: the Amazing Telephone (making contact with valued others); the Bag of Gold (the acquisitive, the needy, and the introspective sides of the personality); the Curious Bag (feminine symbol, introspective abilities); the Flying Carpet (passivity needs, nature of relationship to mother, wish to avoid reality); the Lonely Wall (nature of defenses, representation of life difficulties); the Magic Shoes (nature of impulses or compulsions); the Special Gold Key (availability of treasures of life, male sexual symbol); the Talking Mirror (reflection of inner life); the Treasure Chest (availability of life treasures); the Wonderful Well (symbol of unconscious).

Vegetative Motifs

Growing objects represent various aspects of life and psychic functions, both good and bad. These motifs can nourish or poison human activities (note the role of the apple in the tale of Snow White). They may also connote sexual concerns.

Game board motifs that fit this category include the Astonishing Apple (signifies aspects of life, love, and sex, strong sexual meanings); the Talking Tree (masculine symbol, guiding agent, primitive personality core); the Toadstools (feminine symbols, need for primitive shelter).

Geographical Motifs

Themes in fairy tales involving lakes, springs, ponds, or fountains are common. We may assume they are referents to the nourishing sources of life. They, along with forests, can also stand for areas of renewal (a jumping-off place to another stage of development).

Game board symbols fitting this classification include the Dark Forest (a developmental barrier, transitional area) and the Enchanted Lake (ambiguous transitional area, reflection of unconscious activity).

Case Illustrations

Uses with Individuals

One of the most intriguing characteristics of Sammy (the boy in his fourth foster placement home) was his ability to stand up to me in those matters where he thought he knew best how the game should be played. For instance, he never completely accepted the idea that there was no way to "win." I explained, as best I could, that winning and losing presupposes there are right and wrong ways to make up stories and that some young-sters would be turned off if they thought that to be the case. He bought into this idea of "no win–no lose" game playing only because he knew his stories would be better than any of the tales told by other children!

The comments by Sammy in response to game board stimuli helped me understand the nature of his motives, attitudes, and modes of school and home adjustments. From board responses and office conversations I knew he was intensely concerned and conflicted about the proper roles of parent figures (shown in confusing stories he made up about the King and Queen and the family of Three Bears symbols). The parent characteristics of these motifs, in his estimation, could not be counted on for reliable support and affection. These unhappy responses led me to demonstrate that I was al-ways available to him for reassurance and help (telephone calls immediately answered, school visits whenever needed). I offered him refreshments each time we met (giving food, I thought, equated to presenting him with tokens of affection). I also knew he was afraid of many pupils at school (his sym-bolic defense against his fear: He identified with the Prickly Porcupine who could fight anyone off "even if they were bigger").

But what about this capacity to stand up for his rights, to spar verbally with me, to face up to other kids even though he was frightened of them? It reminded me of military air crew comrades I admired during war service—men who never gave up regardless of the stress facing them. What was the source of this ego strength? My hypothesis was that he possessed a core of psychic resilience. Fostered by what? Early good mothering? He was or-phaned at 3, the parents killed in an auto crash. In those infant years, before the parents were lost, had he experienced satisfactory nurturing?

To test this postulation, I asked him to give me observations about the Curious Bag, the Treasure Chest, the Wonderful Well, and the Interest-ing House. Following are his replies along with my interpretations of the responses.

> *The Curious Bag* (studies it for a long time): "Well, there's something alive in there. I think it is a monkey who might bite you if you reached in. But he's not a really bad monkey—he's just kinda shy and scared. If he liked you he would be a good pet."
>
> *Interpretation:* The bag (feminine symbol) contains something valuable, a monkey that could be a friendly pet (indicating possible optimism on the part of the storyteller). Is Sammy telling us that a disagreeable part of his nature (burned child?) could become more attractive if ap-proached properly? Anyway, a monkey is an interesting figure to put in the story. Monkeys are active, alert, strong, and generally fun loving—all attributes of a healthy personality.
>
> *The Treasure Chest:* "There is something valuable in the chest but there is a big problem. The chest has a lock on it and it is hard to open. Somebody

has the key but nobody knows where to find the guy who has the key. Hey, Doc, maybe you know where the guy is!"

Interpretation: Again, we have a hint about the existence of a positive introject. Sammy possibly indicates a valuable part of his personality is locked in the Treasure Chest. Can it be accessed? A good sign emerges. He looks to his therapist as possibly having a key to this asset.

The Wonderful Well: "Boy, you could fall down that well and really hurt yourself! That's the trouble with wells, you have to have water but you could break your neck falling down one. If you wanted to I guess you could get into a bucket and go down to see what is at the bottom—that is, if someone would help you by winding you down. What's at the bottom? I dunno, maybe some dimes and nickels that people have thrown into the well."

Interpretation: Once again, we have interpretive evidence indicating this youngster is able to discern nourishing unconscious material when he reflects on a symbol directing him to look down (inside himself?). He even finds money at the bottom of the well, a substance that allows persons to fulfill desires. Of course, we must take cognizance of the fact that Sammy is telling us he feels it might be dangerous to examine the unconscious realm (i.e., fall down the well and hurt the self). The clinician is being warned to tread carefully when examining this area of the personality.

The Interesting House: "This house is old. Nobody lives there right now. It's cold in the house—see, there's no smoke coming out of the chimney. (Did people used to live there?) Yes, yes, they did but they went away. (Would people live there again?) Maybe."

Interpretation: Long experience with the House-Tree-Person projective test (Buck, 1948) confirms my belief that the house symbol largely reflects the previous introjection of mother-figure characteristics. The devastating loss of the natural parents is, I think, reflected in Sammy's comments about the house. In a sense, the house is dead to him, but I suppose we must note that he has not entirely given up on the notion that it might be habitable (brought back to life) in the future.

The interpretations given to Sammy's comments to the above game board motifs are interesting but would be useless if they did not bear on therapy outcomes. Did the notion that early developmental experiences (in the main, adequate mothering) give the youngster enough healthy personality underpinnings to allow us to make the assumption that therapy would produce positive results? Yes, I believe it did. Let me summarize the counseling consequences. Sammy stayed in my care for two years. He gradually (according to the foster parents and teachers) became more adjusted to home and school life. His greatest fear, that he would be rejected by his current foster family, was abated when the foster parents and I held a ceremony in the home to present the now 10-year-old Sammy with a gold-embellished certificate vouching he could never be let go by the foster parents. Sammy graduated from high school and went on to higher education. Now and then, for a long time, I received notes from my good friend Sammy.

Every so often, while using the *Imagine* game, I have received a response from an individual that almost perfectly illustrates the nature of a dilemma suffered by the person (Burks, 1993). An 11-year-old male patient came into therapy because the parents were concerned about his unhappiness and lack of friends. Tom suffers from diabetes. He has been placed on a rigid medical regimen. He tells his parents that he monitors his blood sugar levels but actually does not. This upsets the parents. They endeavor to correct his evasive actions by lecturing him. Speeches end with Tom in tears. Everyone is frustrated.

This child appeared apprehensive to me. Talking with him was difficult. He came to therapy with a chip on his shoulder. I finally asked him if he would like to play the *Imagine* game with me. He assented but looked disconcerted on seeing the game. At least, I thought, his decision to perform indicated some degree of ego strength. We sat down on the floor to begin play.

As we proceeded Tom relaxed. He looked more directly at the symbols. I asked him what he thought of the board. He answered by saying that it was certainly different. When queried as to the symbol he liked the most, he replied that he really preferred the Enchanted Lake because "it was so peaceful." When asked what it was he didn't care for, he said, stabbing his finger at the Troll, "I can sure tell you that, it's that troll. He looks mad!"

Eventually, Tom drew a Pretend card with the following message printed on it: "Pretend you put on the Magic Shoes. One shoe wants to do one thing and the other shoe wants to do something else. What happens?" The question stumped this boy for a period of time. He finally said, "Well, I think I remember that when you put on them shoes you can't take them off." He appeared distressed. Struggling with the impasse for a time he said, "Well, I guess the only thing to do is split myself down the middle so that each shoe can do what it wants."

This provocative remark brings us up short. If anything could instruct us about the inner rigidities of this youngster, his stated solution to the dilemma of the two demanding but separate-minded shoes certainly should. He is immobilized by an ethical predicament: how to gratify the contradictory wishes of both shoes. Tom is unable to alter learned symbol rules (i.e., the shoes must not be removed). Powers of imagination are paralyzed. Quite unlike most children and the majority of adults, he cannot lightheartedly say that he would let one shoe do what it wants for awhile and then let the other shoe perform. We may assume, I believe, that his solution, painful as it is, represents the resolution Tom usually employs when facing problems—that is, psychologically to split himself down the middle (and to weep miserably) when confronted with clashing demands. Subsequent talks with this child brought forth the facts that he deeply resented being "different" from peers (forced on him by his illness). He wanted to act just like them. On the other hand, giving in to the parents meant he would have to follow the demands of the medical regimen, which also caused him to feel alienated. His answer? Sob painfully.

The diagnostic—but not the reparative—value of the *Imagine* game is illustrated by the above case. To show possible healing properties, let us consider the following study (repeated from an illustration employed by the author for the manual accompanying the game board; Burks, 1993).

While experimenting with the game I had occasion to record stories from 8- and 9-year-old disturbed youngsters. One boy fixated on the plight of the Little Worm. At the end of a tale about this character he had a large bird dive down to swallow the worm. The surrounding group of children enthusiastically congratulated him for relating such a fascinating story. I could tell, though, that he wasn't completely satisfied. At the end of the meeting he came to me and said, "You know, Dr. Burks, that's not the end of the story. When the Little Worm found himself in the stomach of the bird he started to puff himself up. He got bigger and bigger until all of a sudden, POW! The bird blew up and the Little Worm floated to the ground and crawled away!"

What's going on here? The child was exhilarated by this fresh and ingenious ending to the tale. He was laughing, his cheeks flushed. Evidently, the little Worm (himself?) had outfoxed and defeated a dangerous and stronger figure (symbol of authority?). The creative act of imagining a story had transformed itself into an emotionally gratifying experience because it could be communicated to a compassionate other it was even more satisfying.

Hammer (1975) has emphasized the therapeutic need for this kind of experience. He notes the close relationship between the act of creativity and elemental personality strivings. Hammer also contends that creative expression reveals needs more clearly and directly than other types of human endeavor. Ye Burno (1989), an experienced clinician, encourages his patients to engage in creative acts because, in his opinion, these accomplishments are related to greater emotional stability. DeAngelis (1992) concurs. He narrates positive changes in physiological well-being in those employing verbal techniques to reveal inner emotions.

Apparently, creativity (such as imagining stories) is closely allied to the full and healthy expression of the personality.

The therapeutic (in addition to the diagnostic) value of the *Imagine* game was an unexpected but welcome finding. Does it matter if the clinician fails to understand the projective meanings inherent in a player's statements? Not really. The psychological benefits derived by the child who told the story about the Little Worm and the swooping bird would no doubt have occurred whether or not the clinician comprehended deeper story explanations. Further, it must be pointed out that players, particularly children, do not gain assistance from a psychological analysis of stories. The stimulation a participant derives from dreaming up a story is not improved, in fact, may well be decreased, by listening to an anatomization of narrative meanings. Diagnosis remains suspect. As Ekstein (1989) explains, analysis of verbal free associations do not explain psychological illnesses and do not cure disorders.

The foregoing examples of responses to game symbols by individuals hopefully give the reader some insights into the diagnostic and therapeutic uses of *Imagine*. But the full flavor of the game cannot be grasped until the impact of its employment in group situations is understood.

USES WITH GROUPS

During game construction I deliberately tried to incorporate features that encourage creative group expression. Many ideas were gained from readings by Torrance (1962a, 1962b, 1981). Following is a description of properties that apparently promote imagination:

1. *Players independently choose to play the game or not.* In group work I never push a child to participate. Experience demonstrates that most individuals become so intrigued watching others play they quickly volunteer to participate.
2. *No player is forced to continue play when he or she wishes to stop.* Some children tire quickly. Weary participants concentrate on feelings of fatigue rather than on the wish to free associate.
3. *When enthusiasm for the game diminishes, the game is stopped.* One cannot expect excitement to continue indefinitely. It's a good idea to stop play while players are still stimulated. This tends to ensure they will want to return to the game in the near future.

4. *Environmental stimuli is kept to a minimum.* Fantasy is engendered more efficiently in a nondistracting milieu. Supervising adults are advised to keep verbal participation to a minimum, enabling game participants to concentrate on stories rather than on needs of adults.

5. *Freedom of bodily movement is encouraged.* Children, in particular, need to move about when playing. Williams (1973) found that many youngsters, when focusing on a problem, demonstrate nervous mannerisms (scratching, picking, tapping, etc.). This activity apparently enhances concentration. Some players communicate better through movement than through speech. The game should be played in an informal atmosphere with players coming and going as they wish, perhaps sitting on the floor or walking around.

6. *No one is forced to play in a hurry.* Haste can defeat efforts to fantasize. The process needed to formulate original and complex thought patterns requires time, although the duration of this interval varies from person to person. When a player displays an air of finality and satisfaction after telling a story, we may be sure the necessary time for creative thought has occurred.

7. *A spirit of fun is encouraged.* Genuine creativity resides in the "child" side of the personality structure (Steiner, 1974). The child ego is identified with the characteristics of spontaneity, innovation, and a willingness to take risks. Playful thinking reinforces efforts to be creative (Siegelman, 1990). The child ego can be stifled if adults ask for or demand prescribed responses. Creativity withers on command.

8. *Responses are not monitored.* The native intelligence of small children is discounted when responses are interpreted in a literal, straightforward way. Repetitive questioning can make children uncertain of replies, forcing some to change responses. Critiquing the direction or outcome of stories can indicate story elements are inadequate or inferior. These negative perceptions may stifle imagination. To enhance player comfort, no scoffing at stories is permitted.

9. *Responses are never analyzed.* As has been pointed out, players (in particular, children) do not benefit from psychological story interpretations. In any case, sentence-like external representations of imagery can never fully account for fantasy (Rollins, 1989).

10. *Encouragement is offered to verbalize hidden impulses.* Hiding unpleasant or dangerous thoughts is a universal occurrence. Menacing

thoughts, in particular, are kept out of consciousness because individuals may be afraid they will be translated into harmful actions if admitted into conscious thought. Repression, however, ordinarily exacerbates the strength of morbid impulses, making the threat of their emergence even more troublesome. The game of *Imagine* offers avenues of thinking and expression where these urges can be experienced safely.

The reader may gather a comprehensive feeling for the *Imagine* game as it relates to group interactions if I relate a recent experience with elementary-age students. My son, Tom, teaches a class of fourth-graders. He wanted to see how the children (mostly disadvantaged youngsters, many of Spanish American extraction) would react to the game. When I entered the classroom, Tom explained that I was his father. This created a commotion. The pupils were anxious to know about their teacher's childhood: Was he a good boy? Did I have to spank him a lot? Did I give him many toys? Where was his mother? After this barrage of questions (clearly with projective meanings in themselves), the youngsters wanted to know what kind of game it was that I brought to the classroom. They were intrigued by the game board cover. The cover, containing many colorful fairy tale figures, is intrinsically interesting to youngsters.

At this point, I would like to say that one of the advantages of the game is that it is quick and easy to administer and supervise. Children immediately see it as something challenging and attractive. My personal preference is to let them study the colorful board for as long as they like. Typically, comments such as "Gee, look at that mean old witch!", "I wish I had all the gold in that bag!", "I wonder what's in the Treasure Chest?", and "Look at the stupid little pig!" are forthcoming. Sometimes these observations provide projective material to the clinician who observes which objects seem to have the most meaning to participants and which symbols provoke the greatest number of commentaries.

These fourth-graders reacted to the game no differently than any other group of children I have observed. They inspected the covers with avid interest and then tore off the plastic to get at the board. My son and I divided the class into five groups, each with a game. Many sat on the floor or on and around tables. The six students at my table spent about five minutes studying and commenting on the board symbols. The largest boy in my group (actually the biggest pupil in the room), an African American child, climbed up on my chair, sat himself up against me, and proceeded to run the game. He started out by telling the other players when they could speak and when to keep quiet. These actions, of course, violated the spirit of spontaneity necessary for productive playing. I gently told George that everybody got to speak when they wanted to. He was uncomfortable with this imperative but finally gave in after I interrupted him several times to remind him of the requirement.

Typically, a child or two in every group takes a long time to become involved. In my assemblage, one little Spanish American girl sat quietly for about 10 minutes, but she could not bring herself to stay out of the interplay. She finally crept up to the board and said she liked the princess. The other children studied the symbol, and one girl asked her what she liked about the princess. The reply was that she thought the clothes were nice. Now, this may not sound like much of a contribution, but for this youngster it was an act of constructive aggression not evident in ordinary class participations (this according to my son).

Except for George, the students in my group did not give lengthy stories and the quality of the tales was uneven. George was fascinated with the giant figure and wove a tale about a giant who went about the land forcing his will on others. Fortunately, the giant was benevolent in nature. He simply needed to rule others because they were "too dumb" and because he knew what was good for them. We will hear from George in years to come.

We must not concentrate on final story narratives to the exclusion of other indications of productive mental involvement. The children in my group (much like those in similar gatherings) gave the following indices of creative activity (from a checklist compiled by Torrance, 1962a):

1. Many evidences of *intense animation and physical involvement* (seen more often in younger than older subjects).
2. Many suggestions of *bodily engagement of an intense nature in writing, reading, and drawing* (many children want to write their stories or draw game board symbols).
3. Many intimations that children want to *study and look at symbols closely* (seen in children of all ages).
4. Many signs of *intense absorption in listening, observing, and doing* (seen in youngsters of all ages).

5. Many indications of *eagerness to tell others about discoveries* (children want to tell stories to each other).

6. Many manifestations of the wish to *show relationships between apparently unrelated symbols or ideas* (youngsters bring coherence to the affinity they seen in game motifs).

7. Many intimations of *heightened curiosity* (participants become interested in one another's stories and want to know more).

8. Many wishes to *check story sources* (memories of fairy stories are checked among players).

9. Many demonstrated desires to *consider or toy with strange ideas* (much of the originality demonstrated in stories springs from this desire).

10. Many tendencies to *lose awareness of time* (many players have to be asked to stop play).

11. Many indications of a wish to make an *intense and honest search for truth of inner feelings* (children identify with emotions thought to be felt by game symbols).

12. Many evidences of *excitement in voices concerning game discoveries* (seen mostly in younger children).

13. Many signs of *analogies being employed in speech patterns* (employed by nearly all players, particularly when confronting emotion-arousing symbols: witch can be "old bag," "old grouch," "old hag," etc.).

14. Much *spontaneous employment of experimental approaches* (applies, in the main, to the extent players judge the impact of stories on others).

15. Many indications of willingness to *manipulate ideas and objects to form new combinations* (very evident when players feel free from criticism to do this).

16. Many signs that players want to *take independent actions* (game is constructed to encourage attempts to make up individual stories, to write them down, and to illustrate them).

17. Many indications of *self-initiated learning* (true to the extent that few children want to be left out of the game).

18. An evident wish to *challenge ideas of authority* (happens when child attacks or questions adult authority).

19. Tendencies to *search out and explore new game board possibilities* (children like to change story endings or make up a new hero).

20. Evidence among some pupils to *concoct bold stories* (game encourages children to propose aggressive solutions to story conundrums).

21. Many signs children want to *test story outcomes* (seen when players are interested in the give-and-take reactions of others to invented tales).
22. Many manifestations of *penetrating questions and observations* (stories raise level of curiosity about contents of particular tales).
23. Many signs of wishes to *follow through on ideas set in motion by stories* (players continue to build on stories after game ends).
24. Many expressed wishes to *continue playing after game officially ends* (most groups evidence this desire).

The above phenomena are noted, in the main, during play of groups made up of children but are not generally seen in adult gatherings. This is true for the following obvious reasons: (1) Adults think it somewhat embarrassing to play what to them is a childish activity, almost "silly" in nature; and (2) adults are not as close as children to the primitive or magical side of their natures, the part that can suspend belief about the logical or realistic condition of the universe.

Under particular circumstances, I have found the game useful with adult groups. During marathon sessions, seminars lasting for 24 hours or more, participants tend to let down defenses, lie down on the floor like children, and play *Imagine* in playful and even mischievous ways. Certain game board symbols, like the Amazing Telephone, are capable of eliciting strong emotional responses. One woman, when asked to speak to someone she missed, pretended to call her deceased mother but immediately broke down into tears. This episode precipitated a long discussion about unresolved conflicts with her mother, frictions that had never previously been reviewed. This opened up for inspection personality problems central to the reasons she entered therapy.

The *Imagine* game, I believe, has also proven useful in family therapy interactions. Fairy tales, in the main, involve parent and child ego aspects of the personality (the adult ego is largely ignored), and fables place characters in universally well-known roles (the hard-working mother or father, the neglected child, the authoritarian, nonunderstanding grown-up, the youngster innocently wandering into trouble, etc.), and members can identify with these figures, elaborate on their attributes, and relate to difficulties faced by mythological subjects.

An example illustrates these processes. A father, mother, and two children played the game during a counseling session. The father, the most resistant member of the group and the most unwilling to talk, had to be urged to join in play. The question came up as to what character or symbol the players thought they were most like. When it came to the father's turn, he stared at the board for some time and finally muttered that he thought he was the one-legged Tin Soldier. His wife glanced at him in sharp surprise. The children, with uninhibited ardor, thought his reply explained why he always looked stiff and at attention and, like most sentries, quiet. One child got up, stood on a single leg, saluted the father, and imitated his grim visage. The wife was the one who would not let his choice of game board symbol pass without comment. She had good reason to do this because the principal motive for entering family therapy lay in the displeasure she experienced concerning her husband's reticence and evident discomfort in family relationships. She had told me in a private session that she was thinking of leaving him because he seemed like a stranger to her. "John," she asked, "please explain to us why you feel like a soldier—one with only a single leg." To everyone's astonishment, this man began to tear up. He mumbled, almost incoherently, that he always felt like an outsider, that he was overworked, had to guard the family, and was not gaining enough pleasure from life. Then he started to weep. The children flung themselves on him, telling him that they loved him. His wife also embraced him.

This incident changed the course and outcome of therapy for this family. The husband found he could let down his defenses without catastrophic results; the children were delighted they could comfort and feel closer to their father; and the wife, to her eventual surprise, learned that she was not giving enough solace and understanding to her mate because she was so involved with the children and their interests and with outside duties. The husband later told his wife he had come to feel of no importance in the family circle.

Glowing examples of the efficacy of the *Imagine* game should not obscure the fact that there are limitations to the efficient use of any projective counseling device.

LIMITATIONS OF PROJECTIVE COUNSELING TECHNIQUES

Once upon a time, I had high hopes for a projective technique I entitled "The Path of Life." In counseling sessions I would ask clients to imagine they were on a path in the wilderness. After they visualized this scene and told me about it, I would take them along the path to different situations (e.g., see a house, an animal, a dangerous spot, other persons, etc., and describe possible conflict characteristics of imagined settings). This exercise was an effective diagnostic tool. It gave me significant information about a patient's attitudes, motivations, current emotional conflicts, and so on, but did little for his or her mental health. In short, no reparative process was occurring because *no significant emotional affect accompanied patient statements.* If an imagined scene does not arouse feelings of apprehension, anxiety, fear, dread, or, hopefully, depression (all emotions, experienced and repressed in early years), then the patient *is not experiencing the emergence of unconscious and unwanted motives that must be confronted if therapy is eventually to be successful.*

Of course, not all individuals seen in the counseling office suffer undue neurotic symptoms. Some clinicians working in schools, public health clinics, prisons, or hospitals encounter subjects lacking proper superego controls who are not emotionally conflicted enough. They may also suffer impulse control deficiencies and be unable to reflect inwardly (many refuse to become depressed when frustrated). Is the game of *Imagine* a useful counseling instrument with these individuals? Perhaps to the degree it supplies diagnostic information, but not to the extent it offers therapeutic assistance. Unconforming teens, for instance, may show contempt for game board subjects by flouting accepted rules of conduct (e.g., the advice of the Wise Wizard is ridiculed, wild animals like the Wolf are admired). Outside of diagnostic hints, I have not found the game to be particularly effective as far as helping these subjects acquire insights or change unethical behaviors for the better.

It goes without saying that the genetic makeup of an examined individual influences the quality and amount of diagnostic material derived from the use of any projective device. Most children with normally functioning nervous systems produce satisfactory stories and other evidence of imagery because they are able to employ rich fantasy lives that nourish egos with imagery that can be employed in the service of solving problems and making life tolerable and productive.

This is not so true for many children with attention-deficit (Burks, 1957, 1960, 1964, 1985, 1993). Many of these youngsters cannot enlist the assistance of a functioning fantasy life. As a result, their conduct is characterized by impulsivity, poor attention, and sometimes by hyperactivity.

This style of overreaction to environmental stimulation evidently occurs because an impetus to act is translated at once into muscle action rather than being mediated through imaginative thought processes.

Some physiologically healthy individuals cannot employ active fantasy lives apparently because they have been taught in early stages of development to fear inner imagery. I consider these persons to be "constipated in the head" (Burks, 1993). Sometimes, therapy can free them from bondage to the restrictive rulings. The *Imagine* game can be helpful in this regard, particularly when used with children.

Then there are normal individuals who apparently cannot fantasize. Thinking occurs in literal ways, and imaginative skill training brings few encouraging results. As a clinician for many years, my impression is that most become engineers whose pedantic conduct drives spouses insane.

Finally, we must be aware that some subjects possess an imagination that knows few boundaries. Reality appears to be a nuisance. I have had a few youngsters with proclivities to overfantasize when playing *Imagine* and remain puzzled how to interpret these free flows of consciousness. At times, I think it an indication of pathology; at other times, I believe some have been encouraged to employ unrestricted fantasy. This proved true in one instance: The mother of a 9-year-old daydreaming girl admitted she had immersed her daughter in romantic stories and encouraged her to engage in wild imaginings. I suggested she limit this unusual form of stimulation.

SUMMARY AND CONCLUSIONS

The *Imagine* game, I believe, has withstood the test of usage. It achieves at least two purposes: (1) It obtains significant diagnostic information from game participants; and (2) it enables some contestants to achieve greater emotional stability. Story thought processes transmute contrary preoccupations and hurtful emotions like jealousy, anger, and revenge into creative works, constructive and adapative in nature, leading to positive changes in physiological and emotional health (DeAngelis, 1992).

These aims may suffice for most clinicians, but other, unexpected but welcome aspects of the game must be considered. The *Imagine* game has proven popular with classroom teachers, hospital workers, and parents—most with limited exposure to psychological theory. Why, then, the enthusiasm shown by these individuals? Simply because they felt *Imagine* achieved two other purposes, that the intellectual and social development of youngsters was furthered because: (1) participants became more *creative*, and (2) players learned to *communicate* better with each other.

I will not devote a great deal of space to these apparently agreeable findings, except to say that the act of creativity is closely tied to the need for self-expression (Glover, Ronning, & Reynolds, 1989) and to mention that disadvantaged and unusually silent children are more powerfully affected to use speech by visual stimuli than by auditory cues. Formal instruction (because it tends to inhibit creativity) leaves them unconcerned. *Imagine* encourages communication by allowing players to "run the show" and by encouraging them to fantasize at will.

It is worth pointing out one more time that strivings to be more creative and acts of self-expression apparently contribute to greater emotional stability (Godmun, Smith, & Carlsson, 1990). Sarasan (1990) expands on this reasoning: He holds the urgency to give voice to internal imaginings to be a universal and constructive propensity (even though it is often stifled by social structures). Current educational practices, unfortunately, stress logical-scientific thinking to the detriment of abilities to contemplate and voice the unconscious realm.

SOME CAUTIONARY NOTES

Now, a word of warning to clinicians who use projective game techniques in classrooms or similar situations: Adults, teachers, aides, and other supporting personnel are usually not prepared to understand the sexual meanings inherent in ancient myths. They may even be offended by erotic interpretations. Let me give an example. Some time ago, I gave a talk to a large group of teachers about the mechanics of the *Imagine* game. In discussing the analytic meanings of fairy tales, I mentioned that the story of Little Red Riding Hood was probably a narration about the sexual maturation of females and went on to discuss menstruation and phallic symbols employed in ancient stories. The audience (consisting mostly of younger female teachers) froze. Rapport between speaker and listeners vanished.

I don't give talks like that anymore.

My personal preference, when talking to individuals with limited psychological training, is to discuss game stories in transactional terms (Berne, 1964). Listeners catch on quickly to the idea that there are three major ego sides of the personality: (1) the child state, which is considered to be spontaneous and free and is the origin of creative activities; (2) the parent state, which takes on the task of teaching rules and regulations (much of this knowledge is used in the formation of the superego); and (3) the adult state, which adopts the role of decision making and logical reasoning.

Many *Imagine* symbols are employed to represent the child state, such as the Magic Shoes, Mickey the Monkey, Little Pig, Lost Children, and Little Mouse. The parent ego state is denoted by the King and Queen, the Old Witch, the Talking Tree, and the Giant. The adult ego condition is less easy to classify. I placed the Wise Wizard in the middle of the game board to represent someone who, so to speak, "directs traffic" and is endowed with judicial sagacity. Not many other symbols are seen to embody adult characteristics, although, at times, the King and Queen, as role players in stories, may be allowed to make intelligent choices.

We should be aware that fairy tales are nearly always made up of parent and child figures (scant interest is paid to adult types). This should not surprise us. Fairy stories are faithful chronicles of psychological complications faced by children at diverse stages of development. In the beginning, children must endeavor to control and direct untamed impulses and to deal with adults who govern them. The ability and the necessity to make adultlike judgments occur in later years.

CHOICE OF PROJECTIVE INSTRUMENTS

A final word about effective uses of projective devices such as the *Imagine* game: The basic rule is identical to that employed for other psychological tests: Utilize the simplest and most economical instruments in terms of time and effort. Most disturbed children, for instance, can be identified through the employment of standard screening devices like the *Burks Behavior Rating Scales* (Burks, 1977), an instrument used to screen millions of children over the past thirty years. Most of the youngsters identified by these scales as having social, emotional, and academic problems do not need further elaborate diagnostic testing. But some do. For these troubled individuals, those with problems whose sources remain a riddle to the clinician (Chua-Eoan, 1999), diagnostic instruments should be administered but only if they contribute specific information not obtainable more quickly and easily by other means. In addition, chosen test devices should offer a maximum of information, and this is accomplished when applied instruments can be analyzed in several different ways.

The game of *Imagine,* in certain circumstances, may be an instrument of choice. With withdrawn or reluctant subjects, the game is a good ice-breaker because children see it as a fun undertaking. Unlike most projective devices, the game can be played in association with others, and this allows the diagnostician to note participant social abilities and dysfunctions. Creative thinking abilities and communicative skills can also be estimated. Another possible strength of the game resides in its capability to sustain the interest of subjects. They want to play it again and again, offering the clinician renewed opportunities to analyze projective content. Finally, because game play can incorporate activities like drawing, writing, and bodily movement, the diagnostician is provided additional sources of projective information.

REFERENCES

Berne, E. (1964). *Games people play.* New York: Grove Press.

Bettelheim, B. (1976). *The uses of enchantment.* New York: Alfred A. Knopf.

Buck, J.N. (1948). The H-T-P technique, a qualitative and quantitative scoring manual. *Journal of Clinical Psychology, 4,* 317–396.

Budiansky, S. (1999, July). The truth about dogs. *Atlantic Monthly,* 284.

Burks, H.F. (1957). The effect of brain pathology on learning. *Journal of Exceptional Children, 24,* 186–194.

Burks, H.F. (1960). The hyperkinetic child. *Journal of Exceptional Children, 27,* 18–26.

Burks, H.F. (1964). Effects of amphetamine therapy on hyperkinetic children. *Archives of General Psychiatry, 11,* 604–609.

Burks, H.F. (1977). *Burks Behavior Rating Scales.* Los Angeles: Western Psychological Services.

Burks, H.F. (1985). *Diagnosis and remediation of learning and behavior problems in children using the Burks Behavior Rating Scales: A handbook.* Los Angeles: Western Psychological Services.

Burks, H.F. (1993). *The Imagine game.* Los Angeles: Western Psychological Services.

Burks, H.F. (1999). *Diagnosis and remediation of learning and behavior problems in children using the Burks Behavior Rating Scales* (rev. ed.) Los Angeles: Western Psychological Services.

Chua-Eoan, H. (1999, May 31). How to spot a troubled kid. *Time, 153,* No. 21.

DeAngelis, T. (1992). Illness linked with repressive style of coping. *Monitor,* 23(12), 13–14.

Ekstein, R. (1989). *The language of psychotherapy.* The Netherlands: John Benjamins.

Glover, J.A., Ronning, R.R., & Reynolds, C.R. (1989). *Handbook of creativity.* New York: Plenum Press.

Godmun, J., Smith, W., & Carlsson, J.M. (1990). *The creative process: A functional model based on empirical studies from early childhood to middle age.* Madison, CT: International Universities Press.

Hammer, E.F. (1975). *The clinical application of projective drawings.* Springfield, IL: Thomas.

Heuscher, J.E. (1974). *A psychiatric study of myths and fairy tales.* Springfield, IL: Thomas.

Murray, H.A. (1943). *Thematic apperception test.* Cambridge, MA: Harvard University Press.

Rollins, M. (1989). *Mental imagery: On the limits of cognitive science.* New Haven, CT: Yale University Press.

Rorschach, H. (1949). *Pschodiagnostics.* New York: Grune & Stratton.

Sarasan, S.B. (1990). *The challenge of art to psychology.* New Haven, CT: Yale University Press.

Siegelman, E.Y. (1990). *Metaphor and meaning in psychotherapy.* New York: Guilford Press.

Steiner, C. (1974). *Scripts people live.* New York: Grove Press.

Torrance, E.P. (1962a). *Guiding creative talent.* Engelwood Cliffs, NJ: Prentice-Hall.

Torrance, E.P. (1962b). Non-test ways of identifying the creatively gifted. *Gifted Child Quarterly, 6,* 71–75.

Torrance, E.P. (1981). *Thinking creatively in action and movement.* Bensonville, IL: Scholastic Testing Services.

Williams, D.G. (1975). So-called nervous habits. *Journal of Psychology, 83,* 103–109.

Ye Burno, M. (1989). *Therapy by means of creative self-expression: Psychotherapeutic treatment of psychopathies and slowly pregradient schizophrenic disorders with defensive manifestations.* Moscow, USSR.

CHAPTER TWO

The *Feeling* Word Game

ELYCE A. CRON

T he ability to express emotions has long been regarded as essential for good mental and physical health (Albon, Brown, Khantzian, & Mack, 1993; Easterling, Antoni, Kumar, & Schneiderman, 1990; Pennebaker, 1995; Smyth, 1998; Spiegel, Bloom, Kraemer, & Gottheil, 1989). In addition, to express emotions, it is equally essential to accurately identify and label those emotions with appropriate descriptive adjectives (Brody, 1999; Magai & McFadden, 1996; Oatly, 1992; Shapiro & Emde, 1992).

However, there are very few suggestions in the literature of methods to aid the identification of emotions or to teach labels (descriptive adjectives) that name the emotions being experienced. The *Feeling* word game (Cron, 2000) fills that gap. It teaches a wide vocabulary of expressive words and also encourages free expression of feelings. By framing the skills of identification and expression in a game format, the *Feeling* word game places the learning process in an enjoyable experience and, in addition, gives it a bit of competitive spice. Within the game the task of learning becomes fun.

Other underlying benefits are reaped. For example, game players generally become less guarded in the excitement and energized atmosphere of the competition. As they search their memories for illustrative examples of a feeling, it is not unusual for personal narratives to emerge.

Without consciously trying, whole repertoires of descriptive stories are disclosed by the participants. This, in turn, greatly detoxifies any reluctance or inhibition toward disclosure of personal stories. Another unconsciously gained benefit comes from listening to others' tales. In the listening and telling of each person's stories, all players discover that they are not the only ones who have these feelings.

Stories can, and usually will, be drawn from the personal experiences of the game players' positive and negative experiences, depending on the type of word being described. Those feeling words that are descriptive of positive affect often elicit silly, happy, joyful, proud examples, which, when shared, can increase the positive effect of those pleasant experiences. Both the telling of and the listening to positive stories bond the game players in mutual enjoyment. The feeling words that describe negative affect are frequently illustrated with stories of shame, fear, guilt, or sadness. The potential effect of externalizing the game players' specific experiences elicited by the negative words, in the unguarded moments of sharing in the game play, is to dilute and lessen the negativity of those incidents. In the same way that the telling of positive stories brings mutual enjoyment and bonding, the darker, heavier feelings bring an awareness of not being alone in pain and hurt. In some ways, the negative story bonding is even stronger. Several research studies (Easterling et al., 1990; Oatly, 1992; Smyth, 1998) support the efficacy and benefits of expressing internal affect. The *Feeling* word game provides a natural and fun vehicle for emotional expression of both positive and negative content.

DESCRIPTION OF THE GAME

The *Feeling* word game is deceptively simple in its presentation. The plastic game bag contains 110 cards, approximately the size of business cards. Each card is printed with a single feeling word surrounded by a rainbow border. Examples of the words are angry, calm, silly, worried, hurt, amazed, and flabbergasted. The reverse of each card is imprinted with either a number 1 or 2, signifying the level of difficulty of the vocabulary. The 60 Level 1 feeling words are more likely to be in the vocabulary of younger or less articulate people (e.g., scared, mad, friendly, sick, nervous, happy, and puzzled). The 50 Level 2 feeling words are more likely to be in the vocabulary of older or more articulate persons (e.g., belittled, ecstatic, resigned, suspicious, proficient, indignant, and bizarre). Other, "special use" cards found in the game bag are imprinted with the words seldom, often, almost always, and right now; their use is described in the section below on individual play.

Basic Instructions

Basic instructions for play of the *Feeling* word game are as follows:

1. Before beginning a game, decide how many rounds will be played (e.g., each player will have 4 turns, 6 turns, etc.).
2. Deal each player 1 card for each round, face down.
3. The person whose birthdate is closest to today's date starts the round as the communicator; after that, play continues to the left (clockwise).
4. Communication of the feeling word may be by:
   Telling a story illustrating the word (When I got my cast off, I danced and giggled).
   Using synonyms to describe the feeling (It's a giddy feeling).
5. The communicator may not use the feeling word or any form of it when conveying his or her feeling word. (If the word is *silly,* then *silliest* or *sillier* may not be used.)
6. Each communicator has 2 minutes to convey the feeling.
7. At the end of 2 minutes, if the feeling has not been correctly guessed, the communicator loses 1 point.
8. If the communicator inadvertently uses the feeling word while conveying the feeling, he or she loses 1 point.
9. If the word or the root of the word (e.g., *peace* for *peaceful*) is correctly guessed before the 2 minutes is up, that person earns 1 point. If 2 guessers simultaneously guess the correct word, each earns 1 point.
10. It is suggested the guessers use the formula: "You feel . . ." or "You felt . . ." when guessing the feeling word.
11. The player to the right of the communicator is the timekeeper and gives the communicator a warning when 90 seconds have elapsed.
12. The 60 cards marked with a 1 are easier words for children and beginners. The 50 cards marked with a 2 are harder and for advanced players. The decks may be combined.

13. The main object of the *Feeling* word game is to learn to communicate (send and receive) feelings. Even if you do not get the top score, everyone wins when these goals are met (Cron, 1998).

These simple rules are the basic, core instructions for the use of the *Feeling* word game. However, there are additional instructions found in the game bag, which describe modifications for use in team play, group play, couple play, and individual play.

TEAM PLAY

Team play uses the same basic rules outlined above, only now the competition changes to include a whole team of guessers trying to discover the feeling being conveyed by one member of the opposing team. All points are recorded as team scores. This version of play is suited to atmospheres where the group members are comfortable with disclosure to several people on the opposing team. This version is frequently more boisterous and energetic and has a higher level of competition.

GROUP PLAY

Group play suggests two possible formats. In version A, each player is dealt three cards and may select one feeling word to explore with the group. An agreed-upon time of three to five minutes is suggested for each player to take a turn sharing with the group. This format is especially well suited to those who do not care for the competitive aspect of the basic rules. It can also provide a calmer, more relaxed time frame for sharing. The longer time gives the game play less urgency, and there is no pressure for scoring a point to move on. In fact, no points are gathered in this version. The sole purpose is to communicate and disclose personal stories to the other group members. The game becomes a framework in which the exploration and the sharing of emotions is the norm. Because everyone is doing it, there is less resistance to disclosure.

In the group play version B of the *Feeling* word game, the entire deck is fanned out for one person (perhaps the leader of the group) to draw a card. Everyone shares a personal experience about the same feeling. There is no specific timing for each individual's turn. Once again, no points are recorded; the primary goal is clearly to communicate and to identify the internal emotional experience of that specific feeling.

This version can be a vehicle for the therapist to "load the deck," so to speak. Instead of fanning out all 110 cards for choosing a feeling to explore, the therapist can select specific words that have the potential of opening up topics that are being avoided by individual members or by the group collectively. A progressively more difficult grouping of topics has a good success potential. Group trust can be built by using several softer or more benign topic groupings for the selection pool, slowly progressing toward the more difficult groupings of feeling words. It should be obvious that a creative therapist can modify the use of the cards with a group in many ways beyond the ways described here or offered by the instruction cards found in the game bag.

COUPLE PLAY

Couple play once again uses the basic rules, with the following suggestions for when only two persons are playing the game. The directions clearly specify that the game is not competitive. It is to be used as a tool for communication, a means for deeper understanding, and a method to increase dialogue between the pair. Cards are dealt, feelings and stories are shared, partners guess what the emotion being conveyed is. The focus is on listening to one another, listening especially for the emotional content of the stories. The benefits are both a deeper appreciation of the differences between two people and an increase of the depth of knowledge of each other.

A second version is also proposed for couple use. In this version, no words may be used. In pantomime, somewhat like playing charades, the couple tries to communicate the feeling without verbalizing anything. Obviously, any of the versions of the *Feeling* word game can be played in mime fashion. However, as the group gets larger, the therapist might also need to become a referee to keep the energy in the group from spinning out. In mime play, the ratio of boisterousness increases exponentially with each additional person. It only takes one budding thespian to double the possibility of the group's getting out of control. In some settings and circumstances, the fun and high volume of the mime play can be very beneficial—just be aware of the pitfalls!

When used with just a pair of participants, the mime play can be very worthwhile. The potential is for an increase of the ability of each partner to accurately assess feelings from gestures and facial expressions and body language. Another, more subtle benefit may also be reaped: The partners learn to verbally verify their intuitive and impressionistic interpretations of the partner's body language instead of relying and acting on possibly inaccurate assumptions.

Although this use of the *Feeling* word game might seem, on the surface, to be only for married couples or adults in relationship, it can also be a very effective tool for working with adolescents. One of the case illustrations below describes highlights of using this version in a school counselor's office.

INDIVIDUAL PLAY

Individual play is quite different from the other multiple-person games described above. The goal now becomes very personal. Indeed, in this version, the cards can be used in solitude as a personal exploration to raise self-awareness and understanding. Five extra cards, found in the game bag, are used in this version: seldom, sometimes, often, almost always, and right now. When spread across the top of a desk they become categories under which each feeling word card can be placed. Are there some feelings that the client would like to have more often? Do some appear in the "almost always" category that he or she would choose to make less frequent? Are there here-and-now feelings that need to be discussed? The exploration of these feelings and narratives can, as mentioned above, be done alone. They can also provide a soft, nonthreatening vehicle for opening counseling dialogue across a wide spectrum of feelings.

CASE ILLUSTRATIONS

The following case examples are arranged in the same order as the descriptions of the different uses of the *Feeling* word game outlined above. They are drawn from the author's own experiences with the use of the game. Care has been taken to protect the confidential nature of the stories.

BASIC PLAY

A group of camp counselors were preparing for the summer. They had been practicing good listening skills and found that they were very good at hearing content and information in their practice with their partners. However, when it was suggested that good listening includes attention to the affective content of the stories, several reported that they heard no particular emotional content in their practice listening. Others said that they felt it was prying into personal territory to mention nonverbal cues of feeling content. Still others felt they were repeating themselves: "You felt upset," "That was upsetting to you," or "How upsetting!"

The *Feeling* word game was used with the group of 12 counselors, divided into small groups of four. Each person in each group was dealt four cards and the play commenced. As groups finished their first set of cards, they could continue by drawing one more feeling word card each until all groups had completed, at a minimum, their original grouping of four feeling words each.

During the processing of the experience, comments included "I never realized how many words I could use instead of *upset!*"; "I really felt like my partner camp counselors wanted to understand what I was trying to tell them"; "I think our pretend camper was really able to explore what she was feeling better because we concentrated on finding the exact word for her feeling."

The game was played several more times in the course of the training. At the end of the summer camping experience, when asked to give feedback on what was the most helpful part of the precamp training, playing the *Feeling* word game was given a ranking of either "very helpful" or "outstandingly helpful" by all the camp counselors.

TEAM PLAY

The group of adolescents at the high school had been meeting for almost eight weeks. The stated purpose of the group was to deal with processing the feelings surrounding their parents' divorce. Although the counselor felt that some effective work had been done, there were still some teens who did not share much. The atmosphere had become so heavy with the negative that some of the students had said they were thinking about dropping out of the group. "It's too depressing," and "I dread coming because I always leave feeling worse" were some comments the counselor heard.

The *Feeling* word game was introduced as "something fun we can do." When the instructions were read for team play, one teen expressed disdain for the activity. Others said they'd like to give it a try. One especially shy girl held back from taking her turn, but her team members encouraged her: "You can do it!"; "You'll be fine!"

The play only lasted for half of the session, but the spirited dialogue about the game in the second half of the session was energetic and productive. The teens asked if they could play again and the counselor did use the game several more times. In order not to cause a split in the group, she was careful to divide the group into teams with different members each time. The resultant mutual support, camaraderie, and "can do" spirit permeated the other work of the group. What they learned from the game also helped them learn to cope with the feelings and emotional impact surrounding the divorce they were experiencing in their lives.

Group Play A

The single-parent family had been coming to counseling together. Both children had been diagnosed with ADHD and were on Ritalin. The counseling hour often dissolved into a mutual gripe session with the brother and sister pointing fingers of blame at each other. Mom's voice, attempting to control the squabbling, was usually ignored. No one listened to anyone else. The counselor, to little avail, had attempted various interventions.

The *Feeling* word game was introduced. Each member of the family received three cards from which they were to select one feeling to share. A kitchen timer was used to limit the storytelling to three minutes each. It was passed around so that the person to the right of the communicator was in charge of the time. In the first round the counselor included herself to model the sharing. One small modification to the rules of the game was used for this family. Before the turn was passed to the next person in a clockwise fashion, the new communicator had to first summarize what the previous one had shared. Each person had to really listen to what the previous one had said and be able to summarize it to get a turn.

In the beginning the sharing was superficial and real issues were glossed over. The kids talked over each other and giggled as they told silly and obviously fabricated stories. Then Mom shared on the feeling word "sad." She said, "I am so sad that I have failed to be a good enough mother. I want so much for you two to be happy and enjoy each other, but I have not been able to teach you how, and that makes me very sad."

The boy's turn was next. He shuffled back through his cards, picking a different one than he had originally planned to talk about. "I picked the word 'helpless' because I sometimes feel helpless to control my actions. Like when I yell at my sister. I just can't seem to help it. It's not just Mom who feels helpless and sad, I feel that way too."

Not to be left out, the girl gave the counselor back her three cards and said, "I don't want to talk about any of my cards. I want to talk about 'helpless' and 'sad' too." What ensued was the most productive session to that point that the family had had. Each listened to the other, all agreed that they wanted to do something about the two feelings of "helpless" and "sad," and some beginning plans were made for how they could help each other.

Group Play B

The small group that called themselves Survivors of Suicide had been meeting for about six months. Some had entered the group because someone they loved had chosen suicide, others because they had, at one time or another, been so despondent that they had attempted to take their own lives. The group dynamics were excellent. For those who had attempted suicide it was an opportunity to find out what painful residue would be left for the ones who loved them if they succeeded in their next attempt. For the people who had been left behind by the suicide of a loved one, it was an opportunity to hear how people who take their own lives seem to get caught in a downward spiral from which even a loved one cannot pull them out. The group had told their stories over and over. Some said it was the only place where "someone will still listen. A lot of people don't want to hear about it anymore." The very repetitiveness of the narratives had been healing for the participants.

It had been over six months and the therapist felt the time was appropriate to introduce a more positive element to the sessions. Searching through the Level 1 cards, she selected the following feeling words: hopeful, loved, relaxed, joyful, happy, peaceful, comfortable, loving, affectionate, delighted. She brought this "stacked deck" to the session and suggested that they draw one feeling card. Each member of the group would share a personal story of a time he or she had felt that emotion.

Only 15 minutes of the session was devoted to this new activity. At the end of the session, the counselor asked for a vote on whether to continue to use the "prompt" that the feeling word had given the dialogue. The choice was unanimous. Over the course of the next nine sessions the group shared on each of the positive emotions in the stacked deck, one by one.

It should be noted that the timing of the introduction of the positive emotions was crucial; early foreclosure on the processing of the suicide issues would have been inappropriate. Also, the group's input as to whether to continue was solicited to test their readiness. The grief work was still given most of the session time but, like a breath of fresh air, the positive emotions were given a chance to emerge within the group's dialogue.

COUPLE PLAY

The two girls had been sent to the school counselor's office. Their classroom and hallway spats included name-calling, swearing, and sometimes physical attacks. The counselor's first task was to eliminate or, at a minimum, decrease the behavior. Beyond that the counselor wanted to give each of the girls an opportunity to get to know and appreciate the differences of each other.

To keep the combative atmosphere as low as possible, the girls were asked to sit in chairs that were placed back to back about three feet apart. For the first introduction to the use of the *Feeling* word game, the counselor modeled what she wanted the girls to do. She selected a variety of words for which she gave descriptive stories and synonyms and asked the girls to guess her feeling. Then a carefully selected group of nonvolatile, nonthreat-ening feeling words was given to each girl. Each, in turn, told a story illus-trating a time she felt the feeling on her cards. The other had to guess what the feeling was using only the words "You feel. . . ." or "You felt. . . ." The counselor blocked all sneers, derogatory remarks, and put-downs. The com-municator was asked to tell sincere and true stories. The guesser was not al-lowed to throw in extraneous or negative remarks and barbs.

In the beginning, the body language of both girls revealed both resistance to and ridicule of the technique. However, the lack of eye contact helped over-come the girls' competitiveness and combativeness. Each started to listen more closely to the other's stories, trying harder to guess the right feeling. The girls returned three more times and each time the atmosphere was less volatile. In the last session they were allowed to face each other. Both had learned some appreciation of the other's feelings and how each experienced them. Although they never became friends, their sharing had lowered the competitiveness a great deal.

INDIVIDUAL PLAY

The fifth-grader had experienced many losses: first, the death of a grand-mother with whom she had been very close; then her parents had gotten a divorce; last month her best friend had moved to another state. She was a shy child and found it difficult to talk about her losses. At times, she did not even seem to comprehend what her feelings were.

The counselor sorted the feeling cards, selecting a vocabulary of words she felt confident the fifth-grader would understand. The child was asked to di-vide the cards into the seldom, sometimes, often, almost always, and right now categories while the counselor was out of the room. Returning after the girl had finished, the counselor asked, "Is there one stack of cards you would like to talk about?" After the child signified a negative answer with a shake of her head, the counselor asked, "Is there any feeling card you noticed espe-cially and can talk about?"

"I liked the 'friendly' one. I like to be friendly, and I like friendly peo-ple." After a long pause during which the counselor waited patiently, the girl said, "I don't like the 'scared' word. It makes me feel like there's a hole in my tummy."

"Would you tell me more about the hole in your tummy?"

APPLICATIONS AND PITFALLS

The *Feeling* word game is deceptively simple. It is just a stack of 110 words that are descriptive adjectives for feelings. However, the applications are many, as illustrated in the case studies. A creative counselor could probably find many more applications than are described here. An interesting application that was recently proposed by a group that has used the game several times is to suggest other words that might be helpful to include in the next printing. The members of the group decided that any word that was suggested for use must be accompanied with a story of how it affected the person proposing the word. The creative additions to the 110 feeling words expanded the vocabulary and repertoire of all the group members. As people learn the power of knowing and using the correct words for their emotions, the potential for better mental health grows. In addition, as people learn to share their feelings, they discover that they are not alone or peculiar for having them.

Some cautions are worthy of mention. First, although the playing of the basic game and the team games can be fun and beneficial for almost everyone, the deeper, more uncovering aspect of some of the games are best supervised by an experienced counselor. An atmosphere of safety and security needs to be created. The counselor must protect the players by being alert to and deflect harmful directions the play might take. If those darker, heavier emotions are to be worked through, the counseling session must be a safe haven and the counselor a guardian of the client's well-being. That is not to say that the more negative emotions should not be talked about, only that a tender, caring, supportive atmosphere is best for the mental health of the client.

SUMMARY AND CONCLUSIONS

An essential ingredient of good mental health is an ability to express emotions (Albon et al., 1993; Easterling et al., 1990; Pennebaker, 1995; Smyth, 1998; Spiegel et al., 1989). The *Feeling* word game gives full play to the expression of feeling. Moreover, the game lends a sense of fun and safety to disclosure. As many researchers (Brody, 1999; Magai & McFadden, 1996; Oatly, 1992; Shapiro & Emde, 1992) point out, to express one's emotions accurately, it is essential to identify and label those emotions with appropriate descriptive adjectives. The 110 different feeling words in the *Feeling* word game cover a broad spectrum of emotional vocabulary. Hearing their use in stories and learning to use the words themselves gives players of the game a broader, more accurate way of self-expression and self-understanding. The *Feeling* word game can be a very valuable tool for therapy.

REFERENCES

Albon, S.L., Brown, D., Khantzian, E.J., & Mack, J.E. (1993). *Human feelings: Explorations in affect development and meaning.* Hillsdale, NJ: Analytic Press.

Brody, L.R. (1999). *Gender, emotion, and the family.* Cambridge, MA: Harvard University Press.

Cron, E.A. (1998). *The* Feeling *word game* [Game]. (Available from The *Feeling Word Game*, 316 East Street, Rochester, MI 48307)

Cron, E.A. (2000, October). The Feeling word game: A tool for both teaching and therapy. *Family Journal, 8*(4).

Easterling, B.A., Antoni, M.H., Kumar, M., & Schneiderman, N. (1990). Emotional repression, stress disclosure responses, and Epstein-Barr viral capsid antigen titers. *Psychosomatic Medicine, 52,* 397–410.

Magai, C., & McFadden, S.H. (1996). *Handbook of emotion, adult development, and aging.* San Diego, CA: Academic Press.

Oatly, K. (1992). *Best laid schemes: The psychology of emotions.* New York: Cambridge University Press.

Pennebaker, J.W. (Ed.). (1995). *Emotion, disclosure, and health.* Washington, DC: American Psychological Association.

Shapiro, T., & Emde, R.N. (1992). *Affect: Psychoanalytic perspectives.* Madison, CT: International Universities Press.

Smyth, J.M. (1998). Written emotional expression: Effect sizes, outcome types, and moderating variables. *Journal of Consulting and Clinical Psychology, 66*(1), 174–184.

Spiegel, D., Bloom, J.R., Kraemer, H.C., & Gottheil, E. (1989). Effects of psychosocial treatment of patients with metastatic breast cancer. *Lancet, ii,* 888–891.

CHAPTER THREE

The *Talking, Feeling, and Doing Game*

RICHARD A. GARDNER

Many psychotherapeutic techniques have been devised to help children. Many rely heavily on the elicitation of self-created fantasies, but therapists have long experienced frustration in getting children to take a psychoanalytic stance and attempting to gain insight into the psychoanalytic meaning of their fantasies. Conn (1939, 1941a, 1941b, 1948, 1954) and Solomon (1938, 1940, 1951, 1955) dealt with the problem of children's unreceptivity to psychoanalytic inquiry by responding at the allegorical level. They held that one could impart important therapeutic messages by discussing the child's fantasy at the symbolic level. They were certainly receptive to the notion of helping children gain insight into their fantasies, but believed that important therapeutic changes could be brought about by discussing the fantasy at the symbolic level, for example, "Why did the fox bite the wolf's tail?" or "Was there a better way the fox could have dealt with its anger toward the wolf than biting the wolf's tail?"

This author has also directed his attention to the question of how to utilize therapeutically the self-created fantasies of children who will tell stories but who are unreceptive or unwilling to analyze them. The mutual storytelling technique (Gardner, 1971) deals with this problem by having the therapist create responding stories, using the child's own characters and setting but introducing healthier modes of adaptation and resolution than those inhibited in the child's story. For children who are somewhat unreceptive to telling stories, the author has found that a series of games utilizing standard board game play and token reinforcement (1975a, b, 1992) proved useful in facilitating the creation of stories and other fantasy material of therapeutic value. However, there were still some children who, in spite of these games, were unwilling or too resistant to tell self-created stories freely or to provide other therapeutically useful fantasy material. It was for such children that the author developed the *Talking, Feeling, and Doing Game* (1973, 1998).

DESCRIPTION OF THE GAME

The *Talking, Feeling, and Doing Game* is similar in format and appearance to many of the typical board games with which most children are familiar. The game begins with the child and the therapist placing their playing pieces at the *start* position. They alternate turns, throwing the dice and moving their playing pieces along a curved path of squares that ultimately ends at the *finish* position. If the playing piece lands on a white square, the player takes a talking card; on a yellow square, a feeling card; and on a red square, a doing card. If the playing piece lands on a square marked *spin*, the player spins the spinner, which directs the player to move forward or backward or to gain or lose chips. In addition, there are *go forward* and *go backward* squares. The spinner and the latter squares are of little psychological significance; they merely add to the child's fun and thereby enhance the likelihood of involvement. It is the questions and directions on the talking, feeling, or doing cards, of course, that are of primary importance, and the child is given a reward chip for each response provided. The first person to reach the *finish* position gets five extra reward chips. The winner is the person who has the most chips after both players have reached *finish,* or after the game has been interrupted because the session is over. Active competition for the acquisition of chips is discouraged; rather, the therapist plays at a slow pace and tries to use each response as a point of departure for a therapeutic interchange. Obviously, the greater the breadth and depth of such discussion, the greater the likelihood it will be of therapeutic value.

The core of the game, of course, is the questions and directions on each of the cards. As is implied by their titles, the talking cards direct the child to make comments that are primarily in the cognitive and intellectual realm; the feeling cards focus on emotional issues; and the doing cards involve some kind of physical activity or playacting. There are 104 cards in each stack. The questions in each category range from threatening to very nonthreatening (so that practically any child will be able to respond) to the moderately anxiety-provoking. If the child responds (and the most liberal criteria are used, especially for the very inhibited child), a token reward chip is given from the "bank."

None of the cards directs the child into areas that would be as anxiety-provoking as relating self-created stories or free fantasy expression. The main purpose of the low-anxiety cards is to ensure the child's providing a response and gaining a chip. These enhance the likelihood that the child will remain involved. Some typical low-anxiety questions: "What's your favorite flavor ice cream?" "What is your address?" "What present would you like to get for your next birthday?" "What is your lucky number? Why?" "How do you feel when you stand close to someone whose breath smells because he hasn't brushed his teeth?" It is the questions that provoke moderate anxiety that are the most important, and these make up over 90% of all the cards. Some typical questions: "Suppose two people were talking about you and they didn't know you were listening. What do you think you would hear them saying?" "A boy has something on his mind that he's afraid to tell his father. What is it that he's scared to talk about?" "Everybody in the class was laughing at a girl. What had happened?" "All the girls in the class were invited to a birthday party except one. How did she feel? Why wasn't she invited?" "What things come into your mind when you can't fall asleep?" "If a fly followed you around for a day, and could then talk about you, what would it say?" "If the walls of your house could talk, what would they say about your family?"

The child's responses are usually revealing of those psychological issues that are most important at the time. The questions cover the broad range of human experiences, and issues related to the responses are likely to be of relevance of the etiology of the child's psychological disturbance. One does well to view symptoms as the most superficial manifestations of underlying unresolved problems. The problems that are being handled inappropriately via symptom formation are generally the same problems with which all of us deal. Accordingly, the topics raised by the cards are likely to relate to issues that are at the very foundation of the psychopathological process. Each response should serve as a point of departure for therapeutic interchanges.

The therapist does well to "get as much mileage as possible" from each response. Merely providing the child with a reward chip and then going on with the game defeats the whole purpose of this therapeutic instrument. However, the therapist should use his or her discretion when deciding how much discussion is indicated for each patient. The more resistant and defended child will generally not be able to tolerate an in-depth discussion as well as the child with greater ego strength.

The therapist plays similarly to the child and also responds to the questions, which should be left randomized. The therapist's knowledge of the child's problems, as well as the responses that have been given to previous cards, can provide guidelines for his or her own responses. The game requires considerable judiciousness on the therapist's part regarding responses to the cards. The therapist must always be aware that a response should be selected that is in the child's best interests. Many of the cards ask personal questions about the therapist's life. This brings up an important therapeutic question regarding self-revelation. It is the author's belief that therapists who strictly withhold information about themselves certainly enjoy the advantage of getting more free associations from the patient—associations uncontaminated by the reality of the therapist's life. However, a price is paid for this benefit. I believe that it reduces the humanity of the therapeutic relationship and fosters unrealistic ideas about what other human beings are like. Elsewhere, this author (1975) elaborated in detail on the question of the therapist's revelation versus nonrevelation. In accordance with this position, I answer each question honestly, even when a response involves the revelation of personal material. However, such divulgences are not made indiscriminately. Some personal experience is selected that not only will be relevant to the child, but will not compromise my own privacy or that of my family. I often find it useful to relate an experience that occurred at the time in my life when I was the same age as the child. This generally enhances the child's interest in my response, because children usually enjoy hearing about the childhood experiences of their parents and other significant figures.

It is rare that I do not answer a question. However, I give children the opportunity not to answer if they do not wish to. In such cases, I will often inform such children that failure to answer will result in their not getting a reward chip and thereby lessening the likelihood of winning the game. This can serve to motivate some children to at least try to respond to the card. It is not immediately appreciated by many therapists that the main determinant of who wins the game is more luck than anything else. If each player were to answer each card, the determinant of who wins would be the dice. If a player gets a large number of high throws, he or she will reach *finish* earlier and thereby acquire fewer chips. On the other hand, if a player gets a large number of low throws, more chips will be acquired in the course of going from *start* to *finish*. Because high and low throws tend to average out for each player, the number of wins and losses also averages out over time.

CASE ILLUSTRATIONS

In this section, I present some of the common responses I give to some of the cards. The reader does well to appreciate that these are only examples and not my invariable replies. Each response is tailored to the particular needs of the specific child and his or her problems. These responses, however, are some of the more common ones I provide.

TALKING CARDS

The talking cards, as the name implies, deal with cognitive, intellectual issues. They encourage the child to talk about his or her opinion on a particular issue. I am a strong proponent of the position that thoughts generally precede feelings: One's cognitive interpretation of an event is going to be an extremely important determinant of how one will react emotionally. If one interprets a stimulus to be dangerous, then one is going to respond with a feeling of fight or flight. If, however, one's view is changed and one learns that the stimulus is in no way dangerous, then the fight–flight emotional responses are likely to be reduced and even disappear. Many of the benefits that patients derive from treatment result from their having learned how to better deal with the inevitable problems of life with which we are all confronted. The talking cards help teach these lessons in better living.

It is important for the reader to appreciate that the following responses are to be used as points of departure for discussion with the patient. They are not simply stated and then the dice rolled for the game to continue. Furthermore, although the responses I give are intellectual, my attempt is to engender emotional responses to enrich the efficacy of the conversation and add more clout to the therapeutic communications.

"If You Become Mayor of the City, What Would You Do to Change Things?"

For a child who is insensitive to the feelings of others and may need some help in this regard, I might respond: "If I became mayor of my city, I would do everything in my power to bring about the passage of two laws. One would prohibit smoking in public places and the other would fine people large amounts of money for letting their dogs crap in the streets. Let me tell you my reasons for saying this. I personally find cigarette smoking disgusting. I'm not saying this because smoking causes cancer of the lungs. I'd say this even if smoking *cured* cancer of the lungs. I'm just saying it because I find smoking nauseating. I think that if anyone is stupid enough to smoke, that person should be required to do it privately, in his or her own home. Many people who smoke don't care about other people's feelings. As far as they're concerned, other people can choke or even croak on their smoke. They don't think about the feelings of the people who are suffering because of their smoking. Unfortunately, a lot of people don't speak up and say how the smoke bothers them. But more and more people are doing this.

"The other law, about there being big fines for people who let their dogs crap on the streets, would be for the same purposes. People who let their dogs do this don't think about how disgusted others feel when they step in the dog shit. It's really a disgusting thing to have to wipe dog shit off your shoes. It's too bad there are so many people in this world who don't think about other people's feelings. What do you think about people who smoke and people who let their dogs crap on the streets?"

The major thrust of my responses here is to help an insensitive child appreciate how one's act can affect others and that those who don't think about how they are affecting others are generally scorned. Included also in my response is a message about self-assertion regarding nonsmokers in their relationships with smokers.

"A Boy Wasn't Picked to be on a Team. What Had Happened?"

For the child who shows low motivation in school or in other activities, I might respond: "No one was surprised that he wasn't picked. He just didn't take things too seriously or practice. The others were working hard and practicing, and while they were working hard and practicing they were thinking about the time when the coach would be picking kids for the team. Having this idea in their heads made them work harder. But this kid just didn't think about it. He thought that he could do nothing, or almost nothing, and that he would somehow get picked for the team. Well, the day came for the tryouts and you can imagine how surprised he was when the coach told him that he could not be on the team. He was not only surprised, he was sad. He realized that he was living in a dream world. Do you think he learned a lesson from this experience?"

"Suppose Two People You Knew Were Talking about You and They Didn't Know You Were Listening. What Do You Think You Would Hear Them Saying?"

Identification with the therapist and modeling oneself after him or her is an important part of the therapeutic process. This is very similar to the educational model in which the child learns, in part, because of identification with the teacher and the desire to gain the same gratifications that the teacher enjoys from learning. The therapist not only serves as a model for learning, but should be serving as a model for other desirable attributes as well, for example, healthy self-assertion, sensitivity to the feelings of others, feelings of benevolence toward those who are in pain, handling oneself with dignity, and honesty. This card can enable the therapist to provide examples of such traits. However, the therapist should select traits that are particularly relevant to the child's problems. Furthermore, the therapist must avoid presenting these with a flaunting or holier-than-thou attitude.

For a child with a lying problem, I might say: "I might hear the people saying that I'm the kind of person who is direct and honest. Although people might disagree, at times, with what I've said, they would agree that I am direct about what my opinions are and don't pussyfoot about them. They know that when they ask me a question, they'll get an honest and direct answer with no hedging, beating around the bush, or saying things that aren't true. I am not saying that they would say that I never lied in my whole life and that I never will, only that they are pretty confident that I'll be honest with them. You see, I believe that there is truth and wisdom to the old saying that 'honesty is the best policy.' If you tell a lie, you have to go around worrying that people will find out that you've lied. Also, lots of people feel bad about themselves when they lie; they feel guilty about it. And when people find out that you've lied, then they don't trust you even when you've told the truth. So these are the main reasons why I find it better to tell the truth, rather than to lie. What's your opinion on this subject?"

"What Is the Worst Problem a Person Can Have? Why?"

For children who are unreceptive to any kind of self-observation or self-inquiry, who are too inhibited to look into their own contributions to the problems for which they are being treated, I might respond: "There are many terrible problems people can have. Certainly having physical illness, especially if severe, is a terrible problem. However, if one is physically okay, there are still other kinds of problems that people can have. As a psychiatrist, I am interested in psychological problems. There are many kinds of psychological problems, some of which are very bad. I think that one of the worst kinds of psychological problems is the one in which a person makes believe that there are no problems when there really are. That's a pretty lousy problem to have." I might at that point ask the patient why he or she thinks that making believe there are no problems when there really is one of the worst problems a person can have. In the ensuing discussion, my main purpose would be to help the child appreciate that denial mechanisms prevent one from dealing with a problem, so it is likely to get worse. This could then serve as a good lead into the child's own problems that are being denied.

"Do You Believe That Praying for Something Will Make It Happen?"

Most children who are in therapy are likely to engage in wishful thinking at times and believe that their problems will somehow go away by themselves. Unfortunately, it is probable that the vast majority of adults think along these lines as well. For such a child, I might say: "There are many people who believe that praying for something will make it happen. I personally do not believe that. I believe that if you want something to happen you have to *try* to make it happen. This doesn't mean that it will always happen if you try; it only means there's a better chance the thing will happen if you try to make it happen. I know, however, that there are many religious people who believe that praying for something will make that thing happen. But even those religious people generally say that 'God helps those who help themselves.' What is your opinion on this subject?" Of course, when providing this response, the therapist does well to take into consideration what the patient's family's religious beliefs are. It has been the author's experience that the vast majority of religious patients still subscribe to the 'God helps those who help themselves' principle. Accordingly, it is not likely that a response along the lines provided by the author is going to do more than highlight the significant philosophical differences between the therapist and the patient's family.

   In the ensuing discussion, I might present the following question to the child: "Suppose two boys in the same class had a test the next day. One studied for the test and the other watched television, but during the commercials prayed to God that he would pass the test the next day. Which kid do you think would get a better grade on the test? Do you think God would help the boy who watched television get a good mark on the test? Do you think God would put the answers in his head so that he would pass the test anyway?"

"What's the Best Story You Ever Heard or Read? Why?"

For the child with poor academic motivation (a very common presenting problem), I might respond: "One of the best stories I ever read in my whole life was one I read when I was a teenager. It was about the life of Thomas Alva Edison. Do you know who Thomas Edison was?" At that point, I would discuss Edison with the child and make sure that the child knows what Edison's major contributions were. I would then continue: "As I'm sure you will agree, Thomas Edison was one of the world's greatest inventors. All of our lives were made better by him. I'm sure you'll agree that the world is a much better place because of the electric light. It must have been tough in the old days before they had electric lights. They used to have to burn candles and use lanterns, and they used to have a lot of fires. Also, they never got as much light from those things as you can with an electric bulb. It also makes life happier to have phonograph records and now, of course, we have CDs, but they still work on a similar principle and we have Thomas Edison to thank for that. The whole world admires Edison and the whole world is grateful to him. He can serve as an inspiration for the rest of us. Do you know what the word *inspiration* means?" Here I will discuss with the child the meaning of the word in the hope that he or she will come to appreciate the gratification a person such as Edison can derive and the enhanced feeling of self-worth that such an individual enjoys. Most people who have performed great deeds have done so, in part, because of some model whom they are following. My hope here is to engender in the child some of this desire.

"Someone Passes You a Note. What Does It Say?"

For the child who is unpopular in school, I might respond: "Dear Bill, we're forming a secret club. We're going to have our first meeting behind the back door of the school, right after school at 3 o'clock today. Then we're going to elect a president, vice president, and secretary. We're only inviting a few people, those whom we like best in the class. If anyone asks you about the club just tell them that it's a secret, and if Tom or Bob asks about the club don't tell them anything at all. We don't want those guys in the club." I would then ask the child why he or she thinks that Tom and Bob weren't invited into the club. This may bring about a discussion of the child's own personality qualities that have contributed to his or her alienation. My attempt here also is to engender a certain amount of jealousy of those who are invited into the club. This jealousy may also motivate the child to look into his or her own qualities that have brought about the alienation.

"You've Just Seen Your Friend Steal from a Store. What Should You Do?"

For a child who has a problem putting himself or herself in another's position, I might say: "I would go over to my friend and tell her that she should return what she's stolen. I'd tell her that she should think about how bad the storekeeper must feel that his stuff was stolen. I'd ask her how she would feel if someone stole things from her. I'd try to help my friend put herself in the storekeeper's position. If I was able to do that, perhaps then she would feel sorry for the storekeeper and return what she had stolen. What do you think of that?"

For the child who does steal, I might respond: "I would say to my friend, 'You know, some people have seen you do that. I don't think you're going to get away with it. I think you're going to get caught. I've seen you do it and others saw it also. I think you may get reported. Even if you don't you're going to have to walk around scared that someone is going to tell and then people will find out. Do you think it's really worth it to walk around scared all the time worrying about being found out? Also, if you are found out, people are not only going to be angry at you, but you may get punished. If I were the man who owned the store and found out what you've done, I'd at least call your parents and I might even call the police.' I would hope that after my friend heard that, she'd return the thing that she stole and then would realize that it really doesn't pay to steal things. Do you know what the old saying, 'Crime doesn't pay' means?"

"Say Anything You Want. You Do Not Get a Chip If You Say Nothing At All."

This card, of course, provides the therapist with significant freedom regarding what to say. There is indeed a greater universe of possible responses to this card than to many of the others. The *Talking, Feeling, and Doing Game* is very much a verbal-projective game, and this card can be compared to the blank card on the Thematic Apperception Test (Murray, 1936). For the child who is afraid to enter new and strange situations, to do new and different things, I might respond: "Do you know that many people don't realize that both the brave person and the coward are basically very similar? Both the brave person and the coward are usually afraid at first of the new and even scary thing. However, the difference between the brave person and the coward is that the brave person *does* the scary thing, whereas the coward runs away from it. The brave person also has a lump in his or her throat at the scary time, but he or she doesn't let it get the best of him or her. The brave person swallows the lump in his or her throat, grits his or her teeth, clenches his or her fist, and does the frightening thing because he or she knows it's important to do so. The brave person knows that if he or she doesn't, bad things will happen. The coward just runs away and doesn't accomplish very much, if anything at all. How do you see yourself? Are you more like the brave person or are you more like the coward?"

For the child who cheats on tests in school, I might respond: "A boy used to cheat on a lot of tests. He felt good when he got a high mark and was relieved when he didn't get a low mark. He used to watch a lot of television at night and thought that everything would be all right if he continued to cheat on tests. However, he found himself not feeling good about himself when he would get a high mark. He knew in his own heart that he really didn't deserve it. And then the other kids used to watch him cheating and they would call him 'cheater.' This also made him feel bad about himself. Do you think that these things made him change his mind about cheating?"

FEELING CARDS

The feeling cards deal primarily with emotional and affective topics. They encourage children to express their feelings, and this is particularly useful for children who are inhibited in this area. I consider it important for therapists to appreciate that the therapeutic view that the mere expression of feelings is in itself salutary is somewhat naïve. I believe the expression of feelings to be a good first step toward the alleviation of difficulties. The expression of feelings serves, among other things, to enhance one's efficiency in reaching certain goals. We fight harder when we are angry, we run faster when we are frightened, we mourn more effectively when we cry, we love more ardently when we are sexually excited, we eat more when we are hungry, and we sleep more when we are tired. These principles apply when feelings are expressed at low and moderate levels. However, when feelings are generated at a high level they may work differently. Anger, for example, when expressed in severe states of rage, may perpetuate itself even after the initial goal is reached. A murderer who stabs his or her victim to death may continue stabbing the dead body. Clearly, nothing new or further is being accomplished by such repeated stabbings. The same phenomenon relates to excessive drinking, eating, sleeping, and sexual indulgence. The satisfaction becomes an end in itself and goes beyond its initial purposes.

"Everybody in the Class Was Laughing at a Boy. What Had Happened?"

For the child who is inattentive in the classroom, I might respond: "He wasn't listening to the teacher while she was teaching. Then, while he wasn't paying attention, the teacher called on him and asked him a question about what she had said. Instead of being honest and saying that he wasn't listening and that he didn't know the answer, he tried to guess. Well, as I'm sure you might imagine, he guessed wrong. In fact, he gave a very silly and stupid answer. It was such a foolish answer that everybody in the class started to laugh at him. He felt embarrassed. He was humiliated. He was sorry that he hadn't listened to what the teacher was saying. Do you think that he tried to pay more attention after that?"

Children with neurologically based learning disabilities often become class clowns. They recognize that they cannot gain the affection and esteem of their peers via the usual methods such as high academic standing, prowess in sports, talent at music or dance, or any other special skill that might warrant the admiration of their peers. One way of attempting to gain such a response is via clowning in the classroom. Unfortunately, they don't appreciate that they are much more likely to be laughed *at* than laughed *with*. To such a child, I might respond: "They were laughing at him because he was the class clown. He was always horsing around in the classroom and, even though the teachers would often get angry at him, he still continued to clown around. Some of the children would laugh, but others didn't think he was very funny. He thought this was making him popular, at least with some of the children. He didn't realize that they really didn't like him very much when he was clowning around that way. They might have thought it was a good chance to have a little fun in the classroom, but they really didn't respect him. In spite of the fact that they laughed at him, they still didn't invite him to birthday parties or to join their afterschool secret clubs. Do you think the boy finally realized what was happening?" Many children with neurologically based learning disabilities have difficulty differentiating between people who are laughing *at* them and people who are laughing *with* them. This is a manifestation of their cognitive impairment, and it behooves the therapist to patiently attempt to help such children understand this kind of subtle differentiation.

"A Boy's Friend Leaves Him to Play with Someone Else. How Does the Boy Feel? Why Did the Friend Leave?"

Some children have great difficulty sharing. They have difficulty putting themselves in the position of their peers and fail to recognize that the child with whom they refuse to share is likely to be alienated. Some of these children have neurologically based learning disabilities that interfere, on a cognitive level, with their capacity to project themselves into another's position. Other children may have reached the developmental level where this is possible, but have psychological problems in the realm of egocentricism and narcissism that interfere with healthy functioning in this realm. For children in both of these categories, I might respond: "Bob invited Frank to play with him at his house. But Bob was selfish. He wouldn't share. Frank was his guest. He should have known that it's important to be courteous to a guest. He should have known that it's important to be nice to a guest. Anyway, Frank wanted to share Bob's toys with him and Bob refused. Also, Bob always wanted to decide which game they would play. Finally Frank said that if Bob wouldn't play nicely with him and share, he would leave and go play with someone else. Bob's mother overheard the boys talking and took Bob aside into another room. She didn't want to embarrass Bob in front of his friend Frank. She told Bob, while they were alone, that he wasn't playing nicely with his friend and that he wasn't thinking about how his friend felt. She told him that Frank would go home soon if he didn't start to share with him. She told him that Frank had another good friend, George, whom he could go play with if he wanted. What do you think happened? Do you think Bob listened to his mother? Do you think his mother was right or wrong in this case?"

Some children have a general "sourpuss" attitude. They tend to be unfriendly and expect others to make overtures to them. They don't reach out, and tend to display the hostilities that have originated in their homes onto their peers. For such children, I might respond: "Carol was having a lot of trouble at home. Her parents used to fight a lot and this made her very sad and irritable. Also, her mother and father didn't treat her well at times. But, instead of talking to her mother and father about the things that were bothering her, she just held all her thoughts and feelings inside herself. And she became a sourpuss kind of kid. She wasn't very friendly to other people and would be irritable with them. Accordingly, one day her friend Alice stopped playing with her and said, 'You're no fun to be with. You're not very friendly. I'm going to play with Linda.' And so Alice went away and played with Linda. How do you think Carol felt when this happened? What do you think she should have done?"

"On the Last Day of School a Girl Learned That She Would Have to Repeat the Same Grade. What Had Happened?"

There are many children whose presenting problem relates to their failure to appreciate the consequences of their academic negligence. They float along as if there will be no consequences to their failure to fulfill their school commitments. With such children, I might respond: "Betty had goofed off all year. Whenever her teacher would warn her that she might not get promoted into the third grade, she ignored her. And when her mother and father got upset and told her that her report cards were terrible and that she had better start studying harder, she again made believe that there was no problem. She didn't think they were serious. She couldn't imagine herself not being promoted to the third grade. Anyway, on the last day of school, you can imagine how amazed she was when her report card said that she would have to repeat the same grade. Although she was embarrassed to cry in front of the other boys and girls, she couldn't hold back her tears. And this made her feel even worse because she was crying in front of the other children. Some of the children were mean and even made fun of her. Others understood how bad she felt and told her how sorry they were that she was not being promoted. What do you think happened to her the next year? Do you think she still continued to goof off in school?"

The author fully recognizes that his responses to many of the questions in the *Talking, Feeling, and Doing Game* are relatively "superficial" from the psychoanalytic point of view. The author, a psychoanalyst himself, believes, however, that psychoanalysts in general are not fully appreciative of the role of conscious control in the treatment of psychogenic disorders. In addition, he is not against an analytic-type inquiry and will on occasion use the child's responses as a point of departure for such investigation. However, he appreciates, as well, that most children under the age of 10 or 11 who are of average intelligence are not cognitively capable of meaningful psychoanalytic inquiry. They have not reached Piaget's level of formal operations, the level at which the child is able to cognitively separate an entity from the symbol that denotes it and recognize the relationship between the two. Meaningful psychoanalytic inquiry requires such appreciation. Furthermore, even with analytic patients, much of the treatment involves learning better how to deal with the everyday problems of life and utilizing new techniques that may not have been part of the patient's original repertoire. And the learning of such techniques does not necessarily have to take place in the context of an analytic inquiry; it can be derived in part from more direct advice and recommendations by the therapist. This need not produce infantilization and exaggerated dependency on the patient's part.

"A Boy Was Scared to Make a Telephone Call. What Was He Afraid Of?"

Whereas the *Mutual Storytelling Technique* and other derivative games that involve a child's fantasies are useful to the age of 11 or 12, the *Talking, Feeling, and Doing Game* can be played meaningfully with the average child up to age 15 or 16. Children begin to recognize in the prepubertal years that their fantasies are quite revealing of their innermost thoughts and feelings and may then become defensive about such revelations. The *Talking, Feeling, and Doing Game*, however, because it does not generally delve so deeply, is less threatening and can be easily utilized through the mid-teens. For the teenager who exhibits the usual anxiety about calling up a girlfriend, I might respond: "He was thinking of calling up this girl in his class whom he liked. He wanted to ask her to go out with him. But he was scared. He was afraid that she would turn him down. He even went to the telephone and dialed her number and then hung up before it rang. Later on, he let the telephone ring but then hung up before anyone had a chance to answer. On another day, he called again and was even glad when no one answered, even though he *really* wanted to go out with the girl. What was worse, he thought that he was somehow very strange, different, or weak for having such feelings. He didn't realize that it is normal to have such fears. When he learned that it is normal, he felt better about being afraid. However, he was still afraid. He learned also that it's important to push through one's fears and do the scary thing anyway. He remembered the old saying, 'Nothing ventured, nothing gained.' And so he called her again. What do you think happened?" The child's response will generally be in one or two categories: The girl is receptive or the girl is not. If receptive, I emphasize the joy of the success and how willing one should be to tolerate fears in the service of enjoying certain gratifications. If the answer is in the negative, I emphasize the fact that there are other girls out there whom the boy could call and reassure the child in the course of the conversation that there is likely to be someone out there who will be receptive.

"What Is the Worst Thing You Can Say to Anyone?"

For the child who is inhibited in the expression of anger and self-assertion, I might respond: "I think one of the worst things you can say to anyone is: I wish you were dead. Of course, a wish cannot make a thing happen. However, most people would say that this is a pretty nasty thing to say to someone. I think it's important to know that thoughts like this come into most people's minds, even toward people they love most in the world—like mothers and fathers. It's normal to have such thoughts once in a while, even toward someone you love very much. This is especially true when that person does something that gets you very angry. Some kids think it's a terrible thing to have such a thought. I have a different opinion. I think it's important not to say *everything* that comes into your mind when you're angry at somebody. That can cause a lot of trouble. Accordingly, when people have thoughts like that when they are angry, they do better to use words that are more polite than the ones that come into their minds. They should say things like, That's making me very angry, or What you're doing is very mean and I don't like it one bit! Then, if they talk calmly about the thing that's bothering them, it's more likely they will solve the problem. What do you think about what I've said?"

"What's the Happiest Thing That Ever Happened to You?"

For the child who has little academic curiosity or motivation in the classroom and who gets little joy from learning, I might respond: "One of the happiest things that ever happened to me was the day I graduated from medical school. I was about 25 years old at the time and it was the end of many years of hard work in school. I really felt very good about myself. I was very proud of myself, and my parents and relatives were very proud of me also. I really felt *great* that day. Although that happened many years ago, I still remember the day clearly. Some of the work in medical school was very interesting, but some of it I didn't like too much. I knew I wanted to be a psychiatrist and so wasn't interested too much when they taught about how to help people with broken bones or rashes. However, I knew it was important to learn those things also if I wanted to be a doctor. And I also found that they weren't so boring as I had first thought. Anyway, all the hard work was certainly worth it and I have not been sorry to this day that I had to work so hard in medical school. What do you think about what I've said?"

We speak often of the importance of the therapist-patient relationship in therapy. However, the factors that contribute to the development of a good relationship in this area have not been well delineated. This question can be used to help foster a good patient-therapist relationship with a response such as: "I've had many happy days in my life. Three of the happiest were the three days on which each of my children were born. Of course, that happened many years ago, but I still remember the days clearly. I was so happy on each of those days that I cried. They were tears of joy. I still have those warm feelings when I see little babies. It's hard for me not to touch them, and sometimes I'll even ask the mother to let me hold the baby so I can cuddle and kiss the child. Although my children, like all children, may give me trouble at times, they also give me great pleasure. And the pleasures are certainly greater than the pains." My hope here is that the child's relationship with me might improve (admittedly in a small way) by the recognition that children produce warm responses in me. The response conveys the notion that I have the capacity for such pleasure with children in general and this response is not simply confined to my own children.

"A Boy Has Something on His Mind That He's Afraid to Tell His Father. What Is It That He's Scared to Talk About?"

For the child whose parents are divorced, who finds himself in the middle of loyalty conflict, I might provide this response: "He was scared to tell his father that he didn't agree with him. He didn't think that all of the terrible things his father was telling him about his mother were true. However, because he was scared that his father would be angry at him if he told him that he didn't agree with him, he didn't say anything at first. He was scared that if he told his father how he really felt he might even see less of his father. After all, his father had left the house when he separated from his mother and that made him feel very lonely. Anyway, his father then began to ask him a lot of other questions just to see if he agreed or disagreed with him. Then the boy made a *big* mistake. He told his father that he agreed with him and then he started to make up bad things about his mother that really weren't true. Because his father was so angry at his mother, his father believed every one of these lies. And the father then went and told the mother what the boy had said about her and this, of course, made the mother get very upset at him because she knew that the boy was lying. Then he told his mother that he really hadn't said those things to his father and this made the situation even worse. What do you think about what this boy did?" In the ensuing conversation, I would try to get across the point that whatever discomforts the boy might suffer as a result of his being honest with his father—even if he were to say that he didn't want to get involved and criticize one parent to the other—he would be much better off than handling the situation by lying and telling each parent what he thought that parent wanted to hear from him at that time.

"What Is the Thing about Yourself That You Dislike the Most? Why?"

Many children with feelings of low self-worth are intolerant of any deficiencies within themselves. On becoming aware of even the smallest deficiencies, they may denigrate themselves and consider themselves generally unworthy. This reaction, in part, stems from inordinately high standards about what a person should really be like. Sometimes, significant figures in their environment portray themselves as being perfect, or almost perfect, and the child, of course, can never completely measure up to such individuals. In other situations, significant figures may place inordinate demands on the child for perfection in a wide variety of areas. Not being able to live up to these standards, the child starts to loathe himself or herself. For such a child, I might respond: "I, like everyone else in the world, am a mixture of good and bad things. There are many things I'm very good at but there are also many things I am very poor at. I don't think there's one big thing that I dislike the most in myself, but of all the things about myself that I can think of that I dislike I would say that the one that bothers me the most is that sometimes I work too hard and take things too seriously. Of course, it's important to work hard in life if you want to accomplish anything, but it's also important to enjoy oneself and to relax and have fun. Both are important. Did you ever hear the saying 'All work and no play makes Jack a dull boy?' What do you think it means?" I might then use this question as a point of departure for helping the child appreciate that balance in life is important, not only in terms of work and play but also in terms of accepting the fact that each person has both assets and liabilities. One of the elements that plays a role in successful treatment is identification with the therapist. Here, I am attempting to serve as a model of someone who can accept both assets and liabilities within himself and can comfortably reveal both under proper circumstances. My hope here is that the patient will then become more comfortable admitting his or her own deficiencies, both to himself or herself and to others. This can be useful in lessening feelings of self-loathing.

"When Was the Last Time You Cried? What Did You Cry About?"

This can be a particularly useful question for children with emotional inhibition problems. It is reasonable to say that individuals do not generally suffer with isolated inhibitions in the expression of single emotions; rather, such inhibitions tend to spread so that a person with such difficulties is generally inhibited in expressing a variety of emotions. Accordingly, any easing up that the therapist is able to accomplish in one area of emotional expression is likely to spread into others as well. For such a child I might respond: "I'm the kind of person who tends to choke up in certain movies. I remember seeing a movie recently in which a person whom I admired very much died near the end of the movie. It was very sad. Lots of people in the movie theater were crying. Even though I knew that it wasn't real and that it was only a movie, I still felt bad—not only for the person who died but for the friends and relatives who were crying at the funeral. Some people think that boys and men shouldn't cry. What do you think about that?" If the child's response in any way suggests that he or she is an adherent to the notion that it is unmanly for a boy or man to cry, I try to dispel that idea. Then I'd likely enter into a discussion of the purpose of crying. Here, I first try to elicit from the patient his or her answers to that question. By the end of the discussion, I make sure that we have at least dealt with the cathartic value of crying as well as its value in communicating to another person one's frustrations, disappointments, resentments, and so on.

"A Girl Heard Her Mother and Father Fighting. What Were They Fighting About? How Did She Feel While She Was Listening to Them?"

For the girl who has been doing poorly academically and who has been living in a dream world regarding the consequences of her poor school performance,

I might provide this answer: "Well, the mother and father had spoken to the principal that day. She told them that she was thinking about not promoting their daughter into the fifth grade because she had done very poorly that year. She told them that she and the teacher had warned the girl that if she didn't shape up, she would get left back. She told them that that didn't seem to help and that their daughter ignored these warnings. Now she was wondering whether it might be a good lesson for their daughter to repeat the fourth grade. She asked the mother and father for their opinion and told them that, although the final decision was going to be the school's, she was going to take into consideration their thoughts and feelings on the subject. The reason they were fighting was that the father felt sorry for his daughter and said that he wanted her to go on to the fifth grade because she would feel so bad seeing all her friends being promoted when she had to remain in the fourth grade and be with all the younger kids. The mother, however, said that she certainly felt sorry for her daughter, but she thought it would be a bad idea to promote her if she wasn't ready to do fifth-grade work and that her daughter would probably be embarrassed going there every day not being able to keep up with the others.

"First, the girl was amazed when she learned that they were thinking of leaving her back. She really hadn't taken all the warnings seriously and really didn't think that they would do such a thing. Now she was shocked to learn that the people at school really meant business and that there was a strong possibility that she would have to repeat the fourth grade. She was really sorry then that she had goofed off all year and then began to cry. The mother and father, who didn't know she was listening, heard her crying and came out of the room. She begged them to tell the principal to promote her and she promised that she would start trying very hard to do good work. What do you think happened?" In the ensuing discussion, I generally cover three options: (1) the child has to repeat the fourth grade, (2) the child is promoted into the fifth grade, and (3) the child is promoted on probation with the understanding that she will attend summer school and her work will be reviewed after two months in the fifth grade to see whether she should return to the fourth.

"A Boy Was Laughing. What Was He Laughing About?"

For a child with little academic curiosity and motivation, I might provide this response: "This boy was not only laughing, he was cheering. He was just jumping up and down with joy. He had just gotten his eighth-grade report card and learned that he had gotten into three honors classes in the ninth grade. He was very happy. He had worked very hard to make the honors classes and had hoped that he might make one or two of them. But he didn't think that he would get into all three. He was very proud of himself and couldn't wait to get home and tell his parents. His teacher had written a note on the report card that said 'Robert, I am very proud of you. Good luck in high school.' He was also very happy because he knew that, when he would apply to college, having been in three honors classes would look very good on his record and this would help him get into the college of his choice. And so he ran home from school laughing and singing all the way. It was really a happy day for him. What do you think about what I said about that boy?"

At this point, the reader may be wondering why so many of my responses relate to academic performance in school. Although I must admit a possible bias on my part regarding my commitment to academics, I believe that the high frequency of responses related to academic performance is related to the fact that the overwhelming majority of children who are referred to me have problems in the area of academic achievement. In fact, I would say that the most common reason a child is referred to me is because he or she is not performing up to expectations in the academic or behavioral realm in the classroom.

"Tell About an Act of Kindness."

For the egocentric child, the child who has trouble putting himself or herself in another person's position, I might respond: "A good example of an act of kindness would be visiting someone who is sick in the hospital and giving up a fun thing that you'd prefer to do. Let's say that a boy in a class was in an automobile accident, injured his leg, and had to be in the hospital for six weeks. Even though his mother and father visited him often, he was still very lonely. His really good friends were those who were willing to give up fun things like playing baseball, or watching their favorite television programs, or just hanging around and relaxing, and instead went to visit him in the hospital. He was very grateful when they came to see him. And they felt good about themselves for their sacrifices. Visiting the friend was an act of kindness. Do you know what the word 'sacrifice' means?" In the ensuing discussion, I would try to help the egocentric child appreciate the feelings of loneliness suffered by the hospitalized child. I would also try to engender in the child the feelings of self-satisfaction and enhanced self-worth that come from benevolent acts.

"What Do You Think About a Girl Who Sometimes Plays with or Rubs Her Vagina When She's Alone?"

As the reader can certainly appreciate, the kinds of questions found in the *Talking, Feeling, and Doing Game* are not the traditional *Monopoly*-type questions. Many younger children, even those who may not even have any incipient sexual inhibition problems, may not be familiar with the concept of masturbation. Others may be but are likely to have taken on certain prevalent social attitudes regarding its being a shameful or harmful practice. For these children, I might respond: "I think that that girl is perfectly normal if she does it in private. Most teenage girls do that and many girls do it when they're younger as well. There is nothing wrong with it. It is generally considered very poor manners, however, to do that in public. Most people consider that to be a private thing. What is your personal opinion on this subject?" My aim here, of course, is to lessen any inhibitions a child may have regarding masturbation and to plant the seeds for a more balanced attitude toward the practice in the future if the child has no experience or knowledge of the practice.

"Was There Ever a Person Whom You Wished to Be Dead? If So, Who Was That Person? Why Did You Wish That Person to Be Dead?"

This question can be particularly useful for children with antisocial behavior disorders who have little sensitivity to the pains they inflict on others. For such a child, I might respond: "During my childhood and early teens there lived a man in Germany named Adolf Hitler. He was a madman. He was insane. He was the leader of Germany during World War II and was personally responsible for the deaths of millions of people. He was one of the greatest criminals in the history of the world. He used to murder people whose opinions, skin color, or religion differed from his. He not only had them shot but he gassed them to death and burned their bodies in ovens. Millions of people died this way. When I was a boy, I used to wish that he would die. I wished that someone would kill him. I hoped then that maybe all this crazy murdering would stop. To this day, I and many other people in the world feel sorry for the millions of people he killed and all the millions of friends and relatives that also suffered because of his murders. Even though the war ended in 1945, there are still millions of people who are suffering because of the terrible things Adolf Hitler did. These are the people who were put in his prisons and concentration camps and escaped, or were fortunate enough not to have been killed. And these are also the people who are the friends, relatives, children, and grandchildren of those who died there. He was a very cruel man. I really hated him, and I often wished he would die or be killed. Finally, in 1945, he committed suicide. He knew he would soon be caught and executed for his terrible crimes." My hope here, by elaborating on Hitler's atrocities, is to engender in the antisocial child a feeling for the pain that criminal behavior causes others. It is important for the reader to appreciate that when responding to feeling cards, the therapist does well to try to dramatize as much as possible his or her responses to bring about a kind of resonating emotional response in the patient. To engender these feelings in the child who is out of touch with them or who has not experienced them to a significant degree is one of the goals of treatment.

"What's the Worst Feeling a Person Can Have?"

Most children in treatment are not moving along life's path. They have been diverted into pathological roads and are not gaining the gratifications of life that they might otherwise be enjoying. Children with academic problems are not learning and so are not likely to derive the benefits they would otherwise enjoy from an adequate educational experience. Children with behavioral problems are compromising significantly their capacity to form meaningful and satisfactory human relationships and this too is a significant deprivation in their lives. And there are a wide variety of other problems that individuals become obsessive over and dwell on, often with conscious control, and deprive themselves thereby of the healthier gratifications that life has to offer. For such children, I might respond: "I believe one of the worst feelings a person can have is to know that one is going to die very soon. All of us must someday die, and most people hope that they will live a long and full life. If, however, one is going to die soon and if, in addition, one has wasted a lot of one's life, then the feeling that one is going to die soon is made even worse. It's sad enough to know that you have to die. But it's even sadder to know that you wasted a lot of your life and it's now to be over and you're not going to have another chance. How do you feel about *your* life yourself? Do you think that you're wasting your life? Do you think that if you continue living your life as you are you'll be sorry some day that you didn't do things better for yourself?" The younger the child, the less the likelihood that he or she will be able to project himself or herself into the future and think about the questions I have asked. However, there are children who are capable of doing so and can do so meaningfully if the therapist is able to facilitate an introspective and somewhat philosophical conversation. My hope here is that the painful feelings engendered by the prospect that one is wasting one's life will serve to motivate the child to reduce the wasteful psychopathological behaviors and preoccupations.

"What Do You Think Is the Most Beautiful Thing in the Whole World? Why?"

Healthy pleasure is well viewed to be a general antidote for just about all forms of psychogenic psychopathology. When one is enjoying oneself in a healthy way, one is at that time not suffering the psychological pain attendant to psychiatric disorder. In addition, the pleasurable feelings are esteem-enhancing. Because feelings of low self-worth are often involved in bringing about psychopathological reactions, any experience that can enhance self-worth can be salutary. And aesthetic pleasures are in this category. Accordingly, anything a therapist can do to enhance a child's appreciation of beauty is likely to be therapeutic. In the service of this goal, I might respond: "Watching a beautiful sunset, whether it be from the top of a mountain or at the seashore, is to me one of the most beautiful things in the world. It makes me feel relaxed and happy to be alive. Sometimes I will read poetry while watching such a scene. And the poems also make me think of beautiful things that help me appreciate how beautiful the world can be if one is willing to stop and enjoy them. Sometimes I will bring along a tape recorder and play a tape of some calm, beautiful music while watching such a scene. This is indeed one of the great pleasures of life." Again, children are generally less self-conscious about these pleasures and probably less cognitively aware of them. Certainly, they more often enjoy things without conscious recognition and this may be an advantage they have over adults.

DOING CARDS

The doing cards, as their name implies, deal with actions. As is true of the talking cards and the feeling cards, there are a few cards in each stack that are of little, if any, psychological significance. These can be answered by just about any child ("What's your favorite flavor ice cream?" and "With your finger, make a circle in the air.") and ensure that even the most resistant and obstructionistic child is likely to obtain a reward chip. The remaining cards involve some physical activity and, of course, deal with activities that are likely to touch on important psychological issues. There is a fun element in many of these cards that can make the session more enjoyable and this, or course, can serve to counterbalance some of the less pleasurable aspects of treatment—aspects that are likely to reduce even the more highly motivated child's motivation for therapy. Some involve role modeling, which in itself can be therapeutic. It is important, however, for the reader to appreciate that the author is not in agreement with those who place great emphasis on physical activity as a therapeutic modality per se. Rather, he believes that it plays only a limited role in the therapeutic process. In accordance with this position, he most often uses the doing cards as a point of departure for therapeutic interchanges that are directly relevant to the child's problems. And this is the approach that is utilized in the following examples.

"You're Standing in Line to Buy Something and a Child Pushes in Front of You. Show What You Would Do."

For the child with an antisocial behavior disorder, I might respond: "Let's say I'm a kid and I'm standing here in line and some kid pushes himself in front of me. A part of me might want to push him away and even hit him. But another part of me knows that that wouldn't be such a good idea. I might get into trouble or he might hit me back and then I might get hurt. So the first thing I would do would be to say something to him like, 'Hey, I was here first. Why don't you go back to the end of the line and wait your turn like everybody else?' If that didn't work I might threaten to call some person like a parent, teacher, or someone else who is in charge. But sometimes there are no other people around to call, so I might just say that it's not worth all the trouble and that all it's causing me is the loss of another minute or two. If, however, the person starts to push me, then I might fight back. But that would be the last thing I would try. Some people might think that I'm 'chicken' for not hitting him in the first place. I don't agree with them. I think that hitting should be the last thing you should do, not the first. I don't think that people who hit first are particularly wise or brave; rather, I think they're kind of stupid." As is obvious here, I am trying to educate the antisocial child to the more civilized option that individuals have learned to use to bring about a more relaxed and less threatening society. These options may not have been part of the antisocial child's repertoire. Whatever the underlying factors in such a child's antisocial behavior (and these, of course, must be dealt with in the treatment), such education is also a part of the therapy.

"What Is the Worst Kind of Job a Person Can Have? Why? Make Believe You're Doing That Job."

This question can be useful for children who are compromising their lives via academic underachievement or behavioral problems in the classroom that are interfering with their learning. For such a child, I might respond: "There are all kinds of lousy jobs in this world. And there are all kinds of good jobs. Most people agree that the harder you work to learn a job, the more likely you'll get one of the more desirable and better jobs. I think one of the worst jobs a person can have is to clean toilets. I'm sure you'll agree that it's a very smelly job cleaning out toilet bowls in which are other people's wee-wee and doo-doo. You have to get down on your knees and not only clean the toilet but clean all around on the floor, which is also usually pretty filthy. I'm sure that most, if not all, of the people who have such a job wish that they could be doing something better. I'm sure many of them are sorry that they goofed off in school, or even quit when they possibly could have stayed—which is usually when they were teenagers. Now it's too late. They may have families to support and it may be very difficult for them to go back to school." The hope here is, obviously, that the plight of these people will engender in these children some appreciation of what they are doing to themselves by their impaired commitment to schoolwork and motivate them to try harder to overcome their difficulties.

"Make Believe You're Doing Something That's Smart to Do. Why Is It Smart to Do That Thing?"

Many children with neurologically based learning disabilities exhibit a significant problem in impulsivity. Probably the impulsivity for these patients has a neurologic basic. There are children with psychogenic problems, however, who are also impulsive. Regardless of the etiology for such children, I might respond: "One of the smartest things a person can do is think in advance about consequences. Do you know what *consequences* mean?" For the child who is not familiar with the meaning of the word, I might respond: "Consequences are the things that happen when you do something. For example, if you hit your sister, the consequences may be that your mother will send you to your room. If you do well in school, the consequence will be that you will get a good report card. Anyway, one of the smartest things a person can do is to think about what will happen in the future after one does something. Many people don't think about consequences. They don't think about what's going to happen later on after they do something. They just think about what's going to happen now. And that's a bad idea. That causes a lot of trouble.

"Now I'm going to make believe that I'm playing a game with someone and I'm losing. Because I feel bad that I'm losing I'm thinking of cheating. But then I remind myself that if I cheat I might be caught. Then the consequence will be that the person won't want to play that game with me anymore. Or, I think about the fact that even if I'm not caught I won't feel good about myself for having cheated. So, after thinking about the consequences, I decide not to cheat. And I think that's a smart thing to do. How are you when it comes to thinking about the consequences of the things that you do?"

My purpose here, obviously, is to instill in the child a sense of the importance of thinking in advance. Impairments in this area are not confined to children. In fact, I would go so far as to say that there is hardly an adult (including the author) who doesn't regret at times not having thought about consequences.

"Make Believe You're Smoking a Cigarette. What Do You Think About People Who Smoke?"

My response here is for every patient, regardless of the reason for coming to treatment: "First, to get a chip, I'm going to have to make believe I'm smoking. Boy, is this tough. (Cough, cough, cough.) This is very hard to do. It's really painful to get this chip. I hate smoking. In fact, I never smoked in my whole life. It's hard for me to understand how people would want to do such a disgusting thing. It really burns my mouth, throat, and lungs. You know, of course, that smoking can give you lung cancer and a lot of other diseases as well. But I would say what I'm saying even if smoking cured lung cancer. It's a disgusting and a dangerous habit. It nauseates me. Sometimes, when I smell smoke, I feel like vomiting. Some people who smoke think that everyone else can get sick from it but they won't. You can imagine how surprised they are when they come down with one of those terrible diseases that comes from smoking. Some people who smoke think that others should breathe in their smoke and not say anything. I always tell smokers that it bothers me. We nonsmokers have to stick up for our rights. We can't let people smoke in our face and let them think that they can get away with it. We have to say something or do something about it. Even kids have to speak up if adults smoke and they don't like the smoke. What do you think about what I've said?" My response here does not simply direct itself to the health hazards of smoking. Rather, I also comment on self-assertion.

For some children, especially those who are in the preteen or early teen period, I might also say: "I think one of the reasons people start smoking is that they think it makes them look like bigshots. They think that they're more like grown-ups when they have a cigarette in their mouth. Many boys think girls will like them more if they smoke because the girls will be impressed with how grown-up they look. And many girls smoke because they think that boys will think the same thing. Many kids think it's sexy to smoke. I don't think so. To me it's just the opposite. I once saw a sign that said, 'Kissing a Smoker Is Like Licking a Dirty Ashtray' and I agree with that. I don't think it's sexy at all.

"Some kids really don't like smoking, but they think that if they don't get used to it they'll be different from the others and that the other kids will look on them as babies. Those kids may spend long hours practicing smoking to get over the disgust they have for the habit. I think they're really stupid to do this. I think they would be braver to say that it's a disgusting and terrible habit and that even if they are the only one not doing it, they're not going to do such a stupid thing. That's real bravery." My comments here, of course, direct themselves to some of the major psychodynamic factors involved in the early phases of smoking addiction. My hope here is that my comments will be of preventive value in reducing the likelihood of the child's ultimately becoming habituated.

"Make Believe You're Doing Something That Would Make a Person Feel Sad."

For a child with an antisocial behavior disorder, I might respond: "Teasing and laughing at someone can make that person feel sad. Let's say that a boy is playing baseball and he strikes out and starts to cry. He is probably very sad that he struck out. However, he's probably even sadder now that he is crying in front of everyone. He's probably embarrassed that he's crying. In fact, I can see now that he's trying to hold back his tears because he's so ashamed of himself that he's crying in front of everyone. He's covering his eyes now and trying to make believe that he's really not crying, but everyone knows that he is. Then, if I were to tease him and call him a 'crybaby' or something like that, that would make him feel even sadder. But I don't have the heart to do that to him. So I'm not going to do it, even though I won't get a chip. I wouldn't want to do such a cruel thing." As the reader can appreciate, I attempt to engender feelings of sympathy for the victim of the antisocial child and introduce dramatic elements, repetition, and some exaggeration to get across my point.

"Make Believe You're Having an Argument with Someone. With Whom Are You Arguing? What Are You Arguing About?"

For the child with a neurologically based learning disability who needs some lessons in social protocol and getting along better with others, or the egocentric child who does not appreciate his or her effect on others, I might respond: "I'm having an argument with a kid with whom I'm playing a game of checkers. She was starting to lose and then wanted to change the rules in the middle of the game. We both agreed that a person has to jump when he or she can and now she wants to change the rules and say that you don't have to jump if you don't want to. And then she's starting to lie and say that we never made that rule in the first place. So I'm telling her that I'm not going to play the game unless she goes by the original rules. I'll also tell her that if she wants to change the rules for the next game and play by different rules, I'll be happy to talk to her about that. However, if I agree to different rules, it will only be with the understanding that we will stick with those rules throughout that game. Anyway, I tell her that she has to make a decision: either she's going to play by the original rules or I won't play the game anymore. She gets angry at me and bangs her fist on the table. And that makes all the checkers jump up and down, so that we don't know anymore where they all were. And, of course, that ends the game. What do you think about what happened during that game?" The vignette lends itself well to a number of comments on the child's part regarding the feelings of other people, following the rules, obeying social protocol, and general cooperation.

"Make Believe You're Doing Something That Makes You Feel Very Good about Yourself. Why Does That Thing Make You Feel So Good?"

For the child who is an academic underachiever, I might provide the following response: "As you know, I like to write books. I have already given you one of the children's books that I've written. As I'm sure you can appreciate, writing a book takes a lot of work. It's a very hard job. Sometimes I may work over many years on one single book. However, when I finally finish, I really feel good about myself. I feel that I've accomplished a lot. Although I may be very tired over all the work I've put into it, I'm very proud of what I've done. And then, when the final printed book comes out, that really makes me feel good about myself. I have what is called a 'sense of achievement.' Do you know what I mean when I say 'sense of achievement'?" After this is clarified, I might ask the child to tell me things that he or she has done that have provided him or her with similar feelings of accomplishment. My hope here, obviously, is to provide the child with some appreciation of the ego-enhancing feelings that one can enjoy after diligent commitment to a task.

"Make Believe You're Doing Something That Could Make Your Teacher Proud of You. What Are You Doing? Why Would That Make Your Teacher Proud of You?"

Again, for our old friend the academic underachiever, I might respond: "I'm making believe that I started off as one of the worst students in the class. Let's say that I got mainly Cs and Ds on my report card. The teacher has told me that I've been goofing off, horsing around, and that if this keeps up, I'm not going to get promoted at the end of the year. My parents also have been on my back and are very upset over my poor grades. Although at first I don't listen to what they're saying, after a while I realize that they all mean business and that I'm going to be in a lot of trouble if I don't start to shape up. So I decide to try harder and even stop watching a couple of television programs that I was hooked on. Then, over the months, I start getting better grades and by the end of the year the teacher gives me a special certificate that says that I showed the most improvement of all the children in the class. She says on the certificate that she's very proud of me. And I'm also very proud of myself." My responses here, of course, hope to engender some motivation in the child to enjoy similar feelings of accomplishment.

CONCLUSION

It is important for the therapist to appreciate that the responses provided to each of the selected cards are only representative of possible answers to the question. There is no such thing as a *standard* response to any of the cards. Each response must be tailored to the particular needs of the child and direct itself to the specific problems for which the child is being treated. Just as the responding story in the Mutual Storytelling Technique (Gardner, 1971) is specifically tailored to relate to the particular problems the child is revealing in the story, the therapist's responses to the *Talking, Feeling, and Doing Game* cards should also be designed to the specific psychological needs of that particular child. My experience has been that the *Talking, Feeling, and Doing Game* is a particularly attractive therapeutic tool and will predictably involve the vast majority of resistant, uninhibited, and uncooperative children. Like all therapeutic modalities, it has its advantages and disadvantages. One of the main disadvantages of the *Talking, Feeling, and Doing Game* is that it may be *too* attractive to both the patient and the therapist. The therapist may thereby be deprived of the kind of deeper unconscious material that one obtains from projective play and storytelling. And the child then will be deprived of the therapeutic benefits that may result from this type of activity.

Accordingly, I generally warn therapists not to be drawn into the temptation of using this game throughout the session and to do everything possible to balance the therapeutic activities with other modalities.

REFERENCES

Conn, J.H. (1939). The child reveals himself through play. *Mental Hygiene, 23*(1), 1–21.

Conn, J.H. (1941a). The timid, dependent child. *Journal of Pediatrics, 19*(1), 1–2.

Conn, J.H. (1941b). The treatment of fearful children. *American Journal of Orthopsychiatry, 11*(4), 744–751.

Conn, J.H. (1948). The play-interview as an investigative and therapeutic procedure. *Nervous Child, 7*(3), 257–286.

Conn, J.H. (1954). Play interview therapy of castration fears. *American Journal of Orthopsychiatry, 25*(4), 747–754.

Gardner, R.A. (1971). *Therapeutic communication with children: The mutual storytelling technique.* New York: Aronson.

Gardner, R.A. (1973). *The Talking, Feeling, and Doing Game.* Cresskill, NJ: Creative Therapeutics.

Gardner, R.A. (1975a). *Psychotherapeutic approaches to the resistant child.* New York: Aronson.

Gardner, R.A. (1975b). Psychotherapeutic approaches to the resistant child (2 one-hour cassette tapes). Cresskill, NJ: Creative Therapeutics.

Gardner, R.A. (1992). *The psychotherapeutic techniques of Richard Garner.* Cresskill, NJ: Creative Therapeutics.

Gardner, R.A. (1998). *The Talking, Feeling, and Doing Game* (2nd ed.). Cresskill, NJ: Creative Therapeutics.

Murray, H. (1936). *Thematic Apperception Test.* New York: Psychological Corporation.

Solomon, J.C. (1938). Active play therapy. *American Journal of Orthopsychiatry, 8*(3), 479–498.

Solomon, J.C. (1940). Active play therapy: Further experiences. *American Journal of Orthopsychiatry, 10*(4), 763–781.

Solomon, J.C. (1951). Therapeutic use of play. In H.H. Anderson & G.L. Anderson (Eds.), *An introduction to projective techniques* (pp. 639–661). Englewood Cliffs, NJ: Prentice-Hall.

Solomon, J.C. (1955). Play technique and the integrative process. *American Journal of Orthopsychiatry, 25*(3), 591–600.

PART TWO

USING TRADITIONAL GAMES IN CHILD THERAPY

CHAPTER FOUR

The Use of Competitive Games in Play Therapy

IRVING N. BERLIN

P lay therapy was developed as a way to understand the nonverbal communications of disturbed children whose feelings, thoughts, and conflicts are often more easily discerned through play than through "talking" therapy. H. Helmuth in 1911 (1921) first used play as a therapeutic tool. In different periods in the 1920s, Melanie Klein (1932) and Anna Freud (1928) expanded on the meanings and uses of play in a therapeutic setting. Later, a number of psychoanalysts contributed to the understanding of the symbolic meaning of play in a psychoanalytic context, followed by David Levy (1938) and others, who evolved a play technique called "structured play," in which traumatic events encountered by a child were replicated with toys, much like a stage set, to provide an opportunity for catharsis and working through the specific trauma encountered by the child. Axline (1947) and Taft (1933) developed specific play techniques that reflect their particular theoretical framework for understanding the psychopathology of children.

Today, the use of games as active play to bring about communication has become a frequent part of play therapy. The increased use of games to some extent reflects a change in the kinds of children and adolescents we work with in treatment. We rarely see the neurotic child who, at 6 or so, can play and talk out his or her conflicts and benefit from interpretations. Much more often we see children with more serious psychopathology resulting from severe neglect or abuse, and these children seldom communicate in words. Among older children, preadolescents and adolescents, it has become commonplace to find they come from homes where talking with parents and among other adults is unusual. The behavior problems that bring these young people to us point strongly to an orientation that emphasizes action rather than talk. Thus, play therapy, and the use of games in that context, has become an increasingly important method of establishing therapeutic communication.

Over the past decade, a number of child therapists have employed various game strategies to break through the communication barrier, with various results. It has become apparent that certain attitudes about the self are readily displayed in game playing. Bettelheim in 1972 described his use of poker and chess for specific purposes in play therapy. Others have used the games of *Monopoly* and *Risk* to focus on specific aspects of feeling helpless and the need to feel powerful and aggressive. Winnicott (1971) introduced the squiggle game as a means of quickly reaching the child's fantasies, which otherwise could not be talked about or were slow in emerging. Gardner (1971) and other child therapists devised storytelling games in which the therapist collaborates with the child to tell a story that usually helps reveal hidden feelings and conflicts; these same child therapists developed structured games, like Gardner's *Talking, Feeling, and Doing Game,* in which each participant draws a card with instructions on what to do or talk about. The impersonal nature of being instructed by a card to describe a feeling or a thought or to engage in an action, combined with the equal participation of the therapist, seems to make expression of ideas and feelings easier. Gardner has commented that the structure of this game helps bypass the superego and permits the ego greater freedom of expression.

Most of us in our training in play therapy have been warned specifically against playing competitive games, such as checkers, because they inhibit the free associative aspects of free play and its accompanying fantasy. Though these anticipated drawbacks may be true to some degree, I have found competitive games very useful in certain therapeutic situations. Further, I think with few exceptions we often find in practice that children who need to use competitive games easily find ways to introduce them into the playroom, often in the rudimentary forms of tic-tac-toe and hangman.

WHY AND WHEN COMPETITIVE GAMES ARE USEFUL

It has been my repeated observation over a number of years that competitive games permit many silent children and preadolescents easier access to unacceptable feelings of hostility, hate, and vengeful feelings toward parent figures and siblings, as well as broader competitive feelings with adults. They also provide an opportunity for dealing with the need to win and feel powerful and competent, in contrast to the actual feeling of helplessness. The therapist as competitor becomes not only a person to defeat, but also one to identify with, especially in the therapist's expression of attitudes about losing and winning. The child may identify as well with many other feelings expressed by the therapist in the play of a game.

An important aspect of game playing is how both therapist and patient deal with the universal need to cheat. An equally important aspect is the patient's opportunity to experience the therapist's regard and respect, which are clearly demonstrated by his or her various attitudes toward the patient in the patient's efforts to learn the game, his or her need to cheat, and so on. Also, the therapist's empathy with the patient's feelings when the patient wins or loses is important to the therapeutic alliance. The game provides repeated opportunities for the therapist to model how a variety of feelings can be openly expressed.

I prefer to play those games in which each move permits the therapist and later the patient to express feelings. Thus, I prefer to play the card game war with very young children, dominos with somewhat older children, and checkers with the most mature children. I avoid chess because it is difficult for children to learn and requires too much concentration on the therapist's part to play a good game and attend at the same time to the variety of details in the therapeutic interaction.

It is critical that the game be played in such a way that each player has a good chance to win. In doing this, the therapist shows respect for his or her competitor and enhances the patient's self-esteem. The methods of promoting such attitudes in competitive play will be described.

SOME CONCERNS ABOUT THE DIFFERENCE BETWEEN PLAYING AND PLAY THERAPY

One of the major obstacles to the therapeutic use of competitive games is the need of many therapists, who are themselves very competitive, to win. This may reflect a strong need to assert and be reassured about their own competence and power. Such therapists very easily slip into playing the game only to win. If being defeated by a child arouses anger in the therapist, or hurt, or a sense of loss of status, he or she can be sure that what is occurring in the session is not therapeutic. Play therapy of all kinds requires an ability and effort to understand the child's behaviors as they are expressed by posture, gesture, speech, and affect. Such attentiveness to the patient is not possible if the therapist is playing the game largely for his or her own satisfaction.

On the other hand, therapy falls just as far short when the mutual enjoyment of the competitive game precludes the kind of attentiveness just described. Naturally, mutual pleasure in playing often occurs in therapy; however, in the nontherapeutic instance, the enjoyment of the game and often the relief at having the child engaged with the therapist, rather than sullenly silent, may lead the therapist into seeing the competitive game as being sufficient if it provides mutual fun. This greatly reduces therapeutic effectiveness.

Young therapists who have not resolved their own competitiveness with siblings and parents and are not yet sure about the process of play therapy are most vulnerable to using the competitive game as an end in itself rather than a means to an end. They still need to learn and experience that the essence of play therapy is the facilitation of communication. Their efforts must be to follow the child's activities closely to comprehend the expression of conflict, no matter how disguised. They must also attempt to communicate a personal receptiveness and a desire to understand the child's troubles and to help the child reduce his or her distress and troublesome behavior.

A DEVELOPMENTAL APPROACH TO COMPETITIVE GAMES

By age 4 many children are aware of the existence of rules; certainly the 6-year-old knows that rules exist for behavior at home, school, and in other organized settings. Problems with observing rules often stem from laxity at home about the necessary rules for living, especially noted in a very permissive home setting with what amounts to no rules. Conversely, an overly strict, harsh, unreasonable, and punitive family attitude tempts the child to overtly comply and covertly defy the rules. In the case of the abused and neglected child, the difficulty is often compounded in that the rules may be terribly harsh and punitive but enforced at one time and not at another, so that the child learns to do as he or she pleases, as punishment may occur under any circumstances and at any time.

Competitive games, in common with other games, have rules. At their simplest, the rules require taking turns. The working through of the use of a set of rules may be the first area of conflictful interaction the therapist must face. This must be done in accordance with the child's cognitive development. How does one begin to deal with taking turns? One way is to inquire whether the youngster understands the idea of taking turns so that a game can be played. If this is hard, and there is no taking of turns, then the child is playing the game alone, which is fine if the child wants to play that way for a while. Most children find that playing alone is no fun, as there is no interaction. If the therapist initiates the turn-taking and compliments the child on being able to wait for his or her turn, the child experiences some real pleasure at the interaction. I have found that the problem about taking turns occurs most often in games such as war and some board games in which the child must amass cards or much reach "home" to win. When one emphasizes that the youngster didn't really beat the therapist and, therefore, didn't really have the fun of winning, most children quickly become eager to win by actually beating someone.

CHEATING IN COMPETITIVE GAMES

Many children and adolescents need to win at all cost in any competitive game. These are youngsters who are very unsure of themselves and have a very poor self-image. They frequently are very angry at the adults in their life. Often, the anger stems from intense sibling rivalry and a feeling that the sibling is preferred and gets the parents' attention, love, and also material things as signs of preference. Their need to win, by forcing others to give in to them, often represents being successful or triumphant over siblings and parents. At times, the need to win may represent being the victor in an oedipal struggle. The parent of the same sex is frequently hostile and threatening. More often than not, this characteristic results from a developmental arrest, usually during the separation/individuation stage as described by Mahler, Pine, and Bergman (1975). The most needy of these children appear to be those who were neglected and/or abused around age 2. Most of these young people have not enjoyed the experience of being cherished and valued as an individual: Their efforts at exploration were not stimulated; their charming ways and engaging comments were neither applauded nor encouraged. Thus, the practicing subphase and subsequent phases are not lived through in a benign and caring environment. Children who must win appear to convince themselves that they are superior and deserve to be admired and cared about.

In time, the therapist's emphasis on making the game fair and competitive, as well as efforts to teach the child to win fairly, will reduce the need to cheat. With some youngsters in whom the need to cheat is overpowering, it may be important to extend oneself to provide a means for winning. For instance, if the therapist is ahead in the game, he or she can exchange the piles of cards, reverse the board in checkers, or change places in dominos so that the child or adolescent can experience the therapist's desire to help him or her to win.

Often, youngsters will want to play the game by their own rules. Such alterations in rules may profitably be permitted, but there must be a clear understanding that any change in rules will apply to both players. The therapist's understanding comments about the child's need to win, while permitting and encouraging winning, is perhaps more effective than sticking to the game rules at the outset. Helping the patient stick to whatever set of rules are established at the beginning of the game with candid comments about how the therapist feels (i.e., angry and frustrated that a real game cannot be played) helps the child play by the rules.

At some point in the therapy, the child will be receptive to being helped to learn to play effectively and to win legitimately. The therapist must be alert to use this moment of the patient's willingness to play correctly. The therapist needs to acknowledge pleasure in helping the child or adolescent to learn, and to compliment the young person on his or her courage in wanting to learn.

Because I use each game to dramatically express my feelings, I take care to show the children a different affective partner when they cheat: I say I don't enjoy playing that way. My protests with no major affective displays are a sharp contrast to the free expression of affect that is pleasurable to the child or adolescent and that results in his or her responsive behavior of either smiling or mild derision. In such situations, playfulness is a powerful aid to playing fairly.

THE PRESCHOOL CHILD IN THE PLAYROOM

Very frequently, we begin by playing war. For the uninitiated, in this game the players divide the deck in half, each taking a stack of cards. The individual piles are placed face down. Simultaneously, the players turn over the top card in their stack, and the highest card takes the trick. When each player exposes the same card, they both shout "War!" and the next turned card determines who wins both piles of cards. The therapist helps the child recognize the number printed on the card by calling out his or her number and encouraging the child to call out his or her card. This game permits the therapist a great deal of emotional expression: "Oh, darn it, your queen is taking my best jack; you're skunking me!" or "Oh boy, my king is taking your queen; I'm really going to beat you!" The therapist's loud declaration of "War!" when the same numbers surface is soon imitated by the child, as are other exclamations. A good deal of affective interaction can occur with each turn of a card. When the therapist has amassed a much larger pile against a young child who *needs* to win, he or she can offer to exchange piles with the child to help the child win. However, the therapist needs to be clear that on each turn of the card, the player with the highest number on his or her card does in fact take both cards. Sticking with that rule shows respect for the child's ability to play and win by the rules.

With some young children I use dominos as a competitive game. Though a game of chance, learning how to block an opponent is important in winning the game. To block, my opponent must first figure out that I do not have any dominos with a certain number of dots and then play those numbers; then I must hunt for more pieces because I can't match any of the dominos in play. If the child can continue to block, I will have to keep hunting, which increases his or her chances of winning. When the therapist assists the young child in learning how to block, the child's self-confidence is bolstered. I always mention aloud what numbers are open to be played on. The triumph of a 4- or 5-year-old who understands how to block is a delight to observe. The expressive possibilities are rich: gleeful when you can match the dominos in play, or dejected and fearful that you will lose if you must hunt for more dominos and increase your pile. The winner is the one who is out of dominos first, and the loser must add up the total number of dots on his or her remaining dominos. Each player keeps a total until the end of the contest; often, the therapist must help children count the number of dots and add it to the total for them. In preparation for this game, I may play several games with both players' piles turned face up so that the manner of playing the game becomes clear to the child.

VIGNETTE 1: ALICE

Alice, a bright 4-year-old, came to treatment because she had been hitting other children at the preschool and attacking her infant brother at home, as well as refusing to obey her mother. Her father, a trucker, was rarely home. When he was, she obeyed him. Alice had nightmares about creatures from outer space taking her away to another planet.

In the playroom, I explained the rules about being able to play with any toys as long as she didn't break anything or hurt herself or me. She soon tried to smash a toy truck with a long block. When I prevented this and held her so she could not hurt me or break anything, she screamed and kicked the floor, but then relaxed. In preschool and at home, Alice was a nonverbal child, and it soon became clear that there was little talking at home by either parent.

In the second session, I prevented her abortive attempt to stamp on a doll and I held her again. She was relaxed in my arms. I reached for the dominos and tumbled them out of the box. I picked one up with a 6 and a 4 on it and asked if she could find a domino that matched either end of the one I had. She counted the dots on each end silently and finally found a 6/3 and laid it next to my 6. We continued to match dominos and created a nice pattern on the floor. Toward the end of the hour, she whispered the numbers on my domino that she had to match, imitating my calling the numbers of each domino aloud. At the next session, she came in, sat down, picked up the dominos, and began the matching play, enjoying taking turns and my comments of "Oh my, where will I find a 7 to match yours?"

Then I explained the game to her, how we each started out with seven dominos, and so forth. Because I knew how to play, I handicapped myself by taking ten instead of seven dominos. We played one "open" game and then a regular game; she won both. She chortled triumphantly whenever I would lament, "You've really got me stuck!" as I hunted for a matching domino. When I would find a match and loudly exclaim that I was going to beat her, she'd say very softly, "Oh no, you're not." In a few weeks she was screaming that she'd squash me when she matched my domino and crying out, "You stinker, you!" when I managed to block her. These were words I'd used at various times, and the affects were good imitations of feelings I had voiced.

As Alice's verbalizations became louder and more fervent, her hostile behavior lessened considerably at preschool and at home. When she learned to block me, she very proudly told her mother when she went into the waiting room.

After about four months, Alice began to use some of the Flagg family dolls to enact a number of themes.* But when she began to feel threatened by what she was playing out with toys, she'd return to the game of dominos. Her joyous, triumphant cries or mock cries of horror if I had a good run, which were appropriately responded to by me, seemed to ease her tension and she could return to play with the dolls and dollhouse. This repetitive play dealt with sibling rivalry and oedipal themes. After two years of therapy, Alice was a much changed girl, doing well in school, at home, and with peers.

At age 8 Alice came back to see me for a short time when her father was hospitalized after an auto accident. She had been immobilized and very depressed. In the playroom she picked out the dominos for us to play, but she also began to talk about her fears of her father's death and how her mother was so scared and helpless that Alice felt she had to take care of everyone. While we played a perfunctory game of dominos during each session, the game was primarily a means Alice used to talk out her anxieties. When her father came home, and I was able to convince both parents that couple therapy was in order, Alice stopped seeing me.

The dominos were useful as a way of getting angry, hostile, fearful, gleeful, and victorious feelings out in the open, as well as the sad feelings that accompanied losing. As Alice learned to play well, and especially to block, her self attitudes became positive and her self-image changed from a frightened, insecure child to a self-confident, effective one. Playing dominos led to her ability to express feelings in symbolic play.

VIGNETTE 2: TED

Ted is 5.5 years old, the only child of wealthy, elderly parents. He was always given his way to avoid his crying, and later his tantrums. At age 4 he was sent to preschool, where his demands to have his own way and his tantrums antagonized his peers and teachers and he was asked to leave after a few weeks.

At age 5 he entered a private kindergarten, where his behavior resulted in many conferences with his parents. They were unable to alter their behavior with Ted. The kindergarten director suggested therapy.

One of Ted's most pleasurable activities was to play board games with his father. Ted dictated the rules of the game and insisted on winning each game. His father, to avoid tantrums, always gave in.

---

*Small 3 to 5 inch rubberized dolls with clothes on them.

In the playroom Ted picked out a game because he was intrigued by the popgun. *Annie Oakley* is a game invented and named by a former patient. It involves a popgun and cards numbered one through five. The cards are leaned against a low rack on a table with blank sides out. During each turn, the player shoots a cork until he or she knocks over any two of the cards and their numbers are totaled to become the player's score. The one with the highest score wins the game. During the first session, we simply took turns shooting down two cards each without declaring a winner.

During the second play therapy session I began to total the scores so that after each turn I would declare a winner. At first, Ted said that I cheated in adding up the numbers. I discovered that he could add up the numbers easily. He then insisted that the cards he shot down were the numbers he said they were. At this point, I ended the game, saying that he understood the rules. "It is no fun playing with children who cheat." Despite Ted's tantrum, I then started the game over, this time taking the roles of both Ted and myself, saying, "Now I'm Ted" and "Now I'm Dr. B." After a few moments of screaming and jumping up and down furiously, Ted quieted and watched me play for both of us. He was, of course, fascinated by the popgun and wanted to shoot it at other objects in the room. I made it clear that the cards and the popgun went together. He noticed that when I played for him and he won, I proclaimed loudly that Ted had a total of so many points and he won that game, and as Dr. B. I bemoaned my poor luck. When I won, I proudly announced my good luck and said, "That's tough, Ted. Better luck next time."

At the beginning of the next session, I again set up the cards and popgun and invited Ted to play. When he again insisted that a card with a one on it was a four I took the popgun away from him and continued playing for both of us, with accompanying comments as I had the previous session. Ted sat watching me. We had eight corks, and after two complete turns I would find them for the next round of play.

Ted never volunteered to find and pick up the corks and I did not make it an issue and always did it myself. Toward the middle of the third session, when I ran out of corks, Ted said softly, "I'll get them." I thanked him matter-of-factly and continued playing for both of us. Without saying a word, Ted continued to pick up and return the corks to me. He smiled when I thanked him. Toward the end of the session, when I was playing for Ted and he won, he uttered a weak "Yeh!" to my gleeful "Ted wins!"

At the beginning of the fourth session, I again set up the cards, put a cork in the popgun, and matter-of-factly handed him the popgun. Ted shot down two cards and added the 3 and 4 to make 7. I took my turn and added the 5 and 2 to make 7 and exclaimed, "A tie. How's that?" Ted smiled and said, "A tie. Great." Ted won the next game to mutual exclamations of "I won" and "Ted, that's great!" He quickly scrambled to find the corks and loaded the popgun for the next game. When I won he looked downcast but did not try to cheat, and I said enthusiastically, "It's so nice to play together. It's really no fun playing alone." Ted nodded and for the rest of the session joined me in "Hurrahs!" when he won and smiled when I won. At the end of the session, I told both his parents what a great sport Ted had been and how proud I was of him.

We continued this game for another two sessions. I complimented Ted on his sportsmanship when I won and his "Hey, that's great" got more and more genuine as the sessions continued. At the end of each session, I praised Ted in front of his parents.

Ted had been eyeing the children's dartboard during the last session. I took it off the wall and showed him the numbers in each colored circle around the bull's-eye, with the biggest number, 50, being in the bull's-eye. I explained the rules and placed my calculator next to us on the sofa and showed him how to enter the numbers and how to total them. Ted quickly learned how to use the calculator. We played a trial game. We each took a turn with the four darts. Ted added up both our totals and announced them. We then discussed the technique of throwing the blunt darts and I tried to teach Ted how to step forward to the line and throw hard. As he learned how to throw more effectively his totals increased. I praised his increasing skills and told him how proud I was of him for playing fairly. At the end of the session, Ted gave me a tentative hug. When we walked to see his parents, I commented on his sportsmanship and how well he was learning to throw the darts as well as his skillful use of the calculator. In subsequent sessions, I told his parents how much fun it was to play with Ted, who now easily played by the rules. At the end of each session, he gave me a warm hug, which I warmly returned. These hugs were a clear expression of our developing relationship.

Before the next session, Ted's father phoned me and described that Ted had played their favorite board game by the rules and enjoyed his father's praise and did not fuss when he lost. This marked a turning point in Ted's slow shift in his behavior. He began to want to please his parents during the day.

During the next two sessions, after a few games of darts, Ted wanted to explore the other games in the room. I taught him to play *Give Away Checkers,* which he enjoyed with much laughter when I lost and no complaints when he lost. When it was clear that he was going to win the game, I would smile and call him a "stinker." Ted laughed, and at the end of the session gave me his usual warm hug as he left. During a dart game, one of my darts missed the board, hit the wall, and bounced to the floor. Ted quickly picked up the dart, handed it to me with a smile, and said, "Try again, maybe you'll have better luck."

Ted's father phoned me before a session because Ted had insisted that when they played a board game, his father should imitate Ted's loud and joyous comments on winning and his "Too bad" when he lost. For the first time, his father played a board game with Ted with affect and they both enjoyed it. It was clear from Ted's comments during our hugs that his parents were not physically demonstrative.

For a child with an inactive elderly father who was interested only in sedentary games, the large and small muscle involvement provided Ted additional learning experience and kinesthetic pleasure.

Ted returned to kindergarten, and the teachers remarked how much more playful and what a good sport he was and how well he applied himself to learning.

The next five sessions ended our work. In three of those sessions we played ring toss. Ted quickly learned to toss the rings close to the peg. He jumped up and down with joy when his ring fell over the peg so that he won the game. In the fourth session, we divided our time between ring toss and my antiquated version of *Battleship.* While we played *Battleship,* Ted told me how "good" he did in kindergarten and that his teachers and the kids liked him. In an aside, he confided that now when he hugged his dad or mom they seemed to like it and hugged back.

In our last session, Ted brought his new electronic version of *Battleship.* We played with it for a few minutes and then he said that he liked my old-fashioned version better. It was clear that the slower pace permitted us to talk about how well he was doing in school and about the friends he was making in school. With joy he told me he found a playmate in his neighborhood. As a parting gift, I gave Ted a new game of ring toss so that he could teach his father how to play. He gave me a long, warm hug as he left. For some months I received cards from his parents recounting how well Ted was doing. Ted always drew a face with a smile on each card.

I continued to hear from the family on Ted's birthday and at Christmas. In one note his father wrote that he was learning to catch a softball and to throw it to Ted so that Ted could learn to catch, throw, and hit the ball in preparation for Little League play.

The active play helped Ted to experience and enjoy the kinesthetic pleasure of the activities. My continuing a game and playing for both of us with accompanying affect modeled for Ted the feelings that could be expressed on winning or losing. Primarily, it helped him to enjoy the relationship created by the interplay of vocalized emotions whether one won or lost, with less and less premium on winning. The active games of darts and ring toss required the acquisition of both small and large motor skills never before experienced by Ted. He also learned to express his pleasure in the relationship by warm hugs at the end of each session. Importantly, he taught his parents to enjoy his hugs and to hug him in return: the beginning of affectionate interchanges between these not very demonstrative, elderly parents and their son.

THE SCHOOL-AGE CHILD

School-age youngsters are well aware of rules, and their need to win is not clouded by lack of understanding how games are played. In my experience, children of this age who are unable to talk easily and tend to be silent and withdrawn have often suffered serious abuse and neglect. To trust an adult will take time. For school-age children, playing checkers is usually of interest, although playing with an adult may be anxiety-producing. Sometimes, an evident need to cheat reflects the parents' or other adults' lack of concern about the child, particularly in terms of helping him or her to become a competent, effective person. This may lead, and often does, to the child's conviction that beating someone else and winning at any cost is the important goal, not being an effective human being.

Children are keenly aware of adult superiority in games, and they are sensitive to the lack of respect for them shown by an adult who gives them permission to play unfairly or to win illegitimately. The therapist who communicates a lack of respect or concern for the dignity of the children or adolescents is repeating their previous experiences with adults and damaging the therapeutic relationship. The therapist must also be aware that there are some children whose need to win—even when knowing they are being allowed to win—is symptomatic of serious neurotic oedipal conflicts. Their omnipotence may need to be deliberately bolstered early in treatment as a therapeutic phase.

It is important with school-age children to play a trial game to find out how good each player is and to determine how much of a handicap is necessary to have a good, hard-fought game. By doing this through one or more trial games, the therapist lets the children know that he or she really wants them to have a good chance to win the game and to learn to enjoy playing. Therapists must also convey that they don't want to win through the opponent's lack of skill or by thoughtless errors by either player. When a child makes a silly or haphazard move, the therapist should ask the child to reconsider the move. In checkers, the youngster sometimes needs to be shown repeatedly how a particular move will lead to being jumped and perhaps beaten, and alternative moves should be suggested. Occasionally, a child will insist stubbornly on an original move no matter what the consequences, and the therapist must decide whether to go along with the move or to demonstrate once more how this move will probably end in the youngster's loss. After asking the youngster several times to reconsider the move, the therapist may need to say he or she cannot play this way, and that perhaps they can play another game of checkers at the next session.

The therapist's choice in this situation may well depend on the child's developmental stage, as well as on the degree of characterologic impulsiveness. For the child who is beginning to want to learn to play by the rules—at age 7 or so—it may be better to stop the game. The therapist should make it clear that it is no fun for him or her and that the child seems not to be ready to learn to play a good game or to enjoy playing. With very impulsive children, the therapist's willingness to stop the game and begin another may demonstrate to the children that their mistake has not lost them the game, although their impulsive, angry behavior has prevented their winning. Readiness to try again expresses the therapist's hope that the children will want to learn how to play better next time. In either case, the children get the message that the therapist wants them to play well. This is a message they may have seldom or never received from an adult. Their desire to be the equal of the adult, even in a few areas, rarely has been understood or encouraged. Once the children recognize the therapist's concern in helping them achieve mastery in a game, they will begin repeated testing of the sincerity and extent of that concern.

Most competitive games permit the therapist to demonstrate how one can fully express feelings of anger and hurt on losing, and triumph, glee, or pleasure on winning. Checkers, however, permits such demonstration of feelings with almost every move. When I am jumped, I scream with anguish and anger about possibly being beaten or almost losing, and I playfully accuse my opponent: "You skunk, you're trying to smash me!" When I jump my opponent, I chortle with glee about how I will demolish him or her. I crow when I win a game, usually bragging about how good I am. If I lose, I'm equally dramatic in my dejection. Because I exaggerate the affect, with obvious enjoyment of my own histrionics, the youngsters seem to enjoy it. It does not take long for even a very silent, withdrawn child to begin to imitate my behavior, at first tentatively, and to begin to express hurt and anger on losing a game after a bad move and pleasure on winning or at a good move.

In the following clinical material, the youngsters I describe are developmentally delayed in some cognitive, social, sensorimotor, or psychologic-interpersonal areas as a result of psychopathology and the resulting conflicts arising at various periods of their development. Exacerbation of conflict with major maladaptation occurs when conflicts in the current developmental stage reinforce the original trauma and maladaptation of previous stages of development.

VIGNETTE 1: HERB

Herb, a 6-year-old boy who was very hyperactive, hostile, aggressive, and had a poor attention span, was referred by the school. At the time of treatment he was in a foster home, but had been severely abused till age 4. He came sullenly and worriedly into the playroom, sat down at the low table, and would not accompany me to look at the toys available for him to play with. When I asked him what he'd like to do, he shrugged his shoulders and looked both scared and hostile. I took down the checkerboard and checkers and asked him if he knew how to play; he barely nodded yes. I explained our playing a test game to find out how many checkers I needed to take off for it to be a good and fair game. He withdrew and looked uncomfortable. It was clear he knew the moves of the game. When I stopped his moving his checker because I'd get a double jump, he seemed surprised. When I complimented him on a good move, he stared suspiciously at me. After handicapping myself three checkers, we played a close game. Herb reacted with a slight smile when I moaned, "Oh no, you're not going to jump me again." Thus, while we played for four weeks in near silence, Herb seemed to be less apprehensive each time and also appeared to appreciate my instructions, which helped him make better moves, and my warning him of potentially bad moves. After about a month, Herb whispered after me comments like "Darn it, you're going to trap my man" or "Oh boy, have I got you!" Each time he whispered he looked fearfully at me. In another few weeks, he moved from echoing my words to exclaiming with muted glee when he was about to jump me or expressing annoyance. In time, he became very boisterous as he imitated my remarks. He'd greet me joyously when he came in. He learned to play well for his age. His foster father once inquired with a mixture of annoyance and pleasure how I had taught Herb to play so well that he could often beat him. Through our playing checkers, Herb worked out a great deal of his anger, hostility, fear, and hate, and his behavior at school improved markedly. He was clearly more trusting of adults. He also learned to express feelings of closeness, saying "This is fun," as he enjoyed those moments. Herb's learning improved, his attention span increased, and there was no evidence of hyperactivity.

VIGNETTE 2: SAMMY

Nine-year-old Sammy was brought to treatment because of hyperactive, destructive behavior in school. He was frequently ejected from his classroom and sent home, and had fallen two years behind in basic subjects. He displayed aggressive, overactive behavior with his mother and two younger siblings, but was less aggressive and overactive around his father. However, he inadvertently broke things when he and his father worked in the yard or on the car or made appliance repairs. These were activities that

Sammy usually enjoyed. At the time I saw him, repeated expulsions from class, along with the anger of teachers, administrators, and parents, had resulted in Sammy's becoming a sullen, defensive child.

He was brought in to be evaluated for minimal cerebral dysfunction. There were no developmental data to confirm the diagnosis and no abnormalities revealed by neurologic and neuropsychologic examinations.

Sammy was very large for his age and demonstrated some of the clumsiness of large 9-year-olds, as well as an inability to sit still; but his coordination in physical games and his gross motor skills were excellent. Developmentally, Sammy was not yet ready to spend much time sitting still. His fine motor skills, though good, were not refined, so that he could not write easily. Although he could read and concentrate, he needed to be up and about frequently. Given a model to build, however, he spent an hour without interruption.

After several introductory sessions, Sammy was still uncommunicative, wandering from toy to toy, silently discarding tinker toys, trucks, and the like, just moments after he picked them up. I asked if he would like to play checkers. He nodded glumly. I explained our trial games, and after I had beaten him handily in several, he agreed to my being handicapped by playing with two fewer checkers. In our first game, after a few opening moves that showed he knew how to play, he made an impulsive move that would give me a triple jump. I refused to move and asked him to reconsider, explaining that it would be no fun to beat him simply because of a careless mistake. He refused to reconsider or change his move. I removed the checkers from the board and said we would play another time. For the remainder of that play session, Sammy wandered around the playroom disconsolately kicking at toys. I said several times that I was sorry we could not continue the game, but it was no fun unless he played well enough to make it tough for me to win.

At the next session, Sammy heeded my warnings and even asked my advice about a move. We both tried to figure out which move would be better. On one occasion, he tried to cheat by moving a checker straight across squares so that he could make a double jump. When I mildly remonstrated, muttering, "I sure do know how much you want to win," he shamefacedly replaced the checker. He narrowly lost this game, and at the end I praised him for the great fight he had put up. In the 10 minutes left in the session, he began to arrange furniture in the dollhouse quietly and systematically, without comment.

In a session sometime later, he stopped me when I made an unthinking, stupid move, saying he could not move until I had reconsidered. When I soberly thanked him, he grinned and approved my next move. Sammy learned to play well and became less concerned with winning than with playing a good game.

His subsequent play with other toys became more serious, and he began to talk about the behavior and feelings of the dolls in the dollhouse. He seemed to take it for granted that I would listen attentively, try to understand him, and treat him with dignity. At this juncture, he had made the transition from essentially nonverbal, concrete, competitive play to verbal fantasy, and we entered the next phase in therapy.

VIGNETTE 3: CHESTER

Chester, at the age of 13, used checkers to communicate in various ways. He was a brilliant boy from a brilliant family, but emotionally he was very constricted and depressed. He was brought to treatment because he had begun to stay in his room, refusing to go to school or to see his friends. He complained of assorted aches and pains and was eating little. His symptoms had begun shortly after the onset of puberty and his promotion to high school.

I suspected developmental problems, especially the recrudescence of previous conflicts about self-worth that had previously led to depression combined with adolescent anxieties as he was being flooded with sexual impulses. There was also evidence of rebellion at unrelenting parental demands for scholarly excellence, which in no way reflected his parents' pride in his talents and achievements, only in fulfilling their expectations.

Chester was passive and silent in the interviews. After failing to get him talking by commenting several times about the kinds of feelings adolescents might experience, I suggested a game of checkers. He snorted, saying it was a child's game and he had been the state junior chess champion in junior high school. I said that I did not play chess well enough to make it interesting. Grudgingly, but curiously gracious, he sighed and humored me. In our trial game of checkers he won easily, so I suggested a handicap of one checker for him.

In the ensuing game, he reacted with subdued glee to my agonized cries when he jumped me. When I beat him occasionally, my triumphant cries were met with his half-angry, half-derisive comment, "You were just lucky."

When I had made it clear that we could not allow stupid moves, he began to stop me when I was making an error with the expletive "Stupid!" Then he would show me some alternative moves. Gradually, when he began to realize that I wanted to learn and did not resent his teaching me, he stopped me more gently. When he won, he began to crow with increasing expressions of pleasure. Once my playing clearly showed I had benefited from his ever more patient teaching, we began to play without handicapping him. Our games were fairly even, though "Chet," as he now asked me to call him, won most of them.

Chet could predict who would win after two or three moves, just as he had learned to do in chess. Because I did not have this capacity to visualize the end of the game, I would insist we play the game out, with all the attendant drama I initiated. After a time, Chet enjoyed the opportunities for expressing feelings himself, and he stopped making predictions. As he more freely expressed feelings of dismay, hurt, anger, pleasure, and victory, it became easier for him to laugh and enjoy my histrionic displays in victory and defeat, which he had earlier labeled childish.

At this point, Chet began to use our game of checkers in a new way. When it was time for him to move, he would pick up a checker, hold it or toss it thoughtfully in the air, and talk, as if to himself, about something that concerned him. I was careful to hear him out and follow his lead, making my comments, questions of clarification, or interpretations while I also thoughtfully considered a move. Most of our therapeutic work was done while ostensibly playing checkers.

It was evident that the game permitted communication at several levels, as well as gave Chet permission to identify with me. My communication of respect for his brilliance was not coupled with any demands, except for my request that he help me play a game that would be mutually challenging and interesting. Thus I, a feared and despised adult, wanted and needed to learn from him. He felt superior to me in this role and, as I've noted, quite early imitated my displays of feeling in a limited way, which generally meant deriding me or expressing anger that someone as "stupid" as I should win. When I did not retaliate, he recognized the metacommunication: I was not disturbed by his derision, was not tempted to retaliate, and enjoyed both his instruction and the excellence of his playing.

As he began to imitate my more open and exaggerated expression of feelings, which seemed to him a safe, make-believe way of expressing deep, disturbing, and dangerous feelings of anger, he watched guardedly for my reactions. To express open anger toward me when I won a game seemed frightening; he cut his comments short and suggested starting another game. But when he saw that his anger did not alter our relationship, he seemed to accept my laconic comment, "It feels pretty good to me when I get angry." As he became more open about his feelings, he began to tease me when I made a poor move or was trapped. The difference was that it was a healthy, gentle teasing that led to his trying to be helpful. By the time he initiated talking over checkers, expression of affect seemed less difficult for him.

During the seven months of therapy, Chet's behavior at home changed markedly. He went to school, worked, took gym, studied, and again began to associate with friends. Attitudes toward both parents became more relaxed as some of his early anxieties and fear of his father's irrational, unexpected, explosive anger and of his mother's seductiveness emerged and were discussed, and he was also able to repeatedly open up the conflicts about whom he had to please with his schoolwork. He finally decided that if he worked effectively for himself, his parents would also be satisfied. These discussions occurred while we played checkers. Chet was also able to work out some of his anxiety about the enormous anger he had to suppress, and at the same time to express his concurrent anxiety about retaliation and loss of support and nurturance from important people, as if he were a small and vulnerable child. The safer it became for Chet to experience and express many of his feelings, the more gentle and nurturant his teaching of me became in the game situation.

CONCLUSIONS

Competitive games, especially checkers, can provide a developmentally appropriate means of communication between a therapist and a nonverbal child or adolescent patient. With school-age children who are cognitively beginning to learn the use of rules, the rules in checkers provide a basic framework for the relationship. A number of therapeutic issues can be approached and explored in the context of the games. The child's need to win at all costs, often by cheating, can be worked through. Moreover, cheating can be made unnecessary by handicapping the more expert player. Refusal to permit impulsive or obviously thoughtless moves helps the youngster to think about strategies and to accept help in planning his or her moves. Also, such efforts to enhance the competency of the children and to build their self-esteem reflect the adult's respect for them. When the children are able to play well enough so that the therapist can learn from them, there is a major opportunity to experience and later express mutual respect and pleasure.

One of the problems in playing competitive games is the therapist's need to win. Feelings of competitiveness from the past, usually sibling rivalries or rivalry with a parent, may interfere with playing the game therapeutically. Such interferences need to be worked out by the therapist, usually in supervision. Another interference may be that enjoying a competitive game with a previously sullen, uncommunicative child may become an end in itself. In both instances, the therapist is not able to carefully observe the patient's interactions and respond therapeutically to the youngster's need.

Checkers and some other competitive games provide a medium by which the therapist can model feelings of hurt, anger, and hopelessness after a poor move or defeat by therapist or patient. Similarly, feelings of pleasure and triumph can be demonstrated in relation to excellent moves and winning. Both victory and defeat present opportunities to model ways in which attendant feelings can be expressed fully. Each game is a separate opportunity for modeling, and encouraging children to behave similarly when they experience the same kinds of feelings during the game. Youngsters see that they can display feelings that are accepted by the therapist without being labeled silly or bad. Because the experience is repetitive, the child begins to feel safer about the fuller expression of feelings.

Feelings generated and expressed in the context of playing checkers often are generalized later to other aspects of play therapy. With older children, feelings can be generalized by the way children talk about their difficulties and problems, perhaps during the actual game.

Nonverbal children are difficult to work with in psychotherapy. They may not speak easily because of the severity and type of their psychopathology or because of their sociocultural background. Under the conditions of play described above, there is no pressure or demand from the therapist for children to participate in exposing or talking about their feelings and thoughts before they are actually ready to do so. Thus, the negativism resulting from expectations and demands, which these children have experienced with other adults, may be reduced.

In summary, then, the rivalry of competitive games like checkers, dominos, and the card game war can be utilized so that adult and child are on relatively equal terms. Full expression of feelings can be demonstrated by the adult and later imitated by the child. Such capacity to experience and communicate on a feeling level in the therapeutic situation is critical to therapeutic effectiveness and often extremely difficult to achieve with nonverbal children and adolescents. Competitive games provide a reliable means for therapeutic engagement of youngsters who, by virtue of their developmental problems, their particular psychopathology, or their sociocultural antecedents, are difficult to engage in ordinary play or "talking" therapy.

REFERENCES

Axline, J. (1947). *Play therapy.* Boston: Houghton-Mifflin.

Bettelheim, B. (1972). Play and education. *School Review, 819,* 1–13.

Freud, A. (1928). Introduction to the technique of child analysis. New York: Nervous and Mental Disease Publishing.

Gardner, R. (1971). *Therapeutic communication with children.* New York: Aronson.

Hug-Helmuth, H. (1921). On the technique of child analysis. *International Journal of Psychoanalysis, 2,* 287–305.

Klein, M. (1932). *The psychoanalysis of children.* London: Hogarth.

Levy, D. (1938). Release therapy in young children. *Psychiatry,* 1, 387–389.

Mahler, M., Pine, F., & Bergman, A. (1975). *The psychological birth of the human infant: Symbiosis and individuation.* New York: Basic Books.

Taft, J. (1933). *The dynamics of therapy in a controlled relationship.* New York: Macmillan.

Winnicott. (1971). *Playing and reality.* London: Tavistock.

CHAPTER FIVE

Therapeutic Uses of Fine Motor Games

JAMES N. BOW and FRANCELLA A. QUINNELL

Games are commonly used to engage children in the therapeutic process because they are familiar activities and a natural medium of expression. They also create an informal atmosphere and reduce the intensity of the interpersonal interaction between therapist and child, which alleviates initial discomfort and anxiety. Beyond engaging children in psychotherapy, games have other important purposes: They may be used diagnostically and in the promotion of therapeutic growth. These aspects of games are often overlooked, though they are active ingredients that contribute to psychotherapeutic efficacy.

Many different types of games are used in psychotherapy. Some are ordinary games children play every day; others are therapeutic games developed to address particular issues. The present chapter focuses on the former group, with an emphasis on games with a fine motor component, such as *Pic-Up Stix,* jacks, *Operation, Tiddly Winks, UNO Stacko, Perfection,* and penny hockey. As outlined by Bow and Goldberg (1986), fine motor games have certain advantages. First, fine motor games provide an avenue for learning to curb impulsive behavior, which is a common referral problem to mental health clinics. Second, they allow an outlet for hostility and anger, thereby allowing the child to appropriately discharge and ventilate feelings. Third, they allow a variety of roles to be created, such as the grandiose winner and angry loser. Fourth, fine motor games are not overengrossing and allow for discussion of therapeutic topics. Fifth, these games improve attention span and frustration tolerance. Last, fine motor games typically take 5 to 15 minutes to play, allowing numerous learning trials to occur during a therapeutic hour.

DIAGNOSTIC ASPECTS

SOCIAL-EMOTIONAL FUNCTIONING

Fine motor games provide an array of opportunities to assess social-emotional functioning within a therapeutic setting. Table 5.1 outlines 12 major areas to assess.

Cognitive strategies refer to the approach a child takes during a game, for example, trial and error or insightful problem solving. Some children randomly try different strategies, without any clearly defined plan, whereas others carefully analyze options and possible strategies. The particular approach employed is reflective of the child's problem-solving skills and intellect. The child's ability to learn from mistakes or failed attempts also reflects on cognitive strategies. Is the child flexible and able to employ new, modified strategies versus rigid and inflexible? Some children will try the same strategy time and time again, even though it has been unsuccessful, whereas others will quickly adjust and try new tactics.

Table 5.1
Social-Emotional Factors to Assess

1. Cognitive strategies
2. Response to feedback
3. Drive for mastery
4. Sense of competency
5. Self-control
6. Attention span
7. Frustration tolerance
8. Competitive drive
9. Willingness to follow rules
10. Ability to deal with pressure
11. Reaction to success and failure
12. Locus of control

A child's response to feedback is another important area to assess. Does the child accept or reject input from the therapist? Some omnipotent conduct disordered children will ignore the therapist's input, thinking they know best. In contrast, dependent children will listen attentively and follow any suggestion a therapist provides. Also, it is important to gauge the child's reaction to praise. Is praise readily accepted and appreciated or discounted as invalid or insincere? Depressed children often react to praise with indifference, whereas anxious children seem reassured.

The drive for mastery reflects the child's degree of investment, persistence, and desire to accomplish. Many children are highly driven to succeed, wanting to continually practice and excel. On the other hand, some children lack drive and desire and sometimes even fear success. This may surface as self-doubt, avoidance, and anxiety. A child's sense of competency can also have a direct bearing on the drive for mastery. When children are confident and comfortable with their abilities, their investment and desire to accomplish is greatly enhanced. When self-doubt and feelings of inferiority surface, declining self-confidence occurs and avoidance follows.

The degree of self-control a child has over drives and impulses is an important area to analyze with fine motor games. Is the child able to stop and think before acting? Is the child able to delay responding, without impulsively moving? Does the child become aggressive and destructive? Impulse-ridden children will have great difficulty with self-control. In contrast, obsessive-compulsive children will approach tasks in a very deliberate manner, with much forethought and caution.

Another area to analyze is the child's attention span. Is the child able to focus on the assigned task? How distractible is the child by extraneous stimuli and to what degree do they interfere with performance? ADHD children have great difficulty with attention, as do children with anxiety or depressive disorders. Another area that ADHD and oppositional defiant children experience difficulty with is frustration tolerance, which is the ability to deal with mishaps, delays, failures, and disappointments. These children often became explosive, argumentative, and negative when faced with frustrating situations. In contrast, some children display unbelievable patience and are able to cope well.

Competitive drive is reflected by the desire to win. Some children are highly competitive, with a strong desire to win. A preoccupation with the score, number of victories, and margin of victory are ways in which competitive drives surface. This is best reflected in conduct disordered children, who want to control and humiliate the therapist, often "talking trash" about their victory. Passive-dependent children are fearful of victory over the therapist because of possible rejection or retaliation.

A child's willingness to follow game rules is another important area to assess. Externalizing children (e.g., those with ADHD, conduct disorder, or oppositional defiant disorder) often attempt to take extra turns, change or ignore basic rules, and add/delete points to players' scores. They attempt to gain an unfair advantage at the expense of other players. In contrast, most internalizing children (e.g., anxious, depressed, or obsessive-compulsive) are overly concerned with following rules and expectations.

Success at fine motor games often depends on a child's ability to deal with pressure. This may involve making a critical move or performing in the clutch. Some children excel in such situations; others deteriorate. After the game is completed, it is important for the therapist to assess the child's reaction to success or failure. Some children react to success with a sense of grandiosity and omnipotence, whereas others experience fear of retaliation from the therapist. Failure may bring forth feelings of inferiority or anger. Another area to assess is the child's locus of control. Does the child attribute success or failure to internal factors he or she can directly control, such as working harder, being smarter, or using a better strategy? Or do external factors beyond the child's control, such as the therapist's having more practice, the game's being rigged, or luck, seem to determine success? A simple question such as "What reason do you think you won (or lost)?" helps address this issue. The causality children attribute to their success or failure greatly influences their motivation.

Through analyzing these social-emotional factors, therapists will gain valuable diagnostic information, which will assist them in the treatment process. They will also be better able to develop therapeutic strategies to address specific problem areas, such as impulsivity, poor organization skills, and low frustration tolerance.

VISUAL-SPATIAL ABILITY

Fine motor games provide a unique opportunity to assess a child's visual-spatial ability. This is important because children with a mental health diagnosis have a higher rate of frank or presumed brain damage (Rutter,

1990; Rutter, Graham, & Yule, 1970). As a result, they may present as clumsy, impulsive, disorganized, and inattentive.

A variety of components and subprocesses constitute visual-spatial functioning. Two major components are visual-perceptual and motor, which are separate but often interrelated. The visual-perceptual area includes recognition, discrimination, closure, and figure-ground relationship, whereas the motor area includes dexterity and manual manipulation. Specific analysis of discrete skill areas is not usually possible because most fine motor games involve a combination of skills. Nevertheless, the therapist should be able to identify the child's general proficiency, along with major deficit areas.

PROMOTING THERAPEUTIC GROWTH

Fine motor games create a natural, informal setting that blurs the purpose of the activity. Children enjoy games and games put them at ease. As a result, fine motor games reduce children's defenses and engage them in the therapeutic process.

Fine motor games also promote a therapist-patient relationship because the therapist becomes an active participant and role model. The therapist's reaction to pressure and frustration, ability to follow rules, and response to success and failure offer direct learning experiences for the child. Furthermore, the therapist is provided the opportunity to teach specific skills, such as anger control, problem-solving strategies, and social skills. For example, a game of *Pic-Up Stix* provides an ideal opportunity to teach and reinforce problem-solving techniques, like the Think Aloud Method developed by Camp and Bash (1985). Prior to each move, the player can identify possible moves, weigh the pros and cons of each move, make a selection, and then evaluate the success of his or her selection. Anger control techniques, such as Goldstein's (Goldstein & Glick, 1987) Aggressive Replacement Training or Robin's (Robin, Schneider, & Dolnick, 1976) Turtle Technique, are useful when children become agitated, irritable, and frustrated. Having the child pull back, identify feelings, use relaxation techniques, and problem-solve about possible solutions help the child learn appropriate ways of coping.

The opportunity for ego-level interpretations of the child's behavioral style is another advantage of fine motor games. Such interpretations encourage a child to reflect on his or her behavior. The willingness to accept such interpretations reflects the child's insight or resistance, along with the desire to change. For example, to a child who continually refuses to obey game rules, the following may be said: "It appears you are having difficulty following the basic rules of the game. We all like to win, but the real enjoyment is just playing the game and having fun. If you fail to follow rules when playing with your friends, they won't want to play with you. Let's review the rules again so we have a better understanding of them."

An additional advantage of fine motor games is that therapists usually have some degree of control over the course and outcome of the game. Depending on the child's presenting problem(s) and stage in therapy, a variety of therapeutic situations can be created. Critical moves, stressful situations, success or failure, and disappointment can all happen during the course of the game. The opportunity for therapists to provide guidance, support, encouragement, and ego interpretations during the game further enhances the therapeutic process.

Last, transference and countertransference issues need to be closely monitored during fine motor games. These competitive games can create a variety of feelings and thoughts, along with a high degree of intensity. It is critical that therapists are aware of these issues and familiar with ways to address them therapeutically.

DESCRIPTION OF GAMES

Many fine motor games are available on the market. However, they vary in complexity, cost, size, and therapeutic value. The fine motor games described below are classic games, which have a high degree of therapeutic value. They are readily available at most toy stores and inexpensive, that is, less than $20. They are generally small in size and easily transported. Also, they are easy to learn, even for young children.

TIDDLY WINKS (PRESSMAN & GABRIEL)

A classic and widely used childhood game is *Tiddly Winks*. It consists of differently colored and sized "winks" and a circular game board. The game board is divided into different sections according to point value, with the center section having the greatest value. The object of the game is to shoot the small winks onto the game board, aiming for the highest point area. The game is recommended for children age 6 and older. The therapeutic value lies in assessing eye-hand coordination, frustration tolerance, and persistence.

PERFECTION (LAKESIDE GAMES)

The object of *Perfection* is to match as quickly as possible 25 geometric shapes with their analogous "cutouts" in a plastic tray. After 60 seconds the tray pops up, scattering the pieces, and no score is made. The winner is the person who completes the game in the shortest time period. The game is recommended for children age 5 and older. It provides good opportunities to assess organizational skills (reflective versus impulsive), cognitive strategies, and visual-spatial skills. In additional, the game is time-limited which increases psychological pressure. The game can be modified; less time can be allotted for advanced levels, and fewer shapes can be used for beginners.

Two other games, *Superfection* (Lakeside Games) and *Numbers Up* (Milton Bradley) are similar to *Perfection* but involve matching pairs of designs and numbers, respectively. *Berserk* (Cadaeo) is a similar game that uses color pegs and offers three different skill levels: color matching, color sequencing, and counting from 1 to 20.

PIC-UP STIX (STEVEN MFG)

Twenty-five sticks of assorted colors, including one black stick, are held in one hand and dropped, forming a pile of overlapping sticks. The object is to pick up the sticks, one at a time, moving only the stick being touched. If any other stick moves, the player's turn ends. A player may remove sticks only with his or her fingers. However, the player who obtains the black stick may use it to flip and tip other sticks. The game is finished when all sticks are picked up. Each player's score is calculated according to the number of sticks obtained, with different point values being assigned to each color. The highest point value wins. The game is recommended for children age 5 years and older. The game is highly dependent on eye-hand coordination, cognitive strategies, and the child's willingness to follow rules. The latter provides ample opportunity for cheating, which can be dealt with therapeutically. It is important to assess if the position of the stick or point value is more important to the child. In addition, it is worthwhile to note how the point value of different colored sticks and the special utility of the black stick impacts the child's approach.

OPERATION (MILTON BRADLEY)

This game consists of Cavity Sam, the "patient," who is on a plastic-framed platform. He has 12 holes or cavities in his body, which represent operations to be performed. A player attempts to remove an object from each hole, such as Spare Ribs, Wish Bone, Adam's Apple, or Charlie Horse, with a pair of surgical tweezers, when the respective *doctor* card is selected. The player must insert the tweezers and remove the object without touching the edges of the cavity with the tweezers. If done successfully, the player collects the designated fee on the card from the banker. When unsuccessfully done, a buzzer will sound and Sam's red nose will light up, and the player's turn ends with the part being dropped back into the cavity. The player with the *specialist* card for that particular operation then has an opportunity to remove the object, with payment at a higher rate than the *doctor* card if successful. If the *specialist* is unsuccessful, the object is returned to the cavity and that particular *doctor* card goes to the bottom of the pile. A time limit of one minute is recommended for any operation. The game ends when all 12 operations have been successfully completed. The winner is the player with the most money. The game is recommended for children age 6 and older. This game assesses eye-hand coordination, patience, frustration tolerance, and self-control.

UNO STACKO (MATTEL) AND JENGA (MILTON BRADLEY)

UNO Stacko consists of a tower of 51 plastic blocks that are stacked on a flat surface in layers of three blocks. Each layer is at a right angle to the layer below it. A loading tray is provided to straighten the tower into position. Each block has a number (1, 2, 3, or 4) and color (red, blue, yellow, or green). The first player rolls the UNO cube, which has number/color combinations along with draw two and reverse. If a number is rolled, a block of either the same color or number on the cube must be removed from the levels below the highest level. Only one hand may be used. The block that is removed is then placed on the top of the tower at a right angel to the level beneath. If a reverse is rolled, a block is not drawn by that player; instead, he or she passes the cube back to the previous player. If a draw two is rolled, the next player must draw and stack two blocks of any color from the tower. After the first player completes his or her turn, the cube is passed to the player on the left. If a player causes the tower to collapse, he or she loses and the previous player wins.

Jenga is very similar to *UNO Stacko*. It consists of 54 hardwood blocks that make an 18-story tower, with three blocks making up each layer. The traditional game does not use numbers and colors. The player who built the tower goes first. He or she removes any block below the highest completed level using only one hand. The removed block is placed at a right angle to the previous highest layer. Play continues to the left, with the next player removing a block and stacking it. The game ends when the tower falls. The last player to take a turn without the tower falling wins. A new edition of *Jenga, Throw'n Go Jenga*, is very similar to *UNO Stacko*. A roll of a die determines which color or block position is selected, which requires greater problem-solving skills.

These games are recommended for children age 8 and older. They provide good opportunities to assess problem-solving skills, eye-hand coordination, planning ability, frustration tolerance, and impulse control.

PENNY HOCKEY

This game requires three coins (usually pennies) and a table surface. Players position themselves across the length of the table top. One player is initially selected as the shooter, and the other player is the goalie. The goalie creates a three-sided goal by placing his or her hand at the edge of the table, with his or her index and little finger extended onto the table. The shooter, starting on his or her side of the table, slides the three coins together. This is called the "break." The object of the game is to score a goal by moving the three coins across the table by sliding one coin through the space created by the other two. A slide is created by flicking, not pushing, the coin with the index finger. The shooter may slide the coin in any direction, that is, sideways, backwards, or forwards, but he or she cannot slide the same coin consecutively. If the shooter eventually scores by flicking a coin into the goal, he or she is awarded one point and the shooter becomes the goalie and vice versa. A shooter loses his or her turn if (1) the coins touch each other after the break; (2) a shot is not possible; that is, three coins are parallel; or (3) any of the coins fall off the table. The winner is the first player to score 10 points. However, this score criterion can be varied depending on the age of the participants, time constraints, and skill level. The game is recommended for children age 8 and older. Enjoyment of penny hockey is highly dependent on eye-hand coordination, problem-solving skills, ability to deal with pressure, and willingness to follow game rules. The plan of attack should account for such factors as the number of flicks and distance of shots on goal.

A commercially produced game, *Rebound* (Mattel), is similar in many ways to penny hockey and is set up like a miniature shuffleboard game. It involves flinging a puck down a game board, with point values at the end. The challenge is to land on the highest point values, with the winner being the first to reach 500 points.

JACKS (STROMBECKER)

This classic game uses 5 to 12 metal or plastic jacks and a small rubber ball. It has many variations. The most popular version is baby game. It is played by scattering the jacks on the playing surface with one hand. The first player tosses the ball and picks up one jack with his or her preferred hand, then catches the ball after one bounce with the same hand. The jack is then transferred to the other hand. The player then tosses the ball again, another jack is picked up, and the ball is caught in the same manner. All jacks are picked up in this way. The next round involves players picking up two jacks at a time, called twos. When using six jacks, future rounds consist of threes, fours (four and then two, or two then four), fives (one and then five, or five then one), and sixes (all at once). A player loses his or her turn when fouls or misses occur, which include any of the following: catching the ball with the wrong hand or both hands, failing to pick up the correct number of jacks, allowing the ball or jacks to touch the body or clothes, dropping the ball or jack(s) by mistake, double bouncing the ball, touching other jacks while attempting to pick up a specific jack or group of jacks, or trying twice for the same jack(s).

A popular variation is upcast, which is very similar to baby game, but after catching the ball with the jack(s) in the preferred hand, the ball is tossed again. The jack or jacks are then transferred to the other hand and the ball is caught again with the preferred hand after it bounces. Again, rounds continue through ones, twos, threes, and so forth.

Another variation is called eggs in basket. It is also very similar, but more difficult. Before catching the ball with the preferred hand after one bounce, the jack(s) must be transferred to the other hand.

This game is recommended for children over the age of 3. It taps eye-hand coordination, planning ability, frustration tolerance, obedience to rules, and self-control.

SLAM BAS-KET (CADACO)

This tabletop version of full court basketball creates much excitement and action. The game consists of a molded base with seven quarter-sized holes on each side of the court, with backboard baskets at each end. When the table tennis–size basketball lands in one of the holes, it can be flicked toward the basket by one of the three flip-up levers on each side. When the right amount of pressure is expressed, a basket is made. If too much pressure is used, the ball may leave the court, which results in the opponent's getting a shot from center court. Two points are given for court shots and one point for free throws. The winner is determined by the number of points scored in a time period or by the first player to a designated point value. This game taps fine motor control, dealing with pressure, frustration tolerance, and willingness to follow rules. Other versions include *Hot Shot Basketball* (Milton Bradley) and *Move 'N Hoops 3* (Manley).

TIP IT (MATTEL) AND TOPPLE (PRESSMAN)

These games involve balance and tap fine motor coordination, problem solving, and frustration tolerance. They are appropriate for children age 5 and older. *Tip It* involves a three-prong structure balanced on a center pole, which extends about one foot. At the top of the pole, a plastic clown is tenuously balanced. Eight colored disks are placed on each prong in various color sequences. The player spins the spinner and uses a fork to remove a disk of the color indicated. During play, if the structure becomes unbalanced, the clown falls and the player must return one of the disks previously earned to a prong. The first player to remove four disks is the winner.

Topple consists of a multilevel tower balanced on a stand. Disks are placed on the levels according to the roll of a die, with the aim of keeping the structure balanced. If the tower becomes unbalanced and falls, the player loses the game.

CASE ILLUSTRATIONS

During the game *Perfection,* Tom showed good visual-spatial skills. He was able to correctly match up shapes with the cutouts. However, he had great difficulty dealing with pressured situations. After about 30 seconds, he became preoccupied with the timer and easily frustrated. As a result, his performance greatly deteriorated. Three techniques were tried. First, he was taught some relaxation exercises to assist him in pressured situations. Second, anger control techniques were introduced to help him deal with frustration. Third, systematic desensitization was used: Only 15 shapes were initially used rather than 25; when he completed the task, he was asked to wait until the timer was almost ready to ring before turning it off. This was done to desensitize him to the time pressure. Tom quickly progressed from 15 to 18, then to 21, and finally to 25 shapes. He showed better organizational skills and a higher tolerance level to pressure situations. These same strategies were also used when playing *Superfection* and *Numbers Up.*

Sally, age 12, had great difficulty during a game of jacks. Her eye-hand coordination was very poor. She had problems coordinating the bounces of the ball and picking up the jacks. While playing the game *Perfection,* Sally had problems differentiating shapes and fitting shapes into the cutouts. During the game *Operation,* she was constantly hitting the edge of the cavity and activating the buzzer. These observations, along with a long history of specific academic problems, resulted in a learning disability referral. A learning disability was confirmed through formal testing.

While playing *Tiddly Winks,* it became obvious that Brenda was a timid, shy, and nonassertive girl. With prompting, Brenda finally acknowledged that she was fearful of pressing too hard on the winks, noting that she did not want to break them. The game was briefly interrupted. Brenda was requested to press as hard as possible on the wink, with the intention of sending it as far as possible across the room. She was initially apprehensive, but gradually found enjoyment in flicking the winks. She quickly learned that the winks were indestructible and could go a great distance. She also became more carefree and less fearful. The game was then reintroduced. Brenda rapidly found enjoyment in playing the game. She developed strategies to win and started to display a competitive drive, which was strongly encouraged.

Derrick was an impulsive and driven boy, who had difficulty following rules. He requested to play *Pic-Up Stix.* The rules were briefly reviewed at the beginning of the game. Derrick dropped the sticks to start the game. He immediately attempted to pick up the black stick instead of other sticks that were much easier and less risky to pick up. Derrick was unsuccessful, but continued to employ the same approach rather than attempt to modify his strategy. He became frustrated and angry. Also, he often argued that other sticks did not move while he attempted to get the black stick. He became more negative as the therapist accrued numerous sticks, finally winning the game. Derrick then wanted to quit. Anger control techniques were used to calm down. The therapist also decided to review the rules, especially with regard to the point value for each stick. Strategies for approaching the game were discussed and the Think Aloud method was used to facilitate problem solving. Another game was played. The therapist went first and modeled the techniques, explaining his options, rationale, and decision making. Derrick then followed and showed much better planning ability and self-control. He was able to explain his approach and rationale. Derrick won the game, which reinforced his approach and use of the various techniques. A discussion then followed about applying these strategies and techniques to other games and real-life situations. *Tip It* was then played with the intention of utilizing the problem-solving techniques he had just learned. Derrick was able to analyze his options for disk placement and made appropriate selections. He showed much satisfaction and success, which fostered self-esteem.

The game *Operation* was played in a group therapy situation. Because there were six group members, including the therapist, three teams were selected. Rules of the game were reviewed and *specialist* cards distributed. The team of John and Mark was selected to go first. Mark selected a *doctor* card, and John elected to do the operation. He was successful at removing the Spare Ribs and the team earned $200. The next team of Glen and Tim could not decide who would select the card and who would do the operation, and much arguing ensued. Problem solving was utilized to address this issue, which was resolved by quickly playing the paper, rock, and scissors hand game. Tim won and chose to do the operation. Glen drew a *doctor* card, which requested the repair of a broken heart. Tim attempted to remove the heart, but the tweezers touched the edge of the heart cavity, setting off the buzzer and lighting the red nose. Glen immediately started berating Tim, which escalated into mutual name calling. A brief time-out from the game was called. Appropriate social behavior was reviewed, along with anger control techniques. The games was then resumed with John and Mark attempting to remove the heart, as they had the *specialist* card. Because John had done the previous operation, the team decided Mark would attempt this one. He was successful and the team earned $1,200. This caused another flairup in Glen's behavior; he complained that Mark and John had $1,400, and he and Tim had nothing. Ego support was given in regard to dealing with frustration and disappointment. The third team of Dr. Bow and Matt went next. Dr. Bow drew a *doctor* card, which involved connecting the ankle bone to the knee bone. Matt was able to do this successfully and the team earned $200. John and Mark went next. Mark drew a *doctor* card, which requested he "pluck the wishbone." John was unsuccessful. Because Glen and Tim had the *specialist* card, Tim attempted the removal and was successful, resulting in the team collecting $1,200. Glen immediately boasted of his team's accomplishments, noting they still had another turn. Tim drew the next *doctor* card. It requested the removal of the "bread basket." Glen was successful and the team was awarded $1,000. Now they were in the lead with $2,200, which increased Glen's boasting. Ways of handling happiness, without offending others, were reviewed, along with how emotions can change from disappointment to happiness with persistence and hard work. The game continued, with John and Mark finally winning. Each team was asked the reason they won or lost. Glen and Tim showed an external locus of control, accusing others of cheating and being lucky, which initiated a discussion about locus of control and sportsmanship.

During the game *UNO Stacko*, Lisa, age 11, was timid and indecisive. She ruminated about possible moves, taking two or three minutes to make a move. The first step involved switching to the game *Jenga*, which is very similar but does not involve color and number combinations, so less problem solving is involved. Second, a time limit of 30 seconds per move was instituted. Initially, Lisa seemed overwhelmed and frustrated by the time limit, but gradually she adjusted. After she mastered *Jenga*, *UNO Stacko* was reintroduced. Again, the 30-second time expectation was instituted. Initially, Lisa had difficulty adjusting to the greater problem-solving requirements of this task, especially within the time limit. However, with ego support and encouragement, she was able to master the task. Gradually, the time limit was reduced to 25 seconds, then 20 seconds, and finally 15 seconds.

During a game of penny hockey, Montez showed much impulsivity along with poor planning ability. He used a trial-and-error approach, with little forethought. In response, problem-solving skills were taught, which involved the following steps: First, analyze each possible move; second, evaluate the pros and cons of each move; third, make a selection; finally, evaluate the selection. While the game was played, each step was verbally rehearsed. The technique helped improve his self-control and problem-solving skills. His performance greatly improved over time. These techniques were also generalized to other games, such as *UNO Stacko* and *Pic-Up Stix*.

Thomas was a highly competitive child, who requested to play *Slam Bas-Ket*, noting that he was the best basketball player in the world. As the game was played, Thomas became frustrated and angry, complaining that the "game ain't acting right" because he was not scoring many points. The game was briefly interrupted at this point to review some anger control techniques. Also, ego interpretations were provided regarding his externalization of blame for his poor performance. When the game was resumed and the therapist shot the ball, Thomas started blowing air in an attempt to throw the ball off its course. When confronted about his misbehavior, Thomas initially denied it, but then rationalized his behavior by stating that the rules did not forbid it. Ego interpretations were made about the intent of rules, along with the impact of bending or violating rules. Gradually, over time, Thomas showed less limit testing and better frustration tolerance. He also accepted greater responsibility for his performance.

SUMMARY AND CONCLUSIONS

Fine motor games are highly effective therapeutic tools. They easily engage children in therapy, provide valuable diagnostic information, and promote therapeutic growth. Fine motor games create an informal, natural medium of expression, which reduces the intensity of the therapeutic interaction, thereby enhancing the therapeutic relationship. Much diagnostic information is provided by observing a child's performance. A variety of social-emotional factors can be assessed, including cognitive strategies, response to feedback, drive for mastery, attention span, frustration tolerance, self-control, competitive drive, ability to deal with pressure, willingness to follow rules, reaction to success or failure, and locus of control. All of these provide valuable information about a child's functioning and assist in developing therapeutic strategies for specific problem areas. Also, fine motor games provide diagnostic information about visual-spatial functioning. Therapeutic growth is promoted through the therapist's being an active participant, role model, and educator during fine motor games. This process is further enhanced by the therapist's opportunity for ego-level interpretations and ability to control the course and outcome of the game to some degree, depending on the child's presenting problems and stage of therapy. Overall, fine motor games have many active ingredients that contribute to diagnostic and therapeutic efficacy.

REFERENCES

Bow, J.N., & Goldberg, T.E. (1986). Therapeutic uses of games with a fine motor component. In C.E. Schaefer & S.E. Reid (Eds.), *Game play: Therapeutic use of childhood games* (pp. 243–255). New York: Wiley.

Camp, B.W., & Bash, M.A. (1985). *Think aloud: Increasing social and cognitive skills: A problem-solving program for children.* Champaign, IL: Research Press.

Goldstein, A.P., & Glick, B. (1987). *Aggression replacement training: A comprehensive intervention for aggressive youth.* Champaign, IL: Research Press.

Robin, A., Schneider, M., & Dolnick, M. (1976). The turtle technique: An extended case study of self-control in the classroom. *Psychology in the Schools, 13,* 449–453.

Rutter, M. (1990). The Isle of Wight revisited: Twenty-five years of child psychiatry epidemiology. In S. Chess & M.E. Hertzig (Eds.), *Annual progress in child psychiatry and child development* (pp. 131–179). New York: Brunner/Mazel.

Rutter, M., Graham, P., & Yule, W. (1970). *A neuropsychiatry study in childhood.* London: Lavenham Press.

CHAPTER SIX

Therapeutic Use of Card Games with Learning-Disabled Children

STEVEN E. REID

Learning-disabled children are those who demonstrate marked academic underachievement whose cause cannot be traced to intellectual limitations, sensory deficits, motor impairments, socioeconomic disadvantage, inadequate instruction, or emotional disturbance (Rourke, 1985a). These children not only present problems in terms of designing adequate educational programs, but also are likely to constitute a significant proportion of mental health problems. Many of these children go on to develop difficulties in conduct, self-esteem, and depression as a result of years of frustration and failure in school. A substantial percentage of learning-disabled children drop out of school, thereby contributing substantially to the population of juvenile delinquents in this country (Brown, 1978).

Despite the significance of the problem of learning disabilities, it remains one of the most confusing areas in the literature of child psychology. For example, as many as six different diagnostic labels have been used to describe this problem, including "minimal brain dysfunction" (Millichap, 1977), "dyslexia" (Benton & Pearl, 1978), and "brain-injured" (Strauss & Lehtinen, 1947). Only recently has the term "learning disabilities" gained widespread usage. Accordingly, estimates of the prevalence of this disorder have varied, ranging from as low as 3 percent (Ross, 1976) to as high as 10 percent (Millichap, 1977) of the school-age population.

For many years, the inability of children to learn despite adequate educational opportunities and intellectual ability was believed to result from underlying emotional conflict. Although this notion has fallen into disrepute, there remains considerable debate in regard to the causes of specific learning disabilities. The etiological theories encompassing genetic factors (Boder, 1973), social-environmental influences (Denckla, 1979), attentional problems (Ross, 1976), and visual-perceptual deficits (Orton, 1937) have not received much empirical support. Support has been growing for the notion that neuropsychological immaturity and/or dysfunction is the cause of the learning problems of a large number of these children (Barkley, 1981; Rourke, 1978, 1985a). Central nervous system dysfunction may take two general forms: diffuse brain damage, resulting in widespread cognitive and behavioral deficits, or highly focal lesions, resulting in highly specific disruptions in cognitive functioning. The term *learning disabilities,* in its current usage, refers to those children whose learning problems are attributable to neurogenic origins.

The literature on identification and classification of subtypes of learning disabilities easily exceeds other related research in terms of general confusion, disorganization, and controversy. Recent research (see Rourke, 1985b, for a review) has at least made it possible to coherently summarize existing knowledge about learning disability subtypes, as follows: (1) Children with learning disabilities represent an extremely heterogeneous group with regard to their pattern of cognitive skills and level of academic achievement; (2) specific disorders of reading, spelling, mathematics, or written expression are also not homogeneous subtypes of learning disorders; (3) the various subtypes of learning disorders do not result from simply a critical deficit in any one cognitive skill; and (4) at least four general areas of cognitive development appear to be important to adequate achievement skills: linguistic-conceptual, visuospatial-constructive, sequential-analytic, and motor planning, execution, and regulation. Where these skills develop out of synchrony from one another, problems with achievement are likely to occur.

To appreciate the complexity and breadth of the conceptual and research issues regarding learning disabilities, the reader must understand that the above constitutes only the briefest of overviews of the literature of these disorders. Familiarity with these issues is a first step toward greater understanding of the psychological world of the learning-disabled child. Interest in the psychological functioning of these children remains high. It is widely held that socioemotional difficulties often occur in conjuction with childhood learning disorders. Inefficient learners are commonly referred for psychological counseling and represent a substantial proportion of referrals to mental health clinics (Adams, 1975). Early investigations into the secondary emotional problems of learning disorders were poorly designed and yielded little reliable information. However, recent well-controlled research has brought the psychological functioning of learning-disabled children into clearer focus. The research can be divided into three general areas: the behavior of learning-disabled children, their interpersonal environment, and their emotional and personality functioning.

AREAS OF RESEARCH

BEHAVIOR

A number of studies have documented the greater frequency of behavioral problems of learning-disabled children in and out of the classroom. Conduct problems, such as aggression, hyperactivity, social withdrawal, anxiety, and school phobias, are more commonly found among learning-disabled children than those achieving at a normal rate (Douglas & Peters, 1979; Klinsbourne & Caplan, 1979; Peter & Spreen, 1979; Rutter, 1978). Cunningham and Barkley (1978) have demonstrated how academic failure can create classroom behavior problems, inattentiveness, off-task behavior, and aggression in children. Although these behaviors may occur simultaneously with learning disabilities, they may also develop in response to extended failure in the classroom. A number of learning-disabled children also suffer from hyperactivity. Children whose primary diagnosis is hyperactivity, or attention deficit disorder (*DSM-III*, 1980), typically are underachievers and manifest behaviors, such as distractibility, that interfere with classroom learning.

INTERPERSONAL ENVIRONMENT

In general, the literature indicates that learning-disabled children must deal with an environment that differs significantly from that of their normally achieving peers. In contrast to normal achievers, learning-disabled children tend (1) to be perceived as less pleasant and desirable by parents, teachers, and peers; (2) to be ignored and rejected more often by their teachers; (3) to be the recipients of more negative communications from their parents, teachers, and peers; (4) to be treated in a notably more punitive and derogatory manner by their parents; and (5) to live in families that resemble in certain crucial ways those of emotionally disturbed children (see Porter, 1980, for a review of this literature).

Socioemotional Functioning

Considering the apparently negative environment facing learning-disabled children, one would certainly expect to find that they have difficulty functioning emotionally and socially. Researchers have consistently identified secondary emotional problems—such as low self-esteem, lack of drive for mastery, helplessness, and depression—among these children (e.g., Black, 1974; Bryan & Pearl, 1979; Zimmerman & Allebrand, 1965). However, some studies (e.g., Connolly, 1969; Silverman, 1968) found no significant differences in levels of emotional adjustment and self-esteem between learning-disabled children and their normally achieving peers. Ribner (1978) found that underachieving children in regular classrooms were likely to have low self-esteem, but that those segregated in a learning-disabled classroom were not likely to have a negative self-view. In their summary of the literature in this area, Porter and Rourke (1985) suggest that a substantial proportion of children with learning disorders do not experience emotional difficulties.

Although this notion certainly goes against established opinion, it is nevertheless plausible. Because learning-disabled children are an extremely heterogeneous group with regard to their pattern of cognitive deficits, it seems likely that these children are also not homogeneous in terms of their emotional functioning. Some may have adapted to their limitations, whereas others clearly suffer a great deal from the loss of social status. A number of factors, in addition to pattern of cognitive deficits, probably impact on the overall emotional adjustment of the learning-disabled child. Unfortunately, investigators are only beginning to identify relationships between socioemotional functioning and such factors as subtype of learning disorder and educational placement. One consistent finding is that children with language-based disorders tend to be more socially responsive and emotionally flexible, but, predictably, less verbally expressive compared to children with visuospatial-based disorders. The latter groups tends to exhibit stereotyped and constricted emotional responses (Ozols & Rourke, 1985). Clearly, there is a need for more research into the nature and patterns of emotional disturbance among learning-disabled children.

TREATMENT

The neurological impairments that presumably underlie many children's learning difficulties are not easily detected by existing neurodiagnostic methods. Damage to the brain and spinal cord cannot be directly treated or cured. Thus, treatment approaches to learning-disabled children have necessarily focused on the overt academic, behavioral, and emotional manifestations of the neurological deficits. Treatment of the academic problems includes both retraining through use of the child's cognitive strengths and a frontal assault on the deficient areas (Rourke, 1976). Modification of related behaviors, such as attention span and impulse control, have also been part of efforts to improve academic performance.

The question of treatment of the secondary, emotional and behavioral problems that occur simultaneously with learning problems has not received much attention in the literature, largely because of the relative recency of the learning disabilities diagnosis. Only play therapy has any sort of established history of use with this population. The goals of play therapy are broader than those interventions designed to modify specific behaviors. Play therapy is designed to relieve the child's emotional distress and engender a more positive attitude about achievement in general. This approach involves, essentially, permitting a child to play freely with a variety of expressive and imaginative play materials, such as dolls, puppets, art materials, miniature objects, sand, and clay. The therapist responds empathetically to the child and sets limits on his or her behavior, but otherwise does not actively intervene during the child's play. The assumption here is that children will express and work through emotional conflicts on their own within the metaphor of play.

In their books on play therapy, both Axline (1947) and Ginott (1961) describe the application of nondirective play therapy with learning-disabled children. Guerney (1983) elaborates on the curative aspects of play therapy with this population. She states that the "special physical and interpersonal environment can permit learning disabled children to succeed and develop a feeling of satisfaction with themselves and their competences" (p. 424). The atmosphere of the playroom is one of playfulness and permissiveness, in which fantasy expression is encouraged. As a result, a special environment is created that allows for expression of feelings and experimentation with situations that in "real life" are experienced as threatening. The repetition inherent in play permits the child to work through and master uncomfortable feelings.

One assumption inherent in the play therapy approach is that a child's feelings and attitudes about learning and academic achievement will surface in his or her play. Therefore, no attempts are made by the therapist to elicit expression by the child of particular emotions or concerns. The open-ended quality of this approach may have its drawbacks with learning-disabled children. Primary is the problem of generalization. Play therapy may help children strengthen their general sense of self, but this feeling of competence may evaporate in the school setting. For many children with learning impairments, the very concepts of school and learning are strongly associated with failure and with feelings of inferiority compared to "normal" children.

Game playing is an activity that appears to have potential to more directly address the learning-based emotional and behavioral problems of learning-disabled children. Game therapy is a form of play therapy that utilizes formal, organized games, such as checkers and *Monopoly.* Common board games, fine motor games (e.g., *Tiddly Winks, Pic-Up Stix*), and card games are among those that have been brought into the therapy situation. It is only recently that games have gained recognition and acceptance as psychotherapeutic tools. Games, like free play, are separate from reality and thus provide a context for fantasy experience. Games are seen as a natural medium for expression (Nickerson & O'Laughlin, 1983) and the preferred play activity of school-age children (Piaget, 1962). Thus, a playful and open atmosphere similar to that strived for in play therapy can be generated using games. Throughout history, games have been created and played not only for leisure, but as a vehicle for dealing with specific anxieties. For instance, *Monopoly* was created during the Great Depression of the 1930s, when many dreamed of escaping the economic hardships of the times.

It follows, then, that the primary advantage of games for learning-disabled children is their focusing potential. Games are structured, rule-bound, task-focused, and goal-directed activities. However, they do not possess the same evaluative quality as other task-focused activities, such as schoolwork. Games provide an opportunity to learn basic skills necessary to attend to and complete a task, such as concentration, impulse control, and persistence. Additionally, games are more "cognitive" than free play. Most games require logical thinking and strategy (the exceptions being pure chance games, such as adult gambling and *Candyland*, among others). Others tap motor dexterity (e.g., target games) and visual skills (e.g., many card games, such as concentration). Games are structurally analogous to academic tasks. Unlike schoolwork, however, games are inherently pleasurable, and children will learn more readily from activities that are enjoyable.

A second advantage of games is therapist control. The therapist can control the outcome of the game to provide the learning-disabled child with a success or failure experience, depending on the child's particular therapeutic needs at the time. During game play, the therapist can encourage and reinforce experimentation, attempts at mastery of skills, and actual successful responses. The therapist can stop the play temporarily to explore issues that may come up during the game. The child's sense of competence, feelings of trust toward adults, and defenses are likely to be revealed by the competition involved in playing the game. The therapist can thus formulate diagnostic impressions during game play and make ego-level interventions within the framework of the game.

The number of publications on the therapeutic potential of games has increased dramatically in recent years, but there has been little evaluative research to date and only a few reports on game play with learning-disabled children. Gardner (1973) discussed the use of his *Talking, Feeling, and Doing Game* with underachievers. Goldberg (1980) has used the *Battling Tops* game with children who have cerebral dysfunction. He argues that the game, in which tops are spun and collide in a bowl-shaped area, is useful to promote success experiences and curb the impulsive behavior exhibited by many learning-disabled children. The game is also thought by Goldberg to have value in rehabilitation of fine motor deficits, attention problems, and in providing a sense of mastery, as small increments of improved performance are highly visible. Goldberg cautions, however, that *Battling Tops* or other fine motor games must be used only as a limited therapeutic modality and not as a complete therapeutic program per se.

CARD GAMES

An important consideration in game therapy is choosing a game or set of games that maximize therapeutic efficiency for the individual client. For the learning-disabled child referred for therapy, the game(s) selected should (1) provide opportunities for intellectual as well as emotional growth, (2) require of the players a wide range of neuropsychological abilities, and (3) have varying levels of difficulty so that children can start at their own level and experience increasing increments of success. One set of games, those that use a regular set of playing cards, has been found by the author to meet these requirements and to be of particular therapeutic value with learning-disabled children.

Card games are an extremely flexible therapeutic tool. Scores of different games exist and new ones are easily created, all from a finite and fixed set of stimuli: the 52 playing cards. The advantage of using the same props over and over is that children gain a sense of comfort and safety with what is familiar. Later, the repetition involved in card playing enables children to acquire a sense of mastery and competence that will generalize to other task-focused activities. Most card games can be played more than once during a therapy hour, thus increasing the likelihood of the child learning from the previous game. Card games vary widely in terms of intellectual ability required. Therefore, they can be used with children of all ages and of various intellectual capacity. The most simple games can be used with younger children or those with more severe intellectual impairment. More complex games can be introduced as children master the easier games. Older children and adolescents may be more motivated to participate in card games than in traditional play activities, as the latter are often viewed as being childish forms of amusement.

With card games, learning is "painless" because games are intriguing, challenging, and fun. They are not usually resisted when offered as a part of therapy. Card games are intrinsically motivating and are not usually viewed as hard work by children, despite the fact that they require a variety of cognitive abilities and real intellectual effort from the participants. The following is a brief discussion of the skills that card games can help develop. Specific card games that can be used for developing different skills are also named, but a description of each game is prohibited by considerations of space. The reader may wish to consult Golick (1973) for a complete description of the specific card games mentioned.

MOTOR SKILLS

Handling, shuffling, dealing, and learning to form a hand of cards all offer practice in an extensive range of hand and finger movements. Fine motor skills are essential to handwriting, drawing, painting, crafts, and other school activities. Some games, such as stinker, slap jack, bow to the king, and spit, require quick reflexes and fine motor speed and agility.

RHYTHM

Some children with learning disabilities exhibit little awareness of the orderly timing that is needed in physical activities, that underlies fluid speech, and that is essential to the appreciation of music and poetry. Card playing exposes children to a variety of simple rhythms. Efficient dealing of cards involves a steady rhythm pattern. Having a child close his or her eyes can help him or her learn to *hear* these rhythms, and with practice to develop a good sense of rhythm. Games that proceed in rhythmic patterns include war, pisha paysha, and Earl of Coventry.

SEQUENCE

Sequencing problems are common among learning-disabled children. Many seem unable to understand the order or arrangement in time or space of a series of sounds, movements, or ideas. Card games provide opportunities for learning sequence concepts. Orderly dealing and turn-taking teach temporal sequencing. Some games, such as stop and go, rummy, poker, kings in the corner, up and down, cribbage, and spit, involve number sequencing.

NUMBER CONCEPTS

Card games offer opportunities to learn a wide range of number concepts. Simpler games such as go fish and war help with identification of numbers as well as the concept of greater/lesser. A variety of sensory modalities are invoked during game play. Seeing numbers, hearing them called out during dealing, and feeling the number of separate movements as one deals the cards all help the child form associations between numbers and tangible phenomena. The finite and intriguing properties of a deck of cards—52 cards, 4 suits, 13 cards in each, 2 pairs of every denomination, and so forth—also entice children to use numbers. Sharing a group of objects among several individuals is a precursor to understanding the concept of division. Handing the cards out two or three at a time (e.g., as with manville or euchre) or counting up pairs after a game of go fish provides beginning counting exercises. Addition is practiced in keeping score, especially in games where cards have different values (e.g., casino, Yukon, and rummy). In games such as blackjack, adding numbers is a part of the game. A final mathematical concept that can be practiced is categorization, which helps a child learn about sets. Go fish, old maid, and hearts involve categorization.

VISUAL SKILLS

All card games require visual discrimination. Simple matching games (e.g., go fish) give practice with color and form discrimination. Visual tracking is involved every time a player scans his or her fan-shaped hand to select a card. In slap jack, bow to the king, and spit, players are rewarded for speed and accuracy of visual recognition and response. Concentration is a game that requires good visual memory.

VERBAL SKILLS

In a card game, verbal stimuli are reduced and particular verbal responses are practiced over and over again. A new vocabulary is often created during card play. The experience of learning a new word and using it meaningfully has a stimulating effect on overall vocabulary growth. Receptive language skills are also practiced in processing verbal instructions and comments made by the therapist.

GENERAL INTELLECTUAL SKILLS

Logical thinking, planning, and organization of ideas are all rewarded in card playing. Another intellectual asset fostered by playing cards is the ability to hold many factors in mind at once. Mental flexibility is also tapped in card games, in that a player must be ready to change his or her mental set during a game or from game to game.

It is clear, then, that card games provide many opportunities for learning and practicing of a wide range of intellectual and neuropsychological abilities. Card games also strengthen nonintellective factors that impact on learning and academic performance. Card games demand attention, mental alertness, concentration, self-control, and active participation. All these factors are important for learning of any sort.

Card games can also stimulate emotional growth. As mentioned previously, card playing within a therapeutic framework can enhance children's self-esteem, build a sense of mastery and self-confidence, and increase motivation toward academic achievement. Other therapeutic ingredients of game play include the following.

THERAPEUTIC ALLIANCE

The enjoyable and familiar aspects of games lure children into therapy. As children become more comfortable, they also become more willing to discuss uncomfortable topics. Children also experience a sense of trust and safety in the therapist who plays fairly but is not overly competitive.

PLEASURE

Pleasure in moderation has the power to soothe and to reduce an individual's overall level of distress. Games are, above all, fun to play and are meant to be enjoyed.

SELF-EXPRESSION

Games are not "for real," so players are more likely to express feelings and attitudes in this context. To prove this point, one need only observe how emotional some usually reserved children become during the course of a game. Games entice children to relax their defenses and become affectively involved with their immediate environment.

SOCIALIZATION

There are many opportunities for social learning through game play. Games are thought to parallel many real-life social situations. Games, like life, require obedience to a fixed set of rules for behavior, recognition of and compliance with group norms and expectations, self-control, acceptance of authority, and controlled expression of aggression and competitive feelings. During game play, players must communicate with each other about the rules and procedures of the game and are expected to compete with a friendly and respectful attitude.

GENERAL THERAPY CONSIDERATIONS

Repetition and practice are crucial for developing the cognitive skills described previously and for engendering a feeling of special competence. The therapist should encourage repeated use once the child starts playing cards. I have found that children do not become bored during prolonged intervals of card playing; rather, they tend to become more confident and interested in mastering new games.

An atmosphere of fun and joy must be maintained if children are to challenge themselves to improve. With many learning-disabled children, a sense of inadequacy and defeat pervades their thinking and prevents them from risking failure in many endeavors. These children are likely to view any competitive situation as threatening. Others may express their fears in the form of chronic cheating or testing of the rules. The therapist can downplay the competitive aspects of the game to entice children to play. Success can be built into the child's performance by creating handicaps for the therapist. The therapist may need to let the child win during the initial stages to help him or her gain confidence. The therapist can also structure the game play so that children "graduate" to games of higher complexity and challenge, thereby building their self-esteem. Cheating is thought to be a manifestation of a child's urges toward fantasy gratification and anti-social adaptation (Meeks, 1970). Cheating should not be permitted, but the therapist must be open to exploring the child's need to cheat.

The therapist must keep in mind that the game is not an end in itself; it is only a vehicle for learning and emotional expression. The basic receptive and understanding stance of the therapist should not be compromised for the sake of continuing the game. The therapist should encourage temporary departures from the game for discussion. If the therapist's own need to win becomes primary, then the original goals of the game therapy are lost.

Card games are not a panacea. They should be used only as one intervention tool within a broader context of psychological therapy. Some learning-disabled children are not ready to engage in game play. A number of these children are so convinced of their own incompetence that they refuse to enter into any competitive situation. Others are so emotionally distressed or impulse-ridden that they cannot engage in structured, organized play. Still others have specific cognitive deficits that are more efficiently addressed with specific games or learning devices. For instance, children with isolated motor difficulties might benefit from playing several fine motor games, which would offer a wider range of hand and finger movements than card games. A final limitation of card games in therapy is that there are some children who simply do not like to play cards.

CASE ILLUSTRATION

Robert (fictitious name), a 10-year-old boy of average build, height, and general appearance, had a history of learning problems. Educational testing done when Robert was 6 revealed a board range of deficits, including underdeveloped expressive skills, poor comprehension and concept formation, visual-motor problems, and difficulty processing auditory stimuli despite intact hearing. On the Weschler Intelligence Scale for Children–Revised (WISC-R), Robert obtained the following scores: Verbal IQ 80, Performance IQ 74, Full Scale IQ 78. A number of "soft" neurological signs were evident in Robert's overall output. Projective testing found a good deal of internal emotional turmoil, an active fantasy life dominated by aggressive themes, and a poor self-concept. Robert was seen as being "at high risk for future academic problems." He was placed in special education classes in a public school, where he remained for three years.

Robert made little academic progress during these three years; in fact, his records suggest that his overall functioning deteriorated. His classroom behavior usually consisted of fluctuations between extreme social withdrawal and provocative, attention-seeking behaviors, such as teasing others and defiantly refusing to comply with teacher requests. Aggressive behavior gradually increased over the three years. These behaviors seriously interfered with learning and prompted his being transferred to a private school for children with emotional and learning problems.

On entering this school, Robert was retested. His math skills were at the 1.9 grade level, and his reading was at the kindergarten level. He knew basic adding and subtracting skills. He recognized primary numbers but not all the letters of the alphabet. His new Verbal WISC-R score was 15 points lower than his score of two years earlier. Though Robert's behavior stabilized at his new school, he remained highly distractible and had a very short attention span. His teachers remarked that he had no desire at all to learn and did everything he could to avoid schoolwork. On the other hand, Robert attached much importance to working with his hands. He prided himself on being a "fix-it man."

During the initial stage of therapy, it became apparent that Robert was a very well-defended young man with a very strong denial system. Although he related to the therapist, he would not self-disclose or otherwise examine himself for fear of compromising his "macho" image. Initially he spent much time building castles and houses with a Lego building set. He became interested in cards after watching the therapist shuffle the deck. Robert wanted to learn how to create the "bridge" while shuffling.

The only card game Robert knew how to play was war. His style of play was revealing. He attributed success in this game to skill; when he won, he couldn't control his glee; when he lost, he accused the therapist of taking advantage of a child. Repeated reminders that the game involved nothing but chance and luck finally got through to Robert. His more realistic outlook was followed by less extreme emotional reactions to the outcome and by his giving up his rather transparent attempts to cheat. I attempted to draw analogies from the luck-skill concept of the game to real-life situations. These attempts met with only limited success. Robert seemed to absorb the notion that some things in life result from nothing more than chance and that one cannot blame oneself or others for chance events. However, he quickly backed off when direct references were made to his life.

Robert sharpened his visual and number skills during the course of play. At first he had trouble distinguishing sixes and nines, was unsure of many greater/less than pairs, and didn't understand how the picture cards fit in. He mastered these concepts rather quickly. He also learned how to count to 52 by doing his share of dealing. After about two months of playing war, it was clear that Robert was more affectively involved with the therapist. He began to relate stories about his home life. He identified strongly with his father, who in Robert's eyes embodied all the qualities of a macho super-hero. Robert made few references to his mother, but they were thematically consistent; he disappoints her often and somehow must redeem himself to win back her favor.

Robert became so comfortable with war that he refused to try new games. Finally he agreed to a game of crazy eights because he believed it to be a pure chance game like war. He need a good deal of support to finish the game. The concepts of a wild card, of different suits, and of following suit during play did not come easy to Robert. For the first few games the therapist spent much time helping Robert arrange the cards by suits and hold the hand in fan style. With a little help from the therapist, he won his first game after several defeats, and seemed ecstatic. I pointed out his improvement and suggested that he must be getting very good, as I do not get beat in this game very often. This seemed to heighten Robert's sense of accomplishment. As time passed, he became more aware of the different strategies involved, such as holding a wild card (an 8) until it is really needed, or anticipating a change of suit several turns ahead. Robert's improvement was rather striking: This normally scattered and impulsive child would spend up to 40 minutes in quiet and relaxed concentration during card play, all the while exhibiting the kind of cognitive organization and flexibility in his play that was nowhere to be found during his four-plus years of school.

Robert's teacher observed that he had particular difficulty remembering visually presented material. Auditory cues had to be used often to aid his learning of basic reading skills. The teacher felt the auditory processing problem identified by a previous psycholinguistic examination was an artifact of Robert's motivational and emotional problems, which resulted in his blocking and resisting the verbal commands of others, especially adults. The teacher also thought that Robert's distractibility contributed to his problem with visual tasks.

Because his visual memory was not tapped to any great extent by the two card games Robert and I had been playing, I decided to introduce the game of concentration to Robert. Interestingly, Robert was much less resistant to changing games than previously, perhaps reflecting his growing sense of competence and willingness to risk failure. However, he felt that there were too many cards to remember, so I suggested we play a modified game using only the picture cards and those numbered four to seven (28 cards). Robert also felt he could not beat me, so I handicapped myself by halving the value of my tricks won. Robert made noticeable gains in his ability to remember cards he had seen. These gains were reflected in the classroom; he exhibited improved attention during reading, and his sight vocabulary subsequently increased.

Robert began to discuss himself more in therapy. He confessed that he never believed that he would be able to play cards so well. Robert also offered that he would never be good at schoolwork, however. I reminded him that he had had trouble learning card games at first, but that he mastered all the games by sticking with them, and that it never hurts to at least try to do your best. This was a message that I imparted from the beginning of therapy: that Robert was a capable student who only needed to give learning a better shot.

By the end of Robert's first year at the private school, he had shown considerable growth. His teacher observed that he no longer anxiously avoided schoolwork. He was able to work for an entire period without distracting himself or putting his head down in defiant noncompliance. Robert's reading and math scores improved almost two grade levels. He seemed more "connected" and less hostile in his interactions with other people. He also seemed more self-confident and did not rely on his "macho" defenses as frequently. Most significantly, Robert's mother reported that he really appeared to enjoy school, whereas previously he found it boring.

Of course, there were factors other than game therapy that were helpful to Robert. The classroom teaching focused on engendering positive attitudes and on individualized learning rather than on performance per se. Family dynamics also contributed to Robert's problems. His mother had unrealistic expectations for his academic achievement and seemingly had not yet dealt with the narcissistic injury involved in having a handicapped child. These issues were addressed in family therapy and some progress was made.

This case illustrates how card playing within a therapeutic environment can help children gain a sense of competence and mastery with task-focused activities. The parallels between card playing and academic tasks facilitate generalization of attitudes about learning, feelings about the self, and actual cognitive skills from the play situation to the classroom.

SUMMARY AND CONCLUSIONS

It is only recently that children who do not learn despite adequate educational opportunities and intellectual capacity have been identified and labeled as a distinct clinical entity. Our knowledge about and understanding of learning disabilities have greatly increased over the past 20 years. The current thinking is that a large group of children with learning difficulties have neurological deficits that interfere with normal cognitive processes. At least four general areas of cognitive development are important to acquiring achievement skills: linguistic-conceptual skills, visuospatial-constructive skills, sequential-analytic skills, and motor planning and execution.

It has been empirically demonstrated that many learning-disabled children also suffer from emotional, interpersonal, and behavioral problems. Although these problems may develop simultaneously with the learning disorders, they are more easily explained as responses to extended failure in the classroom. The loss of social status and negative feedback from the environment exacerbate the adjustment problems of learning-disabled children. Many of these children begin school as highly motivated students only to lose interest in—as well as develop aversive associations to—academic material after several years of classroom failure. When emotional difficulties appear to dominate the clinical picture, they are often mistakenly viewed as the cause, rather than the result, of academic failure.

Treatment of learning disabilities is limited by the fact that neurological impairment is, with our present state of knowledge, for the most part permanent and incurable. Treatment has instead been directed toward the cognitive, behavioral, and emotional manifestations of the neurological deficits. Cognitive training has generally been the domain of educators, whereas behavioral psychologists have developed programs to modify specific learning-related behaviors, such as attention span. Treatment of the emotional problems of learning-disabled children has been left to mental health personnel and has tended to focus on relieving emotional distress and enhancing children's self-esteem. Traditional forms of therapy with these children, including play therapy, typically do not directly address their specific cognitive and behavioral problems.

In this chapter, a specific therapeutic medium—card games—for use with learning-disabled children is presented. Card playing appears to have considerable potential for helping these children deal with their specific learning-related emotional and motivational concerns. Card games present children with "mini-learning" situations in which they can experience success, experiment with new roles and behaviors, and develop a sense of mastery and competence. Card games tap a wide range of neuropsychological processes and cognitive abilities that are also important to academic learning. Playing card games requires persistence, attention to task, impulse control, and concentration, all of which are crucial to classroom learning. Children are likely to actively engage in card play because it is intrinsically enjoyable and carries none of the pressure or evaluative qualities of school tasks. Children will be more willing to risk failure and attempt to learn something new in therapy because of the sense of trust and safety that is provided by the therapeutic relationship. Generalization of new learning to the classroom situation is facilitated by the similarity between card playing and other task-focused activities.

Card playing does not constitute a self-contained therapeutic program. Rather, it is a specific intervention to be used within the broader context of psychological therapy and educational remediation. The value of card play is its potential to simultaneously address children's problems across the areas of academic, emotional, and behavioral functioning.

REFERENCES

Adams, P.L. (1975). Children and para-services of the Community Mental Health Centers. *Journal of the American Academy of Child Psychiatry, 14,* 18–31.

Axline, V. (1947). *Play therapy.* Boston: Houghton Mifflin.

Barkley, R.A. (1981). Learning disabilities. In E.J. Mash & L.G. Terdal (Eds.), *Behavioral assessment of childhood disorders.* New York: Guilford Press.

Benton, A., & Pearl, D. (Eds.). (1978). *Dyslexia: An appraisal of current knowledge.* New York: Oxford University Press.

Black, F.W. (1974). Self-concept as related to achievement and age in learning-disabled children. *Child Development, 45,* 1137–1140.

Boder, E. (1973). Developmental dyslexia: A diagnostic approach based on three atypical reading-spelling patterns. *Developmental Medicine and Child Neurology, 15,* 683–687.

Brown, B.S. (1978). Foreword. In A. Benton & D. Pearl (Eds.), *Dyslexia: An appraisal of current knowledge.* New York: Oxford University Press.

Bryan, T., & Pearl, R. (1979). Self-concepts and locus of control of learning disabled children. *Journal of Clinical Child Psychology, 3,* 223–226.

Connolly, C. (1969). The psychosocial adjustment of children with dyslexia. *Exceptional Children, 46,* 126–127.

Cunningham, C.E., & Barkley, R.A. (1978). The role of academic failure in hyperactive behavior. *Journal of Learning Disabilities, 11,* 15–21.

Denckla, M.B. (1979). Childhood learning disabilities. In K.M. Heilman & E. Valenstein (Eds.), *Clinical neuropsychology.* New York: Oxford University Press.

Douglas, V.I., & Peters, K.G. (1979). Toward a clearer definition of the attentional deficit of hyperactive children. In G.A. Hale & M. Lewis (Eds.), *Attention and the development of cognitive skills.* New York: Plenum Press.

Gardner, R.A. (1973). *The Talking, Feeling, and Doing Game.* Cresskill, NJ: Creative Therapeutics.

Ginott, H. (1961). *Group psychotherapy with children.* New York: McGraw-Hill.

Goldberg, T. (1980). Battling tops: A modality in child psychotherapy. *Journal of Clinical Child Psychology, 9,* 206–209.

Golick, M. (1973). *Deal me in! The use of playing cards in learning and teaching.* New York: Norton.

Guerney, L.F. (1983). Play therapy with learning disabled children. In C.E. Schaefer & K.J. O'Connor (Eds.), *Handbook of play therapy.* New York: Wiley.

Klinsbourne, M., & Kaplan, P.J. (1979). *Children's learning and attention problems.* Boston: Little, Brown.

Meeks, J. (1970). Children who cheat at games. *Journal of Child Psychiatry, 9,* 157–174.

Millichap, J.G. (Ed.). (1977). *Learning disabilities and related disorders.* Chicago: Year Book Medical.

Nickerson, E.T., & O'Laughlin, K.S. (1983). The therapeutic use of games. In C.E. Schaefer & K.J. O'Connor (Eds.), *Handbook of play therapy.* New York: Wiley.

Orton, S.T. (1937). *Reading, writing and speech problems in children.* New York: Norton.

Ozols, E.J., & Rourke, B.P. (1985). Dimensions of social sensitivity in two types of learning-disabled children. In B.P. Rourke (Ed.), *Neuropsychology of learning disabilities: Essentials of subtype analysis.* New York: Guilford Press.

Peter, B.M., & Spreen, O. (1979). Behavior rating and personal adjustment scales of neurologically and learning handicapped children during adolescence and early adulthood: Results of a follow-up study. *Journal of Clinical Neuropsychology, 1,* 75–92.

Piaget, J. (1962). *Play, dreams, and imitation in childhood.* New York: Norton.

Porter, J.E. (1980). Identification of subtypes of learning-disabled children: A multivariate analysis of patterns of personality functioning. *Dissertation Abstracts International, 41,* 1125B.

Porter, J.E., & Rourke, B.P. (1985). Socioemotional functioning of learning-disabled children: A subtypal analysis of personality patterns. In B.P. Rourke (Ed.), *Neuropsychology of learning disabilities: Essentials of subtype analysis.* New York: Guilford Press.

Ribner, S. (1978). The effects of special class placement on the self-concept of exceptional children. *Journal of Learning Disabilities, 11,* 319–323.

Ross, A.O. (1976). *Psychological aspects of learning disabilities and reading disorders.* New York: McGraw-Hill.

Rourke, B.P. (1976). Issues in the neuropsychological assessment of children with learning disabilities. *Canadian Psychological Review, 17,* 89–102.

Rourke, B.P. (1978). Reading, spelling, and arithmetic disabilities: A neuropsychological perspective. In H.R. Myklebust (Ed.), *Progress in learning disabilities* (Vol. 4). New York: Grune and Stratton.

Rourke, B.P. (1985a). Overview of learning disabilities subtypes. In B.P. Rourke (Ed.), *Neuropsychology of learning disabilities: Essentials of subtype analysis.* New York: Guilford Press.

Rourke, B.P. (Ed.). (1985b). *Neuropsychology of learning disabilities: Essentials of subtype analysis.* New York: Guilford Press.

Rutter, M. (1978). Prevalence and types of dyslexia. In A. Benton & D. Pearl (Eds.), *Dyslexia: An appraisal of current knowledge.* New York: Oxford University Press.

Silverman, R.G. (1978). An investigation of self concept in urban, suburban, and rural students with learning disabilities. *Dissertation Abstracts International, 38,* 5398A. (University Microfilms No. 78–01, 877)

Spitzer, R., & Williams, J. (Eds.). (1980). *Diagnostic and statistical manual of mental disorders.* Washington, DC: American Psychiatric Association.

Strauss, A., & Lehtinen, L.S. (1947). *Psychopathology and education of the brain-injured child.* New York: Grune & Stratton.

Zimmerman, I.L., & Allebrand, G.N. (1965). Personality characteristics and attitudes toward achievement of good and poor readers. *Journal of Educational Research, 57,* 28–30.

PART THREE

GAME PLAY FOR CHILDREN IN CRISIS

CHAPTER SEVEN

Lifegames

Games Children Play; When Life Is Not a Game

ISABELLE C. STRENG

L ifegames are a series of therapeutic board games for children and adolescents. The games have been devised to facilitate the understanding and disclosure of the complex feelings experienced by children and young people when they are confronted with traumatic life events. The Lifegames series (Searle & Streng, 1996) consists of four games: the *Grief Game*, the *Divorced & Separated Game*, the *Social Skills Game,* and the *Anti-Bullying Game.* This chapter portrays the ideas and theories underpinning the games and what experiences colleagues and I have had using these games in our work with children and young people.

Lifegames originated from a game Dr. Yvonne Searle made while working with Lisa, age 7, who had recently lost her mother. Lisa, an only child, had over a period of several months become more and more withdrawn both at school and at home. She didn't take part in activities at school and she interacted very little with her peers and family. Lisa was referred to the Child and Family Psychiatry Services by her family doctor. Following an assessment, Dr. Searle was asked to see Lisa for bereavement work. Establishing rapport with Lisa turned out to be difficult. Lisa seemed to be "stuck" in her grief and soon Dr. Searle felt stuck herself in working with this little girl. At this point, Dr. Searle created a board game with questions about memories, feelings, thoughts, wishes, dreams, and facts, all relating to death, grief, and bereavement. It turned out to be the use of this board game that enabled Lisa to start working on her inner turmoil. The notion to design other games to help troubled youngsters was very much prompted by the dramatic effect and success of using the board game as a therapeutic tool in working with Lisa.

Dr. Searle and I had already worked together, primarily running social skills groups in a child and adolescent psychiatric unit. I joined Dr. Searle in refining the board game that ultimately resulted in the *Grief Game*. Besides thinking about what other games would be useful to develop, we found Jessica Kingsley Publishers willing to publish our work. We managed to get the games on the market for less than 30 English pounds, the petty cash limit at the time, allowing staff working for the Health Service, Social Services, and Educational Authorities to buy equipment needed for their work.

Following the *Grief Game,* we developed the *Social Skills Game,* the *Divorced & Separated Game,* and the *Anti-Bullying Game.* The themes for these games derived from our clinical experience, where we saw many children referred as a consequence of family breakups, peer relationship difficulties, or the loss of a loved one.

Interventions through group work are effective (Yalom, 1975) also with children and adolescents (Corder, Whiteside, & Haizlip, 1981; Tijhuis, 1993). Groups, first the family group and later the peer group as well, are children's natural habitat, and it is conceivable that this familiarity with groups enables children to work particularly well in this format (Eykman, 1999). Games, a medium familiar to children, are a natural group activity and serve children to have fun, to explore, to learn, and to interact with others. Lifegames combine group work and games to help children and young people address and work through their difficulties.

Each Lifegame was devised utilizing an integrative psychotherapy model, incorporating systemic, cognitive-behavioral, humanistic, and psychodynamic orientations. The games focus on emotional (self-)expression, behavioral responses, relationships, belief systems, and cognitive processes. We considered Lifegames a therapeutic tool, which could be used during therapy with children and adolescents who had been referred to child psychiatry services, mental health centers, or social services establishments. We aimed to make the games flexible enough to be tailored toward the pace of the treatment process and stated that the games should always be played with a therapist. However, after several years of experience with the games, it seems that especially the *Social Skills Game* and the *Anti-Bullying Game* can be used very effectively in educational settings, by (remedial) teachers or school counselors, where both these games can serve a preventive function as well. The games turned out to be even more flexible than we had anticipated.

DESCRIPTION OF THE GAMES

The format of all four games is similar. Each consists of a board, which has a blue background, with colored shapes arranged in a squiggly line. There is a *start* and *end* position. There are two dice, six counters, and four sets of cards with questions corresponding to the four different categories about the theme of the game. Each colored shape in the squiggly line corresponds to one of the four stacks of colored cards. Cards that may be too difficult for younger children are marked with an asterisk, so they can either be removed when working with younger children or players can be informed that they have the option to take another card if they feel the question is too difficult.

In all four Lifegames the questions on the cards generally address the players directly about their thoughts, feelings, behavior, or predicament (e.g., *Have you ever been to a funeral? Would you ever stick up for another person who was being bullied? Do you have a stepmother or a stepfather?*).

The different shapes in the squiggly line are, at several points, connected by "islands." Each island contains a statement. Players docking on an island move their counter forward or backward, according to the instruction given on the island. Several islands in the *Social Skills Game* and the *Anti-Bullying Game* contain instructions to play a separate game.

As in other traditional board games, players roll the die in turn and move their counters forward according to the number of steps indicated on the die. On the board of the four Lifegames, each colored shape in the squiggly line represents one step. The player takes the top card from the stack of cards, which corresponds to the color on which his or her counter landed. The player then has to carry out the instruction on the card (e.g., answer a question). When a player docks at an island, he or she must respond to the given instruction.

When introducing one of the Lifegames, the therapist must emphasize that the players are joining in a game and not a test of knowledge. There are not always right and wrong answers and players should not feel pressured to find the "correct" answer. It is important to stress that the position of the players' counters is not contingent on their responses. Conventionally, the player who gets to the finish first is technically the winner. However, it is crucial to explain at the beginning of the game or even before, when assessing children for their suitability to work on their difficulties in a group format using a game, that the purpose of playing the game is to assist players to work on their difficulties and that participation with the other player(s) is most salient, not winning.

Experiencing the universality of a problem is one of the "curative" factors of group work (Yalom, 1975). Resistance to receive help or treatment from professionals is usually high in children, particularly adolescents. When they discover that there are peers who have the same problem, they are often relieved to know they are not the only one, that they are not so different or strange as they thought. Still, the step to actually join a group remains huge. Seeing a box with a board game focusing on their difficulties is often the concrete proof, before joining a group, that they are not the only one with a particular problem. Often, an initial amazement ("There is a game about it?") is followed by curiosity, resulting in a positive effect on the motivation to join a group.

THE ROLE OF THE THERAPIST(S)

The principal role of the therapist(s) is to facilitate the game by providing a safe, boundaried space where players are encouraged to share and explore their thoughts, feelings, and behavior. In groups, there are usually two therapists coworking. When one of the Lifegames is being used in group work, there should also be two coworkers; after all, it is not just playing a game.

A therapist may join the game as coplayer, but he or she should always take the role of facilitator. When therapists do participate as coplayer, they must feel comfortable about revealing personal material. If the therapist has experienced similar life events, he or she could provide children with a helpful role model. However, it is important for clinicians to make a considered judgment regarding the therapeutic value of their comments throughout the game. Too much self-revelation may be collusive and unhelpful. When working with a group, the therapist has a choice whether or not to be a coplayer. When using the game with individuals, there is no choice and therapists must carefully consider whether they are able to be both coplayer and facilitator at the same time.

The games have greatest therapeutic value providing the clinician facilitates a discussion with the group following a player's response. Whenever a question is answered, the therapist may extend that point for general discussion. The therapist must address any misconceptions and encourage the individuals or the group to express themselves further. This can be done by asking supplementary questions, which should be phrased so as to enable continuing discussion. The therapist needs to be aware that the answers given are affected by the players' cultural backgrounds, their families' belief systems, and the players' understanding and conceptions. A large component of the therapeutic effect is the sharing and comparing of participants' individual belief systems and coping strategies. Whereas on the one hand it is important for children and adolescents to experience the universality of their problems, it is also essential to emphasize their (developing) individuality and to explore differences due to cultural or religious diversity.

DURATION

The games take a number of sessions to complete. The recommended length of a session is 75 minutes for group work and approximately 45 minutes for individual work. It is possible to speed up the game by utilizing both dice, or to slow it down by using just one die. The game may be played over consecutive sessions or may be interspersed with other therapeutic activities.

The recommended maximum number of players is six. The approximate age range for participation for the *Grief Game* and the *Divorced & Separated Game* is 6 to 16 years; for the *Social Skills Game* and the *Anti-Bullying Game,* 6 to 14 years. The *Grief Game* and the *Divorced & Separated Game* will be described first, as both these games have similar objectives (self-expression, communication, peer support) and address the themes of grief and family breakup in a comparable way. Subsequently, the *Social Skills Game* and the *Anti-Bullying Game* will be outlined, as their aims and function are alike (peer interaction, practicing [new] skills, fun).

THE *GRIEF GAME*

The therapeutic qualities of the *Grief Game* are:

- Understanding and sharing the many different feelings involved in grief.
- Enabling disclosure and expression of emotions.
- Providing a safe, boundaried space where children may explore their inner feelings.
- Exploring cognitive processes, including fantasies and dreams.
- Clarifying adaptive and maladaptive belief systems.
- Facilitating discussion of emotional and behavioral reactions.
- Examining the impact of the many changes in the child's world.
- Encouraging the accommodation and assimilation of life experiences.
- Revisiting the past and bringing memories to the fore.
- Answering questions that children need answered but have not felt able to ask.
- Removing some of the taboos surrounding death.
- Realizing that other children (and grown-ups) may have similar reactions.
- Providing a clear message that it's okay to have fun (again).

The *Grief Game* is intended for group work but can also be played with individuals. A group may be constituted by peers, siblings, or a family. The game facilitates the understanding and disclosure of the diverse emotions experienced by young people who are struggling to come to terms with a bereavement. The game addresses factual issues and focuses on emotional expression, belief systems, cognitive processes, behavioral responses, relationships, memories, fantasies, and dreams.

The *Grief Game* is one of the Lifegames where it is of utmost importance that the facilitator is a therapist, bereavement counselor, or experienced practitioner, because working with bereaved children requires distinctive skills and knowledge (Newman, Black, & Harris-Hendriks, 1997). A good comprehension of the impact of grief and loss, particularly in relation to the age and developmental level of the player(s), and knowledge about the often incomplete understanding of the concepts of death and dying (Landsdown & Benjamin, 1985; Speece & Brent, 1984) is an absolute necessity.

The *Grief Game* contains four categories of questions, examples of which follow:

1. Facts—What is a cemetery? How old were you when your special person died? How many different religions can you name?
2. Thoughts, wishes, and dreams—What do you think about when you go to bed? If your special person had a wish for you, what would it be?
3. Memories—What was your special person's favorite music? Say three things about your special person. How tall was your special person?
4. Feelings—Name three feelings. How do you show others that you care about them? What do you do when you are feeling sad?

APPLICATION AND PITFALLS

Prior to considering the *Grief Game* as an option to use as a therapeutic tool in working with a child, the clinician should carry out an assessment. When children are referred to child and adolescent psychiatric services, there often are multiple problems within the family (system) all intertwined with each other. This differs from bereavement services, where adults and children are all being referred for the same reason: one or more bereavements affecting their lives. Often, there are no multiple problems troubling the family, but help is needed in coming to terms with the loss of a family member or a friend. The assessment in child and adolescent psychiatric services needs to establish what kind of treatment (if any) is indicated, about what issues, at what time to benefit the child and the family most. Therefore, it is important to include the whole family in the assessment. Families might have difficulties with discussing death in general or the person who died in particular (Newman et al., 1997). Playing the *Grief Game* with a family can be beneficial to facilitate intrafamilial communication about death or about the person who has passed away.

When the *Grief Game* is the appropriate therapeutic tool in the treatment, it is important to substantiate whether the game should be played one-to-one, with siblings, with the family, or with a peer group. Should the *Grief Game* be used as the sole therapeutic tool or as an adjunct to other treatment? Over several consecutive sessions or tailored to the pace of the treatment process? These questions need to be answered before starting to work with the child.

The child and adolescent psychiatric services in the United Kingdom have long waiting lists for treatment and often for assessments and intake as well. A pitfall might be to focus on a known fact and subsequently offer group work too quickly, thereby ignoring other problems. Another potential risk is that overstretched services might allow less experienced members of staff to use the game in group work all by themselves. Games are sometimes considered to be simple (because children can play them), they are structured, the rules and boundaries are clear, and therefore they provide a certain safety not only for the players but also for the facilitator. But group work is not a simple exercise. To facilitate expression of feelings and ideas, to contain feelings within the group, and to encourage group interaction require a skilled and experienced professional.

Another pitfall of the *Grief Game* is the name of the game. There are people, including colleagues, who are of the opinion that it is inappropriate to use the term "game" when dealing with grief and bereavement, as these are serious and complicated matters not fit for play. Our intention has never been and will never be to trivialize or oversimplify grief. The contrary is true. In our clinical work we have seen both children and adults deeply affected by and struggling to come to terms with the loss of a family member or friend. In naming this game, we felt it to be more important to state clearly what the game is about rather than mincing words to play it safe.

The *Grief Game* is particularly effective when children (and adults) have difficulty expressing themselves or are less able or willing to open up to their therapist. Most clinicians working with children and adolescents will have the experience that a large proportion of their clientele does not consist of the junior version of the so-called YAVIS adult (young, attractive, verbal, intelligent, and social). Games can be a practical tool to facilitate communication and may assist to motivate children to work on their difficulties; in other words, games can serve "as a way of engaging resistant children in meaningful interactions" (Schaefer & Reid, 1986, p. ix).

CASE ILLUSTRATION

Jeremy (9 years old) was referred to the clinic by the family doctor because he was acting out to such an extent that his mother had great difficulty handling him. He had been violent toward both his mother and his younger brother, Paul (5). Jeremy's father had suddenly died nine months previously and the family had had to move, resulting in a change of school for Jeremy.

Jeremy was attending individual play sessions with a male community psychiatric nurse (CPN) and his mother was being treated for depression by a psychiatrist. At a later stage in both their treatments, it was noted that Jeremy and his mother needed help to communicate with each other. A complicating factor in both their grief was that Jeremy's father and mother had had marital difficulties and were about to separate when Jeremy's father died.

I was asked to join the CPN to play the *Grief Game* with Jeremy and his mother. We manipulated the stacks of cards (a mode of flexibility) to have "safe" questions on top (e.g., *Did you ever go on holiday with your special person? What TV program did your special person like best? Have you ever dreamt about your special person? What shape is a coffin?*). These examples illustrate that not all questions are emotion-laden. The term "special person" refers to the person who has died. Several questions—*Think of three ways of letting your anger out. How would you like to be comforted when you are upset? Who cares for you right now?*—generated discussions between mother and son, which were followed by ideas for coping strategies to deal with some of their distress. At home they would practice these strategies and report their experiences to us the following week. Jeremy and his mother were working together rather than fighting each other.

By coincidence, school holiday, and no child minder available, Jeremy's brother joined us for one session. This turned out to be a success as Jeremy felt he was the expert and explained the game to his brother and assisted him in reading out the questions on the cards. Jeremy's mother was pleased to see her two sons cooperate with each other. The *Grief Game*, as an adjunct to other interventions, helped Jeremy and his mother start talking and listening to each other again.

THE *DIVORCED & SEPARATED GAME*

The therapeutic qualities of the *Divorced & Separated Game* are the same as those for the *Grief Game*, but this game was designed to help children deal with the experience of divorce and separation. Family breakup confronts children and adolescents with many changes in their lives (Mcfarlane, Bellisimo, & Norman, 1995). In particular, the period immediately after a divorce or separation is stressful due to the multitude of changes. The impact of parental divorce and separation has been well documented in research focusing on both short-term and long-term effects regarding emotional, social, and academic functioning of children, adolescents, and adults (Amato & Keith, 1991; Astone & McLanahan, 1991; Chase-Lansdale, Cherlin, & Kiernan, 1995; Chase-Lansdale & Hetherington, 1990; Fergusson, Horwood, & Lynskey, 1994; Guttman, 1993).

The *Divorced & Separated Game* aims to explore the belief systems of children regarding their family breakup. It intends to stimulate (self-)expression of feelings and events experienced by children and young people who are coming to terms with the turmoil and pain surrounding family breakup, especially in the immediate aftermath of a divorce or separation.

The game can be played with peers, siblings, or children from reconstituted families. It is possible to include adults (parents) or younger children when the game is being used to work with a family.

The four sets of cards in the *Divorced & Separated Game* contain questions about the following topics:

1. Facts—Do parents ever say bad things about each other? Do children have to do what their stepparents tell them to do? Is it ever the child's fault when parents separate?
2. Changes—Has your last name changed at all? Do you still see your grandparents? Think of two good changes now that your parents are divorced.
3. Feelings—Do you ever miss the parent you are not living with? Ask one of the other players how they felt when their parents split up? Is it okay to show your love for one parent in front of the other parent?
4. Wishes, dreams, memories—Do you keep hoping your parents will get back together? Have you ever dreamt about your parents? What is your best memory about your parents?

APPLICATION AND PITFALLS

Before introducing this game to a child, the clinician should assess the suitability of the *Divorced & Separated Game* as a therapeutic tool for that particular child and should investigate whether the child or family requires any additional treatment. When children might benefit from working on their difficulties through this game format, a decision needs to be made whether the game should be played with a peer group, sibling group, or the (reconstituted) family. Including a parent in a sibling group can assist to improve intrafamiliar communication and can aid to make family members aware of each other's feelings or concerns. However, a potential risk is that the parent's comments might be counterproductive. It is not recommended to have both parents joining the game. The risk here is that playing as a whole family might increase children's wish of reunification. Also, it is possible that the (negative) interactions between parents might be so strong that they are difficult to control, risking a small-scale war and jeopardizing the therapeutic objectives of the game. Playing the game with siblings can be very effective because siblings can, and often do, provide important support for each other in disharmonious homes (Dunn & McGuire, 1992; Jenkins & Smith, 1990; Newman et al., 1997). Siblings have encountered the same situations but have their individual interpretations and understanding depending on their age, gender, and temperament.

The *Divorced & Separated Game* is being used, for example, in family divorce centers, mental health centers, child and adolescent psychiatric services, and family court welfare services. All these services will encounter the problem of split loyalties within families, a dilemma particularly difficult for children. Children are regularly asked for their opinion when a decision needs to be made regarding with which parent the child is going to live. Of course, children are being informed that the adults will make the final decision but that the child's viewpoint needs to be heard as well. Despite the most friendly and careful approach, it is "Sophie's choice reversed" when children are asked to choose between their parents. Questions from the different categories ask, either directly or indirectly, about experiences, concerns, and feelings regarding split loyalty issues. Other questions refer to or open the possibility to discuss themes such as peer ridicule, blame, guilt, reunification/reconciliation wishes, and parents saying unfavorable things about each other to the children. Children get an opportunity to examine the impact of the many changes (both positive and negative) in their lives. They can hear and learn from their peers about how they have coped with similar situations. The realization that other children have similar experiences emotionally relieves children and helps them to open up about their own situation.

It is important that the group is run by an experienced clinician who is aware of the predicaments children find themselves in with regard to family dynamics/systems in dysfunctional families. Knowledge about the court system and procedures with which parents and children can be confronted is imperative.

To get the most out of the game, it is crucial to ask supplementary questions, inviting group members to share their experiences and to inform each other about coping strategies. For example, the question from the category Changes, *Did your parents argue a lot?*, could induce the group facilitator to ask the following supplementary questions: How did that make you feel? Have anyone else's parents argued? Did anyone in your family get hurt? Where were you when you heard your parents arguing? What did you do when your parents argued? What kinds of things made them argue? Who would win these arguments? Did you ever feel you had to take sides? What happened after the argument? Do your parents still argue? Did your parents sometimes get cross with you when really they were angry with each other?

It is not suggested that the facilitator ask as many supplementary questions as given in the example above, nor should the facilitator ask supplementary questions after every player's turn. This would only hamper the flow of the game. It takes professional judgment to decide when to ask more questions and when to encourage group discussion in order for children to participate with interest and pleasure.

CASE ILLUSTRATION

Four half-sisters, Gemma (13), Anna (12), Carol (8), and Samantha (6), played the *Divorced & Separated Game* with a community psychiatric nurse and myself during weekly sessions over a period of several months.

Gemma had been referred by an area social worker because she was not attending school, had run away from home several times, and had a poor relationship with her mother. The family consisted of mother Eileen, the four daughters (by three different fathers), and mother's cohabitee, Ben.

The relationship between mother and Ben was under great strain. Gemma's behavior was said to be the source of many difficulties within the family. Also, the father of Gemma and Anna did not want Ben living with his ex-wife and the children. The arguments between Ben and the father of both girls had escalated into physical fights resulting in police involvement. The children had witnessed violence within their home on a regular basis, usually against their mother.

Playing the *Divorced & Separated Game* with the sibling group was one of several interventions in the treatment plan for this family (e.g., individual therapy for mother, partner therapy for mother and Ben, family sessions). Engaging with Gemma during the assessment period had been difficult because she was reluctant to attend sessions. Both by not singling her out for treatment and the idea of playing a game about a subject she had a lot of experience with encouraged her to join her sisters in playing the game.

One of the recurring themes during the sessions was that Gemma, at several times during her and her sisters' childhood, had taken over the mother role. Very different questions from different categories (e.g., *Do children have to do what their stepparents tell them to do? Are there different rules in each parent's house? Do you ever worry about who will take care of you?*) would result in discussions with Gemma behaving like a mother to her sisters when their natural mother was not fit enough to care for the girls herself. Usually after a new cohabitee had moved in, mother took over her role again. Now that Ben had moved in, Gemma was reluctant to let go of her mother function (again). With permission of the girls, this theme was discussed and addressed during one of the family sessions. Of course, playing this game did not resolve all the problems this family was experiencing. However, it did contribute to improving intrafamilial communications, and the girls were provided with an opportunity to talk about their (traumatic) experiences without repercussions regarding issues like visiting rights. Also, the sisters became more aware of how much support they provided for each other, creating a rather special bond.

In contrast to the above two games, the *Social Skills Game* and the *Anti-Bullying Game* are active and lively games. They contain role plays and fun games, all geared toward positive peer interaction, ego enhancement, problem solving, and cooperation. They strive to teach children (new) skills to interact with peers and adults; the *Anti-Bullying Game* focuses on how (group) dynamics cause and maintain the power differential between victim and bully.

THE *SOCIAL SKILLS GAME*

The therapeutic qualities of the *Social Skills Game* are:

- Developing interpersonal relationships.
- Practicing verbal and nonverbal communication.
- Assertiveness training.
- Practicing adaptive behavioral responses in peer groups.
- Facilitating discussion of emotional and behavioral responses.
- Exploring cognitive processes.
- Clarifying adaptive and maladaptive belief systems.
- Understanding group processes and facilitating group membership.
- Enabling skill acquisition via a medium with which the child is familiar.
- Providing a safe, boundaried space where children may experiment with effective social skills.

- Encouraging the generalization of newly acquired skills.
- Encouraging the accommodation and assimilation of life experiences.
- Realizing that other children have similar experiences.
- Providing a clear message that it's possible to have fun in a social setting.

The *Social Skills Game* has been developed for children and adolescents who experience difficulties with relationships (e.g., peers). It aims to enable participants to explore adaptive interaction styles within a safe environment and helps improve self-concept while encouraging the generalization of newly learned skills in other settings. The game addresses behavioral responses, cognitive processes, belief systems, interpersonal relationships, verbal and nonverbal communication, and assertiveness. The *Social Skills Game* is most efficacious when used with groups. It is not advised to play this game with individuals, as the principal aim is for children to practice, learn, and have fun while interacting with each other.

The *Social Skills Game* has the following four categories:

1. Why?—Why do some people find it hard to look others in the eye? Why do some people care so much about what others think of them? What is the worst thing about being popular?
2. Knowing yourself—Have you got a soft or a loud voice? What do you do when other children don't let you play with them? What smell do you like best?
3. Communication—Ask the person to your left how many brothers and sisters he or she has. Who do you think is the chattiest person in this group? Who has the biggest smile in this group?
4. Being assertive—Tell everyone to move round to the left. Introduce yourself to the group. Say your name, your age, and what school you go to. What should someone do when a teacher tells him or her off?

Most islands of the *Social Skills Game* contain a game for all the players. Their sequence on the board has been planned according to various criteria; for example, earlier games help to break the ice, and later games are of shorter duration. All the island games have been devised to create lively action. The island games have a competitive element in that players may be allowed to move forward on the board depending on winning certain games. Some cards in the categories Being Assertive and Communication entail role plays. In these instances, the player is instructed to ask the group leader for help to set up the role play.

APPLICATION AND PITFALLS

Social isolation results in negative peer perceptions and peer relation difficulties, causing an unfavorable level of self-worth and feelings of loneliness (Hymel, Rubin, Rowden, & LeMare, 1990). Children and adolescents who qualify for joining a social skills group usually have low self-esteem and find relating to other people, especially peers, difficult. Managing to establish good peer relationships is important, as "social support plays a vital role in promoting mental health across the lifespan" (Kashani, Canfield, Borduin, Soltys, & Reid, 1994, p. 819).

Considering the particular difficulties of children attending a social skills group, the group leader may want to do a few introductory warming-up games, which might enable the players to feel more at ease in the group. The group leader's role is to facilitate the group, but he or she can join as a coplayer as well. The group leader is required to help players throughout the game. This entails addressing misconceptions, stimulating group discussions, and organizing the island games and role plays. With each role-play card, the group leader should first facilitate a group discussion about the presented situation and stimulate the players to generate adaptive and maladaptive responses. Subsequently, he or she helps the participants set up the role play. The player who drew the card will have the role of the protagonist. At the end of each role play, the group leader facilitates feedback.

Clinicians, school counselors, or (remedial) teachers can use the *Social Skills Game* when running social skills groups either in schools or at mental health centers. It is essential to first assess each child's needs and strengths to establish the suitability of a group-oriented experience for that child. The assessment should also consider whether additional treatment might be required.

Like the other Lifegames, the *Social Skills Game* should not be played for the sole purpose of winning. However, as the island games in the *Social Skills Game* have competitive elements, the group facilitator needs to be extra aware that the players do not become determined to win the game. The aims of the island games progress as the players move along the line on the board. The learning objectives of the first island game are related to listening, observing, copying, concentration, and body control. The next game promotes eye contact, concentration, and group interaction. Later, the learning targets move on to reducing inhibitions, voice awareness, and understanding nonassertion, assertion, and aggression. The categories Being Assertive and Communication contain role plays, which intend to teach children assertiveness and communication skills. An accompanying booklet provides the group leader with brief details of the island games and role plays.

Participation is the most therapeutic aspect of the game. Due to the nature of the participants' difficulties, they may find it difficult to join in at times. It is important to encourage rather than to insist on participation.

The *Social Skills Game* is the most adaptable game in the Lifegames series. It is so flexible that it is even possible to opt for not utilizing the board game and only make use of the island games and role plays when running a social skills group. The game can be tailored to the needs of the group or of individual participants, helping them to participate more successfully in group processes.

Although the game comes with an instruction booklet, allowing the players to think of their own rules can be most efficacious, particularly with this client group. The players could, for example, be asked to think of a different way to decide who can start the game, rather than just throwing the die to see who has the highest number. A modest (problem-solving) task like this means that the players need to listen to each other, negotiate with each other, and include each other in brainstorming ideas and in making a decision. At the same time, an exercise like this gives the group facilitator an opportunity to observe the behavior of the individual children and thus provides him or her with a chance to stimulate the above mentioned conditions to complete the task.

Another possibility is to let the participants play the *Social Skills Game* in pairs. This encourages children to work together.

The format of a board game, with its clear rules and boundaries, provides safety and structure for the children; however, when a group is more established, and taking into account the behavior of individual players, flexibility with rules and boundaries can work particularly well with social skills groups.

A colleague and I used to run social skills groups on a weekly basis using the *Social Skills Game*. A group would run for 10 sessions. In the *Social Skills Game* most cards ask the players to carry out an instruction. In a group of young adolescents, David (13) found it difficult to join in; he was shy and spoke in a soft voice. We had just had a group discussion following the question about why some people find it hard to say no. The group had come up with all sorts of ideas and participants had been giving examples of situations when they had found it difficult to say no. David had been listening but had not said a word during the discussion. Next it was David's turn to throw the die. He landed on Being Assertive and the question on his card was "Ask one of the group members if you can look at his or her watch. Tell everyone what the time is." David looked at the floor and kept quiet. Before my colleague or I could intervene, one of the participants said, "He could just say no." I saw David smile while still looking at the floor. Other players joined in and agreed that David could just not follow the instruction. David lifted his head a little and followed the participants' comments with interest. The final decision was that David could just say "I am not going to do it," and one of the participants offered this option to David. In a soft-spoken voice, David stated he was not going to do it. Everyone smiled, including David, and the game continued.

The many games in the *Social Skills Game* create action and fun in the group, while children learn about making eye contact or listening to each other. For some children it is their first time having fun in a peer group. Once, I was called out to the waiting room before the group started. A mother of one of our group members wanted me to witness her young son playing a card game with two other boys (not group members) in the waiting room. She had never known her son to spontaneously play with other children.

THE *ANTI-BULLYING GAME*

The therapeutic qualities of the *Anti-Bullying Game* are the same as those for the *Social Skills Game,* but this game was developed for children and adolescents who experience difficulties with bullying (both as victim and as bully). In the past decade, bullying has been highlighted as a serious problem that should not be dismissed. Dawkins (1995, p. 274) states that "professionals have a duty to detect it [bullying], take it seriously, and ensure that it is dealt with to reduce the child's suffering." Several programs and information packages have been developed to help teachers address and deal with bullying (Elliott, 1991; Johnstone, Munn, & Edwards, 1991; Smith

& Thompson, 1991). The *Anti-Bullying Game* can serve as an adjunct to these approaches and offered to schools to address bullying. The game endeavors to provide a positive group experience within a safe environment, and facilitates participants' understanding of the causal and maintaining factors that underpin bullying and victim behavior. At the same time, players are helped to explore adaptive interaction styles and encouraged to generalize their behavior into other settings. The *Anti-Bullying Game* helps to increase confidence and raise self-esteem. It assists to identify the mechanisms that underlie passive and provocative behavior and focuses on interpersonal relationships, behavioral and cognitive responses, belief systems, communication, and assertiveness. It is recommended that both victims and bullies play the game together, as victim and aggressor often share similar experiences. However, it can be most constructive when played with a homogeneous group of victimized children.

The four categories of the *Anti-Bullying Game* are:

1. Standing up for yourself—Why is it good to stand up for yourself? Why do some people find it hard to say no? What is the difference between assertive and aggressive behavior?
2. Making friends—Keeping friends—What could be scary about meeting other people? Where could you go to make friends? Why do some people find it hard to make friends?
3. What about me?—Think of something other people don't like about you. Have you ever bullied someone? How is bullying dealt with in your school?
4. Understanding bullying—What different kinds of bullying are there? Have bullies got problems? Is it ever the child's fault if he or she is being bullied? How do bullies feel about themselves?

In the *Anti-Bullying Game,* only some islands involve games for all the players; others just give a statement instructing the player to move steps forward or backward. The island games have a competitive element. The categories Standing Up for Yourself, Making Friends—Keeping Friends, and Understanding Bullying contain role plays. When a player draws a role-play card, he or she is instructed to ask the group leader for help. Like the *Social Skills Game,* the *Anti-Bullying Game* requires the assistance of the group leader to organize the role play: first to facilitate group discussion about the presented situation, then to assist the group to generate adaptive and maladaptive responses, and at the end to prompt feedback.

Again, the player who drew the card has the role of the protagonist. In contrast to the *Social Skills Game,* the *Anti-Bullying Game* focuses more on the influence of group dynamics and the components that generate and maintain passive and aggressive (victim and bullying) behavior.

APPLICATION AND PITFALLS

A paramount aspect of the *Anti-Bullying Game* is to have fun together in a constructive rather than a destructive way, whether working with a homogeneous group of victims or a heterogeneous group of bullies and victims. Individual group members need to gain insight in their own and each other's behavior and its potential effect on others. With all group work it is important to establish and maintain a safe group environment. However, when working with bullies and victims together, the safety in the group plays an even greater role as all group members have difficulties with feeling safe in groups. Especially in a heterogeneous group, the understanding that often victim and aggressor share similar experiences enables the group to function in a positive way together. When setting up a heterogeneous group, the bully-to-victim ratio needs careful consideration (e.g., avoid having one victim and the others bullies, or vice versa).

As with all the other Lifegames, it is important to assess the potential participants to establish if, or what kind of, a group-oriented experience is most beneficial for them. Questions like the following need to be answered before introducing the game: Can the child cope with group work? Are any other interventions needed? Is the child motivated or can the child be motivated to join a group?

The group leader, clinician, schoolteacher, or counselor facilitates the group and can take the role of coplayer as well. The group leader will be required to help the players throughout the game to organize the games and role plays. The leader needs to encourage the players to share their ideas and thoughts so they can learn from each other's experiences. The games and role plays provide the players with opportunities to learn and practice adaptive behaviors. The role plays also ask the participants to project themselves into different roles (e.g., victim, bully, teacher). In the role play "The Staff Meeting," the participants take on the role of teachers and have to work out ways to deal with bullying in their school.

The *Anti-Bullying Game* can also be used in schools with all (new) pupils (not only victims of bullying and bullies). Children can be helped to have knowledge about the dynamics underlying bullying and can be taught skills to deal with bullying as a victim or as a bystander. The game can assist schools to inform their pupils about policies regarding bullies (including adult bullies) and bullying behavior.

CASE ILLUSTRATION

When using the Lifegames with primary school children it is important to involve them in an active way. Rather than having long discussions following a question, children can be asked, for example, to make a drawing, individually or as a group. The drawing(s) can be discussed in the group when finished. A colleague and I ran a group for victims of bullying (age 8 to 10 years) using the *Anti-Bullying Game*. The question "What does a bully look like?" came up. After a short brainstorming of ideas we asked the children to draw a life-size bully as a group. This bully turned out to be a big fellow with knives, hand grenades, and a lot of teeth in his mouth, in all a very nasty and aggressive-looking person. Although all five participants had been bullied, we were rather sure none of them had encountered a bully like the one in the drawing. This demonstrates how aggressive bullies are in the eyes of their victims. The rest of the session focused on what the participants could do in reality when they were being bullied and what they would like to do to a bully in their fantasy. They were allowed to act out their fantasy on the drawing of the bully. In the following session, more constructive strategies to deal with bullies were practiced through role play.

I was once invited to join a group of six primary school children who were all admitted to a child psychiatric unit for the day treatment program. The children attended the unit four days a week during a period of several months. These children, with a wide range of difficulties, played the *Anti-Bullying Game* weekly as an adjunct to other therapeutic interventions. The group consisted of both bullies and victims of bullying. A nurse and school counselor facilitated the group. Soon after starting the game, there was an incident "over nothing." Brian, one of the participants, had moved the counter of Thomas, whose turn it was. A physical fight followed between the two boys. The group leaders intervened. Dealing with this incident took a lot of persuasion and time. Thomas had left the room and had to be brought back by another member of staff. Finally, the group leaders managed to each sit with a boy on either side of the board. Both Brian and Thomas were instructed to think about the incident. What was it about? Is moving another player's counter always intended to pester that person or could there be other reasons (e.g., trying to be helpful)? Rather than fighting, what else could they have done? The other players were allowed to join in the discussion and also had to think of constructive solutions for incidents they had been involved in themselves in the unit earlier that week. Almost half of the session had been taken up "over nothing," but many topics regarding bullying behavior had been covered before the game was continued. I was impressed by how well the two group leaders facilitated this boisterous group and how they managed as a group to have fun together as well.

SUMMARY AND CONCLUSIONS

Lifegames are a therapeutic tool to help children and adolescents who have experienced adversity in their lives as a consequence of bereavement, family breakup, poor peer relationships, or bullying. These games are a means to assist professionals in their work with children and young people. As is true of the tools of an artisan, the more skilled and experienced the artisan, the better the results that can be obtained with the tools. Lifegames are no exception to this.

All four Lifegames are flexible and can be utilized either as a separate intervention or as an adjunct to other approaches. An assessment of the candidates is needed to make a considered judgment about the suitability of group work using a board game format. It also needs to be established whether there are any other problems or conditions that need to be addressed as well. The Lifegames are intended for group work, although the *Grief Game* and the *Divorced & Separated Game* can be played on a one-to-one basis as well. The composition of the group (e.g., peers, siblings, or family) needs careful consideration to allow the best possible outcome for the participants.

Lifegames are useful and effective games to play with children and adolescents "when life is not a game."

REFERENCES

Amato, P.R., & Keith, B. (1991). Parental divorce and adult well-being: A meta-analysis. *Journal of Marriage and the Family, 53*, 43–58.

Astone, N.M., & McLanahan, S.S. (1991). Family structure, parental practices and high school completion. *American Sociological Review, 56*, 309–320.

Chase-Lansdale, P.L., Cherlin, A.J., & Kiernan, K.E. (1995). The long-term effects of parental divorce on the mental health of young adults: A developmental perspective. *Child Development, 66*, 1614–1634.

Chase-Lansdale, P.L., & Hetherington, E.M. (1990). The impact of divorce on life-span development: Short- and long-term effects. In P.B. Baltes, D.L. Featherman, & R.M. Lerner (Eds.), *Life-span development and behaviour* (pp. 105–150). Hillsdale, NJ: Erlbaum.

Corder, B.F., Whiteside, L., & Haizlip, T.M. (1981). A study of curative factors in group psychotherapy with adolescents. *International Journal of Group Psychotherapy, 31*, 345–354.

Dawkins, J. (1995). Bullying in schools: Doctors' responsibilities. *British Medical Journal, 310*, 274–275.

Dunn, J., & McGuire, S. (1992). Sibling and peer relationships in childhood. *Journal of Child Psychology and Psychiatry, 33*, 67–105.

Elliott, M. (Ed.). (1991). *Bullying: A practical guide to coping in schools.* Harlow, England: Longman.

Eykman, J.C.B. (1999). De groep als behandelingsmogelijkheid [The group as treatment option]. In F. Verheij & F.C. Verhulst (Eds.), *Kinder- en Jeugdpsychiatrie III: Behandeling en Begeleiding [Child and Adolescent Psychiatry III: Treatment and Guidance]* (pp. 76–93). Assen, BV: Van Gorcum.

Fergusson, D.M., Horwood, L.J., & Lynskey, M.T. (1994). Parental separation, adolescent psychopathology, and problem behaviours. *Journal of the American Academy of Child and Adolescent Psychiatry, 33*, 1122–1131.

Guttman, J. (1993). *Divorce in psycho-social perspective: Theory and research.* Hillsdale, NJ: Erlbaum.

Hymel, S., Rubin, K.H., Rowden, L., & LeMare, L. (1990). Children's peer relationships: Longitudinal prediction of internalizing and externalizing problems from middle to late childhood. *Child Development, 61*, 2004–2021.

Jenkins, J.M., & Smith, M.A. (1990). Factors protecting children living in disharmonious homes: Maternal reports. *Journal of the American Academy of Child and Adolescent Psychiatry, 29*, 60–69.

Johnstone, M., Munn, P., & Edwards, C. (1991). *Action against bullying: A support pack for schools.* Edinburgh, Scotland: SCRE.

Kashani, J.H., Canfield, L.A., Borduin, C.M., Soltys, S.M., & Reid, J.C. (1994). Perceived family and social support: Impact on children. *Journal of the American Academy of Child and Adolescent Psychiatry, 33*, 819–823.

Landsdown, R., & Benjamin, G. (1985). The development of the concept of death in children aged 5–9 years. *Child: Care, Health and Development, 11*, 13–20.

Mcfarlane, A.H., Bellisimo, A., & Norman, G.R. (1995). Family structure, family functioning and adolescent well-being: The transcendent influence of parental style. *Journal of Child Psychology and Psychiatry, 36*, 847–864.

Newman, M., Black, D., & Harris-Hendriks, J. (1997). Victims of disaster, war, violence, or homicide: Psychological effects on siblings. *Child Psychology and Psychiatry Review, 2*(4), 140–149.

Schaefer, C.E., & Reid, S.E. (1986). Preface. In C.E. Schaefer & S.E. Reid (Eds.), *Game play: Therapeutic use of childhood games* (pp. ix-x). New York: Wiley.

Searle, Y., & Streng, I.C. (1996). Lifegames: The grief game. London: Jessica Kingsley.

Searle, Y., & Streng, I.C. (1996). Lifegames: The Anti-Bullying Game. London: Jessica Kingsley.

Searle, Y., & Streng, I.C. (1996). Lifegames: The Social Skills Game. London: Jessica Kingsley.

Searle, Y., & Streng, I.C. (1996). Lifegames: The Divorced and Separated Game. London: Jessica Kingsley.

Smith, P.K., & Thompson, D.A. (Eds.). (1991). *Practical approaches to bullying.* London: David Fulton.

Speece, M.W., & Brent, S.B. (1984). Children's understanding of death: A review of three components of a death concept. *Child Development, 55,* 1671–1686.

Tijhuis, L. (1993). Inleiding groepstherapie met kinderen en adolescenten [Introduction to group therapy with children and adolescents]. In T.J.C. Berg, M.P. Bolten, E. Glans, & H.G.Y. Koksma (Eds.), *Handboek groepspsychotherapie [Handbook of group psychotherapy]* (pp. 1–36). Houten/Zaventhem: Bohn Stafleu Van Loghum.

Yalom, I. (1975). *Theory and practice of group psychotherapy* (2nd ed.). New York: Basic Books.

CHAPTER EIGHT

My Game

Rebuilding Hope for Children in Placement

RICHARD KAGAN

T his chapter addresses the dilemma of helping children in placement who desperately need a home and yet sometimes seem to do
everything in their power to be sent away from their families or
communities. These are often children with long histories of aggressive
or self-destructive behaviors who have frequently moved back and forth
over the years between their families and foster homes, group care facili-
ties, or psychiatric hospitals. For such children, separations and placements have led to intolerable feelings of loss and abandonment, overt
denial of problems, and acting-out of conflicts. These children have often
experienced repeated traumas through neglect, physical abuse, sexual
abuse, and emotional abuse as well as rejections. Without a secure attachment, they often remain stuck emotionally and socially at the point in
their development when they experienced the worst traumas and lost
hope for the nurture, security, and affection they needed to overcome
hardships.

The author would like to thank Nadia Finkelstein, Steven Sola, Shirley Schlosberg, Adele
Pickar, Peter Watrous, Jan Silverman-Pollow, and David Nevin for their help in the preparation of the original version of this manuscript and *Cast Adrift*.

190

Traumatized children in placement often have learned to cut off the normal grief process to avoid the pain of what has happened or continues to happen in their lives. Behaviorally, they often provoke others—their parents, their teachers, child care workers, and clinicians—to reject them and confirm once again that everybody hates them. In this way, they gain a fleeting sense of mastery over their destiny while repeating tragic separations from the past.

Effective treatment programs must assess the meaning of a child's behaviors in the context of interpersonal, family, and intrapsychic factors. It is essential to evaluate the impact of significant relationships on children's behaviors and utilize the potential of families for promoting growth and development. Therapeutic interventions for children in placement must address the needs of these children for consistent, nurturing family ties now and in the future.[1] Games can be utilized within an integrated therapeutic program to (1) engage resistant children and their parents in therapy; (2) identify significant attachments and messages children have received; (3) facilitate expression of beliefs and feelings to significant others; (4) help parents to validate children; (5) identify and test out the reality of discharge goals, for example, return home or adoption; (5) make often covert behavioral patterns involving children and family members overt with identifiable consequences; and (6) help children and parents to rebuild trust and enjoyment in their lives. Individualized games can help children and their families explore new models of interpreting their world. Broadened perspectives can, in turn, lead to more adaptive behaviors in and out of placement.

ACTING-OUT CHILDREN AND THEIR FAMILIES

Acting-out children typically display a very constricted range of behaviors characterized by a narrow perspective, little thought of the future, intense feelings of loss, and a reliance on aggression or running away to solve problems. From the child's perspective, acting-out behaviors generate excitement and can provide enticing feelings of control in a chaotic, abusive, or depressing environment. Acting-out children often feel a responsibility to maintain a fragile family balance through negative behaviors they have

---

[1] Please see *Turmoil to Turning Points* (Kagan, 1996) and *Families in Perpetual Crisis* (Kagan & Schlosberg, 1989) for a permanency-based model for work with children in severe crises.

learned over the years (Ausloos, 1978). These behaviors may function to unite parents who are threatening divorce, to energize a depressed parent, to block an unwanted marriage by the youth's parent, to elicit help for family members, or to avoid the risks inherent in developing attachments with a prospective adoptive family.

When family conflicts and problems are unable to be resolved within the family, they frequently become acted out with community agents of control (e.g., teachers, police, case workers, etc.). The penalties imposed on a child by a community often appear insignificant from a child's perspective in contrast to the necessity for protecting one's family, the excitement of stimulating powerful forces in the community, and the need to release intense feelings of anger and fear. When no one seems to care enough to help a child in distress, the child adopts the same attitude toward his or her family and community. Stealing, running away, and fighting may seem to be a youth's best chance to get what he or she needs. Getting into trouble with authorities can also bring in help for a family by leading to court mandates for counseling or involvement of supportive services for a family.

PLACEMENT OF ACTING-OUT YOUTH

Without a secure attachment and a safe, nurturing home, children are likely to continue to defy parents, teachers, and other adults. As children become embroiled in progressive cycles of defiance and punishment, they may experience threats from parents (or authorities) to send the child to a "home," or institution, as a punishment. Even the threat of placement can elicit feelings of abandonment in children (Moss & Moss, 1984). Children will often experience placement as a message confirming that they are unloved and worthless. Children are likely to distrust their parents out of fear of further rejection and to hide their feelings behind a mask of indifference or belligerence (Moss & Moss, 1984).

Residential treatment centers for emotionally disturbed and acting-out children typically provide a group living environment in which adaptive social and academic behaviors can be learned and where parents can be helped to understand their child's difficulties and how they can better deal with them (Finkelstein, 1980). Community authorities (e.g., county departments of social services) refer children to child care agencies to provide the structure, control, and nurturing environment that may be lacking in a child's home. A PINS (person in need of supervision) petition will likely be filed in family court, with custody of the child transferred (temporarily) from the parents to the county department of social services.

Parents, however, often feel "put down" by contracts imposed by state authorities, which essentially say You as a parent have failed; now we "professionals" will help your child. Parents who accept this implicit contract often give up and further distance themselves from their sons or daughters. Such children often carry the label of "identified patient" and come to represent the locus of a family's problems.

In other situations, parents may resist taking responsibility for their child's behaviors and may covertly support a child's continuing to act out in a child care agency or foster home. This can help the family to regain their self-respect, as even the "professionals" are eventually proven unable to help such a difficult child. In such situations, progress is often slow, and families frequently end up labeled hostile, resistive, or unworkable (Finkelstein, 1980).

Despite the behavioral gains made during placement, children may still face enormous pressures and conflicts in their family environment when they return home. Children may feel more detached from their parents and may be given increased power in the family as a result of their growing reputation as an "ungovernable," disturbed, and even dangerous individual in the community. Further incidents of acting-out may occur, and the youths are likely to experience the inner terror of feeling disengaged from their family or having more power and responsibility than they can tolerate (Haley, 1973). Consequently, replacement in a psychiatric facility becomes highly probable. In fact, the recidivism rate of children returning from foster care systems to their families has been reported to be as high as 43.6 percent for youth age 13 to 15 and 22.6 percent for children age 10 to 12 (Block, 1981).

A COMMUNITY SYSTEMS PERSPECTIVE

The aggressive and self-destructive behaviors of acting-out children reflect the intense conflicts and feelings of anger, fear, and emptiness experienced by these children and their families. These behaviors will be experienced as dangers by "helping adults" in governmental or private agencies, who may then feel an obligation to impose stringent controls on the child (Ausloos, 1978) to protect the community, the family, and often the child from further injury or harm. Such children will often be given a diagnostic label reflecting an intrapsychic disorder and be placed in a treatment center with responsibility for the child transferred from the parents to a governmental authority. These are well-intentioned efforts to provide help and control for acting-out children. Nevertheless, these efforts frequently backfire by undermining families and the agencies that seek to serve them. Children, parents, and public and private agencies frequently become locked into dysfunctional relationships that serve to maintain children in powerful but dangerous roles.

DYSFUNCTIONAL ROLES THAT MAINTAIN PROBLEMS

Game therapy can highlight the interactional systems that have led to a child's behavioral problems and placement in a dynamic way that can allow children and parents to develop solutions. The responses of parents, public agency workers, private agency staff, and children often fit the classic triangle of victim, rescuer, and persecutor (Karpman, 1968). The child or parents may be initially identified as a victim, with the public or private agency operating as a rescuer. Blame for problems may be placed on any of the individuals or agencies involved: the police, school officials, a negligent parent, or an aggressive child. At the same time, "victims" may be perceived as relatively helpless to resolve their problems without the assistance of professionals.

When the child is identified as the victim, parents are frequently blamed and the youth is frequently seen as harmed or hampered by the environment of his or her parents' home with relatively little control over his or her behaviors. This frequently leads to public agency workers or staff of child care agencies telling parents to do things that are felt to be helpful to the child. Parents in turn often react with anger to these messages and by their mandated (i.e., court-ordered) involvement with public and private agency workers. Parents often become resentful of repetitive demands that they must do more when they, too, have suffered through years of physical abuse, neglect, and chronic instability in their relationships with their own parents, extended family, and spouses. Such parents often feel that their own needs are not being considered and that these personal problems and needs are overwhelming. As a result, they may resist making any substantial changes despite the pleas (or threats) of professionals.

In other situations, *parents* may be seen as victims, and the child (or other individuals) may be blamed for problems. The behavior of the child may be seen as unmanageable by anyone but professionals. In some cases, parents may be seen as physically or mentally disabled; as a result, minimal expectations will be made of them. In such cases, it is not unusual to find up to 10 agencies involved with a given family. Family members may be preoccupied with traveling from appointment to appointment with public or private agency workers. Often in such situations, diagnostic evaluations lead to recommendations for still more services to help such parents with their problems. This further supports parents in their role as victims who need an ever increasing array of services. If parents do take more control, they may lose some of these social and financial services. Families thus experience a strong disincentive for change.

In other situations, a family service agency or psychiatric hospital may feel that it is a victim of uncooperative parents, aggressive children, unfair funding cutbacks, and repressive demands for accountability from governmental authorities. In such agencies, morale will frequently be poor, with agency managers pressed into "freezing" positions, increasing caseloads, eliminating raises, or accepting questionable placements of youths in order to "fill beds." When an acting-out child is involved in such an agency, he or she will likely repeat aggressive or self-destructive behaviors with staff members. The stress caused by a troubled or troubling child (or family) will often appear to be too much for the limited resources of the agency. As a result, the child will frequently be sent to another, more restrictive, institution. The child, parents, and staff will experience this last placement as another in a long series of failures.

ENGAGING FAMILY COMPETENCE

Effective foster care, hospital, and residential treatment programs must assess the impact of community and family systems on maintaining problem behaviors. Triangles of relationships involving children, parents, practitioners, and state authorities become fixed through repetitive crises and efforts to determine (diagnose) a focused cause of current problems (i.e., some person, thing, condition, or entity to blame). Triangular relationships, in effect, help families and professionals to avoid facing painful issues and consideration of each one's own participation in behavior patterns (Fogarty, 1977) that lead to a child's repeated placements. Intense fears of loss, abandonment, and past (or ongoing) violence can be diverted through well-intentioned efforts to address the isolated needs of an acting-out child (or parents).

A community systems approach involves a collaborative effort with public and private agency staff to utilize the power of a child's family to facilitate the growth and development of a severely disturbed and acting-out child. Triangular relationships are viewed as involving the overt (or covert) participation of parents, children, and often practitioners (Fogarty, 1977) and community authorities. At the same time, each person involved is considered to have some potential for changing his or her own behaviors within significant relationships.

Group care is often needed when children and youths cannot safely live in a family setting. In these cases, group care can easily end up being seen by youths and parents as a punishment, with the core family issues remaining "on hold" until the youth is about to return home. In contrast, practitioners can use group care to engage parental competence and free a child from a powerful but dangerous role in his or her family and community (Kagan, 1983). This involves bringing out behaviors on the part of family members and community agents that again and again demonstrate that parents are in charge of their homes and their lives (Haley, 1980; Madanes, 1980), that parents can acknowledge responsibility for what happened and take steps to protect family members, and that parents can help their children overcome the traumas of the past. Children need to relearn how to behave in ways that can help them succeed. They need to see that their parents will maintain rules for safety and utilize appropriate consequences for inappropriate behaviors (see Dreikurs & Soltz, 1964) without threats of rejection or violence.

In this approach, parents are asked to decide whether they are willing to do the hard and often painful work necessary to rebuild a nurturing relationship with their child. Parents are considered to be equal partners engaged in a change process, rather than victims or persecutors whom professionals must change in order to save children from placement. At the same time, parents can be coached to give children age-appropriate responsibilities (and consequences) in their homes and may benefit from learning parenting skills through group sessions or classes.

The thrust of this approach is to help parents and children avoid repetitive behaviors (beliefs and actions) that may serve to maintain problems

(Watzlawick, Weakland, & Fisch, 1974). From a systems perspective, most problems are assumed to be caused by "habitual but ineffective cycles of behavior" in individuals and organizations (Blake & Mouton, 1976, p. 4). A child and family service agency or psychiatric hospital can play a major role by helping children, parents, and governmental agencies avoid being locked into such dysfunctional roles as the rescuer, the victim, and the persecutor.

GAME THERAPY FOR CHILDREN IN PLACEMENT

Children have always used fantasy and creative processes to help them work through difficult problems and intense feelings. Family conflicts, rejection by parents, losses and deaths can be found in many classic children's stories, for example, Hansel and Gretel (Grimm & Grimm, 1980). In group care, games can be used to help children communicate both verbally and nonverbally fears and resentments. Such "play" activities can provide the child in placement with an appropriate means for self-expression and self-help (Klein, 1975; Uhlig, Plumer, Galasy, Ballard, & Henley, 1977).

Therapeutic games provide an effective medium for engaging otherwise resistant children and can be utilized conjointly with parents (Gardner, 1975). Within the community systems perspective outlined above, games can be used to identify in a concrete visual format some of the covert behavioral patterns repeated by a child in the home and in placement. Triangular roles can become overt choices with clear consequences rather than the inevitable problems of helpless "victims" and unchangeable "persecutors."

Therapeutic messages that foster a child's (or parent's) confidence can be dramatized through a participatory (and enjoyable) process. Perspectives of children and families can be expanded to include multiple options. Games can help a child and his or her family see that they need not be trapped by problem behaviors (Gardner, 1975).

In therapeutic relationships, games can also be utilized by a therapist to show that professionals, too, have had problems and feelings (e.g., anger, sadness, etc.) similar to those that may be troubling a child. Careful expression of the therapist's own problems can raise a child's and parent's self-esteem (Gardner, 1975). This is especially effective with families who have been labeled negligent and have come to expect professionals to tell them to behave better or be better parents. Lectures and direct advice often lower the self-esteem of clients (Gardner, 1975) and promote distrust and resentments toward the therapist.

Games can also be an effective approach for helping children who must face the trauma of losing their parents. For children who have been or are in the process of being freed for adoption, games can provide permission and safety for experiencing and expressing feelings of rage, abandonment, fear, and grief. Games can also be used to engage such children in therapeutic processes designed to stop repetitive and antisocial behaviors that offer protection from dealing with painful losses but block the grief process (Kagan, 1980).

CAST ADRIFT

Cast Adrift (see Figure 8.1) was originally based on the feelings, beliefs, and behaviors of Cindy, a 12-year-old girl who had lost her biological mother as an infant, and the foster family who raised her for 11 years. She had been surrendered as a child and placed in an emergency shelter and then a residential treatment program after her foster parents decided they could no longer manage her. In residential treatment, Cindy had an individualized educational program, art therapy, and activity group therapy. A life road map tracing her various "homes" and a life story (Jewett, 1978) illustrating her history was drawn up with her help. Gardner's (1971) mutual storytelling techniques were utilized in individual counseling along with other interventions. At the same time, efforts were made to find a prospective adoptive family.

Like many rejected children, Cindy had a very limited perspective on what she could do. She seemed to be almost continually "oozing with anger" toward her foster parents and everyone else who came near her. Beneath this anger, Cindy was extremely frightened of losing her foster family. However, in her view of the world, things were "crummy" and always would be. She couldn't trust anyone. She saw herself as a mean kid and thought she would always be a mean kid. Everybody hated her, and her problems were caused by everyone else.

As Cindy's foster family withdrew from contact, she became more and more distressed. She panicked at the thought of losing her foster parents and at the anticipation or reattachment to a new adoptive family. Cindy internalized messages she had received from her foster family about how terrible she was, her destiny of becoming a prostitute like her biological

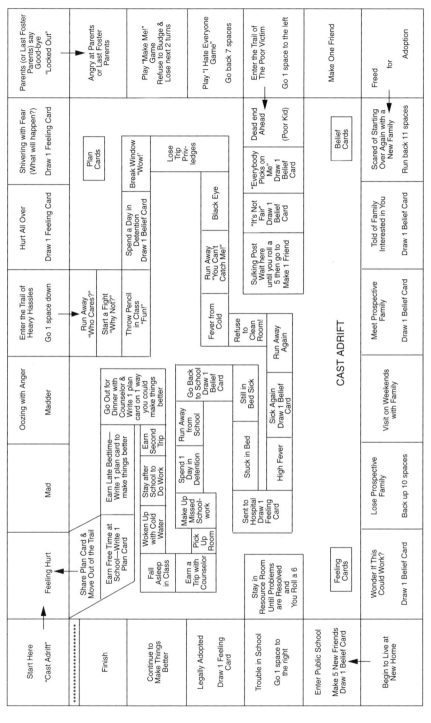

Figure 8.1 Cast Adrift. Reprinted with permission of Human Sciences Press from Kagan, R.M. (1982). Storytelling and game therapy for children in placement. *Child Care Quarterly, 11,* 280–290.

mother, and her culpability for past violence in her foster family (suspected abuse that was never indicated by county authorities). Her behaviors became more and more dangerous to herself and others; and she eventually had to be moved from a residential treatment center to a locked psychiatric ward.

GAME DESCRIPTION

Cast Adrift was created to help Cindy get a more positive outlook and more control over her behavior. The game stressed the difficulties of her situation, that is, rejection by her biological and foster parents, and helped to normalize typical feelings of children experiencing loss and grief (e.g., denial, rage, withdrawal, and depression). The game also diagrammed the typical results of Cindy's usual approaches to her problems. For instance, running away usually led to such outcomes as the loss of privileges or sickness; sulking put her away from the fun others were having; swearing, cursing, and hating everyone usually led to angry encounters and the loss of privileges. The game also emphasized the sense of going in circles, which went along with Cindy's typical behavior. Finally, the game stressed that Cindy, her foster parents, and prospective adoptive families had some control over what happened. Beliefs and behaviors involved choices with predictable consequences.

Considering Cindy's rejection by her foster parents and lack of contact with them or her biological mother, the game was called *Cast Adrift*. The game was played with players moving along the outside squares of the board by the throw of the dice.

Squares were designed to reflect common behaviors and feelings of children (like Cindy) in placement. Players moved from the first square, marked *Feeling Hurt*, to such crucial squares as *Parents (or Foster Parents) Say Good-by (locked out)*, to *Freed for Adoption*, to *Begin to Live at New Home*, to *Continue to Work Out Problems with New Family*. Players took turns throwing the dice and moving until one player made it to *Finish*.

Along the way, players were rewarded (by moving ahead) for positive behaviors and suffered (moved backward) for negative behaviors. For instance, a player could land in several detours. The *Trail of Heavy Hassles* typified a cycle of running away because *Who Cares?* and led through several consequences such as *Detention* and *Sickness*. The *Trail* came back to the first square after a player earned back privileges and made a positive plan (on a plan card) to make one thing better in his or her life.

Consequences were set up to reflect children's typical reactions to realistic events in their lives. Landing on the *Make Me* square involved refusing to budge for two turns. The *I Hate Everyone* square moved a player back seven spaces to *Oozing with Anger*. The *Trail of the Poor Victim* involved going to a *Sulking Post* after passing through squares marked *Dead End Ahead, Everyone Picks on Me,* and *It's Not Fair!* Players who landed on the *Sulking Post* had to wait there until they threw a five, after which they moved directly to *Make One Friend.*

When a player landed on *Scared of Starting Over with a New Family,* he or she went back 11 spaces to *Oozing with Anger.* Landing on *Losing a Prospective Family* moved a player back 10 spaces to *Angry at Parents or Last Foster Parent. Trouble in School* could lead to *Staying in Resource Room until Problems Are Resolved and You Roll a Six.*

On several squares, players had to draw belief cards that stated either a positive or a negative belief and gave a consequence. For example, a player might draw "It's everybody else's fault!" and had to say this out loud and move back three spaces. Or a player might draw "I can figure this game out!" and was asked to keep thinking ahead as he or she moved ahead two spaces. The list of messages for belief cards is printed in Table 8.1 on page 202.

On other squares, players had to draw feeling cards that stated a feeling and a positive or negative way of dealing with that feeling with a resulting consequence. For example, a player may draw "Feel sad and tell someone something that makes you feel sad. Say it softly . . . then move ahead two spaces." On the other hand, another feeling card states "Feel sad but keep it all to yourself. Go for a long, lonely walk and miss your next turn." Messages from feeling cards are listed in Table 8.2 on page 203.

Cast Adrift was specifically designed for Cindy. She was willing to make up her own stories and to play the game but steadfastly refused to discuss any of the implications of the stories or games for her own situation. Her refusal to verbally discuss her situation was accepted; however, Cindy was repeatedly confronted by the dilemmas of characters (like herself) in stories and the frustrations of going around and around in circles on *The Trail of Heavy Hassles.*

Use of this game and of storytelling (Kagan, 1982) helped Cindy to return within two weeks from a locked psychiatric ward of a general hospital to a residential treatment program and avoided a long-term, more restrictive placement. She was soon introduced to a prospective adoptive

Table 8.1

Belief Cards for *Cast Adrift*

---

1. I am in charge of my life and I choose to move ahead four spaces.
2. I am a bad kid. Everybody hates me. Repeat two times and go back seven spaces.
3. Life is crummy and always will be! Say this two times as you go back two spaces.
4. I don't have to be perfect; I will just do my best. Move ahead four spaces.
5. I can be good or bad. It's up to me. Move ahead three spaces.
6. I don't need to get people to hate me. I can make friends and make it in a new family. Say this as you move ahead four spaces.
7. I can figure this game out! Keep thinking ahead as you move ahead four spaces.
8. I can't trust anybody! Repeat two times and go back four spaces.
9. It's everybody else's fault! Say this again and move back three spaces.
10. I know two good things that I am able to do. Name two things you can do and move ahead five spaces.
11. I am a mean kid and always will be! Think about this as you go directly to "The Trail of Heavy Hassles."
12. I am proud of what I can do. Share something that you are proud of with another person and move ahead four spaces.
13. 1 know two good things that I am able to do. Name two things you can do and move ahead four spaces.
14. I can make it! Say this three times as you move ahead three spaces.

Adapted from Kagan, R.M. (1982). Storytelling and game therapy for children in placement. *Child Care Quarterly, 11*, p. 287.

parent, showing Cindy that staff and county workers still believed she deserved a family. Within six months, she was living in a preadoptive home.

Use of *Cast Adrift* and *Heading Home*

Cast Adrift was intended for children who are being freed for adoption. For children in placement who have the goal of returning to their original families, a revised version can be substituted (see Figure 8.2, p. 204). In this game, the last 11 squares have been altered to reflect a child's

Table 8.2

Feeling Cards for *Cast Adrift*

1. Feel scared but don't tell anyone. Instead "run away" (go back three spaces).
2. Feel sad but keep it all to yourself. Go for a long, lonely walk and miss your next turn.
3. Share with someone the saddest thing that happened in your life and as you do move ahead four spaces. What happened?
4. I can let myself feel scared without running away from my feelings. Instead of running away, move ahead three spaces.
5. Tell someone about one of the angriest times in your life and move ahead three spaces. What happened?
6. Tell someone about one of the happiest times in your life and move ahead three spaces. What happened?
7. Tell someone about one of the scariest times in your life and move ahead three spaces. What happened? What did you do?
8. Feel sad and tell someone something that makes you feel sad. Say it softly. Move ahead three spaces.
9. Feel scared and share something that scares you with one person. Move ahead three spaces.
10. Feel angry and show everybody by smashing your radio! Go directly to "The Trail of Heavy Hassles."
11. Feel angry and tell someone. I feel mad because . . . Move ahead four spaces.
12. Feel happy but don't ever let anyone know. Keep a straight face. Don't laugh and get ready to feel angry as you move back three spaces.
13. Feel angry and show everybody by doing something to get someone else to become mad at you. And as they get angry, move back two spaces.
14. It's okay to feel sad. I can let myself be sad and still be okay. Think of one thing that makes you feel sad as you move ahead two spaces.

Adapted from Kagan, R.M. (1982). Storytelling and game therapy for children in placement. *Child Care Quarterly, 11*, p. 288.

beginning visits home, weekend visits, and returning to his or her family. The title was also changed to *Heading Home*.

Cast Adrift or *Heading Home* can be introduced as games that have been used with other children and serve as models to help children to develop their own game (see below). Optimally, a therapist can serve as a coach,

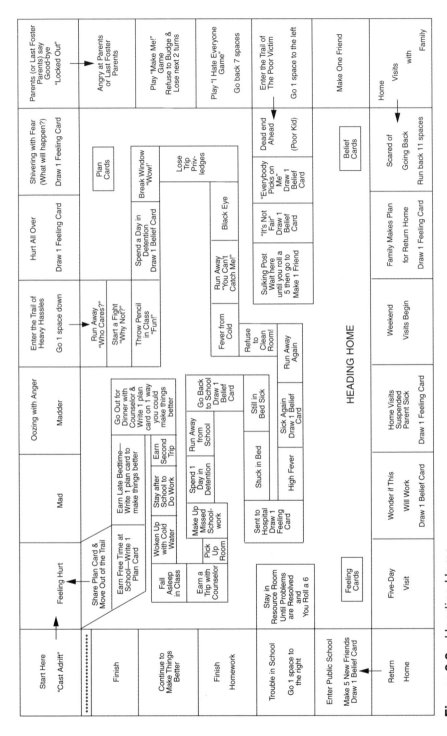

Figure 8.2 Heading Home.

guiding parents (or prospective parents) to help their child to master typical conflicts. This process provides a framework for a caring adult to validate a child's experiences and to reinforce the message that *together* they can overcome the problems of the past and build a better life. The intent of this approach is to move beyond specific problem situations and problem behaviors, to bring out the meaning of these behaviors in the child's life, to help a child see old behaviors as an adaptation to the abuse and neglect experienced, and to expand solutions. The practitioner and caring parent can help a child develop a new ending to his or her own story, a solution that offers hope. This process serves to build (or rebuild) a bond between a child and a biological or adoptive parent. The game model opens up possibilities for changing beliefs, feelings, and actions.

Playing these games can help parents understand typical feelings of children in placement and the cyclical nature of problem behaviors. Games can be incorporated into ongoing family sessions designed to help a child develop a positive identity within or apart from his or her biological family. Use of the game in family sessions can also be helpful for dramatizing how a child's behaviors fit with his or her needs for security within the original family or a prospective adoptive family. The behaviors included in the games are also helpful as a way of predicting and thus detoxifying typical behaviors displayed by children who are in the process of returning to their families or moving into adoptive families. Playing a structured game such as *Cast Adrift* with a family also can be helpful in promoting sharing of otherwise unstated beliefs and feelings within family sessions. The family can then be encouraged to make up their own game and in this way to promote understanding of each other's feelings as well as a commitment to work together in dealing with both good times and bad.

Rules for these games include a time limit, with the winner being the one who has advanced the farthest or reached the finish square in that amount of time—typically 30 to 40 minutes. A player is not required to express a feeling or belief at any time. If a player does not wish to do so, he or she simply does not get to move ahead as indicated on the card. In any case, however, a player will have to move backward if so indicated on a given card or game square. In this way, players are reinforced by expressing positive feelings or beliefs but are not put in a situation of being forced to change.

Cast Adrift and *Heading Home* were designed for children under the age of 13. These games, however, can be utilized with adolescents who are socially and cognitively at a younger age. It often helps to say to older children that this is a game for younger kids, but the practitioner wonders if they'd like to try it out just for fun.

SAFETY STEPS

Cast Adrift and other therapeutic games must be adapted to the abilities, needs, interests, and problems of each family and should not be used as isolated interventions. Use of this or other games without addressing the child's family and interpersonal relationships could inadvertently serve to maintain a child (or parents) in dysfunctional roles. Simply repeating a child's traumatic life experiences can serve to perpetuate a child's hopelessness.

A child needs to be able to trust a parent (biological or adoptive) to be able to benefit from working conjointly on these games. A conjoint approach should not be used if a parent is unable or unwilling to validate a child's experiences and grant the child permission to honestly express memories and feelings. Validation by a parent is essential for a child to work on rebuilding trust and is a prerequisite for a parent to successfully work on reuniting. When a parent continues to deny abuse and neglect, children are faced with a conflict among their wishes to be close to their parent, their loyalty to the family, and the reality of their own experience. Children may then deny their experience; however, the conflict and dishonesty will undermine any work the parent does to rebuild the home. Practitioners need to be well versed in the mandates of the Adoption and Safe Families Act and to be sure that incidents of past abuse and neglect have been addressed by authorities.

Games like *Cast Adrift* are also not recommended for psychotic children or children who do not have the capacity to deal with the anxiety created. In these situations, a child typically lacks a safe relationship with anyone and may be living with injunctions that prohibit any disclosures and leave a child living with threats that the child or someone the child loves may be hurt.

For fairly secure and well-balanced youngsters, games may involve very realistic situations. For more anxious children, it may be necessary to use much more obscure and milder situations and consequences on the playing board, belief cards, and feeling cards. Belief and feeling cards can be carefully selected to utilize less threatening items, or other items may be substituted, for example, adaptations can be made from Gardner's (1975) *Talking, Feeling, and Doing Game.* However, games should embody the important themes that affect the child and family.

Cast Adrift can be used by skilled practitioners working individually with children or youths. These games can also be utilized in small groups of two to four children who are fairly secure and well-balanced. Most children will quickly grasp elements of the game that apply to themselves and thus will have an opportunity to deal with personal issues. Individual sessions minimize the contagion effect of children's anxieties on each other.

Practitioners should have a solid understanding of the stages of grief, loss, and separation (Bowlby, 1960; Thomas, 1967), an introduction to developmental disturbances in childhood (e.g., Kessler, 1966; Wicks-Nelson & Israel, 1984), and a basic understanding of family systems (e.g., Nichols, 1984). These techniques must be used as part of a comprehensive team approach to helping a child deal with grief, loss, and reattachment within the context of his or her family.

As with any therapeutic approach, game therapy must be based on a comfortable relationship among practitioner, child, and (if possible) parents. It is important to provide each child with a safe environment where he or she will have opportunities for appropriate ventilation of feelings as well as a great deal of structure and consistent limits. If children become tense or agitated, they can be encouraged to express their feelings and concerns directly to their parents or significant parent figures through letters, tapes, or in conjoint or subsequent sessions. If this is impossible or unsafe, a child needs to be given a sense of hope by authorities that they understand the child's predicament and will not force the child to return to a dangerous home. Ongoing individual therapy sessions can be arranged to offer the child a special time, place, and relationship within which he or she can safely express intense feelings and learn new behaviors.

DEVELOPING *MY GAME*

After *Cast Adrift* or *Heading Home* is played a few times,[2] practitioners should encourage children to develop their own personal game. This can be

---

[2] With some children, simply showing *Cast Adrift* or *Heading Home* as a model may be sufficient. The goal of this approach should be to help a child to develop his or her own personalized game.

done on blank game grids (see Figure 8.3). It is helpful to encourage children to highlight important goals for themselves, such as adoption, and to put these in key places, such as the corners of the game board. Corner squares can thus be used to represent goals for the child in working through conflicts with the family. Side trails and special cards to be drawn can then be developed, and many of the situations, feeling cards, and belief cards from *Cast Adrift* or *Heading Home* can be incorporated into the child's own game. It is important that a child's own game be relevant to his or her current interpersonal dilemma as well as internal feelings. For instance, a child coping with the loss of his or her parents will need to work through stages of the grief process (Bowlby, 1960; Thomas, 1967), including denial, rage, anxiety, withdrawal, and reattachment. Each of these feelings and behaviors is tied to interpersonal relationships in the child's life. Denial and rage may distance a child from past and potential family relationships as well as from developing bonds to group care staff, teachers, therapists, or foster parents. Experiencing anxiety within a safe relationship may allow the beginning of new connections or the renegotiation of bonds to a child's family. Withdrawal reflects a child's need to experience feelings of emptiness (Fogarty, 1977) and also may serve to protect a child from the risks involved in renewing attachments or developing new attachments to another family. The child's personal game can reflect these feelings and interpersonal relationships. By doing so, the game can facilitate expression of painful feelings to significant people in a child's life who can show a child that those feelings can be managed. This helps a child to reduce the intensity of previously secret feelings and to regain trust. At the same time, key squares on the game board (e.g., corners) come to represent a child's goals in terms of his or her family situation.

Use of games in this way provides children with an opportunity to express their own perception of their behaviors and situation with an opportunity to work out better consequences for themselves. A child's own game also can provide significant clues to important attachments, for example, to past foster parents who may continue to have an impact on the child's behaviors. Messages from parents (or foster parents, etc.) may also be revealed, for example, a parent's message that a child should grow up in a specific institution just as the parent did. Children's own games typically reveal relationships that are causing them a great deal of trouble and visually dramatize their difficulties in working through feelings of

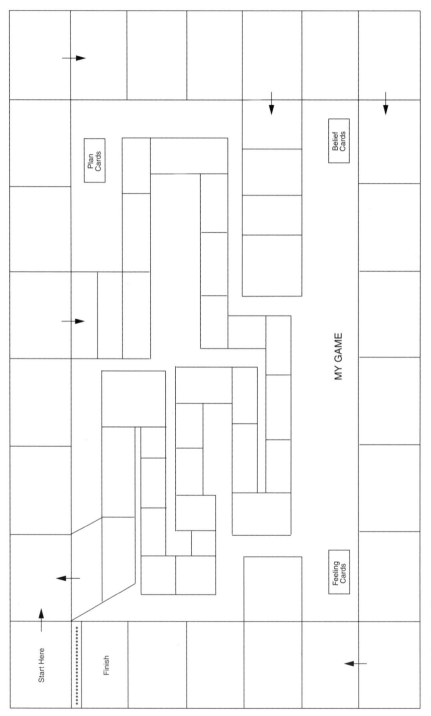

Figure 8.3 My Game.

grief and loss. Personal games can also clarify a child's goals (e.g., to be adopted) and his or her assessment of whether this is really possible.

SUMMARY

Children in placement are frequently mired in repetitive cycles of denial and aggressive or self-destructive behaviors that reflect feelings of loss and intense rage following repeated losses, neglect, and/or abuse in their families. Returning to their families or moving into adoptive homes involves changes in their relationships with their family or families. This in turn involves changes in their perspectives on their world, changes in parental behaviors, and changes in their own behaviors. Therapeutic games such as *Cast Adrift, Heading Home,* and *My Game* can be valuable interventions for use, along with family therapy, activity group therapies, and individualized educational programs, as part of an integrated treatment program for families that addresses both interpersonal and intrapsychic needs. Games can be utilized to help these children to find or renew security and commitment within families they can call their own.

Games can be effective tools in engaging resistant children in counseling relationships as well as in identifying significant attachments and conflicts in a child's life. Games can provide a child with permission to deal openly with some of the painful covert issues (e.g., loss, grief, rejections, abuse) that have led to ongoing aggressive or self-destructive behaviors. With some of these issues identified, therapists can then deal more effectively with a child's need to work on significant relationships with family members or past parent figures (e.g., foster parents). Children can use games such as *Cast Adrift* to experiment with a variety of adaptive and maladaptive beliefs and to see the results of various behaviors. Children can then make choices for themselves as they develop *My Game.* Playing *My Game* can reinforce more adaptive goals, beliefs, and actions that help a child to succeed.

Games can dramatically illustrate the difficult situation of children in limbo. This can be very helpful in preparing prospective adoptive parents or in redefining children's behaviors to their biological family so that change can occur (Watzlawick, Weakland, & Fisch, 1974). Therapeutic games can also emphasize children's and families' many choices about their beliefs and their methods of dealing with feelings through overt behaviors. Family members can then experiment with new models of interpreting their world and also have an opportunity to share otherwise hidden feelings and beliefs. Painful conflicts may thus be addressed through a concrete visual format: the game board. As conflicts are addressed by the family, children can be freed from their role as a "bad" or "crazy" youth. Dysfunctional roles (e.g., victims, rescuers, persecutors, etc.) are highlighted and parents engaged to develop competence in coping with their lives and in managing their children.

In summary, game therapy can be used to help families of children in placement to broaden and clarify their perspectives on their world. This involves illustrating how a child's and family's behaviors fit in with consequences. Game therapy makes covert beliefs, feelings, and behavioral cycles of a child and family overt. *Cast Adrift, Heading Home,* and *My Game* present a child and family's situation in a visual and kinesthetic mode and highlight choices among alternatives of beliefs and behaviors. By presenting maladaptive behaviors in a way that a child or parent will find unacceptable (Papp, 1981), family members will be inclined to experiment with more adaptive behaviors and to take responsibility for their choices. For the child in placement, game therapy can facilitate moving on with the terribly difficult task of facing past traumas, creating safety plans to prevent retraumatization, and helping children cope with losses and grief (Kagan, 1982). Developing *My Game* can provide children and parents with an activity-based approach for rebuilding broken ties and trust, or helping a child to build a new attachment to adoptive parents.

REFERENCES

Ausloos, G. (1978, October). *Delinquency and family dynamics.* Paper presented at the International Psycho-Education Seminar, Paris.

Blake, R.R., & Mouton, J.S. (1976). *Consultation.* Reading, MA: Addison-Wesley.

Block, N.M. (1981). Toward reducing recidivism in foster care. *Child Welfare, 60,* 597–610.

Bowlby, J. (1960). Grief and mourning in infancy and early childhood. In R.S. Eissler, A. Freud, H. Hartmann, & M. Kris (Eds.), *Psychoanalytic study of the child* (Vol. 15, pp. 9–52). New York: International Universities Press.

Dreikurs, R., & Soltz, V. (1964). *Children: The challenge.* New York: Hawthorn Books.

Finkelstein, N.E. (1980). Family centered group care. *Child Welfare, 59,* 33–41.

Fogarty, T.F. (1977). Operating principles. *Family, 5,* 35–42.

Gardner, R.A. (1971). *Therapeutic communication with children.* New York: Aronson.

Gardner, R.A. (1975). *Psychotherapeutic approaches to the resistant child.* New York: Aronson.

Grimm, J., & Grimm, W.K. (1980). *Complete Grimm's Fairy Tales.* New York: Pantheon Books.

Haley, J. (1973). *Uncommon therapy: The psychiatric techniques of Milton H. Erickson, M.D.* New York: Norton.

Jewett, C. (1978). *Adopting the older child.* Harvard, MA: Harvard Common Press.

Kagan, R. (1996). *Turmoil to turning points: Building hope for children in crisis placements.* New York: Norton.

Kagan, R., & Schlosberg, S. (1989). *Families in perpetual crisis.* New York: Norton.

Kagan, R.M. (1980). Using redefinition and paradox with children in placement who provoke rejection. *Child Welfare, 59,* 551–559.

Kagan, R.M. (1982). Storytelling and game therapy for children in placement. *Child Care Quarterly, 11,* 280–290.

Kagan, R.M. (1983). Engaging family competence to prevent repetitive and lengthy institutionalization of acting-out youth. *Residential Group Care and Treatment, 1,* 55–70.

Karpman, S. (1968). Script drama analysis. *Transactional Analysis Bulletin, 26,* 39–43.

Kessler, J. (1966). *Psychopathology of childhood.* Englewood Cliffs, NJ: Prentice-Hall.

Klein, A.F. (1975). *The professional child care worker: A guide to skills, knowledge, techniques, and attitudes.* New York: Association Press.

Madanes, C. (1980). *Strategic family therapy.* New York: McGraw-Hill.

Moss, S.Z., & Moss, M.S. (1984). Threat to place a child. *American Journal of Orthopsychiatry, 54,* 168–173.

Nichols, M. (1984). *Family therapy concepts and methods.* New York: Gardner Press.

Papp, P. (1981). Paradoxes. In S. Minuchin & H.C. Fishman (Eds.), *Family therapy techniques.* Cambridge, MA: Harvard University Press.

Thomas, C.B. (1967). The resolution of object loss following foster home placement. *Smith College Studies in Social Work, 37,* 163–234.

Uhlig, R.H., Plumer, E.H., Galasy, J.R., Ballard, G., & Henley, H.C. (1977). *Basic training course for residential child care workers.* Washington, DC: Department of Health, Education, and Welfare, Office of Child Development, Children's Bureau.

Watzlawick, P.W., Weakland, J.H., & Fisch, R. (1974). *Change.* New York: Norton.

Wicks-Nelson, R., & Israel, A.C. (1984). *Behavior disorders of childhood.* Englewood Cliffs, NJ: Prentice-Hall.

CHAPTER NINE

The Use of *The Goodbye Game* with Bereaved Children

EVA M. NETEL-GILMAN, SUSAN CORKINS SIEGNER, and ROLLIN GILMAN

Separation and loss are unavoidable realities that everyone encounters at some time in their life. When separation and loss occur in the world of the infant or child, especially the death of a primary caregiver, the consequences of this loss can have devastating effects. This is an outcome that all too often occurs. Painful emotions in grief and mourning sometimes seem to disappear, only to show up in adulthood in another, more complex form. This chapter will examine the phenomenon of the grief and mourning process with special emphasis on how to help children navigate these difficult waters.

Grief, bereavement, and mourning are terms that are often used synonymously in the field of grief counseling. This has sometimes led to confusion among the various therapeutic interventions and theories within the domain of grief work. Zisook (1995), in discussing the terms "bereavement" and "grief," has utilized the definitions agreed upon by the Committee of Health Consequences of the Stress of Bereavement. This committee was appointed by the Institute of Medicine and consisted of researchers and clinicians from several disciplines. The definitions developed by this committee are as follows:

Bereavement: loss through death.

Bereavement reactions: psychological, physiological, or behavioral responses to bereavement.

Bereavement process: the umbrella term for bereavement reactions over time.

Grief: the feelings (affects) and associated behaviors, such as crying, accompanying the bereavement.

Mourning: the social expressions of grief, including funerals, visitations, and rituals.

In these definitions it can be seen that the work of the clinician is in assisting the child in dealing and resolving separation and loss. Gilman (1998) reflects this position when he states that the goal of the clinician is to facilitate "the *mourning process* through the management and resolution of the *grief response*," that is, the feelings and behaviors that present subsequent to the loss.

CULTURAL AND HISTORICAL CONSIDERATIONS

As far back as there are history records there have always been elaborate and specific rites of mourning the death and loss of a loved one. Boers (1999) stated, "The contents of some of the earliest discovered tombs included items such as spears, flowers, and personal items used by the deceased during their lifetime." These were placed with the deceased for several reasons: as a loving gesture to support the deceased in his or her journey and passage in the afterlife, as well as to commemorate and conceptualize the memory of the deceased. Boers explained that "these gestures included recognition of the status or role the deceased played while alive and most likely contained thoughts such as, 'this was his favorite spear.'"

The Egyptians had a very detailed belief system regarding the disposition of the dead. Steindorff and Seele (1957) summarize Egyptian belief in the following statement:

Rooted deeply in the hearts of the people was at least the belief that death was really not the end of everything but rather that a man would continue to live on exactly as on earth, provided that the conditions necessary for continued existence were fulfilled. If he had surviving children or other close relatives, piety demanded that they go forth on the great feast days to the cemetery in order to deposit food and drink offerings at the tomb.

This practice by the surviving children and relatives facilitated a form of relating with the departed family member that continued beyond the transition of death.

In ancient times, each Jewish family had their own burial grounds on their land. Birnbaum (1995) described this custom as motivated by the desire "to sleep with their fathers, that is to be buried in the family tomb." This carried the hope that there would be some type of reuniting with the lost loved one. Eliot (1976) discusses the impact that death and the "forces of destruction" have had on all peoples of the world, so that "a high proportion of world myth concerns itself" with the understanding of what happens to deceased loved ones, namely, that "destruction is only the dark side of a recreative process: life itself."

Many cultures hold that death itself is a personified deity. Campbell (1974) details this theme in his classical work *The Mythic Image*. This idea continues among many peoples today and firmly suggests that any work in grief and mourning must include a change in the nature of the relationship not only with the deceased but with the deity Death as well. Thus, work in grief and mourning necessitates a respect for the presence of any idiosyncratic religious worldviews of those who have lost a loved one. Zisook (1995) reviews the clinical and therapeutic benefits of various cultural beliefs and practices surrounding grief and mourning:

The funeral and the burial service acknowledge the real and final nature of the death, countering denial; they also garner support for the bereaved, encourage tribute to the dead, unite families, and facilitate community expressions of sorrow. Visits, prayers, and other ceremonies allow for continuing support, coming to terms with reality, remembering, emotional expression, and concluding unfinished business with the deceased. Several cultural and religious rituals provide purpose and meaning, protect the survivors from isolation and vulnerability, and set limits on grieving. Subsequent holidays, birthdays, and anniversaries serve to remind the living of the dead and may elicit grief as real and fresh as the original experience; over time, the anniversary grievings become attenuated but often remain in some form.

THEORETICAL CONSIDERATIONS

Clinical focus on the grief and mourning process began in the works of Carl Jung and Sigmund Freud. Jung is the founder of what has become known as analytical psychology. One of the main emphases of analytical psychology is the concept of the self that emerges from the unconscious, both collective and personal, with emphasis on individuation, or the realization of the developmental potential within the individual. Jung wrote, "Myths are the earliest forms of science" (1961). He had quite a bit to say about the role myth and death play in the human psyche:

> Critical rationalism has apparently eliminated, along with so many other mythic conceptions, the idea of life after death. This could only have happened because nowadays most people identify themselves almost exclusively with their consciousness, and imagine that they are only what they know about themselves. What the myths or stories about a life after death really mean, or what kind of reality lies behind them, we certainly do not know. We cannot tell whether they possess any validity beyond their indubitable value as anthropomorphic projections. To the intellect, all my mythologizing is futile speculation. To the emotions, however, it is a healing and valid activity.

Sigmund Freud is known as the originator of psychoanalysis, specifically the theoretical perspective known as ego psychology. This orientation is largely based on the concepts of instinctual drives, conflict in the expression of these drives, and adaptation in the midst of these conflicts. Freud (1917/1963) introduced the now classical expression "the work of mourning" in *Mourning and Melancholia*. Laplanche and Pontalis (1973) define this phrase as the "intrapsychic process, occurring after the loss of a loved object, whereby the subject gradually manages to detach himself from this object." The goal is to withdraw the emotional investment the subject has placed in the lost object, "object" being the unfortunate word used to describe the person with whom the subject has a vested emotional relationship. Golden and Hill (1991) summarize Freud's *work of mourning* concept as

> the process of mourning as a period of grief we experience as we take leave of someone we have lost, and which temporarily disables us from taking an interest in life. This leave-taking involves withdrawing our emotional investment from each link in the complex chain that connects us to the person we have lost.

Freud went on to distinguish between normal mourning and pathological forms of mourning and melancholia. Laplanche and Pontalis (1967/1973) summarize Freud's ideas on various pathological forms of mourning:

> Where the subject holds himself responsible for the death that has occurred, denies it, believes that he is influenced or possessed by the dead person, or that he is himself a victim of the illness that has caused the death. In pathological mourning the conflict of ambivalence has come to the fore; with melancholia, a further step has been taken: the ego identifies with the lost object.

Grief and clinical depression are not analogous. In the mourning process, grief gradually recedes as the person is able to bring closure to the loss and reengage in the process of reinvestment of emotional energy into other relationships. In clinical depression, there is a kind of fixation in sadness that interferes with the person's ability to reengage fully.

Regression is often a characteristic response of mourning in children. Fixation and regression are explained by Freud as going hand in hand. He described regression as a reverting backward to earlier stages of development:

> The impulse [that stimulates psychological development] will find occasion to *regress* in this way when the exercise of its function in a later and more developed form meets with powerful external obstacles, which thus prevent it from attaining the goal of satisfaction. It is a short step to assume that fixation and regression are not independent of each other; the stronger the fixations in the path of development the more easily will the function yield before the external obstacles, by regressing on to those fixations; that is, the less capable of resistance against the external difficulties on its path will the developed function be. If you think of a migrating people who have left large numbers at the stopping-places on their way, you will see that the foremost will naturally fall back upon these positions when they are defeated or when they meet with an enemy too strong for them. And again, the more of their number they leave behind in their progress, the sooner will they be in danger of defeat. (1920/1953)

Melanie Klein, with Fairbairn, Winnicott, and Balint, are credited as being the main clinicians who founded and established the object-relations theoretical perspective in psychology. This theory places the greatest emphasis on the transformation of external relationships into internalized representations of relationships, which exist between the subject, or self, and others, or object. Klein (1930/1975) furthered Freud's theories and understanding of the psychological factors involved in mourning. She felt that during mourning, the subject begins a process whereby the relationship with the actual deceased person (object) is relinquished over time as various memories, experiences, and emotions connected with the lost object are constituted symbolically in an internal representation of the object. This newly internalized symbolic representation of the lost object serves to comfort, soothe, and sustain the subject. Thus, the external object becomes internalized into the psychic reality of the subject. Segal (1974) described this transformation:

> Every aspect of the object, every situation that has to be given up in the process of growing gives rise to symbol formation. In this view, symbol formation is the outcome of a loss; it is a creative work involving the pain and the whole work of mourning. If psychic reality is experienced and differentiated from external reality, the symbol is differentiated from the object, it is felt to be created by the self and can be freely used by the self.

Self psychology is derived from the work of Sullivan and Kohut and emphasizes how external relationships impact and contribute to self-esteem and integration of the self, necessary components for a sense of well-being. Disturbances in primary relationships in the life of the child lead to psychopathology, namely, the subject's sense of self that is defective and fragmented. Gabbard (1994) wrote regarding self psychology: "From the standpoint of the growth and development of the self, others are not regarded as separate persons but as objects to gratify the needs of the self." *Selfobject* is the term used to define the role the caregiver and others play in satisfying the needs of the emerging self. Gabbard states that the fundamental anxiety is disintegration anxiety, "which involves the fear that one's self will fragment in response to inadequate selfobject responses, resulting in an experiencing of a nonhuman state of psychological death."

From this it can be seen that inadequate resolution of the loss through death of a primary caregiver plays a significant role in subsequent pathological development. Empathic attunement and subsequent response to the emotional needs of the child is regarded as being the main function a primary caregiver provides in the establishment of a healthy sense of self. Death of a primary caregiver will have varying effects on the child as determined by the level of development of the child's sense of self. Attachment, trust, and security are critical for a healthy sense of self to develop and be maintained (Gabbard, 1994). In the face of loss of a primary caregiver, the therapist does well to assist the child's continuing needs for attachment, trust, and security.

FUNCTIONS AND STAGES IN THE MOURNING PROCESS

From the above theoretical considerations one can see that grief and mourning can be characterized as consisting of two main functions: restructuring of external relationships following the loss, whereby the lost relationship is let go and new relationships are formed; and a restructuring of the internal psyche, whereby the lost relationship becomes symbolized and internalized within the psychic reality of the subject. Furman (1984) summarized these functions of mourning in a similar way, writing, "It consists of two opposite but complimentary processes: detachment, which serves to loosen our ties with the deceased, and identification, which enables us to keep aspects of the deceased forever by making them a part of ourselves."

There has been extensive research and publishing on the subject of grief and mourning. Many researchers have attempted to develop a comprehensive understanding of the process of mourning that describes and breaks down this process in stages or levels. Elizabeth Kübler-Ross is perhaps the pioneer in this work. She conducted an interdisciplinary conference on death and published her findings in 1969. She developed from this conference a schema of the mourning process whereby the individual progresses through five stages. These are described in her now famous work *On Death and Dying* (1969) as:

1. Denial and Isolation; or, "No, not me!"
2. Anger; or, "Why me?"
3. Bargaining; or, "Yes, me, but . . ."
4. Depression; or, "Yes, me."
5. Acceptance; or, "Yes, me, and I'm ready."

Williams has utilized these stages of grief in his work with children's grief. Tatelbaum (1980) reported on Williams's findings regarding some of the ways children respond to grief while negotiating through those various stages:

> The first phase is denial or isolation. The second phase is anger. (Unlike adults, children may be more openly angry in response to a loss. For example, children may suddenly and unaccountably become angry at a surviving

parent or sibling, or they may be openly hostile to the deceased.) The third phase is the bargaining phase, where children try to change the reality of death, for example, by promising, "I'll be good." The fourth phase, depression, is when the children, like adults, may experience symptoms such as nightmares or other sleep difficulties, appetite or weight loss, or physical aches and pains. The resolution phase, the final phase of mourning, is when a child finally accepts the loved one's death.

Bowlby and Parkes (1970) described what they considered to be the four stages of grief in children:

1. Shock and numbness; or, "I can't believe this is happening!"
2. Searching and yearning; or, "What really happened? Why?"
3. Disorganization; or, "It's hard to go on."
4. Reorganization; or, "I choose to go on."

Rycroft recognized and defined the mourning process as consisting of three stages. These stages are detailed in his work *A Critical Dictionary of Psychoanalysis* (1995) as:

(a) That of protest or *denial,* in which the subject attempts to reject the idea that the loss has occurred, feels incredulous, and experiences anger, reproaching himself, the dead person, or his medical attendants for having allowed the loss to occur. Darwin called this stage "frantic grief." (b) That of resignation, acceptance, or despair, in which the reality of the loss is admitted and *sorrow* supervenes. (c) That of detachment, in which the subject relinquishes the object, weans himself from it, and adapts himself to life without it.

Altschul (1988) held that a grief response is evoked at times of trauma and proceeds along the course of the mourning process. Altschul stated that this course proceeds "through a sequence of disorganization, working through, and reorganization" (p. 10). Pollock (1961) delineates the mourning process into two broad stages: acute and chronic. The acute stage is characterized by three subphases: shock reaction, affective reactions, and separation reaction. Pollock's description of the chronic phase closely resembles Freud's concept of the mourning phase as described in *Mourning and Melancholia.*

Tatelbaum (1980) proposed a model of healthy grief that follows a three-stage process. She described the first stage as "fully experiencing

Table 9.1
Phases of Grief

PHASE 1: Shock and Denial (lasting for minutes, days, or weeks)
• Disbelief and numbness.
• Searching behaviors: pining, yearning, protest.

PHASE 2: Acute Anguish (lasting for weeks or months)
• Waves of somatic distress.
• Withdrawal.
• Preoccupation.
• Anger.
• Guilt.
• Lost patterns of conduct.
   Restless and agitated.
   Aimless and amotivational.
• Identification with the bereaved.

PHASE 3: Resolution (lasting for months to years)
• Have grieved.
• Return to work or school.
• Resume old roles.
• Acquire new roles.
• Reexperience pleasure.
• Seek companionship, relationship, and love of others.

Adapted from Zisook (1995).

and expressing all the emotions and reactions to the loss"; the second stage consists of "completing and letting go of attachment to the deceased and to sorrow"; the final stage is marked by "recovering and reinvesting anew in one's own life."

Despite all of these various models of stages and phases of grief and mourning, the phenomena observed and treated by clinicians are the same. Zisook (1995) recounts the findings of investigators who have attempted a synthesis of the various models of the phases and stages of bereavement and has noted that there are "at least three partly overlapping phases or states: (1) initial shock, disbelief, and denial; (2) an intermediate period of acute discomfort and social withdrawal; and (3) a culminating period of restitution and reorganization" (see Table 9.1).

PATHOLOGICAL OR COMPLICATED BEREAVEMENT

Bowlby (1963) explains that pathological bereavement often is due to several factors, such as the type of death (expected, sudden, after protracted illness, by suicide, or murder) and the aftermath of the death (absent or minimal family or social support network, drastic changes in family lifestyle or residence, or financial crisis). Other factors of import include the developmental and emotional maturity of the child, the level of dependency the child had on a deceased parent or caregiver, the quality of relationship with the deceased, and the quality and level of availability and support of surviving caregivers. Other factors include the personality constellation of the subject, previous history and experiences with significant loss and its subsequent resolution, the nature of the relationship with the deceased person, other life stresses present in the subject, overall medical and health status of the subject, and the significance of the loss to the subject.

Bowlby (1963) found four main variations in pathological mourning among children:

> (1) Pathological yearning with the aim of reunion (often in the absence of outward grief); (2) angry reproaches (displacements) directed at the self or others; (3) overconcern for the suffering of others; and (4) denial of the permanency of the loss usually through the use of ego splitting mechanisms. A greater incidence of symptom formation generally results and includes protracted grief and prolonged, intense yearning, agitated depression and frank melancholia, hypochondriacal reactions, euphoric states, anniversary reactions, and suicide.

Zisook (1995) identified three patterns of complicated and dysfunctional grief as chronic, hypertrophic, and delayed grief:

> *Chronic grief,* the most common, is defined as unremitting distress, often highlighted by bitterness or idealization of the deceased. Chronic grief may be likely to occur when the relationship between the bereaved and the deceased was close or ambivalent, when the personalities were dependent, or when social supports are lacking and friends and relatives are not available to share the sorrow over the extended period of time needed for most mourners. In *Hypertrophic grief,* seen most often after a sudden and unexpected death, bereavement reactions are extraordinarily intense. Customary coping strategies are ineffectual to mitigate anxiety, and withdrawal is frequent. When one member of a family is experiencing a hypertrophic grief reaction, disruption of family stability can occur. Hypertrophic grief frequently takes on a long-term course, albeit one attenuated over time.

Delayed grief refers to absent or inhibited grief when one normally expects to find overt signs and symptoms of acute mourning. The pattern is marked by prolonged denial; anger and guilt may complicate its course. Although family members, friends, and clinicians are often alarmed when a bereaved person shows minimal overt symptoms of grief after losing a loved one, empirical evidence fails to support a relation between delayed or inhibited grief and other negative outcomes.

Volkan and Zintl (1993) have identified four factors that impair the mourning process: the "emotional makeup of the survivor, the specific nature of the lost relationship, the circumstances of the loss, and the modern prohibition against the expression of grief." Tatelbaum (1980) includes other factors, such as lack of knowledge about experiencing and completing the mourning process, exaggerating or prolonging grief for years beyond the actual loss, misguided ideas of courage in our society, unexpressed or absent grief, denial of grief, shutting off the flow of feelings about the loss, delayed grief, inhibited grief, clinging to unfulfilled promises, and hanging on to a particular memory, feeling, or idea. Exaggerated or prolonged grief is often present if the subject were to "overidealize the deceased, or hang on to such feelings as sorrow or guilt," or fail to reengage in life after the loss. Delayed grief is "the pushing aside of feelings at the critical early stages of mourning."

CHILD CONCEPTIONS OF DEATH

Children have various abilities to understand the concept of death, usually determined by the developmental maturity of the child. However, grouping of children into broad categories for the purpose of understanding general patterns and trends is possible. This section describes the age groupings in which the use of thematic therapeutical games, such as *The Goodbye Game,* would be appropriate. These categories can be defined as 3- to 5-year-olds, 6- to 9-year-olds, and preadolescent 10- to 12-year-olds.

CHILDREN 3- TO 5-YEARS-OLD

Children in this group tend to view death as a temporary state (Nagy, 1948). They see death as something that can be reversed. They often believe the deceased is still living, albeit under different conditions than they are. They may report they believe the deceased person is actually only sleeping, or perhaps only temporarily away, and that return is possible. Many times these children believe death is just "another form of existence" (Chesser,

1967). Egocentricity and magical thinking characterize this age. Although they see death as temporary, children of this age still have a fear of death (Nagy, 1959). Lonetto (1980) reports that "children at this stage of development often ask questions concerning just where the person went and how they are getting on." Children in this age group interpret statements made to them quite literally, so statements regarding death should take this into consideration.

There is a pattern of typical responses found among children in this age group. Kroen (1996) described some of these as "bewilderment, regression, ambivalence, expressing grief through play, modeling the behavior of their parents, separation anxiety, and forming of new attachments to other adults."

CHILDREN 6- TO 9-YEARS-OLD

Children at this age begin to understand death and the permanence of its state; that is, they understand that the deceased do not reanimate and come back to life. Death can become personified with attributes. Nagy (1948) summarized some of the personifications children attribute to death in the following synthesis of children's statements:

> Death is scary, frightening, disturbing, dangerous, unfeeling, unhearing, and silent. Death takes you away. If you see death coming at you in time, you can escape. Death can be invisible like a ghost or ugly like a monster or it can be a skeleton. Death can be an actual person, or companion of the devil, a giver of illness, or an angel.

Lonetto (1980) points out that "through personifications, children can locate, identify, and, of great importance, elude death." Piaget (1966) observed that children in this age group understand that death must have a cause, and they are often driven to determine what that cause is. Children at this age may understand the permanence of death, but until death strikes close to them, there is an inherent tendency to believe death will not affect their life or the lives of their family. Common responses among this age group include denial, idealization, guilt, caretaking, searching for the person who has died, and fear and vulnerability (Kroen, 1996).

PREADOLESCENT 10- TO 12-YEAR-OLDS

Preadolescent children understand that death is inevitable for all living things (Childers & Wimmer, 1971). Zeligs (1974) points out that children in this age group know that death is inescapable, though the soul or spirit of the deceased may live on. They become even more curious regarding the causes of death. Children in this age group share similar content with their adolescent counterparts regarding death and dying. The weight of significance of the death to them and their family is the only significant variable noted between this and the two younger age groups (Kastenbaum & Aisenberg, 1972). Children in this age group are more interested in the religious or spiritual consequences of the departed, and will often ask questions regarding heaven, hell, and judgment of earthly behavior.

Children in this age group place a great deal of emphasis on the thoughts and attitudes of their same-sex peers. Status among peers is important, and being "like the rest of the gang" is a motivational directive. There is often a fear of showing grief in public, especially for boys and especially among peers. Kroen (1996) observed that common responses for children in this age group include attempts to "hold off on any outward signs of grief, trying to remain above the emotional pain," excessive caretaking, uncharacteristic anger, fear of their own mortality or that of a family member, somatic complaints, "moodiness, sleep difficulties, eating problems, and a lack of interest in attending school."

DESCRIPTION OF THE GAME

The Goodbye Game was primarily developed to help counselors facilitate children's self-disclosure and understanding of the death or loss. The structure of the game is designed to take the players through the five stages of grief identified by Kübler-Ross: denial and isolation, anger, bargaining, depression, and acceptance. Because anger is sometimes a response to fear, cards relating to a child's fear have been included in the anger stage.

This game was designed to help grieving children complete the mourning process as well as to teach nonbereaved children to communicate about subjects related to death and dying. Experienced counselors may also use the game as a diagnostic tool to learn about the child's underlying psychological processes associated with grief, fear of death, or fear of someone dying.

The number of cards in each section of the board represents the movement among the different stages of the grief process; for example, there are many *Denial* spaces in the beginning of the game but no *Acceptance* spaces. As the player moves along the path, different stages of the grief process are represented. As in real-life situations faced in clinical settings, resolution of grief is an uneven process.

Counselors are given latitude in determining how to play the game with each child, with the understanding that it is more important that children learn to express their feelings and perceptions than to answer the questions correctly. Playing is also an opportunity for the counselor to educate the child and dispel any myths or false beliefs regarding death. We encourage counselors to reward children with a token for staying engaged in the process.

The Goodbye Game was designed for use by mental health professionals, including psychologists, counselors, social workers, and other professionals with training in counseling techniques. It is recommended that adults using this game have a background and training in grief counseling. This game is not recommended for use by parents of a grieving child, who may be too emotionally involved in their own grieving process.

The Goodbye Game contains a game board, *Denial* card deck, *Anger* card deck, *Bargaining* card deck, *Depression* card deck, *Acceptance* card deck, tokens, a six-sided die, 6 pawns, a notepad, and a Cycle of Life poster. It is recommended for ages 4 to 12 and can be played with 2 to 6 players or played with a family with a therapist as facilitator. It is recommended that *The Goodbye Game* be played in approximately 20 to 30 minutes so that there will be time left in the counseling session to talk about the process.

HOW THE GAME IS PLAYED

The game begins with players placing their pawns on the *start* space; the youngest player goes first. The youngest player rolls the die and moves her or his pawn along the leaf path the number of spaces on the die. When the player lands on a colored leaf, she or he chooses the corresponding color card and reads it aloud (or the adult reads it, depending on the age of the child). The player is rewarded with a token if she or he answers the question or performs the task designated on the card. Sometimes the child may not want to respond. This is okay; however, she or he does not get a token. If a player lands on the log, she or he must move in the direction indicated by the arrow (i.e., forward or backward: it's natural to vacillate forward or backward during the grief process). A player can also accelerate the process toward the end by landing on a space that leads up the stream.

The object of the game is to accumulate as many chips as possible by the time the player reaches the *finish* space (sunset). Alternatively, one could be declared the winner if one accumulates the most chips within the therapeutic hour. Finally, at the end of the game, players are encouraged to make a statement pertaining to a special memory associated with the loss for which they are grieving.

CASE ILLUSTRATIONS

Kevin was a 5-year-old boy who was brought to therapy by his mother following the death of his father. Kevin's father battled with cancer for several years. Kevin had experienced the horror of the protracted illness, as well as the emotional turmoil that this type of illness brings to a family.

Kevin was exceptionally bright, able to read at a third-grade level, and verbalized well. He adapted well to play therapy and was able to develop a working relationship with the therapist. His presenting symptoms were nightmares, bedwetting, excessive fears of threatening events, and difficulty separating from his mother. Although Kevin was able to express himself somewhat in art therapy, he was very restricted in his display of affect. There were intense unconscious defenses in place that prevented Kevin from connecting and working through his difficult emotions regarding the death of his father. Kevin showed a strong preference in playing the therapeutic games available in the therapist's office. Although some of his symptoms abated slightly during the initial course of therapy, the therapist was aware that Kevin was not able to access many of the emotions regarding this event. This resulted in his successful avoidance in dealing with the issues relating to the loss of his father.

Kevin was introduced to *The Goodbye Game* in an attempt to penetrate these unconscious defenses. The therapist was surprised at the willingness Kevin showed in engaging in this activity. He played the game with enthusiasm. His previous defensive status was not an impairing factor, and at the end of the session he asked to play *The Goodbye Game* again on the next appointment. *The Goodbye Game* enabled him to process his grief in a safe and nonintrusive manner. His symptoms began to recede almost immediately, and he was able to talk to his mother more openly about his painful emotions. This intervention allowed Kevin to proceed through the mourning process in a relatively short period.

The Goodbye Game can also be used when working with a family. After receiving a call from a mother requesting therapy for her 11-year-old daughter, the therapist invited her to bring the whole family in. In the initial telephone call, the mother explained that the father had died very suddenly from a cerebral hemorrhage at the age of 38. It was clear the mother had not resolved her grief over her husband's death. The other member of the family was a 16-year-old male. After several sessions of assessment, the therapist suggested that they play *The Goodbye Game*. Both children seemed eager to play the game. Playing enabled the family to engage in a purposeful exchange of information, as well as facilitating the release of unexpressed emotions. Many erroneous assumptions concerning death came to light in this way. For example, the son had taken on a protective role in the family and had assumed too much responsibility for the emotional well-being of the family. The daughter was afraid to expand her relationships and activities outside the family, due to her fear that her mother would experience an increase in her sense of abandonment. Through the use of *The Goodbye Game*, the mother was able to assure her children that they could continue to be children in the family and that she did have a support system to rely on. With this bit of work accomplished, the family was able to share memories of the father and to move successfully through the mourning process.

SUMMARY AND CONCLUSIONS

Many school-age children appear to go through stages of grieving much the way adults respond to a significant loss. With children, however, these stages may not be as predictable as in adults, due to the nature of their cognitive and emotional development. In addition, these stages may be masked by a child's seemingly contradictory behavior. For example, depressed children may act irritable and even hostile, rather than sad and withdrawn.

The cards in *The Goodbye Game* roughly correspond to the different stages of mourning as identified by Kübler-Ross. The clinician using this game should be aware that the characteristics of any or all of the stages of mourning might be present in the child's mourning at any given time. These stages include denial and isolation, anger, bargaining, depression, and acceptance.

The denial stage serves as an emotional buffer to the unwelcome and shocking news. However, if denial continues too long, it blocks the normal grief process. Many families have great difficulty talking or even thinking about death and are therefore not able to be of much help to their child in this process. By playing *The Goodbye Game* the therapist is able to help the child move past the denial stage. Examples of denial include the belief that the deceased is just sleeping, pretending the person isn't really dead, denying emotions ("I don't feel bad"; "I'm not sad"), refusing to talk about the death, and pretending not to care ("So what?").

Anger can be a very confusing emotion in regard to loss, and some families do not permit this feeling to be expressed. Helping children express and understand fear and anger helps to relieve the potency of these emotions, as well as assuage any related guilt. Because anger is sometimes a response to fear, cards relating to a child's fear have been included in the anger stage. Examples of anger and fear include thoughts such as "Stupid Grandpa, I hate him!" and "It's not fair!" There may be intense anger at the doctor for not fixing the lost loved one, anger at a significant person for letting the death happen, anger at the therapist for bringing it up, fear of one's own death or a parent's death, a sense of not being "safe," fear of growing old, and fear of the deceased.

Bargaining may be associated with quiet guilt or with an attempt to postpone acceptance of reality. It is an irrational way of keeping the deceased alive. For younger children, it may also be an attempt to make sense out of a concept that is very difficult for them to understand because of the level of their cognitive development. Examples of bargaining include "If I had been a better kid this would not have happened"; "If I had given my puppy more attention, she might not have been hit by a car"; "Will Grandpa come back from heaven for my birthday party?"; "What do people eat when they are in heaven?"; and "Why did this happen?" Compulsive holding on to a possession of the deceased is another form of bargaining.

Depression follows the bargaining stage. It is now recognized that childhood depression may be manifested in many different ways. These include temper tantrums, sleep disturbances, bedwetting, withdrawal and isolation, challenging or oppositional behavior, changes in school performance, and self-destructive behavior.

Acceptance follows when children no longer feel angry or depressed: They have come to accept the loss. At this time, they are able to entertain a wider range of emotions and memories, as well as being able to talk more easily about their loss. The event no longer impacts their life as significantly as it did in the earlier stages of mourning and they are able to go on to age-appropriate developmental tasks and challenges.

The Goodbye Game may also be played by children who are not in the grieving process as part of a "life sciences" or "values education" program. All children experience death in their lives, whether through the loss of a pet or simply hearing about death on the television news. Understanding death and learning to communicate about it is an important part of a child's development and education.

Children who encounter death for the first time have no experience grieving and mourning death. They have no concept of grief as a process, nor do they have the hope that they will be able to accept and to assimilate this experience. Very young children have not developed the mature cognitive reasoning necessary to understand death. *The Goodbye Game* helps children process the loss in a concrete way that makes sense to them. Children are more likely to misunderstand or misinterpret the events and experiences of the death because of magical thinking, ignorance of the facts regarding death, or and discomfort in talking about death. Because of this they may develop the wrong impressions and assumptions surrounding the death.

The therapist must remember that the goal of the therapy is not to take the pain away, but to help children recognize, express, and manage their affective states. Because the questions in *The Goodbye Game* are open-ended, the therapist is able to view the loss from the child's unique perspective. This has the added benefit of lessening the chance of countertransference issues interfering with the therapeutic process. In addition, questions related to religious or philosophical issues are presented in such a way as to be educational and unbiased.

Use of *The Goodbye Game* enables the child to identify the issues surrounding grief and loss. *The Goodbye Game* is fun. It creates a powerful therapeutic intervention in the familiar activity of play, offering a non-threatening atmosphere for children to deal with their often overwhelming thoughts and emotions. The familiar format offers immediate support for the verbalization of emotions and painful affect.

The use of this game serves several purposes for the therapist: It aids the therapist in helping children process their grief; it gives the therapist the opportunity to assess the level of magical thinking children may be engaging in; and it allows the therapist to identify misconceptions, learn family myths, and detect the use of maladaptive defenses.

It is often helpful to include the grieving parent in the game playing. This serves to educate parents and assist them in communicating with their child. Parents often have difficulty talking about death and loss to other adults, and they have an even greater difficulty talking to their children. Grieving parents are often unable to process and contain their child's emotions. As a culture, we tend to be uncomfortable with bereavement: Is it any wonder that we have difficulty helping our children grieve and mourn?

Excellent guidelines for talking to children about death have been gleaned from many clinicians. These guidelines are suitable for clinicians as well as parents. Lonetto (1980) has synthesized some of these guidelines into the following set of principles:

1. Children are ready and capable of talking about anything within their own experience.
2. Use the language of the child, not the sentimental symbols we find so easy to utter.
3. Don't expect an immediate and obvious response from the child.
4. Be a good listener and observer.
5. Don't try to do all in one discussion; that is, be available.
6. Make certain that the child knows that he is part of the family, especially when a death has occurred.
7. One of the most valuable methods of teaching children about death is to allow them to talk freely and ask their own questions.

REFERENCES

Altschul, S. (1988). *Childhood bereavement and its aftermath.* Madison, CT: International University Press.

Birnbaum, P. (1995). *Encyclopedia of Jewish concepts.* Rockaway Beach, NY: Hebrew.

Bowlby, J. (1963). Pathological mourning and childhood mourning. *Journal of the American Psychoanalytic Association, 11,* 500–541.

Bowlby, J. (1980). *Attachment and loss* (Vol. 3). New York: Basic Books.

Bowlby, J., & Parkes, C.M. (1970). In E.J. Anthony & C. Coupernik (Eds.), *The child in his family.* New York: Wiley.

Campbell, J. (1974). *The mythic image.* Princeton, NJ: Princeton University Press.

Chesser, E. (1967). *Living with suicide.* London: Hutchinson.

Childers, P., & Wimmer, M. (1971). The concept of death in early childhood. *Child Development, 42,* 705–712.

Eliot, A. (1976). *The universal myths.* New York: Penguin.

Freud, S. (1953). *A general introduction to psychoanalysis* (J. Riviere, Trans.). New York: Permabooks. (Original work published 1920)

Freud, S. (1963). Mourning and melancholia. In J. Strachey (Ed. & Trans.), *The standard edition of the complete works of Sigmund Freud* (Vol. 14, pp. 237–260). London: Hogarth Press. (Original work published 1917)

Furman, E. (1984). Children's patterns in mourning the death of a loved one. In H. Wass & C. Corr (Eds.), *Childhood and death.* New York: Hemisphere.

Gabbard, G. (1994). *Psychodynamic psychiatry in clinical practice.* Washington, DC: American Psychiatric Press.

Gilman, R. (1998). *Facilitating bereavement in preschool aged children.* Unpublished manuscript.

Golden, G., & Hill, M. (1991). A token of loving: From melancholia to mourning. *Clinical Social Work Journal, 19,* 23–33.

Jung, C. (1961). *Memories, dreams, reflections* (A. Jaffe, Ed.; R. Winston & C. Winston, Trans.). New York: Vintage Books.

Kastenbaum, R., & Aisenberg, R. (1972). *The psychology of death.* New York: Springor.

Klein, M. (1975). The importance of symbol formation in the development of the ego. *Love, guilt and reparation and other works 1921–1945.* New York: Delacorte Press. (Original work published 1930)

Kroen, W. (1996). *Helping children cope with the loss of a loved one.* Minneapolis, MN: Free Spirit.

Kübler-Ross, E. (1993). *On death and dying.* New York: Collier Books.

Laplanche, J., & Pontalis, J.-B. (1973). *The language of psycho-analysis* (D. Nicholson-Smith, Trans.). New York: Norton. (Original work published 1967)

Lonetto, R. (1980). *Children's conceptions of death.* New York: Springer.

Nagy, M. (1948). The child's theories concerning death. *Journal of Genetic Psychology, 73,* 3–27.

Nagy, M. (1959). The child's view of death. In H. Feifel (Ed.), *The meaning of death.* New York: McGraw Hill.

Piaget, J. (1966). *The child's conception of physical causality.* London: Routledge & Kegan Paul.

Pollock, G.H. (1961). Mourning and adaptation. *International Journal of Psycho-Analysis, 42,* 341–361.

Rycroft, C. (1995). *A critical dictionary of psychoanalysis.* New York: Penguin Books.

Segal, H. (1974). *Introduction to the work of Melanie Klein.* New York: Basic Books.

Steindorf, G., & Seele, K. (1957). *When Egypt ruled the east* (Rev. ed.). Chicago: University of Chicago Press.

Tatelbaum, J. (1980). *The courage to grieve.* New York: Harper & Row.

Volkan, V., & Zintl, E. (1993). *Life after loss.* New York: Charles Scribner's Sons.

Zeligs, R. (1974). *Children's experience with death.* Springfield, IL: Thomas.

Zisook, S. (1995). Death, dying, and bereavement. In H. Kaplan & B. Saddock (Eds.), *Comprehensive textbook of psychiatry* (6th ed., Vol. 2). Baltimore: Williams & Wilkins.

CHAPTER TEN

Therapeutic Games for Children of Divorce

YAKOV M. EPSTEIN and HELANE S. ROSENBERG

This chapter is a modification and extension of the chapter written for the first edition of *Game Play*. In this chapter, we describe *The Children's Feedback Game* and the *Could This Happen Game* and present case illustrations of each. The games are an important aspect of the Children Helping Children Program (Epstein, Borduin, & Wexler, 1985), a group-based program for children of divorce, and have been adapted and extended for other purposes and other populations. The games described in the first edition of *Game Play* were developed by Yakov Epstein and Charles Borduin (1984, 1985) for use in the Children Helping Children Program.

Since the publication of the first edition of *Game Play*, several things happened to alter the approach that I (Epstein) used with my patients. First, starting in 1986, I personally experienced a divorce. This personal involvement and what I learned from my own children participating in this process taught me important lessons that I could not learn in any other way despite the countless hours that I worked professionally with children of divorce. Second, I met Helane Rosenberg, a researcher with expertise in children's imaginative behavior. Helane became my research colleague, my cotherapist, and my wife. Third, I accepted a position as associate director and then as director of the Rutgers Center for Mathematics, Science, and

Computer Education. In this capacity, I began to experiment with the use of innovative new technology, including computers, scanners, video-capture equipment, and digital cameras. This technology opened new vistas for psychotherapy. Helane and I incorporated the technology in our therapy sessions with children.

In this chapter, we discuss the original games, briefly review some of the case material presented in the chapter in the original edition of *Game Play,* and then describe how we used ideas drawn from imagination research and new technology to modify and extend these games.

WHY USE GAMES?

Children are frequently reluctant to attend therapy sessions. The meetings conflict with other activities that interest them. Typically, meetings occur in the evening after an exhausting and trying day at school. Candidates for child psychotherapy are also likely to suffer peer ridicule or the reproach of teachers and parents. By the start of the therapy hour, they have accumulated considerable frustration and anger, which they frequently vent on fellow group members. They are likely to tease, taunt, fight, bully, or "put down" others. Not only are these actions a response to accumulated frustrations, they are also an accepted and enjoyable aspect of children's social interaction patterns. Teasing another child is fun—though being teased is anything but fun. Prevailing in a contest of opinions is so universally a cause for celebration that it has created a voluminous lexicon of victory slogans (I owe a debt of gratitude to my daughter, who, over the course of many years, has given me numerous opportunities to observe these patterns), including "Moted" as in "Ooh—you're moted" (a California expression intoned in a singsong voice), "You're beat" (a New Jersey counterpart), and a covey of less polite epithets. Even when children are too tired to concentrate on learning, they have more than enough energy to engage in these contests.

Adults working with children can find these patterns disruptive and annoying. In a therapy session it is difficult to discuss children's feelings or focus on their fears when some children are bickering or teasing others. Our approach is to engage in "psychological jujitsu": Rather than trying to curtail these behaviors, we try to harness them. If children are motivated to tease, then we will give them the opportunity to do so in a manner that promotes learning. Teasing, after all, involves pointing out another person's shortcomings. This is equally true in giving feedback to someone. The difference, however, lies in the destructive intent. We utilize the motivation of teasing as an aspect of *The Children's Feedback Game,* which teaches feedback skills while avoiding the destructive aspects of teasing.

Games are also exciting: They license competition. At the same time, they promote collaboration between teammates who might otherwise be antagonists in an effort to beat the other side. With what sometimes seems like acrobatic skill, group leaders balance the competitive spirit against an incentive system that favors collaboration between opposing teams. Just how this is done will be explained shortly.

The desire to win is also a powerful incentive to discuss topics and engage in actions that would otherwise be shunned. In the guise of a game, children can deny the reality of their words. By invoking the belief that "it's only a game," children allow themselves the luxury of feeling emotions and expressing beliefs that otherwise would be verboten. The *Could This Happen Game* is based on this premise.

We believe that a frequent consequence of divorce is a precipitous diminution of the power of the child. The youngster's oft unheeded plea to the parents to stay together is perhaps emblematic of his or her inability to influence the course of these trying events. Clinicians have targeted the rapid decline in power and influence as an important contributor to mental illness (Ackerman, 1958). Hence, we take every opportunity available to demonstrate to the children in our program that they are not powerless—they will be heard. The structure of the game provides an opportunity to drive this point home. When games are employed in the context of children's therapy groups, the adult therapist recedes into the background, becoming an observer or referee, while the children assume a focal role. This shift in influence diminishes restraints on disclosure and spontaneity that may otherwise occur when children interact directly with an adult therapist. It also increases their commitment to the group and may even enhance their self-esteem.

There are additional reasons for elevating the child's influence in the program. Researchers have recently begun investigating the efficacy of using peer-mediated approaches to promote children's positive social interaction. In a review of this literature, Odom and Strain (1984) conclude: "Numerous studies have demonstrated that socially competent peers who, at times, receive training from teachers or clinicians can effect positive changes in the social behavior of children exhibiting social interactional deficits" (p. 555). Although the basis for the studies cited in this review is largely atheoretical, there is nonetheless literature in social psychology to support the value of using peers as change agents.

In a classic paper dealing with opinion change processes, Kelman (1958) distinguished among *compliance, identification,* and *internalization. Compliance* is changed behavior in response to external reinforcement contingencies. The compliant individual changes his or her opinions to obtain available rewards or to avoid the punishment or censure of others. Compliant change is comparatively easy to engineer with the proper schedule of reinforcement. However, researchers have found that compliant change is superficial, limited only to circumstances in which the change agent can monitor the actions of the subject. The individual does not value the new behavior more than the old habit. Given the opportunity to revert to the old pattern, he or she is likely to do so.

Identification produces changes that are more enduring than those rooted in compliance. The individual adopts behaviors and opinions that are valued by someone he or she esteems and seeks to emulate. Like compliant change, however, the new behavior is not valued in and of itself. Should the esteemed other fall from grace or the relationship deteriorate, the subject is likely to revert to the old behavior pattern.

The deepest and most enduring change is based on newly acquired values that are *internalized.* The person whose values have changed considers the new behavior better and more worthwhile than the old way of acting. Even in the absence of surveillance and despite disillusionment with a former idol, internalized values are likely to maintain changed behaviors.

Adults typically employ compliance- or identification-based strategies to change a child's behavior; rarely do they succeed in creating internalized change. In what was perhaps the most extensive research program dealing with persuasive communication, Hovland, Janis, and Kelly (1953) demonstrated the importance of the communicator's *credibility.* The failure of adults to promote internalized change may stem from their lack of credibility. When adults criticize children, these youngsters attribute the censure to a fundamental characteristic of the adult role. Grown-ups are expected to criticize the behavior of children; peers, however, are not supposed to do so. Therefore, for children, peers may be more credible evaluators.

Festinger (1954) postulated that the desire for social comparison with peers drives social behavior. Children wish to know how they are evaluated by their friends and classmates. Often, they are given the summary comments without being privy to the full review, as it were. Children know when their peers dislike them. They recoil from the taunts of other children, which are often freely offered. But these same peers rarely share information about their reasons for disliking these children. Even when they do, the feedback is usually not offered constructively. Adults must find a way to transform these hurtful communications into productive messages that can stimulate internalized change. *The Children's Feedback Game* was designed to fill this need.

Yalom (1970) postulated a number of "curative" factors in group psychotherapy. Games are an effective vehicle for introducing these factors:

1. Sharing, expressivity, and catharsis.
2. Legitimizing the expression of negative affect.
3. Experiencing the universality of a problem (in this case, the problems created by divorce).
4. Receiving help from peers considered similar to oneself. Help includes advice, skill, training, experimentation with new behaviors, and direct emotional support.
5. Giving help to others in a similar situation. By learning to help others, the child learns to help himself or herself.
6. Instilling hope. This often follows from learning new ways to cope with problems and thus feel less helpless.
7. Receiving feedback from similar peers and learning to take more responsibility for oneself.
8. Using similar peers as models.

In describing the features of the two games, we will show how they incorporate many of these curative factors.

THE CONTEXT IN WHICH THE GAMES ARE USED

The Children Helping Children Program is a two- to three-month program consisting of a children's group and a concurrent parents group each meeting weekly for 1.5 hours. The activities of the children's group are based on a number of assumptions about families of divorce. One such assumption is that these families frequently organize themselves either as competitive systems or as individualistically oriented groups in which each person attempts to satisfy his or her own needs without regard for the needs of others. Children's aggressive or competitive behavior may model the parental conflicts they witnessed. Further, children may also emulate their parents' attempts to satisfy their own social and emotional needs, thereby reducing their commitment to the common goals of the family unit. This individualistically oriented stance results in a sense of aloneness for family members: mutual social support, one of Yalom's (1970) curative factors so necessary for coping with the stress of divorce, is reduced. In an effort to promote a supportive family climate, the Children Helping Children Program attempts to teach cooperation. By creating a cooperatively oriented children's group, the members are able to benefit from the support of other children. Hopefully, the cooperative behaviors they learn in the program can be transferred to behavior at home. However, if children are to behave cooperatively, they must acquire several essential skills. They must learn to (1) take the role of the other person, (2) give and receive feedback, and (3) share and take turns. *The Children's Feedback Game* teaches these skills.

Another assumption is that children are often confused about numerous aspects of the divorce experience and are reluctant to discuss their fantasies and anxieties. Frequently, they experience shame and guilt, thinking that they are unique in their feelings and beliefs. Our program encourages children to air these secret thoughts. We believe that such public expression can foster social comparison and enable children to feel "in the same boat" with other group members. The "we-feeling" is likely to be experienced as social support and contribute to a cooperative atmosphere in the group. The *Could This Happen Game* is used to reduce children's secretiveness and foster an open discussion of beliefs and concerns, thereby incorporating several of Yalom's (1970) curative factors.

Taken together, the two games build on one another. The skills of giving and receiving feedback acquired in *The Children's Feedback Game* increase the effectiveness of communication in the *Could This Happen Game.* Likewise, the discovery of common experience resulting from the *Could This Happen Game* promotes the cooperative group structure that *The Children's*

Feedback Game seeks to develop. As the group becomes increasingly cohesive and supportive, children's initial defensiveness begins to dissipate and the likelihood of sharing anxiety-arousing material in the absence of a specific game format increases.

DESCRIPTION OF THE GAMES

THE CHILDREN'S FEEDBACK GAME

This game was developed by Epstein and Borduin (1984) as a means of reducing the disruptive, silly, and aggressive behavior that occurred frequently in the initial meetings of the Children Helping Children Program. Such disruptiveness seems to be common to group programs for latency-age children. In conjunction with a group program she conducted, Rhodes (1973) observed:

> Authorities in the use of groups with preadolescent children agree that a recurring problem is the handling of aggressive behavior. Certainly, with these groups, *the most difficult aspect was the management of the chaos and disorganization which tended to be present at times.* . . . The leaders found that from the very beginning the children tested the limits of the situation by a wide range of disruptive activity. This included breaking into small groups, whispering, getting up and engaging in individual or joint activity apart from the group and occasionally chasing one another. (p. 212)

Ginott (1961) devoted an entire chapter to discussing the need for the adult therapist to set limits to circumvent children's disruptiveness. However, we believe that peers can be more effective than adults in changing disruptive behavior and that such change is more likely to be internalized. Rhodes (1973) notes, in reference to the group described previously, "When the group could be engaged to confront the group member with his impulse ridden behavior, it was far more effective than when the leader did so" (p. 212). *The Children's Feedback Game* facilitates this process while also teaching the children observational skills, training them to give constructive feedback, and increasing their motivation to attend to their own behavior.

The Children's Feedback Game is data-based. The data consist of salient events pertaining to the group members. The use of the game motivates children to attend to their own behavior and the behavior of others. Group leaders provide summary information to the children to help them recall these events. They videotape and audiotape group sessions and prepare summaries based on this recorded material. A computer-generated summary of the previous session is distributed to the children at the start of each session. The summary contains a separate paragraph for each member as well as a paragraph summarizing what happened to the total group. Each member's paragraph begins with the following heading: "WHAT HAPPENED TO (name of child)."

Reviewing the recorded information is time-consuming (though extremely valuable) and alternative procedures could be substituted. Rather than listening to a recording of the session, leaders could compose a brief paragraph about the salient events that occurred for each child during the session. These paragraphs could be typed and distributed to group members.

The use of summary information is consistent with the program's underlying goal of maximizing the children's likelihood of success. Children may initially be unable to provide feedback to others for lack of information. We therefore supply them with data on which to base the feedback. Alternatively, children may have sufficient information but be ignorant of which items are worth sharing and how to communicate them constructively. The summary models the feedback process while the game motivates the children to read the transcript and learn how to provide the feedback appropriately. In all, providing information and a means of absorbing it increases the likelihood that a child will succeed at giving feedback to members of the group.

The Children Helping Children Program uses an incentive system to promote group member interdependence by increasing the children's involvement in the games. Toward the beginning of the program a point system is introduced. Points accumulated through participation in several different activities are used to acquire items for a group party held during the last meeting of the group. A party chart prominently displayed in the room allows children to determine their current point accumulation. The chart, which looks like a ladder, includes a number of subgoals. Each subgoal corresponds to an item to be acquired for the party (e.g., ice cream, balloons). The group is divided into two teams who compete for points in the various games. The competition is exciting and motivates participation. However, despite the competition, the games promote cohesiveness because points earned by each of the teams are totaled and applied to the common goal of a group party.

The game begins by dividing the group into two teams. Next, the leader reads a description of an incident that occurred in a previous meeting. The description does not identify the child involved in the incident, and the wording of the description omits gender cues. For example, a description might read: "This child made fun of other children in the group and didn't participate in the game we played." The children's task is to guess which child is being described. Typically, the children are eager to demonstrate their ability to identify the *target* child. The leader encourages them to huddle with their teammates to arrive at team consensus. In so doing, each child has to check his or her impulsive tendencies and learn to consider the ideas of other children.

Several rounds are played. On each round, the teams alternate being the guessing team. After the spokesperson announces the team's guess, the leader gives the other team an opportunity to "challenge." The challengers disagree with the guess and offer an alternative name. If the guessing team is correct, they earn one point. However, if the challengers are correct, they earn two points and the guessing team loses one point.

The competition between teams heightens interest in the game. But the competition is embedded in a larger cooperative context. Points earned by each team are cumulated and applied toward the common goal of a group party. Thus, each team is pleased at the success of its opponent. This overarching cooperative goal is consistent with the program's values.

The children also have an opportunity to earn a variety of bonus points. A child can earn a *feeling* bonus point by describing how he or she felt when the target child behaved as described. *Owning* bonus points can be earned by the target child for acknowledging the feedback and guessing how other group members reacted to this behavior. The target child can also earn a *change* bonus point by suggesting changes in his or her behavior in future situations. Finally, children can earn *advice* bonus points by advising the target child about alternative ways of acting. Thus, the use of bonus points motivates the children to engage in behaviors that promote several of Yalom's (1970) curative factors.

Points are recorded on a blackboard. During the game, each child is given a turn to be scorekeeper, a highly desirable role. An equally sought-after job is party chart recorder. The child performing this task fills in "rungs" on the party chart "ladder" with a magic marker to indicate progress toward the group goals. The scorekeeper and recorder roles are used as reinforcers as well as teaching tools. Children learn to cooperate in taking turns at these roles. Appointing children to these roles also affords an opportunity to address children's feelings of deprivation resulting from not being chosen for the task. Other roles can also be created; for example, teams can have captains. The decision to add roles is but one of many choices that should be made after assessing the strengths and weaknesses of each child, his or her distinct familial problems, and the characteristic interaction patterns of group members. The game is an adaptable means to attain therapeutic goals. It can be used most effectively when modified to best meet the particular needs of each unique group.

We capitalize on the ability of games to stimulate discussion and extend the discussion as far as possible. All children are encouraged to participate in the discussion. Indeed, the leader often asks children to share anecdotes in which they acted like the target child. This procedure seeks to help children see themselves through the eyes of others and learn how others react to their behavior. Taking the role of the other toward oneself is a critical ingredient in the socialization process (Mead, 1934) and an important element in developing a cooperative group.

CASE ILLUSTRATIONS

The Children's Feedback Game has been used successfully with several different groups. Some background information about the children described in the case illustrations will provide a basis for assessing the impact of the game.

David, a very bright 9-year-old boy, was caught in the midst of his parents' turbulent and mercurial relationship. The vicissitudes of their relationship are exemplified by the changes that occurred within the space of one two-week period. During this brief time span, they fought so violently that the father called for police intervention lest he literally murder his wife. This incident, witnessed by David, was followed not one week later with a reconciliation: David's father moved back into the home. Shortly thereafter, the fighting resumed and he once again left. Against this backdrop of *Sturm und Drang*, David, who was by nature shy and had difficulty expressing feelings, became confused, antagonistic, and acted out his frustration and anger. In this time of loneliness, when he was most in need of support, his actions in the group served only to alienate him from his peers.

During the third meeting of the group, David frequently left the room, curled up in a bookcase, and played with the microphone. At first, the other children paid attention to David's actions and some even imitated his behavior. The resulting chaos made it difficult for the leaders to involve the children in discussions of divorce-related material. Some of the children complained that David was interfering with the group's activities, yet they did not tell him how they felt about his actions. By the end of the fourth group meeting, David had earned the reputation of group "deviant" and was treated as a scapegoat. In response, he distanced himself even more from group activities, wrapping himself in a mantle of exaggerated indifference to their reaction to him. Less than 30 days after meeting a new group of children, David was mired in an uncomfortable role from which he could not extricate himself.

Joseph's parents separated when he was less than 1 year old. He had limited contact with his father and never witnessed the conflicts that were so much a part of David's world. However, Joseph's mother felt continuously angry with Joseph, primarily because she viewed him as an impediment to fulfilling her career and social needs. In response to her anger, she distanced herself emotionally from Joseph, who, in turn, escalated his demands for attention. Unable to satisfy these needs at home, Joseph's appetite for attention from other adults became insatiable. In the group, he was attentive and delightful when he had the leader's ear, but he refused to relinquish the floor to any other group member. Like David, he too sought a great deal of attention. When he was not in the limelight, he disrupted conversations, attempted to dominate the discussion, or, failing that, acted silly.

During the fifth meeting of the group, the leaders introduced *The Children's Feedback Game*. Whenever we introduce a new procedure, we give the children some practice trials to familiarize them with it. The practice question said: "This child interrupted group discussions several times. Often, when other children wanted to talk this child didn't give them a chance. Instead, this child insisted on talking. When the leaders stopped this child and let other kids talk, this child acted silly. Guess which child we are describing."

The description referred to Joseph. On an index card, each child wrote the name of the child he or she thought was being described. Enthusiastic shouts of "Ooh, I know who it is" had to be contained, and the children were instructed to consult their teammates to reach consensus. The guessing team was unanimous in its belief that the incident referred to David. David's team, the challengers, were likewise inclined to agree with this guess, but David prevailed on them to challenge. Reluctantly, they acceded to his demands and offered Joseph's name instead. To their surprise, the other team's chagrin, and David's utter delight, the group was informed that the incident indeed referred to Joseph. David's dogged determination to resist group pressure and the subsequent vindication of his stance enhanced his self-esteem and contributed to his stature among his teammates. In a productive discussion that ensued, the children examined the reasons for attributing Joseph's behavior to David. The discussion focused on the issue of obtaining a "bad reputation" and being blamed for the misdeeds of someone else. The children realized that their conclusion did not fit the data. They had indicated a child who had steadfastly refused to participate in group discussions as the group member who dominated conversations. They had overlooked this discrepancy because they deemed David the candidate most likely to engage in *any* undesirable behavior.

The discussion provided important feedback to David about the reputation he had earned. It also provided a forum in which he was able to hear not only the negative reactions children had to his disruptive behavior, but also the positive feelings: the caring they felt for him and their wish to be his friend. To earn *advice* bonus points, they suggested ways he could change. Dawn advised David to sit down and refrain from wandering around the room in the future. To earn a *feeling* point, she also told him that she thought he was much more attentive now than he had been in previous sessions and she liked him as she saw him now. David seemed to enjoy the positive feedback. It provided a face-saving means by which to change his behavior. By following the advice of group members, he indicated that he valued their opinions and they, in turn, appreciated him more.

David's behavior changed dramatically in subsequent sessions. He rarely left the room, never again climbed into the bookcase, and stopped playing with the microphone. Although he did not share very many of his feelings during this or other games, he was extremely attentive and actively participated on a cognitive level. Given the inner turmoil that we suspect he was experiencing, it is our opinion that he was incapable of discussing the turbulent emotions he harbored within him. Whereas this agitation had heretofore driven him literally to run from discussions of emotionally charged topics, he was now able to sit quietly and have the opportunity to vicariously absorb therapeutic benefit from the discussions he witnessed. We attribute the change in David to a desire to be regarded favorably by his peers. The game broke the cycle of reciprocal antagonism and afforded an opportunity to bring an otherwise alienated youngster back into the supportive fold of the group.

Silent members are often ignored by other children. Because they do not disrupt ongoing activity, they rarely evoke feedback. The leaders wanted to help Carl, a silent member, break out of his shell. They hoped that the game would provide a forum to discuss Carl's silence and facilitate his entry into the group. Accordingly, they constructed the following item: "This child is very quiet during group meetings. This child almost never says anything when the rest of the group is having a discussion." The children correctly identified Carl as the subject of this description. Carl acknowledged his silence and discussed his view of the situation. He found it difficult to break into existing conversations. According to his recollection, he had attempted to speak several times but was ignored by others who were unwilling to relinquish the floor.

This interchange was the beginning of a productive dialogue between Carl and the other group members. It provided a nonthreatening arena to discuss Carl's silence and an opportunity to consider some ways to change this situation. In an effort to earn *change* bonus points, Allison, Joseph, and Dawn told Carl that they would like to see him talk and participate more. Carl welcomed the opportunity and promised that he would try to change. The leaders praised Carl for making this public commitment and exhorted the other children to increase Carl's chance of succeeding. They taught the children the importance of listening when Carl talked so that he would feel successful. This discussion appears to have been fruitful. For the duration of the program, Carl was the most actively involved group member.

Joseph continued to act the clown and competed for attention paid to other children. During the sixth session, the leaders described a child who tried to focus the conversation on his concerns and, failing to do so, acted silly. The children easily identified Joseph as the culprit. Allison said to him, "When you act silly we get so mad at you we want to beat you up." Carl told him, "When you act silly we think it's because you want to get all of the attention. You just act like a big shot. We don't like that." Joseph agreed that he behaved this way and promised to try to change.

It would be gratifying to report that following this interchange Joseph stopped acting silly and seeking the limelight. Unfortunately, this was not so. However, now the children would say "Joseph, you're acting silly again" or "Cut it out, Joseph," and he would acknowledge his action and stop it. The game seems to have created a mechanism for rapidly bringing Joseph's behavior under control without eliminating its cause. The leaders attributed much of the cause of Joseph's actions to intractable family patterns and were therefore gratified by their limited success.

In addition to modifying disruptive behavior, the game can also be used to help a child appreciate some of his or her positive qualities. This is how the leaders used it to help Dawn. Dawn coped daily with a most confusing family environment. Her parents disliked one another intensely and agreed to separate six months before the start of the program. Dawn's mother was employed in a fairly prestigious professional position. However, the downturn in our nation's economy had cost Dawn's father his job. Financially destitute, he continued to live in the marital home, maintaining separate quarters and waiting for a time when he would be able to rent his own apartment. Each of Dawn's parents was romantically involved with another person and each introduced Dawn to this individual. Dawn's mother had a negative opinion of her daughter. Her description of Dawn as "my little monster" had a critical rather than a playful edge to it. She was quick to dismiss Dawn's good qualities. When the leader complimented Dawn for sharing candy with the other children, her mother quickly dismissed it, explaining that Dawn gave her candy away because she wasn't allowed to eat it at home. This constant belittlement contributed to Dawn's inability to appreciate her good qualities.

The leaders read a description of a child who acted kind in the group and cared about other children. Group members guessed that the description referred to Dawn. She, on the other hand, dismissed the praise, thinking she didn't deserve it. However, the discussion gave the children an opportunity to share with Dawn their positive feelings for her. She seemed to relish this feedback and became centrally involved in the group.

COMMENTS ON USE OF THE CHILDREN'S FEEDBACK GAME

As the program progressed toward its later phases, the children were encouraged to give feedback to one another in the here and now. Indeed, having learned to give feedback in response to the incidents described in the game, the children rapidly developed the ability to point out each other's negative behavior in the present. They described these behaviors and shared their emotional reactions to them. They attended more closely to one another's behavior. Rather than acting out their negative reactions or complaining to the leader about a child's misbehavior, they talked directly with this person. Moreover, children confronted with feedback developed the habit of acknowledging rather than instinctively defending against and denying the information.

Experience using the game demonstrated that it is easier to train children to spontaneously criticize constructively than to praise freely. However, by modeling praise and reinforcing the children's imitation of these behaviors, the leaders succeeded in heightening awareness of positive behavior as well as increasing positive feedback.

Use of the game was beneficial in a number of related ways. Because the children had learned to give and receive feedback, they were often able to rapidly curtail undesirable behavior. By gaining this control over disruptive behavior, the group was able to work more productively and reduce the level of friction in the group. This reduction in tension promoted the development of a cohesive and cooperative group. Finally, the frequency with which feelings were expressed and the depth with which they were explored showed a noticeable increase after the introduction of this game. In all, *The Children's Feedback Game* has been a valuable therapeutic tool in the Children Helping Children Program.

MODIFICATION AND EXTENSION OF THE CHILDREN'S FEEDBACK GAME

The Children's Feedback Game was based on selected segments chosen from our review of each session's videotape. More recently, we have acquired new technology that allows us to take this activity in new directions. Our modifications are based on the imagery research that Helane Rosenberg has conducted and on her work using theatre games. Rather than verbally describing a behavioral incident, we now show an image of the event and include a method of modifying that image and capturing the changed image. The resulting games are called *Moment in Time* and *Statue,* respectively.

In 1962, theatre director Viola Spolin wrote *Improvisations for the Theatre,* a book of theatre games that helped actors work improvisationally. These activities, very game-like in structure, were the source of the work of such troups as Second City, the production of *Story Theatre,* and the television series, *Saturday Night Live.* One of the key aspects of these activities was the ability of the actor to communicate emotions and ideas physically, summarized in the coaching line "Show me, don't tell me." Another key feature was the ability of the actor to distill the action to its essence, to pare down, as it were, the most essential parts of a feeling or an idea that must be communicated. Because of the tremendous success of these techniques, Spolin reorganized these games into the *Theatre Game File,* published in 1975 for use with children and for nonprofessionals. Two primary games from this file were used to provide the basis for the work described here: *What Happened Before* and *Statue.*

Another technique that helped shape the work described here is the notion of the "psychological gesture" from the book *To the Actor* by Michael Chekhov (1953). Also a book used by actors in their training, *To the Actor* details a method that actors can use to get at the essence of a character for the purpose of communicating that essence both verbally through the text and physically through the body. Once an actor finds the psychological gesture of a character, he or she can take the shape of that gesture, experience the emotion called forth by assuming that posture and facial gesture, and communicating those feelings to the audience. The psychological gesture technique is valuable to a therapist because it focuses on both the decoding of physical stances and gestures as well as on creating alternative physicalities.

One additional key aspect of the activity described here is our work in the area of mental imagery. We believe that it goes without saying that images have tremendous power in shaping behavior and stimulating feelings. Although our work in mental imagery does not preclude the importance of verbalizing, we structure many activities in our work with youngsters to differentiate between pictures and words. The *iii framework* (Rosenberg, 1987; Rosenberg, Pinciotti, Chrein, & Castellano, 1985) describes a process by which people acquire images, store images, manipulate images both internally and externally, and create imagination images from memory images, albeit not entirely from memory, that stimulate change in behavior and ultimately through verbalization. We focus on an image that records a moment in time and allows what is ephemeral to become captured and manipulated. The power of a photo captures what is stored internally; the manipulation of that external image, through modification and through discussion, creates a new image, external and then stored, that can spark change in both words and behavior.

For these activities, we use several pieces of equipment: a laptop computer with a PC card slot (PCMCIA slot), a color inkjet printer, a digital camera, a scanner, and a video-capture unit. As we view the videotape of the previous session, we note the location of images that depict the essential features of an important incident. We choose an incident that had a powerful impact on the group. Our focus is on having the children describe what led up to this incident and how each participant was feeling.

Using a simple and inexpensive video-capture device, we are able to freeze and capture important frames from our videotape. We use a device called Snappy (made by Play Inc.). It is a box about the size of a deck of playing cards that attaches to the parallel port on a computer. A cable running from the Snappy attaches to the video-out port on a camcorder. An earphone attached to the audio-out port on the computer provides the sound track. The computer screen displays the session video. When a salient image of behavior is located, a click of the mouse grabs the frame. The isolated image of the *target child* is then saved to disk as a graphic file. We print this image and make copies for each of the children. In our first game, *Moment in Time,* rather than asking children to guess the child being described by an incident, they can look at the image of the child as he or she is involved in the incident. As the children look at the image, the leader provides just enough verbal descriptive information to ensure that the children can recall the incident.

As before, the group is divided into two teams who have an opportunity to earn points that will be accumulated toward points needed for the group party. The team having the target child, is given the first opportunity to describe the circumstances leading up to this incident. We call this information *what happened before*. The information includes both a description of actions as well as associated feelings. When an action description is offered, the group votes on whether they consider it a valid description of what happened before. Valid descriptions are awarded points. Likewise, disclosure of feelings in response to the action also generates points. As in the previous game, if one team is unable to offer observations or share feelings, the other team has a chance to do so.

Following these observations, the leader encourages discussion of alternative ways of behaving under these circumstances. The goal is to develop a way of behaving that leads to satisfying outcomes. When the group has succeeded in identifying a satisfactory alternative, they physicalize this alternative in the next game, *Statue.*

In *Statue,* group members take turns moving the target's body and face to evolve into the desired image. Points are awarded for each move that brings the target closer to the desired final position. Once the target has attained the desired shape, the leader takes a digital photo of this pose. The camera image is downloaded to the laptop computer and copies are printed for each child in the group. They are asked to place the original image and the remolded image side by side and to discuss their response to the differences in these two images.

CASE ILLUSTRATIONS

Matthew's parents separated when he was 4 years old. His parents had worked out a relatively cooperative relationship with one another. Both parents lived in the same town. Matthew alternated between each parent's household on a weekly basis. Both parents tried to maintain an active involvement in Matthew's school and recreational activities. They each attended teacher conferences and religiously attended Matthew's soccer and Little League games. In the group, Matthew was well liked and actively involved in group activities.

During the fifth session of the group, as the children were playing *The Children's Feedback Game,* Matthew behaved in an uncharacteristically disruptive way. Rather than attending to the description read by the leader and trying to offer a reasonable guess about which child was being described, he behaved disruptively. He seemed sullen and when his groupmates solicited his opinion of which child was being described, Matthew suggested a name that clearly could not have been the child in question. His teammates became angry at him. The image we captured from the videotape showed Matthew with his hands crossed over his chest, sitting slumped over with a scowl on his face. He appeared to be both angry and dejected.

The week following this incident, Matthew showed up in his more characteristically chipper and cooperative mood. The group played the *Moment in Time* game. When Matthew saw the picture of himself in his angry pose, he was surprised. His teammates tried to guess what led up to Matthew's behavior. Their guesses couldn't have been more wrong. Jennifer, a girl who had a poor image of herself, guessed that Matthew, whom the group viewed as high-status, had lost interest in the group. Jennifer guessed that Matthew felt the other kids (whose parents were much less supportive than Matthew's) were "losers" and that he did not want to be associated with them. Fred, a second teammate, agreed with Jennifer. Matthew was mortified. He was able to tell them that he was saddened to learn that his teammates thought he felt this way toward them. He went on to share that he really cared about the other kids, that he looked forward to coming to the group, and that his behavior had nothing to do with what they suspected. He told them that just before coming to group last week he had played in an important Little League game. Without any explanation, his father, who always showed up for his games and who had promised to be there for this important game, had not showed up. Matthew owned that when he came to the session the previous week he had been upset and distracted. Until he saw the picture he had not realized how that incident had affected him.

Next, the leaders initiated the *Statue* game. Working from the printed-out image and without talking, the children "molded" Matthew into the stance he had assumed in the printed pose. The key elements were his slumped-over posture, arms crossed across his body, and a scowl on his face. There was much giggling and laughter as the group molded him into this position. Once in this position, Matthew discussed how he felt having been placed in the position from last week. He was amazed to find that despite the good mood he was in when he entered the evening's session, he was now in touch with feelings of anger and dejection that had been associated with last week's incident. Next, Matthew's teammates conferred to decide how to mold him into a body position and facial expression that was more positive. His teammates got Matthew to stand up and uncross his arms but were unable to correct the slumping body and grumpy face. Now it was the other team's turn to complete the transformation. Kristen, a member of the other team, used an innovative technique. She molded her own face into a smiling face and then softly molded Matthew's face into a smile. Matthew's face molded easily. The rest of the team helped Matthew to stand up straighter once he was smiling. Having attained this state, the leader used his digital camera to take a photo of Matthew in the new pose. The image was saved on a flash memory card on the camera. Then the memory card was removed from the camera, inserted into the PCMCIA slot on the computer, and loaded into *Adobe Photo Deluxe* (a software program that is bundled with the

Snappy video-capture hardware). A caption with Matthew's name, the names of the other group members, the date, and a summary description of the change was created. The summary read: "I changed from grumpy to happy by uncrossing my hands, standing up, and smiling." Then multiple copies of the picture were printed, one for each child in the group. They placed the new image next to the image captured the previous week and discussed the differences.

THE *COULD THIS HAPPEN GAME*

The *Could This Happen Game* is introduced after the children have had an opportunity to play *The Children's Feedback Game*. The *Feedback Game* teaches children how to express their feelings; this skill is further honed in the *Could This Happen Game.*

Children of divorce are often reluctant to discuss their feelings concerning divorce-related family problems. Likewise, many of these children have never aired their fears and worries. Some of these concerns (such as a parent's inability to pay bills) may be realistic. Others, however, may be based on misinformation, overheard snatches of conversation, or information they misunderstood and never felt free to check out with an adult. Thus, they may be needlessly burdened with guilt that could be alleviated through discussion with their parents. The *Could This Happen Game,* developed by Epstein and Borduin (1985), was designed to facilitate a discussion of these problems and fears.

The game begins with a division of the group into two teams. Each team selects a name. Pencils and index cards are distributed to each child. The leader posts a newsprint chart containing the following four alternatives:

1. I'm sure this could happen.
2. I think this could happen but I'm not sure.
3. I don't think this could happen but I'm not sure.
4. I'm sure this could not happen.

The leader informs the children that they will be told about a hypothetical situation and asked to guess whether or not it could really happen. The newsprint chart is displayed and each of the four alternatives explained. The leader invites the children to practice playing the game by answering a sample question. Each child writes his or her name on the index card and one of the four numbers listed on the chart. The cards are collected and the leader reads each child's choice. The child is questioned to ensure that he or she understood the meaning of the chosen alternative and that it indeed represented his or her belief. The leader counts how many children voted for each of the four alternatives and announces which of the four was the most popular alternative.

Team representatives ("reps") are selected. They stand in front of the room and, in contrast to their teammates, do not answer the questions. Instead, their task is to guess which of the four alternatives received the most votes (from both teams combined). Their team receives one point for each person who voted for the alternative the rep thought was most popular.

Suppose, for example, that the question asked: *Two brothers share a room and never fight with each other. Could this happen?* If three children select alternative 3 (I don't think this could happen but I'm not sure) and one child selects alternative 4 (I'm sure this could not happen), and Team A's rep guesses that the most popular answer is alternative 3, his or her team gets three points because three children voted for that alternative. However, if Team B's rep guessed that the most popular answer is alternative 4, he or she earns one point because only one child voted for that alternative. It is possible for both reps to select the same alternative.

In addition to points earned by the rep, the other team members can earn bonus points. One type of bonus point is the *evidence* point. A child earns an *evidence* point by presenting "evidence" in support of his or her chosen alternative. In the previous example, a child might tell how he and his brother fight constantly over when to turn off the lights at night as evidence that brothers could not possibly share a room harmoniously. His desire to earn the bonus point and prove to others that he is correct uncovers information that can be used to discuss the sibling relationship.

Building on the skills acquired in *The Children's Feedback Game,* the children are also given an opportunity to earn *feeling* bonus points. Disclosing "evidence" related to divorce often stirs up powerful feelings. The availability of *feeling* bonus points removes many of the restraints against discussing these feelings. As the children begin to express their feelings, the leader praises them, thus encouraging them to be even more forthcoming. Hearing other children express their feelings reassures the listener by validating his or her own experience and contributes to a sense of group solidarity.

The *Could This Happen Game* can be used to explore almost any topic. The initial catalogue of questions was drawn from the concerns voiced by some of the children in the group, from worries that researchers have attributed to children of divorce, and from our concern about children's feelings of powerlessness and disappointment with their parents. Records of children's responses can provide valuable sources of research data.

At the start of the game, a number of "warm-up" items are used. Typically, the content of these items is not divorce-related. Here is one of the warm-up items we have used: *An 8-year-old child runs in a race with members of the Rutgers University track team. The 8-year-old child wins the race. Could this happen?* This warm-up item was selected for several reasons. Its content is nonthreatening, so it is readily answered. Its unlikely outcome encourages the children to consider the plausibility of the question. It also challenges the children to dredge up evidence supporting their answer. We have found that one or two items of this sort are all that is needed to provide a sufficient introduction to the game. However, we attend to the level of anxiety in the group and increase the warm-up time if it seems high.

A second warm-up item is designed to provide a transition between nondivorce- and divorce-related items: *A woman is elected president of the United States. Could this happen?* This is a valuable transition item because it can lead to an important divorce-relevant discussion of the relative power and status of women and of male-female relationships. As children express their opinions about the plausibility of the item's premise, the leaders guide the discussion to a consideration of what parents have said about opportunities for women. The discussion can then be shifted to a consideration of men's views of women and, more specifically, of fathers' views of mothers.

CASE ILLUSTRATIONS

The cases selected to illustrate the use of this game are drawn from the same group of children described in the material illustrating the use of *The Children's Feedback Game*. Using this same group eliminates the need for additional background material and provides a view of additional facets of the psychological world of these children.

As noted previously, we consider the child's feelings of powerlessness an important consequence of the divorce experience. The following question facilitates a discussion of power: *A child wants hamburgers for dinner. His parents hate hamburgers. The parents want spinach pie for dinner. The child hates spinach pie. The family discusses what to have for dinner and the parents decide to make hamburgers. Could this happen?*

The underlying issue posed by this item is a parents' weighting of a child's expressed preferences against their own. The item raises the question of whether parents place their own needs ahead of their child's. Several children believed that the parents would make hamburgers because that's what the child wanted. However, some children disagreed and spontaneously connected this item with their parents' divorce-related choices. Carl noted that parents don't always do what their child wants. He said that parents are often too busy to listen to the important things a child wishes to say. He said, "I asked my mom to help me with homework and she said 'I'm too busy.' When my father was living with us, we asked him to help me and he said 'I'm too tired: I need a rest badly.' They don't have time for me." Then Carl gave a more poignant example to support his contention. He said: "Once, my dad went to Florida without even telling me. We didn't know where he was. He never called me. We asked my mom 'Why doesn't my daddy call?' and she said 'I don't know.'" On his return, his father's lack of contrition precipitated an argument between father and son. Carl discussed how hurt he felt by the way his father treated him during this incident. Were it not for the game, Carl would have been unlikely to describe this incident. Moreover, this initial description led to more painful revelations of other ways his dad had discounted him.

The "hamburger" item is a nondivorce item that stimulates valuable discussion. Careful thought must be given to the transition from the nondivorce to the divorce content items. The children's responses are often helpful in determining the proper pace for the transition. In our opinion, it would be a mistake to suggest a hierarchy of the sequence of items or guidelines about the timing of specific items. Such an overly "uniform" approach might inhibit the children's spontaneity and impede the group's progress.

When the leader thinks the time is ripe, he or she could approach the content of the "hamburger" item more directly with the following question: *A child's father tells his family that he plans to get divorced. The child asks her father to stay married. The father agrees to remain married. Could this happen?* This item could stimulate children to discuss instances in which they asked their parents to stay together and how their parents responded. It is a useful item for generating camaraderie because so many children have tried to reconcile their parents and failed. Hearing other children discuss these feelings can help the child feel he or she is not alone.

The experience of discussing items whose content does not specifically pertain to divorce eases the transition to a discussion of emotionally charged divorce-related items. The content of these items is drawn from background questionnaire material provided by the parents, from the contents of problems that parents are discussing in the parent group, and from problems reported in the divorce literature. The following question deals with one such topic—a noncustodial parent who withholds financial support: *A child's parents are divorced. The child needs braces for her teeth. The mother does not have enough money to pay for the braces. The father has enough money but refuses to pay for the braces. Could this happen?*

Arlene eagerly volunteered to answer this question. She was a bright youngster with low self-esteem. Both of Arlene's parents were angry with one another and attempted to recruit Arlene as an ally in marital conflict. During our first meeting with her prior to the start of the program, she repeatedly informed us that she was incapable of drawing and that she was "no good at anything," that she had no opinions on any topic, and that she had no feelings about any of the tactics her parents were using to involve her in their conflict. However, the game provided a forum in which she was free to express opinions and strong feelings about these actions. Arlene stated that she was sure that it was possible for a father to refuse to pay for the braces. As "evidence" she stated, "My father is supposed to give my mother some money and he refuses to give. My mom has been working the night shift and she hasn't been seeing me that much. Every time we want to see her, there's always a babysitter around instead." In attempting to earn a *feeling* bonus point, Arlene openly discussed her sadness at not seeing more of her mother and her anger at her father's behavior.

The ability to express feelings that was stimulated by this game generalized to other areas of Arlene's day-to-day activities. Indeed, her mother noticed these changes and, several weeks after the conclusion of the program, wrote us to share her observations and reactions. In her letter, she stated that "many people have noted the growth in Arlene in the past few months." To illustrate this growth, she sent us a photocopy of a composition Arlene had written in school. In this essay entitled "Divorce," Arlene wrote:

> People are busy all the time. I never get to see my mom and dad. My mother and father are getting divorced. I feel that they are trying to pull me apart. It's not fair to me. I hate it so much. . . . They both love me. They want me to live with them. . . . It's hard to have to choose my mother or my father. I hate divorces.

Arlene, a girl who six months previously had been unable to express any feelings concerning the divorce, was now able to talk openly and spontaneously about her feelings. The lure of the game induced her to drop her guard and set into motion a self-perpetuating process of change.

For other children, however, the challenge of the game itself may not be sufficient to induce therapeutic movement. However, other curative factors related to the game may provide the needed spark. Lieberman, Yalom, and Miles (1973) report that a group member who is initially reluctant to participate in group activities can assume the role of "spectator." By watching others and vicariously sharing in their experiences, the spectator's motivation

to participate is increased and an opportunity for therapeutic benefits derived from participation becomes available. This, indeed, is what happened
to Craig.

Craig was a butterball whose disposition belied the "fat men are jolly"
adage. In his mother's opinion, he was more "seriously disturbed" than the
other children in the group. She doubted that the program could benefit
a child as "unbalanced" as he. Combative at home, especially with his
younger brother, he was shy and uncommunicative during the first four sessions of the group. But sitting quietly as he was, he must have been an avid
spectator, for Arlene's disclosure unleashed in him an outpouring of emotion that was to change his participation in the group and his behavior at
home. He followed Arlene's disclosure with these words:

> When I was at my old house, Friday night, my dad said he was going to a meeting.
> I said, "Daddy, why do you have to go to a meeting?" and he said "I have to." He
> didn't go to a meeting. He was moving to another place without me. He was lying
> to me, my sister, and my brother. My mother had to call the police and say "I'm
> missing a husband."

Perhaps Arlene's expression of anger at her father demonstrated to Craig that
other children also experience this emotion and that it's okay to express this
feeling. Perhaps Craig connected Arlene's anger at her father's "betrayal"
with his own anger about this issue. Although it is impossible to determine
what caused what, it is clear that Craig's behavior following this incident was
noticeably different. He became much more communicative, affectionate, and
helpful in the group. His mother reported similar dramatic changes at home.

A second recurring problem, ineffective communication among family
members, was the impetus for another game item. In many two-parent families, children are taught that giving feedback to parents is disrespectful
and should be avoided. Likewise, voicing one's concerns may be equated
with complaining, another negatively sanctioned activity. Although these
prohibitions may not cause great problems for children living in a salutary
environment, they are likely to severely hamper children of divorce, who
may refrain from discussing the stresses they are experiencing. To open a
discussion of beliefs about communication, a necessary prelude to training
in communication skills, the following question was devised: *A parent says
something that hurts a child's feelings. The child tells her parent that the parent
hurt her feelings. The parent gets angry at the child and punishes her. Could this
happen?* Discussion of this question is usually accompanied by role plays in
which the child is encouraged to communicate with his or her parent. The
leader provides feedback about the strengths and problem areas exhibited
by the communicator. The viewing children are encouraged to use the skills
they acquired in *The Children's Feedback Game* to share their reactions about
what they observed. Often, they are able to effectively point out that a child

is whining or acting silly when he or she is communicating a serious concern. Children are asked to take the role of the parent and imagine how a parent would react to this entreaty. Following the role plays, the leader asks each child to identify a concern about which he or she suspects his or her parent is unaware. The children are then given a "homework" assignment: They are asked to communicate the concern they identified as effectively as possible. To maximize the likelihood of success, the leader of the concurrent parent group is informed prior to the meeting that the children will be practicing new approaches to communication in the upcoming week. The leader communicates this information to the parents and discusses effective ways they can respond to the new initiatives.

When the children meet the following week, they discuss the outcome of their assignment. The ensuing discussion is often the source of new items for the game. For example, one child mentioned that he talked about how upset he became when his mother constantly described his father as a bad person. A number of children noted that they had similar experiences. Knowing that this problem was widespread, the leaders of a subsequent program constructed the following item to stimulate discussion of this topic: *A father tells a child that the child's mother is a bad person. Could this happen?* As anticipated, this item stimulated a productive discussion. Betty stated that her parents were involved in a custody dispute and shared her feelings about this matter. She stated that her father had urged her to live with him because "my girlfriend and I are better than your mother, who never does things or gets things for you." Betty never told her father how his words affected her. She revealed to the other children, however, that her father's statements frightened her so much that she hid in her bedroom after talking to him. In the ensuing group discussion, she revealed that what most frightened her was the possibility of going to court and being asked to publicly choose between her mother and father. The children offered her considerable support and provided several helpful suggestions related to her difficulties.

As children can sometimes be supportive, they can also be cruel—their cruelty often far outstripping their kindness. Teachers have reported that children from intact families often tease children of divorce. To open discussion of this issue, we posed the following question: *Children in school tease a child because her parents are divorced. Could this happen?* Carl thought this could definitely happen and said, "I don't think it's very nice of the kids to make fun of her because it's not her fault that her parents are divorced. They make fun of me. They say 'Oh Carl, your father doesn't live with you. And he doesn't take you anywhere.'" Arlene chimed in: "Same with me. They tease me: 'Your father's got a girlfriend. Your father's going to marry her. And then your mother's going to be by herself with you.' . . . I don't do anything when they say that but I feel mad." The ensuing discussion revealed that many of the children had shared this same distressing experience. Because knowing the trials of others can provide limited consolation, the children seemed to draw strength from the recognition that they were not unique in their harsh treatment.

We have also constructed questions that help the children recognize the anguish their parents experience. By doing so, we help them take the role of their parent and see their mothers and fathers in a less stereotypic fashion. In this regard, one question we have found useful is: *A father was talking about something sad with his children. Suddenly he started to cry. Could this happen?* All of the children said that it could definitely happen. Joseph mentioned a time when his mother cried and he and his brother tried to console her. The leaders mentioned that it was good for parents as well as children to share their feelings with one another and encouraged the children to support their parents and in turn draw support from them.

The parents often provide us with material for questions. In one parents group meeting, the mothers complained about how they were frequently the recipients of their child's anger while the noncustodial fathers were treated as the "good guys." Based on this information, we constructed the following question: *A child is angry at his father. But instead of acting angry at his father, he acts nice with his father and acts angry with his mother. Could this happen?* We used this question in a special joint session of parents and children together. Discussion of this question helped to strengthen the parent-child bond. The children all felt that the hypothetical situation could definitely happen. Carl stated that he got angry at his father and took it out on his mother. Carl's mom suggested that Carl is worried that if he expresses anger at his father the father will stop seeing him. Carl said, "I feel sorry for my mom because she's the one getting dumped on." His mom expressed how good she felt hearing Carl share this sentiment and grant psychological weight and validity to her concerns.

The items described give a flavor of the types of questions that can be developed and the impact they have on group discussion. It should be clear to the reader that any issue can be phrased as a game item and used productively. We urge others to unleash their imagination and create questions that can be discussed in the *Could This Happen Game*.

USING THE GAME AS A TEACHING TOOL

The game provides the leader with an opportunity to provoke discussions about cooperation, to raise issues about male-female relationships, and to delve into feelings about belonging and rejection. The method of choosing teams is one such opportunity. The leader can choose from among several alternative methods of team composition. If a discussion of male-female issues is desirable, the leader might divide the group into one team of boys and one of girls. Alternatively, if the leader would like to discuss the sociometric patterns in the group as a prelude to discussing feelings of rejection, he or she might allow the children to choose their own teams.

Another excellent teaching opportunity arises when team reps offer their guesses concerning the most common answer. A rep choosing an unpopular answer may be ridiculed by his or her teammates. Should this occur, the leader can encourage the child to discuss his or her feelings and provide feedback to the tormenters using skills acquired in *The Children's Feedback Game.* The discussion can then be focused on experiences of being ridiculed at school and in neighborhood play situations. The group can then explore positive alternatives to ridicule and blame.

SUMMARY AND CONCLUSIONS

The Children's Feedback Game, though specifically developed for use with children of divorce, is equally suitable for use in other situations. Training classmates to give feedback to one another could eliminate much of the time-consuming and emotionally draining disciplinary activities of teachers. Parents too could use this game to reduce sibling rivalry manifested in taunting, teasing, and tattling.

The *Could This Happen Game* could also be used with populations other than children of divorce. The game capitalizes on children's desire to demonstrate to others that they are "correct" and their willingness to offer evidence to prove it. Though we have constructed items that highlight beliefs and anxiety about divorce, different items could be constructed to open discussion about other areas of concern. For example, guidance counselors could use this game to discuss test anxiety. They might offer the following item: *A child got a failing grade on a test. When he told his mother about his grade, she stopped loving him. Could this happen?* Here, the guidance counselor could explore some of the pressures children may feel to perform well lest their parents reject them. Teachers could also use the game to discuss sex-role stereotypes. Here is a possible question: *A girl liked playing baseball and didn't like playing with dolls. None of the girls in her class wanted to be her friend. They all made fun of her. Could this happen?*

The game could also be used to open discussions about prejudice, other stereotypes, career aspirations—the list of possibilities is limited only by the imagination of the user. With judiciously chosen items, productive discussions are likely to ensue. Even children who are silent spectators can gain from these discussions as they listen to the concerns voiced by other children and realize that they are not alone in their worries. Further, the use of this game legitimizes the assignment of plausibility to *any* concern. Thus, it may encourage children who might otherwise think their worry is "ridiculous" and so keep it to themselves to share it with an adult and have the opportunity to discuss their fears and possibly have them allayed.

Although we did not document it, we have used extensions of this activity in other contexts. For example, we used captured digital images in work with clients in individual therapy, rather than in a group context. We also asked clients to bring in photographs that we scanned into our computer and saved as digital image files. We have asked children to place digital images of themselves next to each other and then write a story about themselves and how they felt in picture A and in picture B. We have also asked children to transform the images in a number of different ways. Using a variety of software packages (e.g., *KidPix Studio Deluxe, Adobe Photo Deluxe*), they can create novel and amusing transformations of pictures. For example, using *KidPix* they can import a scanned photograph and create a scene using that image together with "stamps." For children of divorce, for example, the fantasy of reuniting the family is a powerful one. Taking a scanned photograph of their father and one of their mother, they can use *KidPix* stamps of a dog and a cat, add a house and flowers, and use *KidPix* pens to draw arms, which they add to the portrait of their father so that they depict him hugging their mother in this idyllic scene. Then they can save this picture and import it into a word-processing program and dictate a story to the therapist, who types it and prints it out. The story can then become the basis for a discussion of their reunion fantasy. Based on what they learn from this discussion, they can rewrite the story so that it is more realistic. Over the course of the months that the child spends in therapy, he or she would accumulate a collection of pictures and stories. These could then be printed and bound in a book the child has authored. The child would name the book, have his or her picture on the first page, and a section called "About the Author," in which he or she creates an autobiographical statement. The book can become a treasured possession that reminds the child of what he or she learned during the course of the therapy. Children can also choose to show this book to their parents as a way of informing them about the issues of concern to the child.

Throughout this chapter, we have suggested that *The Children's Feedback Game* and the *Could This Happen Game* can be creatively used to positively influence child psychosocial development. We have pointed out only a few of the therapeutic and teaching possibilities the games afford. Before using the game, leaders are encouraged to carefully consider the needs of the children in the group and to exercise much flexibility in adapting the game to meet these needs. Above all, leaders are exhorted to give great weight to the playful attitude with which most children approach games. Although the games were designed as therapeutic and teaching tools, we feel strongly that children learn most when they are given the freedom to laugh and to behave with a large measure of spontaneity. And what could be better than joyful learning?

REFERENCES

Ackerman, N. (1958). *The psychodynamics of family life.* New York: Basic Books.

Chekhov, M. (1953). *To the actor.* New York: Harper & Row.

Epstein, Y., & Borduin, C. (1984). The children's feedback game. *American Journal of Psychotherapy, 38,* 63–71.

Epstein, Y., & Borduin, C. (1985). Could this happen: A game for children of divorce. *Psychotherapy: Theory, Research, and Practice, 22,* 770–773.

Epstein, Y., Borduin, C., & Wexler, A. (1985). Children helping children: A case illustration of a community response to the needs of children of divorce. *Special Services in the Schools, 2,* 73–93.

Festinger, L. (1954). A theory of social comparison processes. *Human Relations, 7,* 117–140.

Ginott, H. (1961). *Group psychotherapy with children.* New York: McGraw-Hill.

Hovland, C., Janis, I., & Kelly, H. (1953). *Communication and persuasion.* New Haven, CT: Yale University Press.

Kelman, H. (1958). Compliance, identification, and internalization: Three processes of attitude change. *Journal of Conflict Resolution, 2,* 51–60.

Lieberman, M., Yalom, I., & Miles, M. (1973). *Encounter groups: First facts.* New York: Basic Books.

Mead, G.H. (1934). *Mind, self and society.* Chicago: University of Chicago Press.

Odom, S., & Strain, P. (1984). Peer mediated approaches to promoting children's social interaction: A review. *American Journal of Orthopsychiatry, 54,* 544–557.

Rhodes, S. (1973). Short term groups of latency age children in a school setting. *International Journal of Group Psychotherapy, 23* 204–216.

Rosenberg, H.S. (1987). *Creative drama and imagination: Transforming ideas into action.* New York: Holt, Rinehart, and Winston.

Rosenberg, H.S., Castellano, R., Chrein, G., & Pinciotti, P. (1983). Creative drama and imagery. In Shorr, Sobel, Robin, & Connella (Eds.), *Imagery: Theoretical and clinical applications.* New York: Plenum Press.

Rosenberg, H.S., Pinciotti, P., Chrein, G., & Castellano, R. (1985). The iii system: Imagery and creative drama. *Journal of Creative Behavior, 19*(2), 142–154.

Spolin, V. (1975). *Theater game file.* St. Louis, MO: CEMREL

Yalom, I. (1970). *The theory and practice of group psychotherapy.* New York: Basic Books.

CHAPTER ELEVEN

Using Games and Game Play in Group Therapy with Sexually Abused Children and Adolescents

BILLIE F. CORDER

Group treatment has often been described as an effective intervention for sexually abused children and adolescents (Berliner & Ernst, 1984; Berliner & MacQuivey, 1984; Burgess & Holmstrong, 1978). Many therapists feel that the ability of victims to deal with their "sense of differentness" and with their devalued sense of self is critical to treatment, and can best be addressed in groups of peers with similar experiences. Berliner and her coworkers approach treatment with these children in a time-limited format that is fairly structured and utilizes treatment goals focusing on cognitive integration and intellectual understanding of the abuse and their reaction to it, developing empathy for and affinity for others who have been abused, enhancing self-esteem, and focusing on learning methods for protecting themselves from further threats of abuse (Berliner & Ernst, 1984).

The author, with coworkers, has developed a format for structuring time-limited groups for children and adolescents that focuses on some of these same goals, and in addition attempts to develop coping skills similar to those shown by the "invulnerable children" described by Rutter (1978) and Anthony and Cohler (1987). The children described in their research had developed defense mechanisms that allowed them to cope adequately despite having experienced trauma, chaotic backgrounds, chronic stress, and some abuse. The observations of Rutter and of Anthony and Cohler suggested that these children's coping mechanisms could be summarized as the ability to use intellectualization and utilize problem-solving skills, capabilities for seeking out support and assistance from others in their environment, use of some types of cognitive relabeling of their negative experiences, and a capacity for maintaining their self-esteem despite many assaults on their self-concept from the environment and their experiences. Our own goals have been to use time-limited groups not only to develop methods for protecting themselves in the future, increasing their self-esteem, and offering opportunity for relating to other victims, but to also develop some of the other defense mechanisms that might increase their "invulnerability" to the effects of their previous victimization. Structured group discussion has centered around game activities and special coloring books to aid in developing cognitive and emotional mastery skills to handle their trauma. In addition to role play, special playing through "chants and cheers" was used to improve their self-esteem and decrease their sense of differentness and isolation (Corder & Corder, 1989). Special board games, role play, and other play-oriented activities were used to structure and practice problem-solving skills and to identify potentially dangerous, abusive situations in the future, for which they would practice possible avenues for self-protection. Coloring books, games, and role play were used to increase children's ability to identify sources of help and how to seek them out in their environment (e.g., identifying how and whom to contact about potential abuse).

Although this chapter focuses on materials used with children and adolescents in the group, conjoint groups and alternate inclusion of mothers were added to many of the treatment groups. At times, mothers joined into the game play or structured activities when included in the child's treatment group. This was seen as an extremely valuable addition to the work of the group, but some groups appeared to function adequately and to have children show changes in follow-up observations and reports without the addition of a conjoint mothers group. However, it should be noted that all groups required weekly "homework" from children which involved their discussion and working through some of the weekly goals of the group with their mother or support person. A more thorough description of the groups may be seen in the author's *Structured Adolescent Psychotherapy Groups* (Corder, 1996) and *Structured Therapy Groups for Sexually Abused Children and Adolescents* (Corder, 1999).

GROUP PROCEDURES AND USE OF GAMES WITH CHILDREN

The Wouldn't It Be Nice—But the Way It Really Is Coloring Book

Generally, groups met for 15 to 20 sessions over a four- to five-month period for one hour per session. The eight group members, age 6 to 9, had already been identified as abused and had attended a number of individual sessions with Department of Social Service staff. In introductory sessions, the children took turns reading information from a special coloring book, with the group coloring on small drawing boards on the floor of the group room. The coloring book was developed to begin intellectual understanding of abuse and to form group cohesion through sharing feelings of victimization. Cathartic sharing of feelings was also encouraged, within a structured format, by asking each child to relate his or her feelings about the issues being addressed by the coloring book. It was felt that using this structured format could encourage verbalization of feelings within the format of a pleasurable activity without raising the anxiety level of the group to an unproductive level, which might result in "shutdown" of these feelings.

Each section of the book was divided into two parts. One page had pictures of the feelings and fantasies children from past groups had described; this was labeled "Wouldn't It Be Nice." An example is: "Wouldn't it be nice if all touches were nice, right touches, and children could grow up and never have an adult or other child touch them with a wrong touch or make them do things that feel bad?" A picture to color showed a person holding a child's hand in a pleasant, relaxed manner with two blanks underneath for which the group member filled in another example of a "nice, right touch."

Facing this page was another page to color labeled "But the Way It *Really* Is," with drawings of faces of many children to be colored, and the following information:

The way it really is . . . that you are not the only child who has had a bad, wrong touch. There are many, many girls and boys that this has happened to. Some people have said that one out of every five children has been given a wrong touch, or made to be things which are bad touches and make them feel bad. When this is on their private (sexual) parts, it is called sexual abuse. Suppose you have 30 kids in your class at school. Many people say that at least 5 or 6 of them have probably had a bad touch or may have a bad touch someday.

While the children color, group leaders continue to emphasize their lack of differentness by saying that if there are X number of children in our city, this means that X number may have been abused or possibly will be abused. In the illustration they are coloring, the children are asked if they can tell from the faces which have been abused. Then all their similarity and lack of differentness is pointed out.

Each of these pages in the coloring book are divided into a section called "What We Can Do about It." Along with information the group reads aloud and discusses, there may be blanks or puzzles to fill in or directions for role play. In the example above, there may be lists of ways to keep safe and what to do if a situation feels potentially dangerous. There are pages with lists of good and bad touches to separate, instructions about how and whom to contact if a child has received a bad touch, and more.

The purpose of this section of the coloring book is to encourage intellectualization and to help children develop specific problem-solving skills. At the same time, reasons why people have not used these solutions in the past are discussed, based on questions such as "Why would a person be afraid to tell their parent about someone who gave them a bad touch?" and "Why would a parent find it hard to believe that a friend or family member might give their child a bad touch?" Each child kept their own crayons and book in a plastic bag in the room and returned to the book over a period of time in the sessions. Topics to be handled and discussed within the group format were often introduced with the use of the coloring book, and then continued through other games and activities.

HOMEWORK

For each session, a page of "homework" was assigned to be used with their mother or parenting figure during the week. The homework served a variety of purposes. The tasks were linked to the subjects covered in the group and were a repetition for the group members, increasing intellectual understanding of the subject. They also allowed for a positive, purposeful interaction between parenting figure and child during which the child could develop feelings of mastery from previous experience of knowing the answers to the tasks and questions. For example, one of the tasks of a specific homework was:

> Ask your parent what they think is a good plan the two of you could make if you thought you might be in danger of getting a bad touch from someone. If you felt uncomfortable and sort of scared about being left alone with someone, even if they were a friend or family, you should: *(mother and child fill in the blank on homework page).* If a person touched you in a way that made you feel bad and uncomfortable, no matter who the person was, you should: *(mother and child fill in the blank on homework page).*

Because the group had already discussed these issues, they would be prepared for the parent's response and even be able to make prompts and suggestions and "coach" the parent in handling the task. Often, these homework sessions led to sharing of feelings between parent and child as well as making specific problem-solving plans.

Homework was read and "graded" each week. This served as another repetition of learning tasks, increasing opportunities for intellectualization and also increased self-esteem, as each child was praised for even attempting to handle the task. In the rare event that a parent did not complete the task, the child was excused and asked to respond with what he or she thought the parent would have said.

STRUCTURED ROLE ASSIGNMENT

The author has experimented with a game-like assignment of certain "roles" for each member in the group as a method for developing feelings of mastery and for increasing group cohesion. These roles were assigned in a game-like fashion each session by filling a basket with eight cards (one for each member) that described various roles and functions within the group. Children closed their eyes and pulled out a card that named their "role" for the session. Some of the roles were:

- Host and Hostess—These members passed out refreshments and cleaned up after the group at end of session. This role also served to teach simple social skills and manners.

- Role Player—These members were assigned to take role-play parts in any of the role-play situations suggested in the coloring book or other materials.
- Homework Grader—This member gave out weekly homework, collected the prior week's work, and helped the group assign a grade to each paper (always an A if the person made any effort to complete the task).
- Rules Enforcer—This member helped the therapist carry out the simple list of "group rules" which were written out at the first session and continued to hang on a large piece of paper in the group room throughout the sessions. These were simple requirements, such as Do not talk while others are talking; Always at least try to complete the things you are asked to do in the group; Always at least try to do your homework before the next group meeting.
- Member Helper—The member helper gave assistance to any member having trouble with a task or in expressing feelings.
- Group Summarizer—With the help of the therapist, this member was asked to tell what the group had learned and what tasks they had done during the session.

All of these roles were handled in a game-like fashion. The roles were perceived as fun by members and appeared to increase their feelings of mastery and control over the group process.

CHANTS, SHOUTS, AND CHEERS

In an activity similar to "brags" used by Berliner and Ernst (1984), group leaders taught members a series of "cheers" related to the task areas being handled in the group sessions. At times, the children played a patty-cake game in pairs while repeating the cheers; at other times, they stood, yelled, and even developed some cheerleader-type movements which they used as a group when they recited their cheers. The purpose of this activity was to engage the children in active, fun movements while they recited statements that were aimed at increasing their self-esteem and feelings of mastery. The children were reminded each session that "sometimes bad things happen to good people, especially when they have not learned to protect themselves," and what they can do to keep this from happening. In addition to specific cheers aimed at the group's weekly session activities, they recited at each session the following cheers: "I'm a good person, I'm proud of me" and "I've been through a lot, but look how strong I've got."

To promote feelings of healthy denial and to encourage their feelings of mastery over their future, as they learned ways to keep themselves safe from abuse, they recited: "That was THEN, but this is NOW. I WON'T abuse, and I know HOW!"

THE MOVING ON AND GETTING STRONGER GAME

Using a simple board game format, the therapist developed another game to assist children in learning cognitive relabeling of their experiences and in developing intellectualization and specific coping skills for dealing with their past victimization and for protecting themselves in the future. The board was illustrated with children who were progressing from "Sad Valley" to "Mixed Up Mountain" and onward to "Learning Lake," "Positive Plain," and finally to "Safe Plain" and "Smart Mountain" because they had learned ways to handle their feelings and to keep themselves safe. Each child had a game piece (usually geometric forms from a party store) and took turns rolling dice to determine the number of places he or she moved on the board. The board spaces were labeled to correspond with stacks of *learning* cards, *practicing* cards, and *telling* cards.

Learning cards were used to promote intellectualization and as a repetition of many aspects of the learning tasks approached in the group. One example of such a *learning* card task (already discussed in coloring book sessions) was, "Ask somebody in the group to guess how many children in our city have been sexually abused. Tell why you think their answer is right or wrong."

Practicing cards involved some role playing to promote mastery and learning coping skills. The member or leader read aloud a situation described on the cards and asked the members who drew role-play cards to help act our their solution to the problem situation. The group member drawing the card "directs" the scene and explains the solution. For example, "Suppose a person in your neighborhood who has made you feel funny or scared you in the past by seeming to start to give you a bad touch, asks your mother to take you to the park on a picnic alone. Let's practice what you would say to your mother and what you could do to feel safe."

Telling cards required group members to tell something personal about their own experience of victimization, to share with the other group members. This was seen as both promoting cathartic expression of feeling and decreasing feelings of differentness among group members. Items progressed in the stack (arranged beforehand by the therapist) from very low levels of intimacy and personal disclosure to more specific and personal information required by the end of the group's allotted sessions. An example of these cards is "Tell how you picked out the person you finally told about the abuse. Why did you choose him or her? If you did not tell anyone about the abuse before, who would you tell now if you were afraid you might be abused?"

THAT WAS THEN BUT THIS IS NOW TELEVISION SHOW

The purpose of this "pretend" TV show was to rehearse mastery activities, encourage growth of positive self-esteem, and promote intellectualization defenses. Members were divided into two teams. Using materials that had been discussed within the group setting, the therapist took the role of a TV game show host, complete with toy microphone and sometimes with a large cardboard TV set frame through which the rest of the group viewed each "contestant." Each member was asked a question related to the mastery tasks handled earlier, while other team members encouraged his or her answer and cheered and clapped. Score was kept for the game, and each member received small prizes (candy, erasers, stickers, gum) for correct answers. Because members received enough coaching from their team members to ensure a correct answer for each question, the TV show always ended in a "tie" for the two teams.

MATCHING FEELINGS AND FACES GAME

The author has developed "Dr. Corder's Feeling Faces," a group of cards with sets of faces that illustrate feelings labeled guilty, sad, confused, mad, happy, mixed up, angry, and scared. A set of these faces was given to each group member for use during several games. Using the game *Wanda's Story* (described below), members were instructed to hold up the card that illustrated the feelings they perceived the story characters were having.

WANDA'S STORY

For this game-exercise, the therapist read aloud a specially written story that centered around the sexual abuse of a girl named Wanda. At significant points, the therapist read sentences with blank spaces in place of descriptions of how Wanda or other characters were feeling. Group members were asked to hold up the card they thought showed how the story characters were feeling. Then the therapist questioned group members about why they had chosen a particular card.

The purpose of the game was to help the group explore and eventually verbalize their own feelings about victimization, as well as develop intellectualization defenses and coping skills that were described by the story's plot. In the story, Wanda grew from feeling fear, guilt, and confusion to understanding some of the reasons persons could abuse others and learning how to protect herself from victimization. The story ended with Wanda teaching the things she had learned to her own daughter.

My Own Story

Following *Wanda's Story,* group members took turns using their set of feelings cards in response to a very general story outline read by the therapist. The outline contained sentences such as "I was abused by _____. The abuse made me feel _____. I didn't know what to do about it, but finally I told _____. They seemed to act very _____ when I told them." Their story followed the plot of Wanda's story. In the end, they were asked to tell what their own plan was to stop further victimization, and what they would tell their own daughter. In addition to encouraging recognition and verbalization of feelings, the game also provided rehearsal of specific mastery and coping skills related to victimization.

Drawing Feelings and Facts about Your Own Story

After the two stories had been read, members were asked to move to separate parts of the room to draw a picture of the "worst thing about what happened to you when you were abused." The therapist moved about the room to each child separately, talking quietly about his or her drawing. Some children were able to produce only abstract, darkly colored scrawls, which they described as showing how angry they felt about the abuse. Others drew a picture of their face looking sad or crying and spoke of being sent to foster homes or separated from their families. After discussing some of these feelings with each child, the therapist asked them to produce a drawing that showed them after they had learned to understand their feelings, and after they were beginning to feel safe and strong and to know how to get help and to protect themselves in the future. This session ended with the therapist's giving many verbal positive strokes for their progress and a repetition of their chants and cheers.

FIRST LADY PICNIC

One of the closing sessions for the group consisted of planning a picnic for the group within the session, to which they pretended to invite the current president's wife (who was role-played by the therapist). The First Lady congratulated members on their progress and asked if there were a message they would like to send to the president for him to take up with Congress about sexual abuse. One of the "messages" was "Tell the President he probably doesn't know how many children have been abused. I thought I was the only one. And tell him that every girl and boy should be able to go to a group like this one."

TRANSITION OBJECT REHEARSAL

As a transition object and to rehearse their learning cues, during the last one or two sessions each group member was given a tiny stuffed animal called "The That Was Then But This Is Now Wise Puppy." The stuffed animal was to serve as a focus for drill and rehearsal of some of the cognitive behavior modification techniques learned in the group. They were told to pretend that the Wise Puppy had been at each group session and knew all the things they had discussed and learned. Then they were told to pretend that the Puppy could whisper to them if they held him to their ear and listened very carefully. The Puppy would whisper their chant to them: "That was then but this is now. You won't be abused and you know how," or "You're a good person, I'm proud of you. You've been through a lot, but look how strong you've got." If they needed to remember ways to keep from being abused, the Puppy could help keep them calm and help them remember what they had learned, as well as remind them of the list of people they had selected who could help them.

If they felt guilty or mixed up about their own feelings and actions related to the abuse, they rehearsed having the Puppy whisper to them "Sometimes bad things happen to good people. The abuse was not your fault, and you are stronger and wiser now." The children appeared to enjoy these cognitive rehearsals and exercises. Examples of problem situations suggested by the therapist were experiencing mixed up feelings toward the abuser, feeling as if they were different from all other children, and handling their anger toward people whom they felt had failed to protect them in the past.

GRADUATION, DIPLOMAS, AND FOLLOW-UP

At group "graduation," members marched to recorded music to receive their "diploma" from the "That Was Then, But This Is Now" group. The diploma listed all the main points they had learned in the group: that they were not alone, that 1 in 5 children suffer some kind of sexual abuse, that the abuse was not their fault, ways to protect themselves in the future, and so on. The therapist sent a monthly group newsletter to members for three months; this reminded them of their progress in the group and their list of helping people they could contact, and listed exercises they could complete with their parenting figure and phone numbers of local social workers.

DISCUSSION OF GROUP TECHNIQUES WITH CHILDREN

The games developed and game play used were centered around attempts to develop cognitive, intellectualization, problem-solving, and other skills described as typical of "invulnerable children" in research by Rutter (1987) and Anthony and Cohler (1987). In addition to encouraging cathartic verbalization of their feelings, the games were seen as an enjoyable technique for structuring exercises through which members could build self-esteem and lose their feelings of differentness from other children. Some aspects of the games were similar to techniques used by Berliner and Ernst (1984), and part of the format for the group process was modeled after stages described by Pynoos and Spencer (1988) in their interviews with severely traumatized children. At times, mothers were included in the groups and assisted the children in playing games, coloring, and so on. For some other groups, conjoint groups were offered for mothers where the group process was discussed and they were able to express their own feelings about the trauma, treatment for trauma, and their role in the child's progress toward mastery.

The games and tools used in this group were developed by the author and are covered in some of her publications (Corder, 1996, 1999). Using the same group format, therapists familiar with groups for sexually abused children should also be able to develop some of their own games, using "blank" formats for board games offered by commercial printers such as Childswork/Childsplay (1999). This company also offers a package of materials titled "A Sexual Abuse Prevention Program to Instill Confidence" (Childswork/Childsplay, 1999) for children 3 to 5 and 6 to 12, which uses a combination of books, songs, puppets, and activity sheets to teach basic safety rules, concepts of good and bad touching, and how to tell an adult about abuse.

GROUP PROCEDURES AND USE OF GAMES WITH ADOLESCENTS

Therapy groups with sexually abused adolescents that were developed by the author were based on the same theoretical approach described earlier. The group process was used to develop some of the coping skills, cognitive behavior modification techniques, self-esteem building, loss of sense of differentness, cathartic expression of feelings, and methods for protection from further abuse that were the basis for the younger children's groups. Some of the specific games and techniques used in these groups are discussed in the author's publications noted earlier (Corder, 1996, 1999). The eight group members ranged in age from 13 to 15 and had been previously identified as sexual abuse victims and seen for various periods of time in individual sessions, typically with staff of a local Department of Social Services. For some groups, conjoint sessions with mothers were offered. At other times, mothers were allowed to attend every other session with their teen. Some groups were held solely with adolescents when there were so many transportation and other problems that the majority of mothers could not be present. Although conjoint and shared groups appeared more intense and moved more quickly, satisfactory work was also completed in groups where the only contact with mothers was through homework assignments.

THE THREE WISHES GAME

Each adolescent group began with the therapist as Special Wishes Fairy granting each member three wishes surrounding issues of the sexual abuse they had experienced. These three wishes were then used as the basis for structuring the activities of the group. For example, all members wished that the abuse had never occurred. The therapist, now as therapist, stated that the wish realistically could not be granted, but that the group would do the next best thing: Members would learn how to handle feelings about the abuse, understand the experience, and learn how to protect themselves in the future. Other common wishes were that abuse would not happen to their siblings or their own children. This wish was "granted" in a limited fashion when the therapist stated that the group would learn ways to protect not only themselves, but others and how to be safe from abuse in the future. Another wish that group members often was, "I wish the first time I had sex, it would be with my husband, not by abuser." Using cognitive restructuring techniques, the therapist stated, "What you had with the person who abused you was sexual abuse. It was not loving, responsible, shared sex between two adult people who care about each other. When you fall in love and marry, you will have the chance to have REAL loving, responsible, shared sex for the first time. Because what you had before was just using you in a sexually abusive way. It CAN be the REAL first time for you and the person you love."

It has been the author's experience that the three wishes of group members typically reflect the format of the planned group, because they deal with the important issues of abuse: anger, guilt, confusion, differentness, low self-esteem, feelings of powerlessness, and lack of information about the facts of sexual abuse. With the Three Wishes Game, the therapist was able to relate the format of the group to the members' own needs in a relevant manner.

THE GROUP ROLE BASKET

In a game similar to one of the children's games described earlier, various roles were written on cards picked randomly from the Group Role Basket at the beginning of each session. The roles were similar for both groups. Eight members chose among Hostess, Rules Enforcer, Summarizer/Recorder (for Group Book, described below), Encourager, Other Side Viewer (person asked to explain how another person might view the situation being discussed, such as how a parent or authority figure might feel and react), Homework Grader, and two Role Players (who act out any problem situations or role play suggested by material being discussed in group).

TEACHING OTHERS ABOUT ABUSE: OUR OWN GROUP BOOK

As one of the tasks of the group, the therapist outlined the development of a little book by the group members to be completed by the end of the group. The purpose of this book was to teach others about abuse. It would contain all the facts and problem-solving skills they learned from the group, and they would be able to have copies to use with siblings. This task required a summary of each session, so the member who picked the role of Group Recorder provided a summary of what was learned and done in the group (with as much assistance and coaching from the therapist as needed).

THE LIFE GAME

The Life Game, a special therapeutic board game developed by the therapist, has been described in other publications (Corder, 1988, 1996, 1999). The game board contains squares labeled *Knowing Yourself, Understanding Others, Dealing with Feelings,* and *Learning about Sexual Abuse,* which correspond with stacks of cards suggesting questions and tasks. After rolling dice, players move about the squares, taking a card required by the square on which they land. The cards themselves contain questions and tasks related to the developmental tasks of adolescence, and can be "stacked" by therapists before the group meets to ensure items relevant to the particular session's task and goal. The *Learning about Sexual Abuse* cards contain information for discussion meant to promote intellectualization defenses as well as to drill on specific information. The Life Game was used throughout the 12 to 15 group sessions for limited time periods. Many similar developmental tasks could be addressed by therapists without access to a specific game board, by simply having a series of envelopes with questions and tasks written on paper and rolling dice to determine from which envelope to pick.

MIRROR, MIRROR ON THE WALL

For this game, a large mirror was set on a table, and each member sat before it, asking a question about his or her sexual abuse experience. These were answered by the therapist as "the mirror." Typical questions were: "Why didn't my mother believe me when I first told her about the abuse?" and "Will my boyfriend (or husband) hold the sexual abuse against me when I tell him about it?" Using this game-like structure appeared to make it easier for group members to verbalize their concerns and questions and seemed to provide a more enjoyable format for promoting intellectualized defenses and drill for specific information on issues of safety and so on.

A Letter to My Abuser

Members were asked to write a letter (not to be mailed, but discussed in the group) to their abuser. For those who had difficulty formulating a letter, a structured format was available to make certain that all issues discussed in the group were covered:

> To My Abuser:
>   I wanted to write you so you would know that I know what you did to me was wrong, bad, and against the law. You need to learn that what you did was really bad because _____. And you know it is against the law because _____. I wanted you to know that what you did made me feel _____. The reason that I wasn't able to do anything about it at first when it happened was _____. What my mother and my family should have done was _____. If I had my way, what I would like to do to you now is _____.
>   Although what you did made me unhappy and hurt me, I am learning how to handle it and I am going to get strong and happy. What you did was wrong and bad, and you need to _____. This is what I would like to see happen to you in the future: _____. I will do everything I can to make sure that you never have a chance to do what you did to me to anyone else, especially anyone in our family. The things I may be able to do to keep you from it are _____. And in ending this letter, something else I would like to say is _____.

These letters were read out loud in the group, and group members and the therapist gave feedback about any confusion or mixed messages and made suggestions of feelings not included in the letter. This technique appeared to allow for a good deal of emotional catharsis without promoting regression and to encourage members to develop coping skills and promote feelings of future safety.

THE 21-YEAR-OLD VISIT

For this game-like exercise, members were asked to visualize and verbalize what they would like to be doing when they are 21, including the type of job they would like to have, the car they would like to be driving, and how they would like to look and dress. Then they were asked to role-play a visit to their abuser, appearing to the abuser as a successful, attractive grown-up. They were to imagine where they would like to confront the abuser and what they would really like to say to the abuser. Group members took turns role-playing themselves and their abusers. The confrontations appeared to be quite cathartic and emphasized members' expectation that they would handle the trauma and get on with their life, while the abuser would probably remain a confused and often frightened person. One group member had read about grown daughters suing their father for abuse, and insisted that she planned to do so; she acted out her announcement to her father and seemed excited by her new sense of power and control, even though she might never follow through on this plan.

LEARNING ABOUT SEXUAL ABUSE TV QUIZ SHOW

Just as in the younger group, members were divided into two teams with the therapist as quiz show host. Teams were allowed to encourage and assist members as they faced the microphone and questions, and correct answers were rewarded with small prizes. As with the younger children, the contest ended in a tie. This not only served as a drill for tasks this promoted intellectualization defenses and coping skills, but appeared to make learning facts about sexual abuse interesting and less threatening for the group.

CHEERS AND CHANTS

These were essentially the same cheers used in younger children's groups. The main difference was the complex cheerleader-type movements and rhythms that the group developed and used while practicing the cheers.

GRADUATION AND TRANSITION OBJECTS

A similar graduation march and party with "diplomas" was planned for the adolescent group members. Their transition object was a thin but sturdy silver chain bracelet donated by a local merchant. They were told to touch and manipulate the bracelet often to remind them of their success in the group, their sense of belonging with other group members, and as a reminder of their new strength, knowledge, safety, and control over their environment with the knowledge and experiences they had gained in their group.

SUMMARY

This chapter has outlined some of the games and game play utilized in structured psychotherapy groups with children age 6 to 9 and 13 to 16. The goals for the groups were to allow exploration and catharsis of feelings, develop cognitive relabeling (causes of abuse, responsibility, effects), rebuild self-esteem (facts about abuse, growth from new skills), and to promote cognitive reorganization and mastery of the trauma experience (avoidance of guilt, identifying support systems), along with the development of specific coping skills for protection from future possible abuse. These goals reflected the coping mechanisms described by Rutter (1978) as typical of those seen in "invulnerable" children who appear able to develop adequately despite trauma and chronic stressors.

Although some of the play utilizes special game boards developed by the therapist, many of the activities can be modified for use by therapists working with similar groups of children.

REFERENCES

Anthony, E.J., & Cohler, B.J. (1987). *The invulnerable child.* New York: Guilford Press.

Berliner, L., & Ernst, E. (1984). Group work with preadolescent sexual assault victims. In I. Stuart & J. Greer (Eds.), *Victims of sexual aggression* (pp. 105–123). New York: Van Nostrand-Reinhold.

Berliner, L., & MacQuivey, K. (1984). A therapy group for female adolescent victims of sexual abuse. In R. Rosenbaum (Ed.), *Varieties of short-term therapy groups.* New York: McGraw-Hill.

Burgess, A., & Holmstrong, L. (1978). Accessory to sex: Pressure, sex, and secrecy. In A. Burgess, N. Groth, L. Holmstrom, & S. Sgroi (Eds.), *Sexual assault of children and adolescents* (pp. 105–124). Lexington, MA: Heath.

Corder, B.F. (1988). Therapeutic games in group therapy with adolescents. In C. Schaefer & S. Reid (Eds.), *Game play: Therapeutic uses of childhood games* (pp. 279–290). New York: Wiley.

Corder, B.F. (1996). *Structured therapy groups with adolescents.* Sarasota, FL: Professional Resource Press.

Corder, B.F. (1999). *Structured therapy groups with sexually abused children and adolescents.* Sarasota, FL: Professional Resource Press.

Pynoos, R., & Spencer, E. (1988). Witness to violence: The child interview. In R. Thomas & M. Hertzig (Eds.), *Annual progress in child psychiatry and child development* (pp. 299–325). New York: Brunner/Mazel.

Rutter, M. (1978). Early sources of security and competence. In J. Bruner & A. Gaston (Eds.), *Human growth and development* (pp. 153–188). Oxford, England: Clarendon.

PART FOUR

THERAPEUTIC GAMES
FOR CHILDREN
WITH ADHD

CHAPTER TWELVE

Use of the *Stop, Relax, and Think* Game with ADHD Children

REBECCA BRIDGES

Recent years have brought high interest and greater focus to the problems of inattention and impulsivity in children. Attention-deficit disorder with hyperactivity (ADHD) is now practically a household term. With the increase in identification and recognition of ADHD indicators in children, the diagnosis appears to be more frequently assigned. Impulsivity expressed by many ADHD children creates concerns regarding their safety and that of others. Inattention generates concerns about their judgment in problem solving, development of social skills and responsibility, and general life management. Additionally, a number of ADHD children also have learning disabilities which compound their difficulties and may contribute to greater frustration and stress.

Mental health and counseling professionals are challenged to find resources to help the average ADHD child and his or her parents. Research indicates that a combination of education and skill training, as well as the use of stimulant medication, offers the greatest benefit in the treatment of ADHD (Barkley, 1988; DuPaul, Guevremont, & Barkley, 1991).

This chapter presents the use of the *Stop, Relax, and Think* game as a powerful tool for the education and skill development of the ADHD child.

First a brief discussion of research and current understandings of the ADHD syptomatology profile is offered. Then, the *Stop, Relax, and Think* game's structure, objectives, and playing details are described. Last, the use of the *Stop, Relax, and Think* game as an intervention tool with ADHD children individually, in groups, and with their parents is presented. A brief description of the process of the game's production for interested readers is offered as an addendum to the chapter.

ATTENTION-DEFICIT WITH HYPERACTIVITY DISORDER

The recent focus on children with ADHD has generated an increase in information regarding its prevalence, diagnosis, and developmental course. Although prevalence estimates vary greatly, a figure of 3 percent to 5 percent is commonly quoted (American Psychiatric Association, 1987). Numerous studies have shown that children diagnosed with ADHD have significant differences from normed youth on measures of attention span, activity level, and impulse control (Ross & Ross, 1982; Whalen & Henker, 1980). Barkley (1988) asserts that "ADHD children have considerable difficulty adhering to rules constructed for them by the social community" (p. 72). In addition, "ADHD children have difficulties in sustaining compliance to the task of instructions, especially when the task is boring and there are few consequences for doing so" (p. 72). Many ADHD children grow into "at-risk" youth, impulsively making decisions without full consideration of the consequences. This acting without thinking during teen years can lead to risk-taking and potentially life-endangering behavior.

Assessment measures and treatment techniques are now more available than was the case in the early 1980s (Barkley, 1988, 1995). Although 70 percent to 80 percent of children diagnosed with ADHD respond favorably to psychostimulants, the exclusive use of medication to address the ADHD symptom complex is often insufficient (CHADD, 1999). A multimodal approach is recommended by research. Children need information that will help them become their own life managers. Alternative and consequential thinking skills (Shure & Spivak, 1981) taught to children have been shown to have a bearing on improvement in their behavior. Levine (1987) states:

Children with attention deficits and their parents are in desperate need of information regarding attention deficits. Such education can alleviate anxiety, guilt, and accusatory crossfire. . . . Thus, a child may be helped to understand his or her impulsivity. Then certain tasks may be designed to enable that child to practice being less impulsive. (p. 128)

In spite of this, according to a recent survey of mental health providers in a managed care network, references to education of the child about ADHD were found only 7 percent of the time in the treatment plans of clients diagnosed with ADHD, and references to education of the family about ADHD in only 26 percent of the cases. "Review of the cases suggested that educating the family and the child about ADHD was quite effective as an intervention; however, most treatment records did not indicate that this education had taken place" (Managed Health Network, 1999, p. 2).

Parent and child education, self-control training, feeling sensitivity awareness, and problem-solving training are indicated by research as important. The use of child self-control training and parent training has been stressed as important to the improvement of the child's self-control in a number of studies. Kendall and Braswell (1984) developed a self-control training program for children. In Barkley's experience (1988), older children who have "satisfactory or better verbal abilities" and intellectual development respond best to self-control training (p. 97). Palkes, Stewart, and Kahana (1968; Palkes, Stewart, & Freedman, 1971) employed self-directed verbal commands to train ADHD 8- to 9-year-old boys in self-control. In cases where the child exhibits noncompliant, oppositional, or defiant behavior as a part of the ADHD repertoire of symptoms, parent training programs such as those by Barkley (1981, 1987), Dangel and Polster (1984), and Forehand and McMahon (1981) have indicated effective results in reducing those behaviors.

Attention training and scanning strategies have been used to change children's information processing and search strategies to more relevant and helpful dimensions (Egeland, 1974; Parrish & Erikson, 1981). More recently, neurotherapy and biofeedback approaches utilizing electroencephalographic (EEG) biofeedback for children to be aware of when they are focusing has been demonstrated to be effective in some cases in increasing attending (Lubar & Lubar, 1984). In a study of 22 second- and third-grade impulsive children (Kelly-Powell, 1990), a positive effect was found in reducing cognitive, behavioral, and psychophysiological impulsivity. This study trained individual students in an individual impulse-control program; an electric train was connected to an electromyograph (EMG) instrument which provided reinforcement for work on impulse control and relaxation training. The program indicated positive results in home, school, and clinical settings.

Problem-solving training focuses on teaching children to think about the results or consequences of their decisions and actions. Children diagnosed with ADHD and children with attentional or impulsive difficulties in general may miss important social learning cues and information. Children with such problems often experience frustration in school and in relating to peers. Such children may benefit from training in feeling awareness and appropriate feeling expression, relaxation, and problem-solving practice. Teaching children specific skills in ways that will maintain their attention and interest, such as are outlined by the concepts in the *Stop, Relax, and Think* game, may be of great benefit.

The *Stop, Relax, and Think* game is one tool that provides a high-interest way to begin educating ADHD children and their parents about aspects of the disorder and skills that can help. Many other resources exist now also, such as the Starbound program, books, and support groups.

ABOUT THE *STOP, RELAX, AND THINK* GAME

The game is designed for children ages 6 to 12; however, it has also been played successfully with adolescents. It can be played in groups of two to six players. Each game now comes boxed and contains the game board, 36 Feeling cards, 33 Think cards, 4 turtle movers, 30 tokens, 1 Stop card, a die, and an 8-sided die (see Figure 12.1). Instructions are simple and include a brief discussion of game concepts. The general purpose of the game is to educate children in self-control skills and provide some opportunity for practice of those skills. Specifically, the game's therapeutic purposes include teaching:

Awareness and expression of feelings.
Motoric awareness and control.
Practice of simple relaxation skills.
Problem-solving.

The object of the game is to proceed through all four sections to the finish line. Players collecting the most tokens during game play win. The player who reaches the finish line first receives an extra token and game play stops. Game time can be shortened by playing with two dice if there is an opportunity to play with more players and time is short.

FEELINGS SECTION

Helping children become aware of their feelings and first signs of stress is essential to self-control. Four key feelings (mad, sad, glad, and scared) are focused on but players may be encouraged to think of as many different feeling words as they can think of that would express their personal experience. (Center for Applied Psychology, 1991, p. 1)

The first section contains landing spaces that require drawing a card. Each card states a situation to which the player is asked to respond with how he or she might feel if that were happening. There are two types of cards in the feelings section. Feeling cards may ask players to think about what feelings they may have in particular situations, for example: "Your

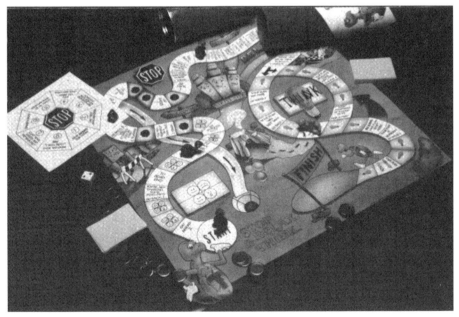

Figure 12.1   The *Stop, Relax, and Think* Game Board.

brother or sister has the stereo on too loud while you are trying to do your homework"; "You struck out and your team lost the softball game"; and "You can't find the pencil you need for math." Or, cards may request that a player identify something about feelings: "How can you tell what someone is feeling?"; "What happens in your body when you feel scared?"; and "How do you show others that you feel sad?" Two blank cards allow for customizing questions by the helping professional.

Tokens are given as rewards for cards answered and as directed in other sections when a skill is performed successfully. The four feeling categories of glad, sad, mad, and scared are illustrated on board spaces indicating that a card is to be drawn if one lands there. Younger players can be encouraged to choose a feeling from those four; older players can be encouraged to begin discriminating their feelings more precisely and to learn new vocabulary words for their feelings.

STOP SECTION

Impulsive behavior can manifest itself in many different forms. This section will help children practice the actual stopping of a behavior and learn the concept of catching themselves before an automatic response or reaction. Naturally without this step learning to relax and thinking through problems will be of little use in appropriate self-control. (Center for Applied Psychology, 1991, p. 2)

A stop sign is represented on the spaces of this second territory, where a skill is required to receive a token. When players land on the stop sign spaces, they must roll the 8-sided die and refer to the corresponding number on the Stop card. On the Stop card are eight behavioral choices to do repeatedly "as fast as you can" until the player on the right says "Stop." The player performing the behavior must stop immediately to be rewarded with a token. Other players evaluate whether the stopping occurred quickly enough to merit a token. The eight options on the Stop card are:

1. Skip around the room.
2. Say "yes" over and over.
3. Pat your head and rub your stomach.
4. Say "I'm mad!" over and over.
5. Count to 10 over and over.

6. Sing a song.
7. Clap your hands and tap your feet.
8. Say "I will not!" over and over.

Players, therefore, practice several skills at this juncture. First, they must follow instructions given. Second, they must risk doing a behavior repetitively that may become quickly "routinized" and therefore keep them from concentrating or focusing on the required directive. Third, they will need to respond immediately to a verbal cue to stop to earn a token.

Other landing spots in this section include affirmations of actions for self-control, such as: "You stopped just in time!" (2 tokens); "You didn't stop in time" (go ahead 1, which leads to the Down Slide); and "Warning, STOP!" (go back 2). The Down Slide and a path to Stress City are "pitfall places" connected to this area of board play. When landing on one of the two Down Slide spaces, players slide their mover down the board to "plop" into a sewerlike hole. As in all pitfall places, players may opt to skip a turn or respond to the request specific to that pitfall place. Players going down the Down Slide may talk about a time they felt down or sad, and what they can do to help their feelings change or to do better. This problem-solving practice offers children the opportunity to make the connection that when feelings are upset, they can be changed; also, it empowers them to think of options that can affect their feelings in positive ways. Impulsive children often receive frequent negative or corrective feedback and cueing, which may predispose frustration, anger, or disappointment with greater frequency than observed in the average nonimpulsive child.

Relaxation Trail

The next board area provides spaces requiring players to practice a number of different relaxation skills to receive tokens. This experiential learning area requires players to do one or more of the following:

"Breathe deeply 3 times" (3 tokens): Deep breathing to get the maximum oxygen is very important for self-control and relaxation training. Players should be encouraged to take deep breaths from their stomach or diaphragm area and release slowly and smoothly.

"Say calmly 'I 'can relax" (1 token): Encouraging self-talk that is positive.

"Tell or do something funny" (1 token): Humor is a useful way to release tension.

"Tell of a relaxing scene" (1 token): Imagery encourages visual pictures to facilitate relaxation and mental escapes from stress.

"Count to 10 aloud to calm down" (1 token): Doing something verbally can help slow down our impulses and gain more control. A player can be encouraged to visualize something he or she is angry about and to imagine being angry and counting to 10 to take the focus off the anger for the purpose of greater control.

"Think of puffy white clouds" (1 token): Use of imagery for relaxation training.

"Tense and relax your muscles" (1 token): Deliberate use of body tensing and releasing decreases stress and allows for better circulation. Players are encouraged to tighten their shoulders by pulling them up toward their ears, making tight arms and legs, with fists and pointed toes, then loosening all body parts like a rag doll.

"You get some exercise" (1 token): Affirms the need to move muscles to relieve stress.

Stress City is a pitfall place that can be arrived at through one path space in the Stop section and two in the Relaxation area. Players sent to Stress City are required to talk about a time when they felt stressed if they wish to return to board play the next turn. If the child has already been trained in relaxation techniques, then the expectation of practice of a relaxation technique can be added; thus, not only is awareness of stress prompted but a response is practiced.

THINK ZONE

Problem-solving training is important for impulsive children, as they often act before they think and create greater problems for themselves. This section encourages systematic thinking that is structured to encourage better choice-making on the part of youth. The Think Zone begins with a choice presented to players of which of two paths to choose. Once the path is chosen, opportunities to draw a problem-solving card occur when landing on spaces illustrated with a yellow lightbulb. The cards contain situations that challenge players to think about solutions to problems that will work, be safe, be fair, and produce good feelings. These contingencies for problem solving were taken from the *Starbound Life Skills Program for Children* (Bridges, Powell, Hampton, & Chapman, 1989). Sample Think Zone questions are: "You are angry at your mother. What are some OK ways of expressing (letting out) your anger?"; "Someone is pushing you and you want the person to stop. What is a plan that will be safe and produce OK feelings?"; and "You had a rough day at school. What happened? How do you feel? What can you do?"

The Think Zone also contains spaces that relate to problem-solving, such as:

"Rethink: your plan didn't work" (arrow sends player back four spaces).
"Your plan was fair—go ahead 1."
"Your plan was not safe—go back 1."
"Your plan produced good feelings—go ahead 2."
"Keep thinking of a good plan—miss a turn."

Confusion Cave is the pitfall place connected to one of the paths in the Think Zone area. Players who go there must miss a turn or talk about a time when they felt confused. If they choose to share their confusion experience, they can return to the path at the spot where they were sent off to the pitfall place.

Tony the turtle, the game mascot, is the mascot of the Starbound life skills training component for impulse control. Three different Tony stories are presented in the impulse control chapter of the Starbound program. Tony represents a fast, impulsive turtle who doesn't fit in with peers and others because he does things without thinking or so quickly that it gets him in trouble at school, with friends, and at home. Tony learns to control his behavior with the "turtle technique" (Schneider & Robin, 1976). The turtle technique is taught in the Starbound program as a cognitive-behavioral skill that encourages children to "pull in" to think at the first internal or external cue to "turtle." Thus, Tony is presented as a figure representative of the average impulsive child who successfully learns to get control of himself or herself and settle down.

One of the most important factors in the use of any psychoeducational game is whether it is fun and engaging to the target audience. "The *Stop, Relax, and Think* game is fun! Children enjoy the high quality graphics, as well as the combination of motoric and cognitive challenges" (Center for

Applied Psychology, 1991, p. 6). It offers a fast-moving pace and a variety of learning activities to sustain player interest and maximize learning potential.

APPLICATION TO ADHD CHILDREN

Although the *Stop, Relax, and Think* game is useful with any child who might benefit from the skills and concepts presented in it, it was designed in particular for children who fit the ADHD diagnosis. It is a game ideal for play with a child individually, with a family or parents and the child, or with a group. This section presents the various player groups that the game can be useful with and the unique advantages to that mode of play.

WITH INDIVIDUAL CHILDREN

With individual children, the *Stop, Relax, and Think* game can move quickly and be personalized to the specific needs for training that that particular child has. The child playing individually can then get a greater number of opportunities for practice, reinforcement, and participation more expediently and personally. Also, the influence of competition with peers may be reduced as compared to play with a group.

Children with ADHD are also often diagnosed with other learning disabilities or differences. The use of a variety of learning approaches is incorporated in the game to help players catch the concepts in the learning style best suited for them. For example, the game is visually attractive and engaging: Cartoon pictures illustrate key game concepts; a stop sign represents the self-control section; Tony the turtle relaxes while reclined and sipping lemonade in the relaxation section; the Think Zone is illustrated with a lightbulb and a choice point of two paths to illustrate "ideas" and "choices" inherent in problem-solving training. ADHD children are often highly kinesthetic. The *Stop, Relax, and Think* game uses a variety of experiential opportunities for practice of skills to promote learning for such children: Deep breathing, joke telling, stopping a repetitive behavior, and getting some exercise are a few of the activities to provide experience and practice target behaviors. ADHD children often require a variety of reinforcement measures to maintain their interest in attending. The variety of skills, responses, and surprises in *Stop, Relax, and Think* board play keep the game highly reinforcing for the typical ADHD child: Chips are earned in a variety of ways and in not always predictable number, as one to three tokens may be earned during a turn.

The *Stop, Relax, and Think* game is, therefore, a cognitive-behavioral educational tool for ADHD children to learn feeling awareness, self-control, relaxation, and problem-solving skills. It can also be useful as an educational opportunity for parents.

WITH PARENTS OF ADHD CHILDREN

The game can be played with parents and families. Concepts can then be reinforced as parents cue the use of self-control and relaxation skills in real-life situations. Tokens or point systems set in place with the assistance of the helping professional encourage the use of skill practice at home. Parents can also be trained in communication skills which take the concepts from the Think Zone and foster problem-solving practice with their youngsters. For example, when a problem situation occurs at home, a parent can ask the child the four problem-solving questions on which the game questions are based:

1. What is my problem?
2. What is my plan?
3. Are there any problems with my plan?
   a. Is it safe?
   b. Is it fair?
   c. Does it produce good feelings?
   d. Will it work?
4. How did I do? (Bridges et al., 1989)

These questions are practiced in the game and presented more thoroughly in the Starbound program.

WITH GROUPS

When played with a group, the rule following and feelings that occur during the game between or among players can become a source of material for therapeutic process. This augments the use of the game as a social skills training tool. Practice in positive social skills occurs in taking turns, moving one's own game piece and not those of other players, rule following, and group negotiating when all other players become the judge of whether problem-solving cards have been answered sufficiently or not. Players are also challenged to make a fair decision and practice assertiveness when becoming the judge of whether another player stops quickly enough to earn a token on Stop Sign behaviors. Players can be encouraged to discuss whether they feel others treated them fairly in playing the game. Resulting feelings from disappointment spots like the pitfall places, where tokens are not earned, are wonderful opportunities for process and greater learning.

With Large Groups

Although using several game boards is likely best for large groups, at times play can occur with positive results with more than four or five players. Playing rounds can be achieved by dividing the large group into smaller groups or pairs of players who take turns answering or performing tasks as a small group for token rewards. This is possible as a classroom activity. With larger numbers of impulsive or ADHD children, this method would probably be difficult in sustaining attention and the structure insufficient for success.

Evaluation of Effectiveness

"The effectiveness of a therapeutic game exists on several levels simultaneously. First is the manifest content of the game itself; its stated goals and objectives" (Center for Applied Psychology, 1991, p. 6). The *Stop, Relax, and Think* game meets the objectives of educating children and parents or other players about the steps for self-control. "Then there is the social context of the game, an opportunity for the therapist to intervene using the power of his or her relationship with the child or group of children" (p. 6). The game offers the opportunity to intervene in the process of impulsive behavior and emotional control in the course of game play as players are encouraged to follow the rules, problem-solve about turn taking, respecting others' boundaries, and listening to answers offered. "Thirdly there is the play value of the game" (p. 6). The play value is determined by the concepts presented and the interest engaged in learning them. The *Stop, Relax, and Think* game is fun and fast moving and presents concepts in a variety of ways for learning.

Prior to its production, the *Stop, Relax, and Think* game was field-tested with over 50 children both in inpatient and outpatient settings. These children rated highly their enjoyment of the game and retention of basic concepts. After 10 years, it still is marketed by Childswork/Childsplay as "ever-popular" and is considered a classic in the field of therapeutic games (Childswork/Childsplay, spring catalogue, 1999, p. 20).

SUMMARY

The *Stop, Relax, and Think* game provides a therapeutic tool for working with children with ADHD behavior profiles to become more aware of and identify their feelings and practice simple self-control, relaxation, and problem-solving skills. It is a game useful for educating children and parents about aspects of ADHD and presents the concepts in a variety of learning methods for those children challenged with learning disabilities. The *Stop, Relax, and Think* game can be used individually, in groups, or with parents or other family members. The long-standing popularity of the game and evaluation by professionals and child players support its effectiveness and its contribution to skill training and therapeutic work with children.[1]

ADDENDUM: GAME PRODUCTION

It was in the midst of leading up to three weekly impulse-control skills training groups for children in the mid-1980s, that the idea for a game was born. The author sketched the four basic concepts and plan for the *Stop, Relax, and Think* game on a paper napkin while traveling. Then the napkin drawing was expanded to a larger piece of paper. The game was drawn as a path, like the *Candyland* format, with a beginning and an ending point. The path was designed to take players through four game territories. Each of the territories represented an impulse-control training concept taught in

---

[1] The *Stop, Relax, and Think* game, as well as the author's second game *Odyssey Islands: An Adventure in Character Building,* are available through the Bureau for At-Risk Children and Youth at 135 Dupont Street, P.O. Box 760, Plainview, NY 11803-0760. 1-800-99-YOUTH.

Starbound: A Life Skills Training Program for Children is available from the author through Fourth Street Project, Inc. at 906 W. Mitchell, Arlington, TX 76013. (817) 265-9438.

Starbound: A Life Skills Training Program for Children groups (Bridges et al., 1989). Four "pitfall places" were included: the Down Slide, Dead End, Stress City, and Confusion Cave. These places were challenge spots, arrived at by chance, to sustain players' interest and provide opportunities for spontaneous responses and skill practice.

After the drawing was expanded by the creator on paper to include the number of landing spots and text to be written on each space, it was given to the artist David McGlothlin, a freelance illustrator and artist in Dallas, Texas, who did the illustration and calligraphy of the text. When the art rendering was complete, a color copy was made and a mockup of the game was made. It was then ready for test play. A questionnaire about players' enjoyment and learning from the game was given to over 50 children in inpatient and outpatient settings. The response was overwhelmingly positive and so production plans proceeded. Funding for the undertaking was provided by Fourth Street Company, a partnership of three therapists who supported the creation of products innovated from practice experience and research at Fourth Street Project, Inc., a parent-child learning and counseling center in Arlington, Texas.

The first printing of the *Stop, Relax, and Think* game was of 1,000 copies. The game playing board sheet was laminated with plastic and sold in green tubes. Turtle movers in five different colors and positions were found at a local novelty dime store. These first movers had movable tiddlywink eyes and were purchased 10,000 per box unsorted by the manufacturer. A sorting party was organized with friends of the creator, to sort the turtles by color and to package them along with two decks of cards, 30 tokens, and an 8-sided and a regular die.

The first 100 games were signed and numbered limited edition prints. Games were sold one at a time by direct mail and at conferences. Arlington Independent School District school counselors bought copies to have in each elementary school and test-played it with multiple children. The counselors gave feedback that it was effective in teaching students concepts of self-control while maintaining high player interest.

The cost of direct marketing inhibited the opportunity for continued sales and distribution of the game, so after a year, the game rights were sold to Childswork/Childsplay in 1990. Childswork/Childsplay is the largest catalogue sales distributor of therapeutic games, and so the exposure of the *Stop, Relax, and Think* game to the market for which it was designed increased greatly. The game has sold over 35,000 copies and continues to be one of the leading sellers. "Since its introduction, the game has proved one of the most popular tools in working with impulsive children, particularly those with ADHD" (Shapiro, 1993, p. 96).

REFERENCES

American Psychiatric Association. (1987). *Diagnostic and statistical manual of mental disorders* (3rd ed., rev.). Washington, DC: Author.

Barkley, R.A. (1981). *Hyperactive children: A handbook for diagnosis and treatment.* New York: Guilford Press.

Barkley, R.A. (1987). *Defiant children: A clinician's manual for parent training.* New York: Guilford Press.

Barkley, R.A. (1988). Attention deficit disorder with hyperactivity. In E.J. Mash & L.G. Terdal (Eds.), *Behavioral assessment of childhood disorders* (2nd ed., pp. 69–104). New York: Guilford Press.

Barkley, R.A. (1995). *Taking charge of ADHD.* New York: Guilford Press.

Bridges, B.A., Powell, D.K., Hampton, M.A., & Chapman, J.E. (1989). *Starbound: A life skills program for children.* Arlington, TX: Fourth Street.

Center for Applied Psychology. (1991). *Stop, relax and think game instructions.* King of Prussia, PA: Author.

Children with Attention Deficit Disorders (CHADD). (1999). Frequently asked questions about ADHD and the answers from the internet. *Teaching Exceptional Children, 31*(6), 29.

Dangel, R.F., & Polster, R.A. (Eds.). (1984). *Parent training: Foundations of research and practice.* New York: Guilford Press.

DuPaul, G.J., Guevremont, D.C., & Barkley, R.A. (1991). Attention-deficit hyperactivity disorder. In T.R. Kratochwill & R.J. Morris (Eds.), *The practice of child therapy* (2nd ed., pp. 115–144). New York: Pergamon Press.

Egeland, B. (1974). Training impulsive children in the use of more efficient scanning techniques. *Child Development, 45,* 165–171.

Forehand, R., & McMahon, R. (1981). *Helping the non-compliant child: A clinician's guide to parent training.* New York: Guilford Press.

Kelly-Powell, D.J. (1990). *The effectiveness of biofeedback-aided relaxation training and cognitive-behavioral therapy on seven- to nine-year-old children with impulsive tendencies.* Unpublished doctoral dissertation, University of Texas at Arlington.

Kendall, P.C., & Braswell, L. (1984). *Cognitive-behavioral therapy for impulsive children.* New York: Guilford Press.

Levine, M.D. (1987). Attention deficits: The diverse effects of weak control systems in childhood. *Pediatric Annals, 16*(2), 117–130.

Lubar, J.O., & Lubar, J.F. (1984). Electroencephalographic biofeedback of SMR and beta for treatment of attention deficit disorders in a clinical setting. *Biofeedback and Self-Regulation, 9*(1), 1–23.

Managed Health Network, Inc. (1999). A study on compliance with ADHD clinical practice guideline. *Network Link, 2*(1), 2.

Palkes, H., Stewart, M., & Freedman, J. (1971). Improvement in maze performance of hyperactive boys as a function of verbal-training procedures. *Journal of Special Education, 5,* 337–342.

Palkes, H., Stewart, M., & Kahana, B. (1968). Porteus maze performance of hyperactive boys after training in self-directed verbal commands. *Child Development, 39,* 817–826.

Parrish, J.M., & Erikson, M.T. (1981). A comparison of cognitive strategies in modifying the cognitive style of impulsive third grade children. *Cognitive Therapy and Research, 5,* 71–84.

Ross, D.M., & Ross, S.A. (1982). *Hyperactivity: Current issues, research and theory* (2nd ed.). New York: Wiley.

Shapiro, L.E. (1993). *The book of psychotherapeutic games.* King of Prussia, PA: Center for Applied Psychology.

Shure, M.B., & Spivack, G. (1981). The problem-solving approach to adjustment: A competency-building model of primary prevention. *Prevention in Human Services, 1,* 87–103.

Schneider, M., & Robin, A.L. (1976). The turtle technique: A method for self-control of impulsive behavior. In J.D. Krumboltz & C.E. Thorensen (Eds.), *Counseling methods* (pp. 157–162).

Whalen, C.K., & Henker, B. (Eds.). (1980). *Hyperactive children: The social ecology of identification and treatment.* New York: Academic Press.

CHAPTER THIRTEEN

Biofeedback Racing Car Game for Children with ADHD

HEIDI G. KADUSON

A DHD is characterized by control deficits of inattentiveness, impulsivity, and restlessness. Other features frequently associated with the disorder include poor school performance and inadequate interpersonal relationships. Despite numerous changes in the diagnostic label and in the relative emphasis given particular symptoms, the core symptoms identified as typical of this condition have remained constant. Developmentally inappropriate attention difficulties, impulsivity, and overactivity are the core features in the diagnostic criteria of the *DSM-IV* (American Psychiatric Association, 1994). Although many of the attributes that characterize children with ADHD are present in all children to some degree at certain times, it is the persistent and excessive preserve of these attributes that labels a child as having the disorder. The distinguishing difference between ADHD children and other children is the intensity, the persistence, and the patterning of these symptoms (Wender, 1987).

At the present time, researchers have been focusing on the attention difficulties evidenced by ADHD children. By definition, children having ADHD display marked inattention relative to non-ADHD children of the same age and sex. However, "inattention" is a multidimensional construct that can refer to, among other things, problems with alertness, arousal, selectivity, sustained attention, distractibility, or span of apprehension (Hale & Lewis, 1979). Research suggests that ADHD children have their greatest difficulty sustaining attention to tasks, that is, vigilance (Douglas, 1983). Manifestations of this type of difficulty include inadequate attending to lengthy visual and/or auditory instructions or presentations and difficulty sticking with an assignment or play activity (Barkley & Ullman, 1975; Braswell & Bloomquist, 1991).

Although attentional difficulties appear to be primary, the hyperactive and impulsive behaviors that these children manifest are clearly the most obvious symptoms. The impulsivity feature refers to a tendency to act before or without thinking. This characteristic is evidenced by behaviors such as blurting out verbal responses in class, having difficulty waiting for one's turn in line or in a game, intruding on others' activities, and shifting frequently from one task or activity to another. Impulsivity can also take the form of engaging in a dangerous activity seemingly without an awareness of the potential for unfortunate consequences, such as failing to look for cars before dashing into the street to retrieve a ball, diving into water without considering the depth and one's ability to swim, or attempting to walk on a high ledge or fence.

Overactivity or hyperactivity is commonly, although not always, observed in children who manifest difficulties with attention and impulsivity. Restlessness, fidgeting, and generally unnecessary gross bodily movements are commonplace (Stewart, Pitts, Craig, & Dieruf, 1966). These movements are often irrelevant to the task or situation, and at times seem purposeless. Hyperactivity is easily observed in the young child who is literally "on the go." Observations of ADHD children at school or while working on an independent task reveal that they are out of their seats, moving about the room without permission, restlessly moving their arms and legs while working, playing with objects not related to the task, talking out of turn to others, and making unusual vocal noises (Abikoff, Gittelman-Klein, & Klein, 1977; Cammann & Miehlke, 1989).

Although all of the foregoing are well-known symptoms of ADHD, it is still not known what causes the disorder. There is no single cause of ADHD. However, in most cases, this disorder is considered to be a physiological problem (Goldstein & Goldstein, 1990). Recent scientific studies

(Zametkin et al., 1990) have found physiological differences from the norm in the brains of ADHD adults. These differences are primarily neurochemical. Another study has found that the prefrontal areas of the brain are important biological determiners of attention (Mensulam, 1986); if these areas are dysfunctional, then inattention, distractibility, and disinhibition are often present.

In addition to the hypothesis regarding biological determinants, there is a debate about the exact nature of the underlying cognitive deficits that produce the primary symptoms of ADHD. Information regarding these deficits has been steadily accumulating over the past 30 years. It has been suggested that some of the cognitive characteristics producing the primary symptoms of ADHD are (1) difficulty adapting behavior in response to situational demands; (2) lack of the inhibition of impulsive responding; (3) difficulty modulating arousal levels to meet situational demands; and (4) an unusually strong inclination to seek immediate reinforcement (Douglas, 1980, 1983). Children with ADHD have also been described as having weak ego functioning, difficulty with rule-governed behavior (Barkley, 1981), and deficits in cognitive control (Kendall & Braswell, 1982).

According to Douglas (1980), ADHD children typically demonstrate difficulty modulating their behavior in response to situational demands. Instead, a careless, disorganized, nonreflective manner characterizes their cognitive and social functioning. This response style, coupled with difficulties in sustaining and directing attention, contributes to the inefficient problem-solving skills displayed by these youngsters (Tant & Douglas, 1982).

Douglas argues that a failure of inhibitory processes is the essence of the ADHD disorder. A weakness of inhibitory processes is easily observed in an ADHD child's impulsive response style. These children respond too quickly and thus fail to use available processing time in a manner that aids their task performance (Douglas, 1983).

Difficulty in maintaining appropriate levels of arousal has also received attention as a possible underlying mechanism of ADHD. In a review of the research, Douglas (1983) suggested that ADHD children do not seem to be different from normal peers in their resting arousal level, but they may have difficulty modulating their arousal level when the situation demands change. In other words, they can become easily bored and quickly excited.

Significant research and theoretical attention have focused on the ADHD child's strong tendency to seek immediate reinforcement (Barkley, 1990; Douglas, 1984; Kinsbourne, 1984). Generally, ADHD children seem to perform as well as others in situations of consistent, immediate, positive reinforcement. When playing Nintendo, these children can sustain attention, stay self-controlled, and maintain appropriate levels of arousal. Most of the differences between ADHD and non-ADHD children are in situations involving infrequent, partial reinforcement schedules or under conditions of negative feedback (Douglas, 1984; Kinsbourne, 1984; Rosenbaum & Baker, 1984).

In general, ADHD children seem to display a weakness of their cognitive-control apparatus. Despite having average or above-average IQs, they show deficits in their ego capacity to tolerate frustration and control impulses. With a weakness in self-regulation and control of their drives, they find it difficult to delay satisfaction and modify their behavior in unexpected situations.

SELF-CONTROL

Perhaps the most important underlying mechanism for reducing impulsivity is self-control. Self-control can refer to a set of procedures used to influence behavior, or the process observed when certain behavior change is occurring (Epstein & Blanchard, 1977). When self-control refers to a set of procedures, the defining characteristic of the procedures is that the variables that influence the response in question be controlled by the subject (Goldiamond, 1965; Kanfer, 1971; Thoresen & Mahoney, 1974). As a process, self-control is considered a function of the basic ego skills that facilitate control over one's actions.

One component of self-control that is applicable to ADHD children is physiological self-control. The basic idea behind this process is to provide individuals with information about what is going on inside their bodies, including their brains. A fundamental principle is that a variable cannot be controlled unless information about the variable is available to the controller. The information provided to the individual is called "feedback" (Ashby, 1963; Mayr, 1970).

Annent (1969) reviewed the evidence that feedback facilitates learning and concluded that biofeedback provides individuals with direct and clear feedback about their physiologic functions, and thereby assists them in learning self-control of such functions. For example, if a person receives information concerning his or her muscle activity from an EMG instrument, it may help that person learn to reduce muscular tension.

Braud, Lupin, and Braud (1975) found that ADHD children have chronic muscle tension and difficulty relaxing. This chronic muscular tension seems to contribute to and intensify the symptoms of hyperactivity. ADHD children appear to be in constant motion as a way of discharging their muscle tension/energy.

To learn self-control, a child must be taught certain skills. In many cases, we can teach these skills to ADHD children, but they do not use them when needed. It is as if they know what to do, but they just don't do it. It is quite common clinically to hear that ADHD children do not listen, fail to comply with instructions, are unable to maintain compliance with an instruction over time, and are poor at adhering to directions associated with a task (Barkley, 1990). All of these behaviors could present problems for teaching a child skills necessary for reducing impulsivity and for self-control. To learn the skills involved in any approach, an ADHD child must be able to attend to the instructions given, must be motivated to comply with the instructions, and needs sufficient reinforcement for doing so. As the therapist attempts to train the child to use the methods necessary for self-control, the ADHD child may become bored and refuse to engage in the treatment. One way to overcome this difficulty is to present the self-control training in a playful, game-like format.

GAME PLAY

A development in the area of child and adolescent therapy has been the utilization of games and game theory (Bobcock, 1967; Crocker & Wroblewski, 1975; Schaefer & Reid, 1986; Varenhorst, 1973). Opie and Opie (1959) noted that organized play with games first appears in our culture when children enter kindergarten at about age 5 or 6. The child's cognitive ability has matured enough so that he or she can plan and carry out long sequences of purposive activities, exercise self-control, and submit voluntarily to restrictions and conventions of the game. In addition, through the use of games, the child experiences a protected way of looking at the world. A "mini life" (Serok & Blum, 1983) is created within the context of a game that provides an opportunity to acquire new information, experiment with new roles and behaviors, and adapt to the demands of the game and to norms of the group (Schaefer & Reid, 1986). What is vague and confusing in real life can be made quite explicit in games through the use goals and objectives of play and the methods of achieving the goal. Games have an "as if' quality that separates them from real life and allows the experience to be non-threatening.

Game playing is particularly relevant to children over the age of 5, when concerns about competence and social interaction are very important. Game play in a therapy setting provides experiences of pleasure and fosters communication and self-expression, reality testing, and insight, and strengthens cognition, socialization, and self-control.

Because playing games is fun, it is intrinsically motivating. Children naturally play, and one need not work at getting a child involved. Play and games represent an educational and therapeutic medium that is naturally attractive and important in the overall development of children (Nickerson & O'Laughlin, 1983).

Games appear to have a unique potential as a teaching tool. Crocker and Wroblewski (1975) delineated six helping functions of games:

1. Games may be used as a projective test. By playing a game, participants may become sensitized to behaviors of which they were not aware. Because of their impulsive behavior, ADHD children typically are not aware of their inappropriate behavior until it is pointed out to them, or after it has occurred.
2. A game may set up a situation in which anxiety about a certain condition can be confronted and dealt with. For many ADHD children, their lack of acceptance by peers is an anxiety-arousing situation. Thus, for them, the game situation can provide a format for working through these anxieties.
3. Playing a game offers a player an opportunity to deal with the rules of the game as an analogy to living by acceptable norms of society. This aspect of game play may be useful in helping ADHD children accept the reality of social rules and the consequent need for self-control.
4. A game situation temporarily allows a player's childlike playfulness to emerge and thus bypass some behaviors that have prevented other interventions from being helpful. For example, ADHD children might oppose the rules governing behavior that they typically find so difficult, but might comply with the rules of the game because they are presented in a fun manner.

5. Games create a safe and permissive climate in which individuals can experiment with new behaviors. In a play format, new ways of dealing with impulsivity and self-control can be tried without threatening consequences.

6. Playing a game may help participants learn coping behaviors. The children learn to cope with the effects that winning and losing have on their feelings of self-worth. In addition, children can learn how to control their expression of these feelings.

Games provide an opportunity for the therapist to avoid the obvious instructional mode of training and to produce a low-pressure method of learning skills. Rapport is easily established through game play. Games are fun and therefore self-motivating. They also provide an opportunity for social learning in several ways: communication with others; respect and obedience to rules; self-discipline; dealing with independence issues; cooperation with others; socialized competition and controlled expression of aggression; and dealing with issues of power and authority (Schaefer & Reid, 1986). While playing games, children can feel relatively spontaneous and free to be themselves (Nickerson & O'Laughlin, 1983).

Self-control is needed for a game to proceed smoothly. The players must learn and perform within the role expectations of the game. Rules require conformity to the norms of the game, and these are reinforced by the other players and the authority of the rules. In addition, cooperation is expected in a two-or-more participant game. The behavior and immediate gratification of the participants must be given up for the good of the team. Players must also concentrate for relatively long periods of time during game play. Many games require a long span of interest, patience, and persistence, even when losing (Serok & Blum, 1983). Therefore, the rules and the norms of the game provide the boundaries within which participants must control their behavior. Finally, the games require a player to understand the task, establish goals, assess alternative paths to a goal and their consequences, follow through with the appropriate behavior, assess the outcome as to the choices made, and use this assessment as feedback as the game proceeds.

Games are ideally suited to children's group therapy because they require interdependent interaction between two or more players. In addition, games with rules are the natural expression of latency-age children's cognitive development in play (Piaget, 1926).

Bow and Goldberg (1986) describe the use of games as being particularly helpful with children who have cognitive self-control deficits. The process of repetitive play and the support and guidance of the therapist enable the child in therapy to master his or her impulses in at least one setting with one set of materials. In one case study, an impulsive and excitable child repeatedly screamed and banged the table during a game involving tops. The therapist was able to teach a "countdown" procedure in which the tops could only be released after the therapist had counted backward from 30 to "blastoff." There was also a "hold" period when the child became disruptive or impulsive. These techniques were generalized to other games, such as penny hockey, tiddlywinks, and shoot-the-moon, with consequent improvement in the child's self-control (Bow & Goldberg, 1986). The teaching of physiological self-control can also be taught in a game-like format through the use of biofeedback.

BIOFEEDBACK TRAINING

The primary intervention used to help children learn physiologic self-control is biofeedback (Attanasio, Andrasik, Burke, Blake, Kabela, & Mc-Carran, 1985). One of the compelling models concerning the etiology of ADHD is proposed by Wender (1971), who hypothesizes a depletion of neurotransmitters as a causal agent. The inability to modulate activity level may be a result of neurochemical dysfunction in the inhibitory and excitatory systems of the brain. The reported success of amphetamines, such as Ritalin, which is the drug of choice in psychopharmacologic treatment of ADHD, is due to their effect on monoamines. The major question concerning biofeedback is whether ADHD children can be taught the physiologic self-control that appears to be lacking in their central nervous system.

Potashkin and Beckles (1990) compared the relative efficacy of biofeedback and Ritalin treatments for ADHD children. Eighteen male subjects between the ages of 10 and 13 were assigned to three groups matched by age, IQ, and race. One group received 10 biofeedback sessions, another Ritalin, and the third nonspecific treatment as the control group. EMG readings, the Conners' Teacher Rating Scale, the Werry-Weiss-Peters Scale, and the Zukow Parent Rating Scale were used to measure treatment efficacy. Results indicated that biofeedback-assisted relaxation significantly reduced muscle tension levels, whereas neither Ritalin nor personal attention produced significant change.

As stated above, relaxation through biofeedback has been used to help children with self-control deficits, including ADHD children (Bhatara, Arnold, Lorance, & Gupta, 1979; Denkowski, Denkowski, & Omizo, 1983, 1984; Dunn & Howell, 1982; Hampstead, 1979; Potashkin & Beckles, 1990). The rationale for biofeedback training is the hypothesis that muscular tension and inability to relax not only contribute to, but actually aggravate, the symptoms of hyperactivity (Braud et al., 1975). Compared to adults, children receiving biofeedback training have been found to exhibit greater self-regulatory abilities, to be quicker to acquire the appropriate response, and to have better overall improvement (Attanasio et al., 1985).

Another advantage of using biofeedback with children is their lack of skepticism about the procedure. Children easily accept explanations of the purpose of physiologic self-control and, although concerned about their ability to perform well, are able to retain the proper perspective about their performance (Attanasio et al., 1985).

Children's lack of skepticism combined with a positive attitude about biofeedback may enable them to learn the desired responses more quickly. Hunter, Russell, and Russell (1976) found empirical support for this hypothesis. They assessed the effects of thermal biofeedback on 60 children (40 boys and 20 girls) age 7 to 9 years, half of whom were learning disabled and half of whom were normal. The children were matched for age, sex, grade, race, socioeconomic status, and IQ. One group of the children (16 learning disabled and 16 normals) received continuous reinforcement for digital temperature increases; the others received mixed reinforcement schedules. Feedback was provided by a variable-intensity light and electric toy train. Learning of thermal control was demonstrated by the consistently reinforced group. The younger children did better than the older, and the girls somewhat better than the boys. A possible explanation for this finding is that younger children often attribute special abilities to themselves and consequently enter biofeedback certain that they can produce the desired response (Attanasio et al., 1985).

Another factor that may contribute to the efficacy of biofeedback is children's familiarity and feeling of competency with high-tech equipment. ADHD children are proficient at computer games such as Nintendo and Game Boy. They come to the biofeedback training with a sense of self-efficacy and positive expectations about their ability to learn this type of task.

As conceived by Meichenbaum (1976), biofeedback relaxation training provides increased awareness of one's maladaptive physiologic responses as well as the experience that these can be controlled voluntarily. Therefore, this training could demonstrate to ADHD children that they have control over their physical behavior, and this perception of self-control may generalize to socioeducational behavior. Biofeedback training may also induce the inhibitory control that Douglas (1984) determined to be integral to therapeutic progress in any treatment of activity problems. That same perception has coalesced a popular clinical belief that interventions that do not promote self-control and decreased impulsivity are largely futile with ADHD children (Ballard & Glynn, 1975; Varni, 1976).

In a study by Omizo and Williams (1982), three extremely disruptive ADHD boys were selected to try the biofeedback approach to relaxation. Two boys were 6 years old, and the third boy was 7. The boys were trained twice a week for a month in 25-minute sessions. After the biofeedback training, the boys were able to sit and listen for longer periods of time and commented that they felt they had a sense of control about their behavior. The teachers also noticed a decrease in disruptive and impulsive behavior.

The effects of biofeedback on ADHD children were noted in a study by Braud (1978). He compared 15 hyperactive children with 15 nonhyperactive children. Both EMG biofeedback and progressive relaxation exercises were successful in that they significantly reduced muscular tension, hyperactivity, distractibility, irritability, impulsivity, explosiveness, aggression, and emotionality in ADHD children.

Another study that emphasizes the importance of biofeedback training was done by Lubar and Lubar (1984). Six unmedicated children were provided with long-term biofeedback. The training consisted of two sessions per week for 10 to 27 months, with a gradual phase-out. All six children demonstrated considerable improvement in their schoolwork in terms of grades or achievement test scores.

To implement self-maintenance of biofeedback, children must be able to influence muscle activity without external feedback (other than self-instruction). Children need to be taught to practice the biofeedback skills. Continual maintenance of the components of self-management is dependent on three things: (1) The child must accurately discern when to implement biofeedback; (2) the child must be able to discriminate changes in EMG activity associated with EMG decreases that indicate success and serve as the occasion for self-reinforcement; and (3) the choice of the reinforcer should be appropriate to maintain biofeedback over long periods of time (Epstein & Blanchard, 1977).

As the above discussion indicates, an impressive body of research has provided empirical support indicating that biofeedback enhances self-control and decreases impulsivity and disruptive behavior.

One of the major drawbacks of biofeedback is the lack of maintenance and generalization of the EMG training. This may be due, in part, to the problems inherent in teaching a skill to ADHD children. The child must be motivated to attend to and comply with the instructions given. These children may become bored and refuse to engage in treatment. To overcome this drawback, a game-like format was created. This game-like quality of the biofeedback helped to mobilize children's interest and motivation. The children actually look forward to coming to the next session to "play" with the equipment.

BIOFEEDBACK CAR RACING GAME PLAY

In the biofeedback car racing game, measurement is taken by the Johnson & Johnson (J&J) EMG (model no. M59A). The machine is used to monitor and display ongoing EMG activity generated by muscle action in the form of audio and visual feedback. The J&J EMG is attached to a cumulative integrator, Biofax model no. S4000, which records the total number of microvolts at any given time. The instrument is recurrently adjusted so that existent tension exceeds the threshold value. For ADHD children, sensitivity is set at .5–15 microvolts. The output of the J&J EMG machine is fed into the Biofax, which then activates a remote-control road racing game. For the car to be activated, the child has to keep the EMG machine below threshold. Baseline thresholds are recorded at the beginning of each session. Surface electrodes are used. Muscle activity at the frontalis is recorded to implement EMG training, as tension at that site seems to be a reliable index of overall systemic relaxation (Schandler & Grings, 1976; Stoyva & Budzinski, 1974). Placement of the two electrodes is standard: two inches on either side of the center of the forehead, and one inch above each eyebrow (Venables & Martin, 1967). The ground electrode is placed between them.

At the beginning of each session, an explanation and demonstration of the instruments is given. Then the therapist asks the child to note the effects that various thoughts and small motor movements exert on the digital display, and to use these thoughts and movements to raise, lower, and stabilize the readings. Using verbal instruction and visual imagery, the child is guided through a progressive relaxation procedure. The child is asked to tighten muscles in his or her feet, followed by leg muscles (by imagining that his or her knees are pushing through the floor), stomach muscles, chest muscles, biceps (by making big muscles with his or her arms), forearms, hands (by making a fist), shoulders (by lifting shoulders to touch ears), and facial muscles (by making a mean, scary face). Each of these muscular tensions are done for 5 seconds, followed by the word "relax" to the count of 5.

After children have completed the relaxation technique, they are told that their task during all sessions will be to induce the biofeedback unit to register the lowest possible reading. The training is always conducted in a fun, game-like atmosphere.

The child plays the car racing game utilizing the J&J EMG biofeedback machine, its connection through the Biofax, and a remote-control device. Each child's goal is to achieve the greatest number of laps during four 2-minute time periods. If the child tenses up, the car slowly goes around the lap until the child relaxes enough to meet the threshold number and hold there for the rest of the race. Each child's number is recorded by the therapist.

EMG readings are taken at the beginning of each session and used to set the threshold point for the client. Each child is his or her own control. Children are encouraged to reduce their threshold point after each weekly session and maintain that reduction throughout the training session. If a child becomes proficient at a certain threshold, the threshold is lowered.

Children who spend 10 weeks on this biofeedback game play show an increase in self-perception of self-control, and many have generalized the behavior to outside of therapy. The sense of control the child feels in therapy is clearly demonstrated by the race car. The more relaxed the child, the faster the car goes.

The biofeedback car game is a valid technique to use with children with ADHD. This game is an intervention where the child competes against himself or herself. Therefore, success is totally due to the child's own effort. The child has to continually practice attaining self-control in order to win the game. In addition, this suggests that practice on a task where success is due to personal effort may be the key to increasing one's sense of self-control.

It is also noteworthy that once the initial technique is taught to the child by the therapist, further refinements of the techniques are essentially self-instructed. Many children, for example, will experiment with different body positions, will repeat calming instructions to themselves, or will share with others (if done in group format) the procedures they used to lower their threshold and hence increase the number of laps of the car race. Another study that utilized biofeedback for clinical use (Attanasio et al., 1985) arrived at similar findings. Specifically, researchers found that children's enthusiasm for learning and increased enjoyment when practicing seemed to result in self-reported increases in perceived self-control. This perceived self-control led to concomitant increases in the children's feelings of self-esteem.

Another factor accounting for the success of the biofeedback car game is the novelty of this type of intervention. Very few children seem to be exposed to biofeedback equipment. When something is novel, especially to an ADHD child, the child puts more effort into learning and mastering the information.

Still another explanation for children's success in this treatment is that of self-reinforcement. Self-reinforcement has been found to be one of the most powerful self-control procedures, equal to or better than external reinforcement for that purpose (O'Leary & Dubey, 1979). It has been shown to be effective both when used alone and incrementally when added to other procedures.

In a study done by this author (1993), the children in the biofeedback car racing group were required to change a physiological response, and they were provided with immediate self-reinforcement for that change. The more proficient the children became at maintaining their current EMG threshold, the faster their car would move around the track. This provided concrete feedback on the success of their own efforts to control their body reactions. Thus, the children received immediate reinforcement each time they decreased the threshold on the EMG biofeedback machines. This game allowed the children to learn by "doing," not just by being told to do something.

SUMMARY AND CONCLUSIONS

Biofeedback is becoming more popular in the treatment of ADHD children. By connecting the biofeedback training to game play, the best of both treatments seems to have a tremendous effect on the child's self-perceived self-control and his or her self-esteem. Being successful at something enhances one's self-esteem and makes one want to persist at doing the action over and over again. It has been found that the same happens with the biofeedback car racing game (Kaduson, 1993). Not only do the children enjoy the therapy, but they want to continue doing it over and over again for the self-reward of success at self-control.

REFERENCES

Abikoff, H., Gittleman-Klein, R., & Klein, D. (1977). Validation of a classroom observation code for hyperactive children. *Journal of Consulting and Clinical Psychology, 45*, 772–783.

American Psychiatric Association. (1994). *Diagnostic and statistical manual of mental disorders* (4th ed.). Washington, DC: Author.

Annent, J. (1969). *Feedback and human behavior.* Baltimore: Penguin Books.

Ashby, W.R. (1963). *An introduction to cybernetics.* New York: Wiley.

Attanasio, V., Andrasik, F., Burke, E.J., Blake, D.D., Kabela, E., & McCarran, M.S. (1985). Clinical issues in utilizing biofeedback with children. *Clinical Biofeedback and Health, 8*, 134–141.

Ballard, K.D., & Glynn, T. (1975). Behavior self-management in story writing with elementary school children. *Journal of Applied Behavior Analysis, 8*, 387–398.

Barkley, R.A. (1981). *Hyperactive children: A handbook for diagnosis and treatment.* New York: Guilford Press.

Barkley, R.A. (1990). *Attention deficit hyperactivity disorder: A handbook for diagnosis and treatment.* New York: Guilford Press.

Barkley, R.A., & Ullman, D.G. (1975). A comparison of objective measures of activity and distractibility in hyperactive and nonhyperactive children. *Journal of Abnormal Child Psychology, 3*, 213–244.

Bhatara, V., Arnold, L.E., Lorance, T., & Gupta, D. (1979). Muscle relaxation therapy in hyperkinesis: Is it effective? *Journal of Learning Disabilities, 12*, 182–186.

Bobcock, S. (1967). The life career game. *Personnel and Guidance Journal, 46*, 328–334.

Bow, J.N., & Goldberg, T.E. (1986). Therapeutic uses of games with a fine motor component. In C.E. Schaefer & S. Reid (Eds.), *Game play: Therapeutic use of childhood games* (pp. 243–255). New York: Wiley.

Braswell, L., & Bloomquist, M.L. (1991). *Cognitive-behavioral therapy with ADHD children.* New York: Guilford Press.

Braud, L.E. (1978). The effects of frontal EMG biofeedback and progressive relaxation upon hyperactivity and its behavioral concomitants. *Biofeedback and Self-Regulation, 3*, 69–89.

Braud, L.E., Lupin, M.N., & Braud, W.G. (1975). The use of electromyographic bio-feedback in the control of hyperactivity. *Journal of Learning Disabilities, 8*, 21–26.

Cammann, R., & Miehlke, A. (1989). Differentiation of motor activity of nor-mally active and hyperactive boys in schools: Some preliminary results. *Journal of Child Psychology and Psychiatry, 30*, 899–906.

Crocker, J.W., & Wroblewski, M. (1975). Using recreational games in counseling. *Personnel and Guidance Journal, 53*, 453–458.

Denkowski, K.M., Denkowski, G.C., & Omizo, M.M. (1983). The effects of EMG-assisted relaxation training on the academic performance, locus of control and self-esteem of hyperactive boys. *Biofeedback and Self-Regulation, 8*, 363–375.

Denkowski, K.M., Denkowski, G.C., & Omizo, M.M. (1984). Predictors of success in the EMG biofeedback training of hyperactive male children. *Biofeedback and Self-Regulation, 9*, 253–264.

Douglas, V.I. (1980). Treatment and training approaches to hyperactivity: Estab-lishing external or internal control. In C.K. Whalen & B. Henker (Eds.), *Hyperactive children: The social ecology of identification and treatment* (pp. 317–335). New York: Academic Press.

Douglas, V.I. (1983). Attentional and cognitive problems. In M. Rutter (Ed.), *Developmental neuropsychiatry* (pp. 414–429). New York: Guilford Press.

Douglas, V.I. (1984). The psychological processes implicated in ADD. In L.M. Bloomingdale (Ed.), *Attention deficit disorder: Diagnostic, cognitive and thera-peutic understanding* (pp. 215–226). New York: Spectrum.

Dunn, F.M., & Howell, R.J. (1982). Relaxation training and its relationship to hy-peractivity in boys. *Journal of Clinical Psychology, 38*, 92–100.

Epstein, L.H., & Blanchard, E.B. (1977). Biofeedback, self-control and self-management. *Biofeedback and Self-Regulation, 2*, 201–211.

Goldiamond, I. (1965). Self-control procedures in personal behavior problems. *Psychological Reports, 17*, 851–868.

Goldstein, S., & Goldstein, M. (1990). *Managing attention disorders in children*. New York: Wiley.

Hale, G.A., & Lewis, M. (1979). *Attention and cognitive development*. New York: Plenum Press.

Hampstead, W.J. (1979). The effects of EMG-assisted relaxation training with hy-perkinetic children. *Biofeedback and Self-Regulation, 4*, 113–125.

Hunter, S.H., Russell, H.L., & Russell, E.D. (1976). Control of fingertip tempera-ture increases via biofeedback in learning-disabled and normal children. *Perceptual and Motor Skills, 43*, 743–755.

Kaduson, H.G. (1993). Self-control game interventions for attention-deficit hy-peractivity disorder (Doctoral dissertation, Fairleigh Dickinson University, 1993). *Dissertation Abstracts International, 50*.

Kanfer, F.H. (1971). The maintenance of behavior by self-generated stimuli and reinforcement. In A. Jacobs & L.B. Sach (Eds.), *The psychology of private events: Perspectives on covert response systems* (pp. 429–444). New York: Aca-demic Press.

Kendall, P.C., & Braswell, L. (1982). *Cognitive-behavioral self-control therapy for children: A component analysis* (pp. 169–190).

Kinsbourne, M. (1984). Beyond attention deficit: Search for the disorder in ADD. In L.M. Bloomingdale (Ed.), *Attention deficit disorder: Diagnostic, cognitive and therapeutic understanding* (pp. 265–280). New York: Spectrum.

Lubar, J.O., & Lubar, J.F. (1984). Electroencephaolographic biofeedback of SMR and beta for treatment of attention deficit disorders in a clinical setting. *Biofeedback and Self-Regulation, 9*(1), 1–23.

Mayr, O. (1970). *The origins of feedback control.* Cambridge, MA: MIT Press.

Meichenbaum, D. (1976). Cognitive factors in biofeedback therapy. *Biofeedback and Self-Regulation, 2,* 201–216.

Mensulam, M.M. (1986). *Principles of behavioral neurology.* Philadelphia: F.A. Davis.

Nickerson, E.T., & O'Laughlin, K.B. (1983). It's fun, but will it work? The use of games as a therapeutic medium for children and adolescents. *Journal of Clinical Child Psychology, 12,* 78–81.

O'Leary, S.G., & Dubey, D.R. (1979). Applications of self-control procedures by children: A review. *Journal of Applied Behavior Analysis, 12,* 449–465.

Omizo, M.M., & Williams, R.E. (1982). Biofeedback-induced relaxation training as an alternative for the elementary school learning-disabled child. *Biofeedback and Self-Regulation, 7,* 139–148.

Opie, I., & Opie, P. (1959). *The love and language of school children.* Oxford, England: Oxford University Press.

Piaget, J. (1926). *The child's conception of the world.* New York: Routledge and Kegan Paul.

Potashkin, B.D., & Beckler, N. (1990). Relative efficacy of Ritalin and biofeedback treatments in the management of hyperactivity. *Biofeedback and Self-Regulation, 15,* 305–315.

Rosenbaum, M., & Baker, E. (1984). Self-control behavior in hyperactive and non-hyperactive children. *Journal of Abnormal Child Psychology, 12,* 303–331.

Schaefer, C.E., & Reid, S.W.E. (1986). *Game play: therapeutic use of childhood games.* New York: Wiley.

Schandler, S.L., & Grings, W.W. (1976). An examination of methods for producing relaxation during short-term laboratory sessions. *Behavior Research and Therapy, 14,* 419–426.

Serok, S., & Blum, A. (1983). Therapeutic uses of games. *Residential Group Care and Treatment, 1,* 3–14.

Stewart, M.A., Pitts, F.N., Craig, A.G., & Dieruf, W. (1966). The hyperactive child syndrome. *American Journal of Orthopsychiatry, 36,* 861–867.

Stoyva, J.M., & Budzinski, T.H. (1974). Cultivated low arousal: An anti-stress response? In L.V. DiCara (Ed.), *Limbic and autonomic nervous system research* (pp. 198–210). New York: Plenum Press.

Tant, J.L., & Douglas, V.I. (1982). Problem solving in hyperactive, normal, and reading-disabled boys. *Journal of Abnormal Child Psychology, 10,* 285–306.

Thoresen, C.E., & Mahoney, M.J. (1974). *Behavioral self-control*. New York: Holt, Rinehart and Winston.

Varenhorst, B. (1973). Game theory, simulation and group counseling. *Educational Technology, 13*, 40–43.

Varni, J.W. (1976). *A cognitive-behavior self-regulation approach to the treatment of the hyperactive child*. Unpublished doctoral dissertation. University of California, Los Angeles.

Venables, P.H., & Martin, I. (Eds.). (1967). *A survey of psychophysiological methods*. Amsterdam: North Holland.

Wender, P.H. (1971). *Minimal brain dysfunction in children*. New York: Wiley.

Wender, P.H. (1987). *The hyperactive child, adolescent and adult*. New York: Oxford University Press.

Zametkin, A.J., Nordahl, T.E., Gross, M., King, A.C., Sample, W.E., Rumsey, J., Hamburger, S., & Cohen, R.M. (1990). Cerebral glucose metabolism in adults with hyperactivity of childhood onset. *New England Journal of Medicine, 323*, 1361–1366.

CHAPTER FOURTEEN

Using Games to
Improve Self-Control
Problems in Children

ARTHUR J. SWANSON and BETHANY E. CASARJIAN

S elf-control problems in children are a common cause for referral to mental health clinicians. Children who exhibit such impairments have been found to be less competent with peers and to experience an array of academic difficulties (Szatmari, Offord, & Boyle, 1989). In a study conducted by Kendall and Braswell (1985), second- through sixth-grade teachers rated 10 percent of their students as having self-control difficulties that interfered with their social and academic functioning. The self-regulatory problems traditionally included under the umbrella term of self-control deficits include impulsive behavior, poor delay of gratification, distractibility, and low frustration tolerance. From a theoretical perspective, recent research suggests that self-control can be conceptualized as an individual trait or construct that exists on a continuum (Barkley, 1997). At the extreme end of this distribution are children who are labeled with attention-deficit/hyperactivity disorder. According to the *Diagnostic and Statistical Manual of Mental Disorders* (*DSM-IV*; American Psychiatric Association, 1994), children who meet the criteria for ADHD have difficulty sustaining attention across settings, often fail to finish tasks, and have difficulty organizing their behavior. In addition, they may demonstrate elevated levels of hyperactive behavior and an inability to inhibit or regulate their behavioral responses to situational demands. Deficits in self-control are considered to be the most "problematic and core" feature of ADHD (Schweitzer & Sulzer-Azaroff, 1995, p. 671).

As with other developmentally bound capabilities, children's ability to exercise self-control typically increases with age as they develop more knowledge about regulatory strategies and skills (Holtz & Lehman, 1995). In contrast to this maturational tendency, 50 percent to 80 percent of children identified with self-control deficiencies including hyperactivity and impulsivity, continue to demonstrate similar behaviors throughout adolescence (Barkley, Fischer, Edelbrock, & Smallish, 1990). Furthermore, marked impairments in self-control in adolescence are associated with externalizing disorders, delinquent and aggressive behaviors, and drug use (Barkley et al., 1990; Krueger, Caspi, Moffitt, & White, 1996).

Over the past decade, considerable progress has been made in identifying the types of interventions and treatment modalities that are most effective when working with children experiencing self-control problems. Given the difficulty that impulsive children experience thinking reflectively about their behavior, a psychodynamic treatment approach is considered to be limited in its utility (Shapiro, 1981). Although behavior therapy has met with some success, the changes that are manifested tend not to be enduring and typically do not generalize to other settings or tasks (Whalen & Henker, 1991). These limitations may be due, in part, to the tendency of behavior therapies to alter specific behaviors without targeting the cognitions that mediate those behaviors.

Cognitive-behavior therapy has been shown to be a promising intervention in promoting the maintenance of behavior change with children lacking self-control skills (Ervin, Bankert, & DuPaul, 1996). Hyperactive and impulsive children tend to act without adequately assessing the cues inherent in the environment, reflecting on the possible outcomes of their behavior, inhibiting maladaptive responses, and reacting to situations in planned ways. Beyond changing a child's behavior in response to academic tasks or social situations, cognitive-behavior therapy addresses the cognitive deficiencies that underlie self-control problems. What follows is a description of three games, derived from cognitive-behavioral principles and methods, that can be used with impulsive children.

Unlike other forms of treatment that may be unpalatable to impulsive children, games offer an engaging and particularly effective treatment approach (Kaduson, 1997). Most children with self-control problems have experienced chronic failure on academic and social tasks, resulting in negative beliefs about their competency and contributing to the development of poor self-concept. Conversely, games offer an opportunity for impulsive children to acquire concrete regulatory skills utilizing an enjoyable and intrinsically motivating format. These games can be adapted to the child's individual needs, modified as the child's skill level increases, and used in a variety of settings by a number of people in the child's life. Furthermore, children with limited self-control skills have been shown to engage in less play than children with better developed impulse control (Alessandri, 1992). Because games are an integral part of childhood social behavior, imparting specific regulatory skills to children through play may have the ancillary effect of improving their peer relationships.

BEAT THE CLOCK: A GAME TO IMPROVE ON-TASK BEHAVIOR

The goal of this game, adapted from one described by Shapiro (1981), is for the child to outlast the clock so that he or she is actively engaged in the task when the clock strikes. Resistance-to-distraction is considered to be a defining characteristic of good self-control (Holtz & Lehman, 1995). Considering that school success is contingent on the ability to sustain attention across a variety of tasks, poor interference control directly compromises academic achievement. Suitable tasks for this game may include reading, writing, or any other school-based activity on which the child is frequently off-task. In the context of the game, behavior is defined as off-task when the child responds verbally or physically to off-task stimuli in the environment or when the child looks away from the task and fails to return to it within 10 seconds. The 10-second time period is intended to give the child an opportunity to stop and think while performing the task and/or to take brief, appropriate breaks as needed.

The child is given a set number of chips at the start of the activity. For example, if the goal is for the child to remain on-task for three minutes, he or she would be given three chips. A response cost procedure is used in which the child loses a chip each time he or she engages in off-task behavior. When the child engages in such behavior, the therapist briefly reminds the child of the contingency and takes away a chip. The therapist then redirects the child to the task without further discussion. At the end of the allotted time period, the therapist discusses these off-task behaviors and draws parallels between them and situations that may occur at home or school.

The time period chosen should be appropriate to the developmental level of the child. It is important that a time period be selected in which the child can succeed. Gradually, this period can be increased as the child's ability to remain on-task improves.

A child has the opportunity to earn chips for each game that is played. Chips can be exchanged for a small prize—for example, a few pretzels or a baseball card—at the end of the session or accumulated over several sessions and exchanged for a larger prize, such as a game or a special outing. The specific prizes used should be ones both valued by the child and appropriate to the amount of work completed.

CASE ILLUSTRATION

THERAPIST: Would you like to play some games today?

CHILD: Yeah.

THERAPIST: Okay, in the first game we're going to do some reading. Go ahead and pick out a book you'd like to read. (Child chooses book.) Got one?

CHILD: Yeah.

THERAPIST: Good, now, we're going to play a game called *Beat the Clock.*

CHILD: Okay.

THERAPIST: Do you know how to play it?

CHILD: No.

THERAPIST: That's Okay. In this game, I want you to work as hard as you can and still be working when the clock goes off. So, you're going to work harder and longer than the clock. That way you beat the clock. Do you understand?

CHILD: Yeah.

THERAPIST: Great. In the first game, I want you to read for three minutes. Can you do that?

CHILD: Yeah.

THERAPIST: Good. When I tell you to start, you begin reading, and when the clock goes off, I want you to *still* be reading, okay?

CHILD: Okay.

THERAPIST: Now, I'm going to give you three chips. Every time you look away from your reading for a long time (10 seconds) or do something instead of reading, I'm going to take a chip away.

CHILD: What are the chips for?

THERAPIST: Well, we're going to see how many chips you can get. At the end of the meeting you can trade your chips in for a small prize or you can save your chips and trade them for a bigger prize later. (A discussion ensues about the available prizes.) Would you like to earn a prize?

CHILD: Yeah.

THERAPIST: Now, what are you going to do? (Child repeats his assignment.) Good. Are you ready to read?

CHILD: Yeah.

THERAPIST: I'll set the timer. Remember, pay real close attention. Ready? Go ahead. (Child begins to read. Therapist may wish to engage in a parallel activity while observing the child's ability to remain on-task.)

CHILD: (In response to distracting noise during minute two) What was that?

THERAPIST: Somebody in the hall. I need to take a chip from you for talking. Go back to your reading. (Child reads for the rest of the time period.) Time is up and you're *still* reading. Good for you. You have two chips. You lost a chip, didn't you?

CHILD: Yeah.

THERAPIST: What happened?

CHILD: I heard something . . .

THERAPIST: And what did you do?

CHILD: I stopped reading.

THERAPIST: Does that happen in school: When someone makes a noise, you stop working?

CHILD: Yeah.

THERAPIST: What happens then?

CHILD: Sometimes I get in trouble.

THERAPIST: How?

CHILD: I tell the kid to shut up.

THERAPIST: What else could you do?

CHILD: Mind my own business.

THERAPIST: That's another thing you could do. What else?

CHILD: Tell the teacher.

THERAPIST: That's good. You were able to think of a lot of things to do when other kids make noise in the class. So, you did really well. Let's play another game where you draw a picture, but this time for four minutes. Do you think you can do that?

CHILD: Yeah.

THERAPIST: Okay, I'll give you four chips. But remember, I'll take one away each time you look away for a long time or you talk, okay?

CHILD: Okay. (Child proceeds with various activities using the same procedure.)

In addition to creating contingencies that increase the child's ability to attend, this game helps the therapist identify the distractions in the child's environment to which he or she is most sensitive. As described in the therapy session, a discussion can ensue regarding ways to cope with these specific distractions.

THE *STOP AND THINK* GAME:
A GAME TO IMPROVE IMPULSIVE RESPONDING

Research reveals that a "coping" model is more effective than a "mastery" model in the treatment of a variety of clinical problems (Kazdin, 1974; Meichenbaum, 1971). That is, models who initially encounter difficulties that they eventually overcome are more likely to be emulated than those who consistently exhibit "perfect" performance. Presumably, coping models demonstrate behavior that more closely approximates the difficulties encountered by the individual, in this case, the child.

The primary purpose of this game, which has been adapted from the curriculum of Kendall and Braswell (1985), is to provide a vehicle by which a child can learn to use self-instruction to complete a task or to solve a problem. Through didactic instructions and exposure to a coping model, the child is taught a series of self-directed statements:

What is the problem? (Task definition)
What can I do about the problem? (Generation of alternatives)
What is the "best" thing to do? (Selection of best alternative)
How did I do? (Evaluation of performance)

The child is encouraged to use his or her own words to describe each step. Once generated, the child's self-statements are written on a note card that becomes a reference tool for use in completing the assigned task.

In a typical session, the therapist models the use of self-instructions while performing the assigned task. The therapist verbalizes each of the self-statements and "thinks out loud" to solve each step of the process. The child then performs the same task, using his or her own self-statements taken from the reference card. Once the child is able to use the four steps consistently, the therapist performs the task while whispering the self-statements. The child is then instructed to whisper while solving subsequent problems. Once successful at this, the child is instructed to think through the steps without verbalizing them. While numerous materials can be used to play the *Stop and Think* game, ones that are particularly suitable include matching familiar figures, mazes, and Pick-Up Stix. Once a child is successful using self-directed statements in the solution of impersonal tasks, tasks of a more personal or interpersonal nature can be assigned, for example, how to solve a conflict with a friend.

In the *Stop and Think* game, one chip can be given for the appropriate use of self-statements and one chip for a successful solution to the given problem. As in the previous game, chips can be exchanged for a small prize at the end of each treatment session or saved and exchanged for a larger prize after several sessions. Including a behavioral contingency, such as token rewards, in these types of cognitive interventions has been shown to increase the effectiveness of the treatment (Hinshaw & Erhardt, 1991).

Case Illustration

THERAPIST: Do you like mazes?

CHILD: Yeah.

THERAPIST: Well, we're going to do some but maybe a little differently than usual, Okay?

CHILD: Okay.

THERAPIST: I'm going to tell you some steps that I use to solve a problem. I have these steps written on a card. First, I ask "What's the problem?" Then, "What can I do?" Then I ask, "What's the best thing to do?" Finally, "How did I do?" When I try to solve a problem, I use these steps. What I would like you to do is put these steps in your own words. How would you say the first step in your own words? (Child writes each step in her own words on a card.) What we're going to do is use these steps to solve these mazes. First I'll do one, then you'll do one. Do you understand?

CHILD: Yeah.

THERAPIST: What are we going to do? (Child repeats assignment.) Good. Now, for each problem, you can earn two chips: one if you use the steps and one if you solve the problem. How many chips can you earn?

CHILD: Two.

THERAPIST: How do you get them?

CHILD: Use the steps and solve the problem.

THERAPIST: Good. Now, I'll do the first problem. Ready?

CHILD: Yeah.

THERAPIST: Okay, let's see. "What's the problem?" Well, I've got to get this guy out of here. "What can I do?" Well, I can go this way—no, that's a dead end. Or I can go this way. (Draw line.) "How did I do?" I got it right. Good work. Now you do one. (Child repeats process, referring to steps on her own card.)

THERAPIST: Good. You used all the steps and you got the mazes right. You get two chips. I find that when I use these steps, I do better in solving problems. Do you think they might help you?

CHILD: Yeah, maybe.

THERAPIST: Okay, let's try another maze. (Therapist repeats process. Child then does maze but begins drawing before deciding on the best route. The sequence went as follows:)

CHILD: "What's the matter?" I've got to get this lady out of here. "What can I do?" Draw a line. (Child draws a line before considering alternative routes and proceeds to hit a dead end.)

THERAPIST: How did you do?

CHILD: I messed up.

THERAPIST: What happened?

CHILD: I went the wrong way.

THERAPIST: Umh, how did that happen?

CHILD: I don't know.

THERAPIST: Did you stop and think before you started drawing the line?

CHILD: No.

THERAPIST: Okay. Well, let's try that next time, okay? I can't give you any points because you didn't use the steps and you didn't solve the problem. Sometimes we forget, but we'll work on that, okay?

CHILD: Okay.

In the early stages of treatment, it is important that the therapist model a careful and reflective use of the steps so that the child can see the effectiveness of good problem-solving behavior. The child will have lapses, however, in the use of these steps, and the therapist's responses to these lapses is crucial to the child's willingness to continue using the procedure. Therapists themselves may wish to gain chips for their performance; they may have their own lapses in the use of the procedure, and then stop themselves, returning to the appropriate step. Children appear to become more involved and learn more when they become both receivers and dispensers of reinforcement.

THE *STACKING BLOCK* GAME: A GAME TO IMPROVE SELF-MONITORING OF BEHAVIOR

The third game is based on correspondence training, a program developed by Paniagua (1992) to increase the connection between a child's verbalization about future or past behaviors and his or her actual behavior. The link between the verbalization about the behavior and the action may occur in either order, for example, a *do-report* sequence or a *report-do* sequence. The goal of correspondence training is to increase an individual's self-control by creating a stronger tie between a planned, verbalized intention and the behavioral manifestation of that thought.

Although many materials can be used with this method, a stacking block game has been found to be appealing to impulsive and hyperactive children. This game, which can be bought commercially, consists of wooden pieces that are stacked in layers to form a tower. Because the tower becomes less stable as parts are removed and restacked, it eventually falls. The goal of each player is to maintain the balance of the tower during his or her turn, a process that is jeopardized by impulsive behavior and a lack of planning. Furthermore, because the structure of the tower changes after each turn, the child must constantly reevaluate the components of the game in a novel way. Although this particular game allows for a specific type of stacking (i.e., the pieces are pulled from the stack and placed on top of the structure), this game can be modified for use with more traditional blocks.

In playing this game, the therapist models the correspondence between one's verbalization and behavior. Although the game is inherently motivating for most children, its effects can be augmented by adding a reinforcement each time the child's verbalization matches his or her behavior.

CASE ILLUSTRATION

THERAPIST: Would you like to play a game that uses these blocks?

CHILD: Okay.

THERAPIST: You might have seen this game before, but we're going to add a step when we play it. Is that Okay?

CHILD: Okay. What?

THERAPIST: Well, before we make a move, we have to say what we're going to do. Everytime what you say is the same as what you do, you get a token. If you say that you're going to make a move to one place and then you do something else, or if you forget to tell me what your plan is, then you don't get a token for that turn. If the tower falls down, we'll start again. Let's see how long we can play before it falls. I'll try first.

THERAPIST: Let's see, I think I'll take this piece on the bottom near the wall and put it on the top. (The required level of specificity in child's verbalization for a reward should be modified based on the child's expressive language abilities.) (Therapist removes block and places it in target spot.) Did I do what I said I would?

CHILD: Yes.

THERAPIST: You go ahead and do one.

CHILD: (Child moves the block successfully without verbalizing the plan.) Done.

THERAPIST: You stacked the block, but you forgot to tell me what your plan was first, so I can't give you a token. Now it's my turn. (Therapist models appropriate report-do correspondence.)

CHILD: Okay. I'm gonna take a block from the middle (points to spot) and put it up here (points). (Child successfully places block.)

THERAPIST: Good job. You made a plan using words and then followed through with your behavior. You get a token for that move. Now I'll go.

THERAPIST: (As the tower gets less stable, the therapist can model more complex planning, taking the changing form of the tower into account.) Let's see, the tower is really starting to lean this way and there aren't many blocks left on this side. I think I'll take a block from here (points) where it seems strong and put it on this side of the top to balance it out. (Performs action.)

CHILD: Uh oh, it's gonna fall. I'm gonna take one from here (points) because the blocks are getting crooked and put it over here.

THERAPIST: Way to go! You really did some careful looking before you made that move. Here's your token. (Players continue until the tower collapses.)

When playing this game with young, motorically delayed, or very hyperactive children, it might be helpful to begin playing with a shorter tower of blocks. This prohibits the child from knocking the structure over very quickly and becoming frustrated. Because the end result of this game inevitably involves the tower falling, the therapist has the opportunity to intentionally allow this to happen during his or her turn in an effort to model an appropriate expression of frustration and disappointment. This can be accompanied by coping statements designed to model a modulated expression of feelings emphasizing the positive elements of game playing, for example, "We really kept the tower standing a long time that time" or "I'm really starting to get the hang of this game." By emphasizing the common purpose of the game (i.e., to keep the structure standing for as long as possible), the competitive element of the game can be transformed into a collaborative exercise emphasizing the "process" of playing rather than the "product" of winning.

SUMMARY AND CONCLUSIONS

Three games found to be effective in the treatment of children with self-control deficits have been described. The requirements placed on the child in each game need to be appropriate to the child's developmental level. These requirements can be increased in difficulty as the child experiences success in the use of these games. In the *Beat the Clock* game, the therapist needs to attend to the distractions to which children respond. Once identified, such distractions can be reduced by teaching more adaptive ways of coping and where possible, isolating the child during perods of concentration. It becomes important that children begin to play *Beat the Clock* in their respective classrooms under the supervision of the teacher or a teacher's aide so that the skills they have learned in the individual treatment sessions can be generalized to the school setting.

In the *Stop and Think* game, children can be shifted from the solution of impersonal tasks, that is mazes, puzzles, and so on, to tasks of a more personal nature. Practice in this game can help children use self-directed statements to guide both their academic and social behavior. In the *Stacking Block* game, the therapist should repeatedly point out to the child that the demands of the task are constantly changing and need to be reevaluated carefully before making a move. Interrupting patterns of nonreflective behavior, encouraging one's observation of the environment, and reinforcing the connection among thoughts, words, and actions are important facets of treatment with impulsive children.

Each of the games described attends to one of the deficits common to children with self-control problems. The games provide the context in which specific behavioral and cognitive skills are taught in the remediation of these deficits. Treatment is most effective in a well-paced program that is sensitive to the developmental needs of the child, combines game playing with instruction in specific behavioral and cognitive strategies, offers varied materials, and brings treatment into the settings for which it is intended.

REFERENCES

Alessandri, S.M. (1992). Attention, play, and social behavior in ADHD preschoolers. *Journal of Abnormal Child Psychology, 20,* 289–302.

American Psychiatric Association. (1994). *Diagnostic and statistical manual of mental disorders* (4th ed.). Washington, DC: Author.

Barkley, R.A. (1997). *ADHD and the nature of self-control.* New York: Guilford Press.

Barkley, R.A., Fischer, M., Edelbrock, C., & Smallish, L. (1990). The adolescent outcome of hyperactive children diagnosed by research criteria: I. An 8-year prospective follow-up study. *Journal of the American Academy of Child and Adolescent Psychiatry, 29,* 546–557.

Ervin, R.A., Bankert, C., & DuPaul, G. (1996). Treatment of attention-deficit/hyperactivity disorder. In M.A. Dattilio, C.L. Bankert, & G.J. DuPaul (Eds.), *Cognitive therapy with children and adolescents* (pp. 38–61). New York: Guilford Press.

Hinshaw, S.P., & Erhardt, D. (1991). Attention-deficit hyperactivity disorder. In P.C. Kendall (Ed.), *Child and adolescent therapy: Cognitive-behavioral procedures* (pp. 98–128). New York: Guilford Press.

Holtz, B.A., & Lehman, E.B. (1995). Development of children's knowledge and use of strategies for self-control in a resistance-to-distraction task. *Merrill-Palmer Quarterly, 41,* 361–380.

Kaduson, H.G. (1997). Play therapy for children with attention-deficit hyperactivity disorder. In H.G. Kaduson, D. Cangelosi, & C.E. Schaefer (Eds.), *The playing cure: Individualized play therapy for specific childhood problems* (pp. 197–227). Northvale, NJ: Aronson.

Kazdin, A.E. (1974). Covert modeling, model similarity, and reduction of avoidant behavior. *Behavior Therapy, 5,* 325–340.

Kendall, P.C., & Braswell, L. (1985). *Cognitive-behavioral therapy for impulsive children.* New York: Guilford Press.

Krueger, R.F., Caspi, A., Moffitt, T.E., & White, J. (1996). Delay of gratification, psychopathology, and personality: Is low self-control specific to externalizing problems? *Journal of Personality, 64,* 107–129.

Meichenbaum, D. (1971). Examination of model characteristics in reducing avoidance behavior. *Journal of Personality and Social Psychology, 17,* 298–307.

Paniagua, F.A. (1992). Verbal-nonverbal correspondence training with ADHD children. *Behavior Modification, 16,* 226–252.

Schweitzer, J.B., & Sulzer-Azaroff, B. (1995). Self-control in boys with attention deficit hyperactivity disorder: Effects of added stimulation and time. *Journal of Child Psychology and Psychiatry, 36,* 671–686.

Shapiro, L.E. (1981). *Games to grow on: Activities to help children learn self-control.* Englewood Cliffs, NJ: Prentice-Hall.

Szatmari, P., Offord, D., & Boyle, M.H. (1989). Correlates, associated impairments and patterns of service utilization of children with attention deficit disorder: Findings from the Ontario Child Health Study. *Journal of Child Psychology and Psychiatry, 30,* 205–217.

Whalen, C.K., & Henker, B. (1991). Theories of hyperactive children: Comparisons, combinations, and compromises. *Journal of Consulting and Clinical Psychology, 59,* 126–137.

PART FIVE

TEACHING SOCIAL SKILLS THROUGH GAMES

CHAPTER FIFTEEN

Teaching Social Skills

A Board Game Approach

CRAIG WINSTON LECROY and JILL C. ARCHER

Increasingly, the healthy social development of children is being recognized as a critical piece of successful development. Indeed, Elias and Clabby (1992, p. 7) emphasize an "inextricable bond linking personal, social, affective, and cognitive development" in children. Past research has documented the long-term negative effects when children grow up with poor social skills. In fact, disturbances in peer relationships are among the best predictors of psychiatric, social, and school problems. Today, mental health professionals and schools are seeking to bolster children's healthy development by promoting social skills. Such efforts can equip children with prosocial skills to help them replace aggressive and withdrawn behaviors with more appropriate responses, and learn interpersonal skills to enhance communication with peers and parents. Children need social skills. Social skills training is an effective treatment model that can help equip children for healthy social development.

In the most general sense, social skills have been defined as socially acceptable behaviors that enable a person to engage in effective interactions with others and to avoid socially unacceptable responses from others (Gresham & Elliott, 1993). Gresham and Elliott (1990) identified five clusters of effective social behavior: cooperation, assertion, responsibility, empathy, and self-control. Guevremont (1990) identified four clusters of social skills: social entry skills, conversational skills, conflict-resolution and problem-solving skills, and anger-control skills. A social skills training program developed by LeCroy (1994) included eleven specific skills: creating positive interactions, starting conversations, making requests, expressing feelings directly, saying no, asserting rights, empathy, dealing with those in authority, responsible decision making, negotiation and conflict resolution, and asking for help. Indeed, there seems to be general agreement among researchers that prosocial skills are necessary to achieve effective social behavior.

Research shows that deficits in social skills may lead to negative outcomes such as low peer acceptance (LeCroy, 1983; Pepler, Craig, & Roberts, 1995), inability to get dates, conflict with authority, aggression, juvenile delinquency, and poor adult mental health outcomes (Gresham & Elliott, 1993; LeCroy, 1983; Morrison & Sandowicz, 1994). Children who lack the ability to express their anger or frustration in socially acceptable ways tend to have aggressive outbursts and disruptive behavior (Morrison & Sandowicz, 1994). This commonly leads to low peer acceptance, which is associated with such negative consequences as lack of companionship, increased likelihood of being victimized by peers, low self-esteem, increased social anxiety, depression, loneliness, lower academic achievement, and increased risk of dropping out of school (Asher & Rose, 1997). It is clear that adequate social skills are vital to ensure positive social, emotional, and academic adjustment.

AN OVERVIEW OF SOCIAL SKILLS TRAINING

Social skills training is a strengths-based approach, focused on building up the child's repertoire of skills rather than eliminating pathological responses (LeCroy, 1994). This model assumes that children are rejected because they have a deficit in social skills. Deficits may be in either the acquisition or the performance of social skills, which may also be influenced by the presence of interfering behaviors such as aggression or withdrawal (Morrison & Sandowicz, 1994).

The most common methods of social skills training include modeling, coaching, rehearsal, role play, and performance feedback (Elliott & Gresham, 1993; LeCroy, 1983; Morrison & Sandowicz, 1994). A metaanalytic review of social skills training programs based on these methods concluded that there is substantial support for their effectiveness (Elliott & Gresham, 1993). In a review of research on social skills training, LeCroy (1994) found numerous studies giving empirical support to this type of intervention. For example, Sarason and Ganzer (1973) found that delinquents who received social skills training had an increased locus of control as well as a lower rate of recidivism after three years. Several comparison studies have shown social skills training to be effective in prevention as well as intervention (LeCroy, 1983). For example, Schinke (Schinke, Gilchrist, & Small, 1979) and Barth (1996) found social skills training to be effective in preventing unwanted teen pregnancy, and Botvin (1996) found social skills training effective in substance abuse prevention.

Social skills training is generally done in a group setting, which is favorable for several reasons. The main reason is that social skills are demonstrated through social interactions and behavior in the social milieu, and a group is a natural setting in which to observe, learn, and practice these skills. Additional benefits include the opportunity for feedback and encouragement when practicing the skills, motivation through interaction with peers, and the opportunity to practice skills with a variety of people possessing different qualities and styles of interaction (LeCroy, 1994).

THE USE OF GAMES AS A SOCIAL SKILLS INTERVENTION

Games are a particularly effective way to teach social skills to children, whether they specifically address social skills or are just everyday childhood games. Utay and Lampe (1995) studied the effects of game play with students who had learning disabilities, and found that the gains were equal for the group playing a game specifically addressing social skills and the group playing various other educational games. Some of the skills used in playing games are initiating interaction, managing disagreement, coping with teasing, asking for help, cooperating, dealing with failure, and dealing with success (Asher & Rose, 1997). Skills learned through game play are more likely to be generalized to other settings, which is clearly the goal of any social skills intervention

(Nevil, Beatty, & Moxley, 1997). Other benefits of using a game as a social skills intervention are that it is generally fun and therefore intrinsically motivating, it fosters a positive mood, it provides an opportunity to learn new game skills, and it provides an opportunity to practice managing emotions such as anxiety, embarrassment, relief, and pride (Asher & Rose, 1997). In an evaluation of the *Social Skills Game,* LeCroy (1987) found no significant differences between a group using the game format and a group using a standard social skills curriculum. The game format appears to be at least equally effective in teaching social skills.

THE SOCIAL SKILLS GAME

ORGANIZATION AND FORMAT

The game was developed to be used within a social skills training program for elementary school children; however, it can easily be adapted to various other settings and populations. The game incorporates common methods of social skills training: role play, modeling, rehearsal, and feedback. It includes each of the eleven social skills identified by LeCroy (1994). The format may vary, but generally the group will meet twice a week for 30 to 45 minutes, and the sessions will run for 8 to 14 weeks, depending on the needs of the particular group. Selecting members for your group will be based on the goals of the group. If the purpose of your group is prevention of some particular negative outcome, you would need to identify those children at risk for that outcome. This may be done by a referral system, a pregroup interview and assessment, or identification of certain risk factors. Similarly, if the purpose of the group is to build social skills in children identified as having social skills deficits, you would most likely have a referral system in place. It is generally preferred to conduct pregroup interviews with all potential participants to ensure they are appropriate for that specific group. This is also an opportunity to assess their current social abilities and explain the nature and purpose of the group.

CONSIDERATIONS IN SELECTING GROUP MEMBERS

It is important to be aware of how well the members of the group know each other, as too much intergroup familiarity can lead to problems with control. Heterogeneous groups tend to function better, especially when there is a variety of ages, genders, and ethnicities. Size of the group is also a concern. The optimum size tends to be between 6 and 10 members; with the larger groups it is beneficial to have two facilitators. There needs to be enough time for each member to practice the skills and receive feedback, which is why having more than 10 participants is difficult.

BEFORE PLAYING THE GAME

The first session should be spent getting acquainted. During this session the participants become comfortable in the group, and the facilitator explains the purpose, objectives, and format of the group. Over the next several sessions, the focus is on problem-solving skills. The steps in the problem-solving process should be taught; these include defining and formulating the problem, generating alternatives, determining solutions, and evaluating and implementing the solutions. The facilitators will then present situations to which the participants can apply the problem-solving steps. The next several sessions should include an introduction to modeling and role play. The steps of role playing include describing the problem situation, selecting participants for the role play, setting the stage, role-playing, providing feedback and discussion, and repeating as necessary for mastery of the skill. Once the participants appear to be comfortable with the problem-solving process and role playing, the social skills board game can be introduced. This is typically between the fourth and eighth sessions, though this will vary. When the game is presented, the facilitator should explain the purpose and share enthusiasm that this will be a fun way to learn and practice skills.

DESCRIPTION OF THE GAME

The game follows a conventional board game format (see Figure 15.1). Each player takes a turn rolling one die and moving a playing piece around the board in a counterclockwise direction. As they move around the game board, players will be asked to pick a card, respond to a question, or initiate a prosocial behavior. The game incorporates aspects of social skills training such as modeling, role play, rehearsal, and feedback. The playing cards cover four areas: situations, feelings, role plays, and fun activities. The *situation* cards give the player a scenario based on situations they may

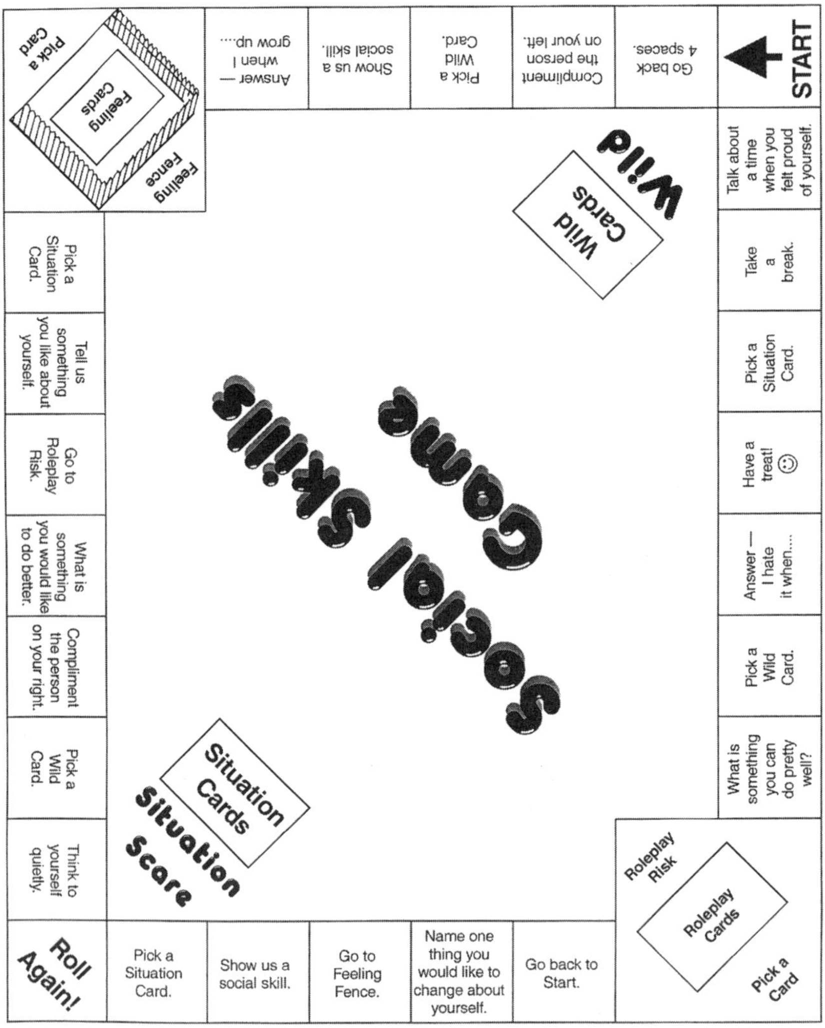

Figure 15.1 The Social Skills Game.

Table 15.1
Situation Cards

---

1. It's Christmas time and Jim wants to buy a present for Scott, his best friend, but he just doesn't have any money to buy one. Scott gives Jim a present in school. Jim doesn't have one for Scott. How would you feel if you were Jim? What would you say to Scott?
2. Name four things you could do to participate.
3. Name three words that mean cooperation.
4. There is a very smart girl in your class. Everyone makes fun of her and calls her the Teacher's Pet. It doesn't seem like she has any friends. How do you think she feels? Tell us how you could help her to make friends.
5. What's the one thing that makes you most angry?
6. What's one way you can show someone else that you're paying attention and listening to them without saying anything?
7. A friend from school is having a party. You find out that you are not invited. Tell us how you think it would feel to be left out.
8. Your friend is feeling bad because someone in your class called him/her a name and made fun of him/her. How can you help your friend? What can you say to help him/her feel better?
9. What are some ways to be friendly or nice to someone else?
10. At home, your parents are out for the night. You and your older brother are the only ones at home. You're having trouble with your homework and you have to get it done or your teacher will be upset with you tomorrow at school. Your brother seems very busy. What would you do? What might you say to your brother?

---

encounter at school, at home, or with friends, and asks them to identify what they would do in that situation (see Table 15.1). *Feeling* cards have a scenario that typically elicits uncomfortable feelings and asks players to identify how they would feel in that situation (see Table 15.2). *Role play* cards give examples of situations that call for assertive responses and ask players to role-play how they would respond in that situation (see Table 15.3). *Wild cards* give the players an opportunity to engage in a fun activity, such as a tongue twister or physical activity (see Table 15.4).

The facilitator must take an active role when the game is played to ensure that the players are achieving their individual goals. For example, children who are isolated and withdrawn must spend extra time learning

Table 15.2

Feeling Cards

---

1. You are at school early one morning. You accidentally break the fish-bowl. The teacher blames another child for breaking it and makes him stay in at recess for a week. You do not like the child the teacher blamed, and you know that he didn't do it. How would you feel?
2. You are playing baseball after school. Your best friend comes to play. He brings his younger brother, who is mentally retarded, to watch. Most of the other kids start making fun of your friend's brother. How do you feel as you see this happen?
3. A friend from school is having a party. You find out that you are not invited. Tell us how you think it would feel to be left out.
4. At school, you do not know how to play volleyball very well. Every time it is your turn to serve, a kid says, "Oh no it's _____'s turn." How would you feel?
5. You have been planning for about a week to have a friend over to spend the night, and you have made plans for all the fun things you will do together. Just before he/she is supposed to arrive, your friend calls to say he/she can't make it. How would you feel?
6. When was the last time that you felt angry? What happened? What did you do?
7. Your teacher is handing back the math tests you took last week. Yours is the last one to be handed out, and your teacher tells the class that you received the highest score. How would you feel?
8. Describe a time when you felt nervous.
9. Show us what you look like when you feel scared.
10. Show us how you look when you feel *(pick a feeling)* and see if we can guess which feeling it is.

---

sharing and friendship-making skills. When a child draws a situation card that covers the friendship-making skill, the facilitator can direct the withdrawn child's attention toward the child role-playing the skill. The facilitator helps the role-playing child to master the skill, but also works with the withdrawn child by helping that child to observe carefully the behaviors modeled by the role-playing child. When the withdrawn child selects a role play card, the facilitator directs extra attention to help the child learn and master the specific social skills.

Table 15.3

Role Play Cards

1. You are taking a test at school. The boy next to you whispers: "Slide your paper over to the side of the desk so I can look at your answers." Show us what you would say and do.

2. You are walking down the hall at school by yourself. Just as you come up to some friends, they start whispering. You think they're whispering about you. How would you feel? What would you do? Show us!

3. A friend of yours in class keeps wanting to pass notes to you and have you write back. You want to pay attention to your teacher. And besides, you know you'll get in trouble if your teacher sees you passing notes. Show us what you would say to your friend.

4. You are at home on a Sunday afternoon and all of your friends are gone. You decide to walk to the park. At the park you see three kids about your age playing a game of keepaway. You don't know any of the kids, but the game looks like fun and you decide you want to play. What would you do or say? Show us!

5. At home, you have your own desk. Your brother or sister uses your desk without asking you. They mess up your desk and you don't like this. What would you say or do? Show us!

6. You're outside your house when your friend Pat comes up to you and wants to play. You don't feel like it and tell Pat that you want to do something else. Instead of leaving, this friend follows you around. You think Pat is being a pest. Show us what you would do.

7. You are in school and you don't know how to play volleyball very well. Each time it's your turn to serve, a kid says "Oh no! It's _____'s turn." How would you feel? Show us what you would do!

8. At school, you notice that your friend treats you a lot nicer when you are alone together than when the two of you are with a group of friends. You have been thinking about this lately and you don't like it! Show us what you would do!

9. You are at a store with your friend. Your friend grabs something off the counter and hands it to you. You don't know what she is doing, but she tells you to put it in your pocket quick! Show us what you would say to her.

10. Pick someone in the group and show us what you might say to him or her in order to make a new friend.

Table 15.4

Wild Cards

---

1. Stand up and, without saying anything, show us what your favorite animal is!
2. Get up and do three jumping jacks!
3. Tongue twister: Rubber Baby Buggy Bumpers.
4. Tongue twister: Silly Sally sold seashells by the seashore. (Say three times as fast as you can!)
5. Run around the group once and sit back down!
6. Show us the funniest face you can make!
7. Tongue twister: Unique New York. (Say three times as fast as you can!)
8. Walk like an Egyptian around the circle once and sit back down.
9. What would you put on your dream pizza?
10. Walk backwards around the group and sit back down!

CASE ILLUSTRATION

Marianne and Dave have been facilitating a social skills training program with a group of seven children. This is their sixth week of the group, and last week they finished learning and practicing role plays. Marianne introduces the game as a fun way to continue learning and practicing the skills they have been working on. Dave sets up the game and lets the children pick their playing pieces.

Stephanie goes first, and lands on the Feeling Fence. She reads the card out loud: "A friend from school is having a party. You find out that you are not invited. Tell us how you think it would feel to be left out." Dave is aware that Tyler is often in this situation, as he tends to be isolated and withdrawn, not having any close friends. Tyler is looking down in his lap and Dave directs Tyler's attention to Stephanie as she says she would feel lonely and disappointed and that no one liked her. Tyler looks as if he wants to say something, but several other children are talking. Dave notices this and asks Tyler if he has a comment. Tyler says, "That's exactly what it feels like, Stephanie." At this point, Carrie chimes in and says, "Yeah, last year when Sabrina had her party at the pizza place, everyone got invited but me. It really stunk."

It's Allison's turn now, and she picks a wild card. She has been fidgeting in her seat since the game started and generally has difficulty staying focused and paying attention. Her card tells her to stand up and show the group what her favorite animal is without saying anything. Allison jumps right up, clearly excited to be out of her seat, and hops around the room on her hands and feet. Everyone easily guesses that her favorite animal is a frog.

James goes next and picks a role-play card. James has a few friends, but tends to get into a lot of fights at school and generally has difficulty with anger management. He reads his card out loud: "At home, you have your own desk. Your brother or sister uses your desk without asking you. They mess up your desk. You don't like this! What would you say or do? Show us!" Marianne asks James to pick someone to role-play with. James has a sister, so he chooses Gwen to be his sister in the role play. James says, "You always mess up my desk and it really makes me mad! Quit being such a brat!" Dave jumps in and offers reinforcement and feedback to James: "James, I really like how you said that it makes you mad when she messes up your desk. How do you think you could improve your response?"

Meanwhile, Marianne sees that Allison is bouncing in her seat and bothering Tyler, who is next to her. Marianne directs Allison's attention to the role play and asks if she has any suggestions for James. Allison says, "Maybe you could find her another place to do her work, or make her put everything back how she found it. That's what I have to do in my dad's office." Dave asks James to try the role play again. This time James says, "It makes me mad when you mess up the things on my desk. Could you please leave it how it is or use a different desk?" Dave praises James for his response and several members of the group applaud. Because there are seven players, they only have time for each player to have three turns. When the game is over, several of the children are asking Marianne when she will bring the game back.

APPLICATIONS

The *Social Skills Game* can be introduced into any existing group or social milieu. It is clear from existing research that social skills training is significantly more effective when done in a group setting as opposed to working with an individual. La Greca (1993) takes this idea further, suggesting that social skills training would be more effective for the individual child if it incorporated his or her broader social milieu. La Greca posits that teaching children these skills in small groups does not necessarily change the reactions of peers and others in their broader social environment. In a classroom setting, this might be achieved by involving that child in playing the *Social Skills Game* with several high-status or nonrejected peers. Other researchers have reached similar findings. In a review of several studies, Pepler, Craig, and Roberts (1995) found evidence that social skills training for aggressive adolescents is ineffective unless it involves the peer group. Morrison and Sandowicz (1994) agree that social skills interventions must be focused at the transactional level, beyond the individual with social skills deficits to the broader context. This may be within the family, in the classroom, on the playground, or in the peer group.

Research has identified certain groups of children, such as those with learning disabilities or mild mental retardation, who are more likely to have social skills deficits (Elliott & Gresham, 1993; Nevil et al., 1997; Utay & Lampe, 1995). Social skills deficits have also been associated with mental health issues such as anxiety and depression, as well as delinquency (Morrison & Sandowicz, 1994; Pepler et al., 1995). Therefore, social skills training commonly occurs in outpatient and residential settings with clinical populations. The *Social Skills Game* is appropriate for use in an outpatient or residential group setting. In fact, social skills training in residential settings has been shown to facilitate the generalization of prosocial behavior (LeCroy, 1983).

Further, it should be mentioned that the *Social Skills Game* could be utilized in conjunction with an existing social skills curriculum. For example, Go Girls is a social skills training psychoeducational prevention program developed for adolescent girls (LeCroy, Daley, & Milligan, 1999). The program teaches specific skills through modeling, rehearsal, feedback, and discussion. The board game could be used later in the curriculum as a tool to practice and reinforce the newly acquired skills.

SUMMARY AND CONCLUSIONS

Social skills training is effective in preventing negative outcomes such as delinquency, poor peer relationships, psychiatric problems, unwanted pregnancy, substance abuse, and victimization. Possessing adequate social skills equips children for healthy social and emotional development.

The *Social Skills Game* is an excellent method of practicing and reinforcing social skills learned through a traditional social skills training program. The game is also appropriate for other group settings, such as a classroom, a family, or residential or outpatient treatment centers. Using the game format enables practitioners to combat the most commonly faced problems in social skills training groups, which have been identified as boredom, inattentiveness, reluctance to learn, and disruptiveness (LeCroy, 1987). Further, skills learned through game play are more likely to be generalized to other settings, increasing the effectiveness of the intervention.

REFERENCES

Asher, S., & Rose, A. (1997). Promoting children's social-emotional adjustment with peers. In P. Salovey & S. Sluyter (Eds.), *Emotional development and emotional intelligence* (pp. 196–224). New York: HarperCollins.

Barth, R.P. (1996). *Reducing the risk: Building skills to prevent pregnancy, STD and HIV* (3rd ed.). Santa Cruz, CA: ETR Associates.

Botvin, G.J. (1996). Substance abuse prevention through life skills training. In R.D. Peters & R.J. McMahon (Eds.), *Preventing childhood disorders, substance abuse, and delinquency* (pp. 81–102). Thousand Oaks, CA: Sage.

Elias, M.J., & Clabby, J.F. (1992). *Building social problem-solving skills.* San Francisco: Jossey-Bass.

Elliott, S.N., & Gresham, F.M. (1993). Social skills interventions for children. *Behavior Modification, 17*(3), 287–313.

Gresham, F.M., & Elliott, S.N. (1990). *Social skills rating system.* Circle Pines, MN: American Guidance Service.

Gresham, F.M., & Elliott, S.N. (1993). Social skills intervention guide: Systematic approaches to social skills training. *Special Services in the Schools, 8*(1), 137–158.

Guevremont, D. (1990). Social skills and peer relationship training. In R.A. Barkley (Ed.), *Attention deficit hyperactivity disorder: A handbook for diagnosis and treatment* (pp. 540–572). New York: Guilford Press.

La Greca, A. (1993). Social skills training with children: Where do we go from here? *Journal of Clinical Child Psychology, 22*(1), 288–298.

LeCroy, C.W. (1983). Social skills training with adolescents: A review. In C.W. LeCroy (Ed.), *Social skills training for children and youth* (pp. 91–116). New York: Haworth.

LeCroy, C.W. (1987). Teaching children social skills: A game format. *Social Work, 32,* 440–442.

LeCroy, C.W. (1994). Social skills training. In C.W. LeCroy (Ed.), *Handbook of child and adolescent treatment manuals* (pp. 126–169). New York: Lexington Books.

LeCroy, C.W., Daley, J., & Milligan, K. (1999). Social skills for the twenty-first century. In R. Constable, S. McDonald, & J.P. Flynn (Eds.), *School social work: Practice, policy and research perspective* (pp. 376–390). Chicago: Lyceum Press.

Morrison, G., & Sandowicz, M. (1994). Importance of social skills in the prevention and intervention of anger and aggression. In M. Furlong & D. Smith (Eds.), *Anger, hostility and aggression: Assessment, prevention, and intervention strategies for youth* (pp. 345–392). Brandon, VT: Clinical Psychology.

Nevil, N., Beatty, M., & Moxley, D. (1997). *Socialization games for persons with disabilities: Structured group activities for social and interpersonal development.* Springfield, IL: Thomas.

Pepler, D., Craig, W., & Roberts, W. (1995). Social skills training and aggression in the peer group. In J. McCord (Ed.), *Coercion and punishment in long-term perspectives* (pp. 213–228). Cambridge, MA: Press Syndicate of Cambridge University.

Sarason, I.G., & Ganzer, V.J. (1973). Modeling and group discussion in the rehabilitation of delinquents. *Journal of Counseling Psychology, 20,* 442–449.

Schinke, S.P., Gilchrist, L.D., & Small, R.W. (1979). Preventing unwanted adolescent pregnancy: A cognitive-behavioral approach. *American Journal of Orthopsychiatry, 49,* 81–88.

Utay, J., & Lampe, R. (1995). Use of a group counseling game to enhance social skills of children with learning disabilities. *Journal for Specialists in Group Work, 20*(2), 114–120.

CHAPTER SIXTEEN

Game Play Therapy for Antisocial Adolescents

MARJORIE MITLIN

I have been playing games ever since I was a child. I can remember playing games with my parents, my brother, my grandparents, my cousins, and, of course, my friends. We played countless games of checkers, chess, jacks, Ping-Pong, pool, *Chutes and Ladders, Candyland, Chinese Checkers, Risk, Monopoly, Scrabble, Pick-Up Stix,* and others. The games, I always believed, were a way of passing the time, a way of structuring my time, as well as a way of socializing with others. These games were a terrific alternative to being bored, a malady that often led to annoying others. Games for me were "the thing." They were a vehicle for being with people, an equalizer, a language that many people could understand. Many games didn't necessarily require talk, yet while playing the games, the space became a safe haven, and talk was inevitable. The talk had safe boundaries in that after a brief amount of time playing a game, the conversation had to stop and you had to refocus on the game play so the next person could "go." Sometimes, even while in mid-sentence, it became your turn and then moments later, someone else's turn. When a new player "went," the players usually had to abandon the earlier conversation and would refocus on the play. Perfect. Safe. Fun.

Another interesting aspect of game play is that many games require you to be in unusually close proximity to the other players. Generally speaking, Americans give themselves more physical space between people than board games allow for. In Edward T. Hall's book *The Hidden Dimension,* he posits that if people are close enough to touch one another (within one foot of one another), this distance is considered to be very intimate in American culture (1969, p. 126). Therefore, because when playing a board game, people are close enough to touch one another, this kind of play commands a level of relatedness and intimacy that is otherwise unusual for most people in this culture.

In playing board games, each player has to depend on the others to follow the rules (even the unspoken rules about not touching one another, even though you are so close to the next player), to play fair, and to follow one another's moves along with the meanings that each move possesses. Each move in a game has an effect on the other players (just as in real life each action of one person in a group or a family affects the others in the group). Each move leaves the player whose turn it is with myriad feelings, including those of success, frustration, disappointment, or triumph. The outcome of a player's move can affect the next player's mood, and, in some cases, it can even affect a player's self-worth. Play is powerful. As I remember it from the perspective of having been a child, it was hardly play. My brother and I played games for hours, playing out our rivalry in contained rule-bound games. Although on a good day, my army would take over his army and crush it (*Risk*), and on other days, his would cripple mine, we always ended up alive and sometimes amiably talking at the family's communal dining table.

My undergraduate degree is in health and physical education, and at the university I went to I was given a huge toolbox (figuratively speaking) of activities, games, and programs. I accumulated more and more games with which to work with children and adolescents. Children seemed to respond best to the structure of those activities while usually being unaware of the skills being developed while just "playing." Children at play—whether organized, structured game play, or imaginative play—are working hard to fit in, contributing something to others, following directions (or not), and developing relationships and alliances with others, while they are also trying to WIN. Competition, a factor in most play, propels children and adolescents (and even adults) to try harder and to do better in an effort to come out victorious. In some cases, on the other hand, competition causes people to withdraw, sometimes even to the point of refusing to play altogether.

During and after graduate school years in clinical social work, I began working with children, adolescents, and their families in a child psychiatry clinic. There, the play was the thing—game play, that is. As part of my training, I was supervised by three different play therapists/supervisors who were skilled at teaching me play therapy. These were the years of plenty: plenty of supervision, plenty of time to work with patients (as long-term treatment was in vogue), plenty of inservice training, and *plenty of games.* We were also taught how to make use of children's drawings as part of the mental status exam in a psychosocial assessment. In addition, we were taught how to interpret children's drawings and how to use all children's artwork as another therapeutic tool with which to work with children and adolescents. We incorporated all of the techniques we could learn from others in the field in our effort to have a bag of tools with which to reach the needs of children and adolescents. We used such tools as "The Storytelling Technique" and "Squiggle" by Richard Gardner, and we also learned how to use all kinds of regular commercial games like *Sorry, Battleship,* and *The Matching Game,* as well as therapeutic games like Richard Gardner's *Talking, Feeling, and Doing Game,* all to help children and adolescents access their feelings and feel safe enough to express them.

During my stint at the child and adolescent clinic, I developed a love and fascination for working with the adolescent population. Many of the patients we saw at the clinic (to whom, over time, we began to refer with a less stigma-laden label, namely, "the clients") came from the inner city of Boston. Many of them came from multiproblem families. There were many families with one or both parents struggling with drug or alcohol addictions and/or mental illness, and there were many who suffered complicated and painful histories of abuse. The patients' histories were laced with childhood memories, including leftover images of physical and/or sexual abuse. Many of these people were coming to the clinic, and, for the first time, trying to heal those old but raw wounds. The clinic, for many, was the first place where they were able to be safe and to begin to feel safe. We played games with them. We talked. We mirrored their behaviors (a technique described in detail by Heinz Kohut), and we talked through characters in the imaginative play, empathizing with their plights. Eventually, together, we would write new scripts with new endings. At times we would rewrite old scripts using familiar players with better habits and safer behaviors, while we offered them a place to experience their feelings in the context of therapeutic play, respite, hope, and laughter (at least during their 50-minute sessions). Throughout these sessions we hoped that, over time, this hopefulness would carry over to the rest of their lives. We primarily worked with these clients through play, using *games.*

My next four years were spent at an adolescent day treatment center where milieu treatment/group therapy was the modality. We worked with adolescents who were struggling with major mental illnesses and/or behavioral problems using art, music, theatre, talk therapy, and *games.* We facilitated games among clients. We played games with the clients. (After hours, the staff played games with each other, such as Ping-Pong and Foosball.) We created new games with the clients. We wrote raps and we choreographed dances and skits. We played games to help them cope with the lot that they were given while creating more possibilities than their lives had previously allowed them to imagine.

EMOTIONAL BINGO

HOW *EMOTIONAL BINGO* DEVELOPED

Soon after this adolescent day treatment center lost its funding, at a time when I was primarily building my private practice, my son's third-grade teacher approached me. She was having trouble with her students, who were having difficulties listening to one another. She asked if I could come into the classroom and do a presentation on "good listening" for the students. I tried to think of some creative way to get them involved in a listening endeavor. I thought that something familiar, something that they had done and had mastered before could be the vehicle. Of course, a *game* would be "the thing." Bingo jumped into my mind: *Emotional Bingo* was conceived, and in 1998, it was published by Western Psychological Services (WPS)—Creative Therapy Store.

THE CONTENTS OF *EMOTIONAL BINGO*

Emotional Bingo consists of 32 bingo boards. Each board has 25 squares set up in 5 rows with a free heart space in the center of the board. In each square, a face is depicted caricaturing a specific emotion. Both sides of each bingo board have the same caricature faces with the names of emotions written underneath them; on one side of the bingo board the emotions are written in Spanish and on the other side they are written in English. There is also a deck of cards with the same caricature faces depicting the same emotions as portrayed on the bingo boards, with the name of the emotion written out beneath each picture. Here, the names on each emotion card are English on the top and Spanish on the bottom. In addition, each game contains a poster displaying all of the emotions depicted on the cards in alphabetical order.

How to Play *Emotional Bingo*

Hang the poster in the front of the group or classroom so that everyone can see it. Explain to the group/class that the emotions on the poster are set up in alphabetical order so that they can find them easily. Explain that after you call out an emotion card, you will point to the correct picture on the poster so that they can identify the picture on their *Emotional Bingo* cards more easily. Hand each player a bingo card and 10 red plastic chips. Instruct them to put a red chip on the free heart space in the middle of the bingo card. Then explain that this game is played similarly to other Bingo games they have played before: For each emotion called out by the leader that appears on their card, they cover the corresponding space with a chip; to "get Bingo," they have to cover a line of five squares on their bingo card (or four in a row plus the free space) in a horizontal, vertical, or diagonal direction.

To start the game, the leader pulls out a card from the deck of emotion cards, reads the emotion out loud, and then points to the corresponding emotion on the poster. Any player who has that emotion depicted on his or her bingo card covers it with a red plastic chip. Here is where the game differs from other bingo games they may have played before: Players who have covered a space with a red plastic chip have an opportunity to give an example of a time in their lives when they have experienced that particular emotion. After players give examples from their lives they are rewarded with two white reward tokens. If players feel too uncomfortable giving a personal example, they can either make up an answer or use an example from someone else's experience (without using that person's name).

The next part of the game involves active listening and empathy. After the first player has given an example of a time when he or she has experienced the emotion, the other players have a chance to respond to that player's example with empathy. For example, if the facilitator picks the emotion card "angry" and the player gives the example, "I felt angry when I had a date and my parents grounded me," another player is rewarded with a white token if he or she is able to respond empathically to the first player's example. Therefore, if a player says, "Of course, you must have been angry when your parents grounded you and you couldn't go out on a date that you had planned," then that player receives one white token. Other players who give additional statements of empathy are also rewarded with a white token. The leader at this point has the discretion to respond to other players who want to give additional examples of times in their lives when they have felt angry, or to move the play along by choosing another emotion card and starting the process all over again.

The play goes on until someone gets Bingo. The player who gets Bingo reads the five emotions in a row aloud so everyone can hear them, and if he or she correctly calls out each emotion, that person gets a red cardboard reward token worth 10 tokens. Play continues to the next round. The winner is the player who at the very end of the game has accumulated the most tokens, including those won for getting Bingo, for giving examples of times when he or she had experienced emotions, and for showing empathy toward other players.

An alternative way of playing this game is for the facilitator to direct the content of the play in a particular direction. For example, if the group has come together specifically to help adolescents focus on issues of sexual abuse, then all of the examples given by the players could be focused on that topic. For example, if the facilitator chooses the card "happy," an adolescent could give an example of this by saying "I was really happy at first when my father was paying so much attention to me." Another example of "happy" might be "I was really happy when I finally told my therapist what was happening to me and he told my mother, who took out a restraining order on my father." Using a game like *Emotional Bingo* to focus on emotionally laden issues could make talking about painful material easier for some adolescents. The game play helps to diffuse the sting a little bit while helping the adolescents stick with the material in a less threatening situation. For some teens, straight talk is too awkward and too direct.

THE PURPOSE OF *EMOTIONAL BINGO*

Emotional Bingo has two primary goals. The first is to reward children and adolescents for being able and willing to give examples of times in their lives when they have felt a particular emotion. The second is to reward children and adolescents for being able and willing to listen to others' examples and for responding empathically. Accomplishing this goal is not a simple task. Children, by nature, are very self-involved. Some of this is developmental, in that children perceive themselves to be the center of their universe. They are bursting with their own needs to be heard, to be understood, and to be the center of attention. Over time, if they are given an adequate amount of love, nurturing, attention, and "mirroring" (Kohut) from their primary caregivers, they become more able to attend to those around them. Without enough of this attention, they remain very needy and self-absorbed, and they have a difficult time being able to listen to others. Given this egocentricism, children and adolescents have a difficult time being able to attend to the needs of others. Therefore, in *Emotional Bingo,* in which paying attention to others is the focus, it is a challenge for children and adolescents to be active listeners.

This need to be the center of their universe at the expense of empathy or support of others shows up during the game. Say the facilitator picks a card with the emotion "disappointed" on it. The player would then give an example of a time of disappointment in his or her life. The player might say something like "I felt disappointed when my father, who lives separately from my mother and my brother and me, didn't come to my football game when he had said he would." A player giving this good example of "disappointed" would then be acknowledged for the good example by being given two reward tokens.

At that point, other players would be given a chance to respond empathically to that original player's example. Typically, children (as well as adolescents and adults) respond to the request for empathy by giving an additional example of a time when they themselves felt that emotion. This is especially true of children and adolescents whose parents are not emotionally available to them for a variety of reasons and, therefore, are not able to provide adequate attention and mirroring. A player might therefore respond to the request for empathy by saying "I felt disappointed when I came home from school, having gotten a part in the play, and my mother yelled at me and told me that she was on the phone and that I shouldn't interrupt her if I didn't want to be grounded." The facilitator would respond to that child by being sympathetic to the situation, stating something like "That is another really good example of a time in your life when you felt disappointed, and therefore, you get one reward token." At that point, however, the facilitator needs to direct the group back to the example that the first player has given and ask if anyone can respond to that player's example of being disappointed when his father did not come to his football game.

My experience is that you may have to go through these steps several times before you get someone who is able to focus on the example of the first player's disappointment and respond with empathy. Examples of empathic responses that the facilitator is looking for are: "That must have been really disappointing for you"; "You must have been really upset when your father said that he would come to your football game and then didn't"; "It must have been disappointing and upsetting for you when your father didn't come." Any player who can respond with empathy gets acknowledged with one white reward token.

Often, in their attempt to be empathic, players give advice to the person who has expressed feelings to the group. An example of this is a person responding to the disappointed football player by telling him, "You should have called your father the day before your game and reminded him." Giving advice does mean that the player has listened to the other person's example, and therefore, it is a step in the right direction. At least he or she has been listening! Therefore, the facilitator should always begin feedback to the player who is giving advice by responding in a positive fashion, saying something like "It is excellent that you heard what so-and-so was saying." Furthermore, the facilitator must acknowledge in a supportive fashion the person's attempt to be empathic: "I can tell that you were trying to be supportive of so-and-so when you gave him advice, and that was really good."

Advice, however, is not the same as empathy. Telling people what to do after they have already experienced the negative results of their expectations or choices does not help them to feel better or to feel understood. When you give advice you are trying to "fix" someone's feelings or situation, which the person with the feelings is not ready for. People who are recovering from hurt feelings are often in need of emotional healing, which involves being able to stay with those hurt feelings for a while before wanting or needing to do anything to change those feelings or the situation. Therefore, when people are upset about something, what they do not need is advice. What they do need, however, is to be understood and empathized with. Given most people's knee-jerk need to "fix" the upset or sadness that other people are feeling, the facilitator may need to reiterate many times over the course of playing this game that empathy is one's ability to listen to what others have said and then to respond to their feelings as if you were in their shoes and could really understand their position.

Over the course of the game, the players begin to respond with empathy, which sounds something like "I'm sorry that your father didn't come to your game. That must have been very disappointing." The expression of empathy by a variety of players often gets derailed by another player's need to give an example of a time in his or her life when he or she felt that feeling too. The facilitator can then reward this player for another good example with one token, and then move the game along, or else the facilitator can get the group to respond empathically to that new example, again rewarding the players for their ability to empathize with the new examples.

At this point, children often want the facilitator to proceed with the game because, although you are helping them to take risks while encouraging them to become better active listeners and to learn how to respond empathically, they are trying to fill up their Bingo boards so that they can win the game. Therefore, when the facilitator notices the players becoming antsy, it is important to move the game along, which happens by pulling out the next emotion card and saying the emotion aloud.

Coleaders Facilitating the Play

Emotional Bingo can be facilitated with one group leader, and there are specific settings in which this might be very workable (as in a school while working with small groups of adolescents). With therapy groups in general, however, and in playing *Emotional Bingo* with behavior disordered adolescents specifically, I recommend two leaders to facilitate this game (and for most therapeutic games). While playing *Emotional Bingo*, it will be necessary for one leader to call out the emotion cards and to hand out reward tokens, while the other facilitator helps to direct the conversation, trying to keep the players on task while helping them to act appropriately with one another. If you are "going it alone," you will have to manage all of this on your own. It is workable but challenging, especially if your charges are antisocial adolescents. Ideally, the group leaders should be seated opposite each other at a round table. If the group chooses to play on the floor, each leader should sit opposite the other in the circle, so that it is easy for them to make eye contact with one another. This positioning is important, as throughout the session, the group leaders need to be in good communication with one another. Also, this arrangement will better enable each facilitator to play a specific role during the game play.

In some therapy groups where coleadership is done, before the group starts, the leaders decide who will play the more supportive role and who will be more confrontational. We used to call this the "good cop, bad cop" system. This way of coleading allows group members to observe two different adult leadership styles with which to negotiate and through which to navigate. In addition, players usually bond to one leader or the other, and different leadership styles allow players to relate to specific styles with which they may more comfortably identify and to which they may be less reactive. Coleadership also makes group members feel more emotionally and even physically secure (as in a functional two-parent family, in which children feel more secure with both parents available). An additional benefit to this coleadership arrangement is that there are two pairs of eyes, two limit-setters, two adults who will support the members, as well as a second clinician who can pay attention to the group process while tuning into the nuances of communications between the group members and the leaders.

Given that working with antisocial adolescents is a constant challenge due to their frequent negativity and oppositional style, having two clinicians involved in the group's game play is unbelievably helpful. It is helpful for the reasons stated above, and it is also helpful as a way to manage the countertransference reactions when an adolescent treats one of the leaders or even other group members in a particularly hostile, disrespectful, or even sexualized way. By countertransference I am referring to the emotional reaction that the therapist has in response to a patient's behavior(s), with the origins of the therapist's reactiveness lying within his or her own unresolved experiences.

For example, when I asked a group member a question that I had inadvertently asked him before, the member blurted out with great hostility and disgust "What do you have, Alzheimer's disease? I already told you that last week!" Countertransference is my reaction to the comment that the group member made to me. In my case, I felt angry that "after all that I tolerate from him, and given how supportive I am of all of them so much of the time, they sure have some nerve for being so hostile to me." I also felt bad that I didn't remember what he had said. These kinds of reactions

sometimes emerge in response to the complex interchanges that are simultaneously going on during the course of each moment during each
group. Therefore, it is very helpful to have a coleader to pick up on the
members' comments to the coleader (who needs a moment to regroup
from his or her annoyance) while directing the members to process the
prior comments that were made. The objectivity that is provided by having a coleader is invaluable.

When working with this population, because the adolescents are often
disrespectful, devaluing, and critical of the other members as well as of
the group leaders, it is helpful to have a second clinician to help diffuse
tensions that readily arise. The coleader's responsibility is to reframe the
hostile commentary into reparative therapeutic interchanges (or at least
to try to).

GAME PLAY WITH ANTISOCIAL ADOLESCENTS IN A HIGH SCHOOL SETTING

For the past three years, I have been working in a traditional high school in
the southeastern part of Massachusetts, specifically with students who
struggle with learning problems. Some of these students have explosive
disorders; others have attention-deficit/hyperactivity disorder. Many
struggle with depression or manic depression, and they all have either conduct disorder or antisocial character pathology.

The *DSM-IV* defines antisocial character pathology as "a pervasive
pattern of, disregard for, and violation of, the rights of others" (APA,
1994, p. 649). The *DSM-IV* goes on to explain that people with this diagnosis use deceit and manipulation as a major mode of getting their needs
met. To be diagnosed with an antisocial personality disorder, the person
has to be at least 18 years of age (p. 650) and have a history of a conduct
disorder since the age of 15 (p. 649). A conduct disorder, according to the
DSM-IV, is "a repetitive and persistent pattern of behavior in which the
basic rights of others or age appropriate societal norms or rules are violated" (p. 85). Given these parameters, the students with whom I work
display behaviors that include a combination of conduct disorder and antisocial personality disorder (depending on their age and the length of
time they have sustained certain patterns of persistent behaviors). Additional behaviors that characterize these adolescents include impulsivity,

irritability and aggressiveness, reckless disregard for the safety of them-selves or others, consistent irresponsibility (e.g., failure to sustain consis-tent work or to honor financial obligations), and a lack of remorse (p. 650).

Aside from these disorders, many of these adolescents also struggle with learning problems, attention-deficit disorder, clinical depression, posttrau-matic stress disorder, and drug and/or alcohol involvement. Frequently, their parents are emotionally unavailable to them, and some of them are drug- or alcohol-involved themselves. Therefore, the diagnostic picture is muddied by these multiple problems. The clearest part of the picture is the behavior that the adolescents display. These antisocial adolescents are fre-quently involved with the police, probation officers, the juvenile courts, the Department of Social Services, foster placements, and so on. Many of them do not have the resources to receive outside psychiatric treatment; those who do have the financial means often do not have parents willing to sup-port their treatment. In these cases, offering treatment in the schools is a blessing. We have, to some extent, captive audiences (except when the stu-dents are suspended or just choose not to attend school), and, therefore, we have some hope of being able to engage them in treatment in school. Also, for some of the students who are involved with the courts, treatment in school is mandated, giving us some leverage in getting the students to com-ply. Many of these students are receiving special education services, and it is written into their educational plans that they receive counseling, which makes accessing them for treatment in the school workable.

In the "regular" school setting where I work, these particular adoles-cents report feeling like outcasts. They frequently talk about feeling like second-class citizens in the school, believing that the students, as well as the administration, consider them to be "trouble," and, therefore, they feel that they are rejecting of them. In truth, antisocial adolescents often have a difficult time complying with school rules. I often hear my stu-dents say, "Why should we go along with the rules? After all, the rules are stupid and ignorant." In addition, many of them repeatedly say "If I was a jock, I wouldn't be getting nailed for these stupid things."

Due to this pervasive attitude about school rules, or any rules for that matter, and due to behaviors that defy the rules at every turn, many of these students are frequently given a variety of disciplinary actions, in-cluding teacher detentions (one hour after school), extended detentions (three hours after school), suspensions (anywhere between 1 and 10 days outside of school), and a Saturday work program held between 9:00 A.M. and 12:00 noon. These students spend an inordinate amount of time in these afterschool programs and on suspension, being punished for a variety of infractions, including not bringing in their gym clothes, not being willing to change into their gym clothes, coming late for class, or swearing. In addition, they are given more severe disciplinary action for such things as carrying weapons, threatening to beat up people, smoking cigarettes, using or selling drugs on school grounds, or for actually assaulting someone.

I began working with these students in individual treatment within the confines of the school. After sitting with antisocial adolescents individually, in more traditional, 42-minute psychotherapy (the time of a typical class period), using "talk therapy" as the primary treatment modality, it became clear to me that while seeing these students individually, I was not seeing the breadth of what these students were really dealing with. Individually, they were smart enough and smooth enough to make a great case for themselves. They were charming and convincing; they were terrific at getting me to see their point of view and to understand how, through their eyes, the system was usually short-changing them.

Again, it did not take very long for me to realize that seeing these adolescents individually wasn't always helpful. They were far too Eddie Haskellesque while I was seeing them alone; they would act overly appropriately, being overly solicitous and overly fake. What I was not seeing while working with them individually was the way they feed off one another. I couldn't see the way their behavior escalates when they are together and how the dynamics shift when they are in a group. Seeing them in the environment in which they collectively function is the ticket, but it is not without its complications and challenges.

In group, these adolescents establish a "pecking order," a power hierarchy in which it is nonverbally decided who is to be in charge and who will be the followers. They function like a family, with traditional roles: one authority figure with a second in command, and then their charges. Together, however, they are not able to listen to one another. They are constantly talking over one another in an effort to be heard. Sometimes they talk over each other in an effort to derail the conversation when it becomes too hot to handle. (That was my interpretation of why they derail the conversation. They would say that they change the subject just because it is boring or because it is none of anyone's business what they think about something.) They have difficulty being with one another without putting each other down.

The group members have little ability to sustain their own separateness. I repeatedly hear about one of the members getting into a fight with someone, and how the others are going to "kick that person's butt." Even though these other adolescents have nothing to do with the original fight, they quickly become embroiled in the conflict, with the same urgency and potential for violence as if some horrible affront were being directed toward them. I was somewhat confused by this behavior that resembled loyalty but was not loyalty. My experience of these students is that, in the end, they would stab each other in the back or sell each other and their families down the river without even flinching. They seem to have little investment in doing right by each other. There seems to be no "standing by their man" mentality. However, they are always ready and willing to get involved with alleged friends in a fight. I began to understand this as their need for stimulation. As with adolescents who self-mutilate (who relieve their numbness by hurting themselves), antisocial adolescents experience a kind of deadness, numbness, or boredom that they can relieve temporarily by being engulfed in fights or arguments.

Additionally, these antisocial adolescents constantly share each other's business in the group and talk behind each other's backs. Together, they lose whatever boundaries they have (the ability to know where each person stops and the next person begins). They constitute one dysfunctional ego, one mass of adolescent hormone surge, and conversations frequently become sexualized or hostile. When these students do infrequently take a risk to share some small but important thing about themselves, they can become emotional punching bags, human targets for fellow group members to devalue.

In the group, these adolescents behave in a much more real way (by real, I mean that they act as they really are, not the way they think they should be when they are with me). What I also learned, however, after not too long a time, is that without some kind of structure within the group session, things quickly deteriorate. Before one has time to ask a question, they are, for example, talking about this great LSD trip that someone had taken or how funny it was when they were smashing people's mailboxes with baseball bats. The other thing that I learned was that even though I had worked with this kind of adolescent for many years and considered myself a seasoned clinician, I did not have a formula for making a group work well with this population. I have found that without structure, this population of adolescents does not seem to be able to sustain itself for more than two minutes before plummeting into hostile, devaluing, boundary-free behavior.

In working with this population of adolescents, I have tried a multitude of techniques and approaches (some more successful than others). I am always trying to give them some of the early experiences that most of them have never had (e.g., being read to, being listened to, believing in them, reading plays together with social themes, watching films and talking about them, talking about relationships, sexuality, and drugs, and of course, *playing games*). Because these adolescents have had few experiences playing games or just "hanging out" with adults, it is impressive that they have tolerated the hundreds of structured activities to which I have exposed them and in which I have involved them.

For about two months, five days a week, I read children's literature to them and processed it with them. Although they initially hemmed and hawed and insisted that they didn't want to read another story, while I was reading, you could hear a pin drop. At times they got stuck on semantics, insisting that, for example, in *Amos and Borus* by William Steig, it was ridiculous to think that a mouse could befriend a whale. "Why not?" I would insist. "Can't you be friends with someone who is different from you? Maybe they have more things in common than you can imagine." Another response came after we read *The Five Chinese Brothers* by Claire Huchet Bishop and Kurt Wiese. One student sarcastically said that it was ridiculous that the brothers could not be killed. Who could stretch their legs all the way down to the bottom of the ocean? These students were very concrete, and had a tough time moving beyond the actual language of the story.

Introducing games into the group sessions became my way of structuring the groups. Although introducing this kind of structure helped to focus and organize the group, the adolescents sometimes complained bitterly of feeling infantalized and victimized by me and my game ideas. It was tough to get it right. At times, they called my games "stupid" and the books "lame" but often referred, in other contexts, to the content of the material that we had been dealing with, which showed me that they were taking in some of this information.

Respecting the fact that they are adolescents and not children is a dance that is constantly challenging because they behave like much younger children in many ways. I have not always found that balance, but to the students' credit, they are excellent about giving me critical feedback when they believe that I have not gotten it right. "That was stupid, Ms. Mitlin. What do you think we are, idiots?" Not too long ago, after I had spent about 60 hours doing research and creating a board game to help adolescents address issues of violence (*Sticks and Stones*, pending publication), they candidly told me (clearly in a weak moment) that they knew I really cared about them and that I wanted them to be successful, which is why they guessed that I even bothered with them, but that having them play this game was really "ignorant." Of course, I knew that the material in the game was anything but "ignorant." In fact, I think that the problem with the game was that it was too affectively laden and therefore too hard for them to tolerate.

I do understand, however, that at times, playing a game at their age feels insulting to them, while at other times, they love it and specifically ask to play. Adolescence is like that, though. This is an age at which teens walk the fence between desperately wanting to be grown up and desperately wanting to be held (figuratively) and cared about like a child. The one aspect of game play that really works well is competition: This population is very competitive and they really want to win. They sometimes respond to game reward tokens, but I have found that they mostly need rewards that meet their immediate needs. When I play games with adolescents, which takes up a good deal of my days, I try to make the winning worth their while. I often reward adolescents with cookies and candy (yes, I admit it!) or by giving them privileges (e.g., getting up and walking around, getting a soda, choosing the next group activity).

As I alluded to earlier, this population is famous for giving you what they think you want to hear as opposed to what they really think or feel. In fact, it is very difficult for them to trust anyone (because of their early histories of being disappointed, abandoned, abused, etc.), especially with their true feelings. Many times I have asked these adolescents specific questions, such as "Have you ever witnessed any violence?" and they have answered the question by saying "That's too personal!" Some of that response is their way of telling me where to go (just to be oppositional), but another aspect of the situation is that their lives have been so filled with losses, disappointments, and pain that they are easily emotionally flooded (overwhelmed) by the most seemingly benign questions. They readily believe, therefore, that it is not safe to answer my questions. In addition, because of their histories, they often misperceive other people's motives for asking certain questions (often attributing some negative motive to people's questions), and they feel distrustful of what others will do with their answers if they dare to be brave enough to answer the questions in the first place. These students come to us with a good deal of baggage that interferes with their ability to trust us. Therefore, they are quick to feel that we are putting them down in some way or just generally out to hurt them or to abandon them (as others have done to them).

For a clinician, the hardest part is to sift through these adolescents' behaviors and ultimately to decipher the true meaning of their communications. These adolescents are savvy and use their own inflated "affective reactions" as a way of getting out of something. A recent example of this was when I was playing a therapeutic board game with a group of adolescents (*Teensense,* which is being produced in 2000 by Western Psychological Services), and one of the questions focused on a male teen's relationship with his mother. One of the students, whose mother had died about six years earlier, bolted up out of his seat and said "I have to leave. I am too upset about my mother's death and I can't sit here for one more moment." He got up and left the classroom and walked out of the school. The next day when I saw the student, I asked to talk with him privately (I should add that I know this student well and have worked closely with him for the past three years). I told him that I understood that his mother had died and that her death had been a big loss for him. As for his reaction during the group, however, I felt that he had given a fine dramatic performance and that his bolting seemed to have little to do with his mother. He laughed and told me that I was right and that he didn't feel like staying in school anymore that day. We talked about how hard it was for me to decipher what was one of his great acting performances and what was real. He just looked at me (with a smirk, I might add). I often say to myself that it is a really excellent thing that I like these particular adolescents, because they do take you for an emotional ride!

PLAYING *EMOTIONAL BINGO* WITH ANTISOCIAL ADOLESCENTS

As stated earlier, *Emotional Bingo* has two goals. One is to help players become better listeners, and the second is for these adolescents to be able to respond empathically to one another. These two skills are very difficult for this population to master, especially the empathy component. By definition, antisocial adolescents do not feel for others. Typically, they feel no remorse for their actions, and therefore, another person's misfortune, losses, sadness, or general pain is usually met with cold emptiness, or worse, with ridicule or sadism. Given this reality, *Emotional Bingo* teaches some basic socialization skills that, somehow, these adolescents have missed. In some cases, the lack of socialization skills is related to their learning disabilities, as some of them lack the ability to pick up on social cues. Others are well aware of the "right thing to do," but are determined not to make the "right choice." Whatever the reason for the poor social skills of this group of adolescents, this game rewards them for making the effort to do right by one another.

It is very important for these adolescents to play the teen version of *Emotional Bingo*, for the teen version has language with which adolescents will more readily identify (e.g., bummed out, freaked out, mellow, turned off). I have also found that if you can direct the game to focus on particular subjects that they are interested in, they are more apt to participate. For example, if the group focuses on drug and alcohol issues, they are likely to be interested. The same might be true of issues around sexuality and intimacy, and also such issues as abuse.

When antisocial adolescents play this game, they sometimes early on "get" the fact that if they are empathic, they will be rewarded (usually with tokens, but also with praise). Therefore, when they figure out how to respond empathically, they often are capable of saying the appropriate words (giving an empathic response), but they are likely to say them in an overly dramatic fashion, sarcastically, or by making a mockery of the situation. Do not be discouraged when adolescents do this. In fact, one should be encouraged because regardless of their less than agreeable attitude in general, in this case they are trying to play the game and are trying to respond empathically. Because responding to one another in a caring or empathic way is so foreign to them, when they do so, they feel self-conscious and awkward. This discomfort is similar to how it feels for anyone in treatment who is trying on a new way of behaving. In the beginning, trying out the new behavior feels fake or contrived. After practicing the new behavior over and over again, however, one starts to feel more comfortable acting differently. Here, too, when the adolescents respond with contrived empathy, it should be embraced and rewarded.

The other point of interest in playing this game with antisocial adolescents (and with most adolescents) is that playing the actual game of Bingo is what they are interested in, not in developing social skills. Therefore, taking the game seriously and making sure they are all playing fair and are not sharing reward tokens (which they sometimes try to do) is crucial. Getting Bingo and winning additional reward tokens, and possibly winning the whole game, is what they are interested in.

With more oppositional adolescents, I find that reward tokens sometimes do not really cut it. This population often needs more incentive to cooperate, specifically, something that gives them immediate gratification. However, here again, it is a fine balance. A recent example of this was evident when I was playing *Emotional Bingo* with a group of behavior disordered adolescents. They refused to play the game except for the Bingo part. When it came to giving personal examples of times in their lives when they felt particular emotions, they refused to play. I yanked out a bag of candy that I had purposefully placed in my sweater pocket, and told them that for each example, I would give them a candy. One of them was quick to respond by telling me that I was trying to bribe them to talk about their feelings. I suggested that I was giving them some incentive to play. Two out of the four boys in the group decided to play (for the candy), and the other two continued to refuse. However, at the end of the game, when there was still one Tootsie Roll remaining, a third boy asked if he could have it. I said that I would be happy to give it to him, that I, in fact, had brought the candy for all of them, but the rule was that he could get the candy after he gave an example. He looked at me, gave me one of those hostile looks that only adolescents can give to adults (and especially to their parents), and then he gave an example of a time in his life when he felt a particular emotion. He said, "I was really upset when DSS (the Department of Social Services) placed me in a foster home." He took the Tootsie Roll and left the room.

The facilitator does not always have to go the "candy route." Depending on the makeup of the group and the willingness of some key players just to play the game, it can be successful with the already built-in reward tokens and praise. The key is to engage a few players who have some influence over the group. Leadership should be praised in the course of this game, because players who are willing to take risks by disclosing their feelings set the stage for the overall group's cooperativeness. The facilitator should always verbally acknowledge any willingness on any player's part to cooperate ("That was a really great answer" or "It must have been very difficult for you when that happened to you").

I have found that it is helpful for the facilitators to play the game with the adolescents. As in other therapeutic games, however, it is imperative that the facilitators' answers respond closely to the needs of the group members, rather than for the therapists to focus on experiences that the cards trigger for themselves. Also, I believe that the less facilitators disclose about themselves to the group, the better. My experience of working with this population is that if you share something personal about yourself, it is often misunderstood, met with criticism, or used as something for the adolescents to retaliate with at some other point. It is better for the facilitator to make up an example that has relevance to the group members' lives. An example of this is that when an "angry" card is picked, the therapist might respond by saying something like "I felt angry when I saw an older high school student harassing a younger student" or "I felt angry when I heard that James was punished for something that he didn't do." It is always important to show them strong emotions in the service of supporting the group members' struggles.

Although this game is fun and is helpful in engaging adolescents who are resistant to traditional talk therapy, when the players share personal examples or if they engage in spontaneous conversation as an outgrowth of the play, it is important for the facilitator to stop the game play and to focus on the issue that is being brought up. For example, once, when I picked the emotion card "angry," one of the players responded by talking about a time when someone spread rumors about him saying that he had had sex with a girl who allegedly really liked him at the same time that he had a girlfriend. He went on to say that this wasn't true and that he had not done anything. Other group members were able to continue to ask him questions about his situation, feeling bad for him that he was being set up in that way, and so on. The conversation went on for a while until the player could no longer tolerate staying with the story. At that point, someone else responded empathically, saying "That is too bad that that happened to you when you did not even do anything," and the game play moved forward.

CONCLUSIONS

I have found that games offer a wonderful vehicle for reaching antisocial adolescents. Games provide structure and a level of intimacy that is new for many of them. Peer acceptance and approval at this stage of their development is extremely important, and even antisocial adolescents in a therapeutic setting are working overtime trying to fit in and to jockey for a position for themselves (preferably one with a little bit of power). Of course, part of what makes this structured game play successful is that there is at least one, and preferably two, adult clinicians who are working closely with the adolescents, acting as positive role models. These adults are taking the time to engage them in game play, to listen to them, to praise them, to laugh with them, and ultimately to teach them, while simultaneously setting limits, challenging blatant disrespectful stereotypes, refereeing, and offering alternative ways to understand situations that this population spontaneously perceives negatively.

I have found that within the context of playing a game, the structure itself creates an environment that is conducive to fostering trust among group members, as well as between the adolescents and the group leaders. It is within the safety of that play around a small board with "directions included" that adolescents can begin to experience rewards. There, they are rewarded for cooperating and for contributing. In addition, the game positively acknowledges adolescents with reward tokens, verbal praise, repeated verbal reinforcement for good manners, for helping a teammate, and for being tolerant of the time that it takes for another player to share an experience with the group. It is while working together in a safe environment that antisocial adolescents can develop social skills and can begin to heal. In the end, *Emotional Bingo* is a therapeutic tool, a vehicle with which to engage adolescents (and children) in discussions about experiences in their lives that elicit their feelings. It also encourages them at least to begin saying the words that at some point may develop into real empathy.

REFERENCES

American Psychiatric Association. (1994). *Diagnostic and statistical manual of mental disorders* (4th ed.). Washington, DC: Author.

Hall, E.T. (1969). *The hidden dimension.* Garden City, NY: Doubleday.

Kohut, H. (1977). *The restoration of the self.* Madison, CT: International University Press.

Mitlin. M. (1998). *Emotional bingo.* Los Angeles: Western Psychological Services.

Mitlin. M. (2000). *Teensense.* Los Angeles: Western Psychological Services.

CHAPTER SEVENTEEN

Prescribing Games to Reduce Aggression in Children

APRIL K. BAY-HINITZ

T he games children play are often overlooked as a powerful tool that will shape a child's behavior. A child's playground, or play environment, is the stage where behaviors are learned, practiced, and tested. When children play together, a setting for interpersonal learning is created. When these children play *games* together, the setting becomes structured and governed by the rules of the game. Hence, the rules of the game become the primary directive for which certain behaviors are learned and developed while others are ignored and punished.

Games can be classified as competitive, cooperative, or individualistic. A competitive interaction is one in which the success of one person requires the failure of others (Kohn, 1983). In contrast, a cooperative interaction requires coordinated efforts of one or more persons such that the success of one can only be achieved with the assistance of others. A third type of interaction, the independently structured activity, differs from both of these. In an independently structured activity, the achievement of one person is unaffected by the achievement of others.

A competitive game is designed to create a winner and a loser. The personal skills reinforced are to do better than your opponent and doing your best is considered good. However, the interpersonal skills are, at minimum, ignored, while usually structured to encourage opposition. With opposition comes aggressive behavior, although not part of the game structure, a significant effect of competitive games (Bay-Hinitz, Peterson, & Quilitch, 1994). Children are learning how to oppose others. Placed in this context, most children are smart enough to discover that lying, deceiving, cheating, and a good hit over your opponent's head will support their cause, that is to win and have your opponent lose. Parents may believe that these are just games and easily differentiated from real life; for children, they are learning the game of life.

The therapeutic and damaging effects of games on children are not often assessed or manipulated. Mental health professionals often treat aggression in children without ever looking at the child's play environment. More often, the child's behavior is consequenced. Underlying causes are also assessed, such as relationship problems within the family, poor frustration tolerance of the child, inadequate limits of parents, not enough "good attention," and other problematic parental techniques. The clinician can make significant impact on the child's behavior through these strategies; however, it doesn't make any sense to ignore the powerful impact of games in a child's life. Therapeutic effects can be found by adjusting a child's exposure to cooperative and competitive games.

HISTORICAL BACKGROUND AND RATIONALE

Aggression is a problem that can begin in childhood and extend throughout a person's life. Aggression is often targeted as a problem behavior that needs to be punished or eliminated in some way. However, aggressive behaviors in young children are, to a large extent, a result of inadequate positive social skills for interacting with peers and negotiating their competing needs with other children.

Lack of social effectiveness is a problem in all ages. Many studies have demonstrated, in fact, that adults have problems in their employment due to inability to get along with coworkers, rather than difficulties with the job itself.

Aggression is a primitive defense for handling frustration, anger, and obstacles in life. In the animal kingdom, we see aggression used as a strategy to handle threat from another animal or situation. A mother bear feels threat to her cubs and becomes extremely aggressive to protect. A lion attacks a hyena for encroaching on his recent kill for food. A 4-year-old hits another child for playing with her toy. Two siblings wrestle to the ground to establish hierarchy and control, and a 6-year-old throws his toy against the wall to reflect his dissatisfaction with his mother's attempt to limit his behavior.

Prosocial skills, such as negotiating, cooperating, and sharing, are more sophisticated forms of behavior. Children need to be taught these skills, just as they need to learn manners or practice the alphabet. Letting children play freely does not provide a direct enough route for training these skills, albeit a child who is exposed to examples of prosocial skills is more likely to role-model this during free-play situations.

Aggressive behavior in a child is often the result of not knowing a more effective way of dealing with a situation. As a result, powerful feedback loops can be created. For example, Johnny wants his toy back and can't seem to get it from the other child, so he bops him on the head with his fist. In the meantime, Johnny learns that he also felt a sense of power or control over the situation. Johnny feels effective, in that he got his toy and he feels powerful, in that he controlled the other child. Children are looking for ways to feel masterful in their environment; this directly affects their self-esteem. Johnny may be punished for his aggression, which in turn will affect his self-concept (i.e., being a "bad kid"). Aggressive behavior can create a vicious cycle extending into self-esteem, self-concept, and self-mastery.

Of course, aggressive behaviors are not only the result of skills deficits but are also created and exacerbated by other factors, such as a lack of resources creating a need for competition (not enough toys to go around or enough attention to go around); a crowded situation; observation of other children, adults, television, and other media sources, that model aggression; and acting out emotional problems.

Play is the primary activity for children and therefore the most salient and accessible time to learn, practice, and reinforce new skills. Teaching children to become effective social beings will not only decrease the likelihood of their being aggressive, but will improve their overall sense of effectiveness, self-esteem, and mastery over their life in all areas. Cooperative games are an effective tool in teaching children to become more socially effective.

RESEARCH

There has been a great deal of research over the years on play, games, and their effects on aggression and prosocial behaviors. Different types of play materials have been found to be associated with prosocial and antisocial behaviors in preschool (Doyle, 1976; Quilitch & Risley, 1973). Research strongly supports the belief that television violence contributes to aggression, violence, and future criminality in children (Hughes & Hasbrouck, 1996). How children play serves an important role in the development of social behaviors, and the choice of materials that facilitate play similarly serves an important function.

COOPERATIVE GAMES: A POSITIVE ASSOCIATION

Cooperative games provide a powerful and significant means to learn prosocial skills. Research has shown that providing cooperative games to young children does indeed increase cooperative behaviors with children and concomitantly decreases their aggressive behaviors. Children who play cooperative games regularly are being provided consistent training and reinforcement for prosocial behaviors.

In addition to cooperative games, the beneficial effects of cooperative activities have been documented in literally hundreds of studies (Johnson & Johnson, 1975). For example, cooperative instruction enhanced liking of school and teacher (DeVries & Slavin, 1978), decreased rejection of newly integrated students (Madden & Slavin, 1983), increased positive relationships with cross-sex and cross-ethnic students (Ames, 1981; Rogers, Miller, & Hennigan, 1981), and reduced prejudice and ridicule behaviors (Johnson, Johnson, & Scott, 1978). Cooperation has also correlated with increased interpersonal attraction (Acton & Zarbatany, 1988), greater empathy (Marcus, 1978), and improved confidence and intrinsic motivation (Johnson, 1975). A review of 122 studies from 1924 to 1980 looked at achievement data resulting from competitive, cooperative, and individualistic activities (Johnson, Maruyama, Johnson, Nelson, & Skon, 1981). Of the 122 studies, 65 found cooperation produced higher achievement than competition, 8 found the opposite, and 36 found little if any difference. As you can see, the literature suggests beneficial effects more frequently associated with cooperative activities.

Negative Impact of Competition: What a Therapist
Needs to Assess

The issue of prescribing cooperative games is secondary to a good assessment of competitive game exposure. The rationale and research behind competitive games should be discussed with parents to increase compliance. For example, research on competition has been correlated with increased fear of failure, decreased academic performance (Kohn, 1983), and greater anxiety (Kernan, 1983), and was found to have an inverse relationship to achievement (Helmreich, Spence, Beane, Lucka, & Mathews, 1985). Competitive attitudes have been found to be correlated with the belief that one is not able to express oneself in class, is not listened to by teachers, and is not able to ask or answer questions in class (Johnson, Johnson, & Anderson, 1976).

In an effort to be balanced, there is a study that shows competitive attitudes were correlated only with problems in younger children and did not seem to have the same relationship with high school students. This study (Johnson & Ahlgren, 1976) found competitive attitudes in high school students to be correlated with positive attitudes, such as motivation to learn and involvement in learning. This study also found that cooperative attitudes were consistently related to these same positive variables across all grade levels from 2 through 12.

Sports is the most obvious arena for competitive activities in schools for older children; for younger children, games provide a competitive arena. In high school students, Quanty (1976) found athletes became more aggressive over the course of a competitive football season, as measured by personality tests. Similarly, a classic study by Sherif and colleagues (Sherif, Harvey, White, Hood, & Sherif, 1961) found that 11- and 12-year-old boys, when divided into competitive teams for baseball, football, and tug-of-war, showed a generalized increase in hostility and aggressive acts. Similarly, in younger children, exposure to aggressive models during competitive play resulted in increased aggressive behavior (Hoving, Wallace, & LaForme, 1979). Aggression has also been correlated with competitive recreation in emotionally disturbed children (Phillips, 1981).

In summary, competitive games and competitive activities are associated with a wide variety of problem behaviors and, in particular, aggressive behaviors. This finding is more consistently found with preadolescent children. Cooperative games are correlated with a multitude of positive behaviors and, in particular, decreases in aggressive behavior. Bay-Hinitz et al. (1994) suggested an inverse relationship between cooperative and aggressive behavior, that is, either by an inhibiting effect of cooperative behaviors, or a replacement of aggressive behaviors by cooperative behaviors.

METHODS OF TREATING AGGRESSION

Over the years, the most popular form of treatment in clinical and nonclinical settings has been to use time-out and resolve the underlying problem, for example, look for aggressive sources that children are modeling and resolving problem relationships at home or school. Interventions aimed at reducing aggressive behaviors in younger children have frequently involved manipulations of the conditions of play. Murphy, Hutchison, and Bailey (1983) found that organized games along with a time-out procedure significantly reduced the frequency of aggressive acts. Another study found decreases in aggressiveness when teachers reinforced cooperative play (Wolfe, Boyd, & Wolfe, 1983). Verbal instruction and a token economy effectively increased cooperative play among these children by 50 percent over baseline. Results suggest very clearly that reinforcement of cooperative play has a powerful effect on problem behavior, even when that behavior is not specifically targeted.

Other manipulations in the play environment include adding or removing certain types of toys. For example, making toy guns available to preschoolers will raise levels of aggression and increase rule breaking behavior. Removing the toy guns or other aggressive toys and replacing them with neutral toys, such as toy airplanes, will decrease levels of aggressive and rule breaking behavior (Sanson & Muccio, 1993; Turner & Goldsmith, 1976). In addition to which toys are available to children, studies have also shown it is important to attend to how much physical space is in their play area. Boe (1977) demonstrated a strong relationship between increased physical space per child and decreases in aggression with problem children.

There are often difficulties in treating aggression through manipulation of reinforcing and punishing consequences. These interventions typically involve a carefully considered individual treatment plan and the use of skilled personnel. Such a program is often labor-intensive and may demand significant amounts of professional time. In addition, one child may be "singled out" for individual treatment which may negatively influence group or family dynamics, for example, increasing the potential for group rejection and ridicule.

These behavioral strategies, along with family therapy, play therapy, and more recent developments in psychopharmacotherapy for aggression (Potenza & McDougle, 1998), are mainstream for inpatient and outpatient settings. However, teaching the child appropriate skills for being with peers, working and playing together, and maneuvering in the social world are lifelong skills that are usually expected to occur naturally or in school and family arenas. As we know, this doesn't always happen. The child is left ill-equipped to deal with others and begins to develop problems.

In contrast to treating behavior problems such as aggression, changing the game play environment (games offered and instructed) can prevent problem behaviors and reduce existing aggressive behaviors by removing many conditions that arise from competitively structured games. Research supports cooperative games as a viable treatment intervention for aggression in preschool children (Bay-Hinitz et al., 1994). In this study, aggressive behaviors that decreased included hitting, pushing, kicking, verbal assaults, and destroying surroundings. The means of aggressive responses decreased 10 out of 12 times following implementation of a cooperative games intervention This study used games as the only form of intervention.

DESCRIPTION OF THE GAMES

Just about any game could be restructured to be a cooperative game. There are many cooperative board games, activity games, and workbooks on the market. Most of these games can be obtained through Animal Town Game Company, P.O. Box 485, Healdsburg, CA 95448; Past Times Publishing, Ontario, Canada; or Childswork/Childsplay, P.O. Box 1604, Secaucus, NJ 07096-1604. Or call 1-800-962-1141. Multiple examples of cooperative nonboard games can be found in Orlick's *Cooperative Sports and Games Book* (1982). These books are helpful for the practitioner, parent, and teacher by facilitating creative thinking and ideas using cooperative goal structures. This is a must for parents who seem unable to fathom that any game could be fun or successful without the competitive edge.

Cooperative board games require that all players work together to move around the board, problem solving, cooperating, sharing, and helping each other to achieve a mutually desired end. Examples of preschool cooperative board games (the ones used in the Bay-Hinitz et al. research study) are *Max, Harvest Time, Granny's House, Sleeping Grump,* and some cooperative nonboard games, such as cooperative musical chairs.

In the game *Max,* all children work together to save the animals of the forest from a cat, Max. Every time Max gets closer to some of its prey, the players can call Max back to home point by utilizing the group's reserve of Max's treats (e.g., milk, cheese). The object of the game is for all players to get around the board and save the forest animals from Max. *Harvest Time* uses four to eight players, all working together to harvest each other's land before "Old Man Winter" comes. The players quickly learn that it is to their benefit to work together to harvest each other's land, not just their own, for the most benefit of all. In the game *Granny's House,* all children work together to move through obstacles to get to Granny's house. To overcome various obstacles, the children must make group decisions using a limited supply of resources. All players either win by reaching Granny's house, or lose by running out of resources before reaching the end. *Sleeping Grump* has children, age 4 to 7, work together to climb the stalk to recover treasures before the sleeping Grump awakes. All players win if they reach the top of the ladder and all lose if the Grump wakes before they finish.

Cooperative musical chairs is the opposite of traditional musical chairs. Children skip around a group of chairs, and when the music stops, they must find a chair or share a chair to sit on. In this form of musical chairs, no one is eliminated from the group; chairs are eliminated. By the last one to two chairs (depending on the size of the group), all children are leaning, touching, and sharing a space on a chair for the group to win. This is a great game to include when children seem to be pairing off, forming cliques, or excluding children. In this game, you will see those same children who normally exclude others helping the "outsiders" by physically pulling them into the group, sharing chair space, leaning on each other, and figuring strategies to include all players. It is evident that this experience benefits the typical outsider and begins to undermine the creation of cliques and impenetrable groups.

Childswork/Childsplay sells various cooperative games for age 3 to 12+. Some of my favorite board games for 6- to 12-year-olds include *Mountaineering,* an adventure game that mimics a real-life mountain experience, where players must work together to reach the summit in freezing weather while avoiding frostbite and snow blindness. *The Secret Door* is a cooperative mystery game, and *Investigators Game* is a fun board game for age 8 and up where kids learn cooperation while solving a crime.

There are some great physical games that can be purchased, such as *Buddy Walkers,* which are platforms that require children to simultaneously lift and move the same leg as they pull up with their hands on ropes. The *Co-Oper Band* is a large latex tube covered with stretchy fabric. A group of children, age 3 and up, stand inside the tube and all children must learn to compensate and cooperate their movements to obtain the desired shape.

Old favorite competitive games such as *Candyland, Chutes and Ladders,* and musical chairs can be restructured by the parent or teacher to have cooperative rules and cooperative goals. For example, in *Candyland* each player takes turns moving around the board to get to the final candy destination and be declared winner. To restructure this game, have all players use the same game piece and take turns moving it around the board. When they reach the end, they have all participated in the final outcome. This is the most simplistic way to restructure a game: It merely removes the competition with a very simple form of cooperative structure (i.e., sharing the same game piece while taking turns).

A more complicated game, however, requires more restructuring and should have more cooperative elements, such as joint problem solving, negotiating, sharing, or exchanging personal resources to benefit another for the overall good. For example, musical chairs restructured removes chairs, not people. Participants must strategize together to create a human lattice atop one or two chairs. Often, removing the "eliminate or do better than the other person" component can be rearranged to eliminating or doing better than a common, nonperson adversary: the race against time or diminishing resources, the highest score achieved together, solving a mystery or puzzle together. Activities such as tennis, badminton, and volleyball are easily played with the goal being the longest volley between each other. It takes some practice to re-create game structures. However, we've found that children become quite adept at doing this on their own. After learning and playing cooperative games, children are able to restructure competitive games to cooperative structures without parent/teacher involvement. The more a child plays by cooperative game rules, the greater the learning and the more reinforcement these concepts gain.

APPLICATION AND PITFALLS

EXPOSURE TO COMPETITIVE VERSUS COOPERATIVE GAMES

Most children are exclusively exposed to competitively structured games. Given the familiarity with these rules, it is sometimes difficult for children, and their parents, to shift to cooperative games. Compliance can be a problem when prescribing cooperative games. Therapy must educate and familiarize parents and children with cooperative rules and structure to facilitate compliance. A description and rationale is usually necessary, followed by an office practice session with parents participating. After children are exposed to cooperative games, they will start to prefer this structure. In fact, research has shown that cooperative games are preferred over competitive games once children are exposed to them (Orlick, 1981).

When working with parents, it is sometimes necessary to educate them on the research. For example, research has shown that cooperative games will increase behaviors such as willingness to share, perceived happiness, and subsequent cooperative behavior (Orlick, 1981). Once a child has mastered the new cooperative goal structures, he or she can teach others in the family. Research supports the generalization from one child's newly acquired cooperative skills onto other frequent play partners (Provost, 1981).

THE CHILDREN (AND THEIR PARENTS) WHO LOVE COMPETITION

Changing the rules on children who are familiar with competitive games can be difficult at first. This is especially true for children who are generally the "winners" and have learned a sense of mastery and identity from winning in competitive situations. Children in general can be resistant to change. The earlier you start to introduce cooperative games, the easier it will be. Parents and adults who interact with the children are often as difficult to change as their "aggressive" children whom they want to help. The people who directly influence young children are not fully aware of the consequences of their game choices and other effects of the environment. A brief explanation to the parents on the primary effects of games on children's behavior and different effects of different games will increase their understanding, and thus compliance.

All children, except the one child that wins, learn to integrate "losing" and "failure" experiences into their identity. Point out that cooperative games allow play and learning to occur in an environment free from failure; instead, feelings of success and camaraderie flourish. Cooperative games also play an important role in the development of more positive social attitudes toward family, peers, and teachers.

When working with parents who are wed to competition, approach the discussion in terms of skills acquisition and their child's interpersonal skill deficiencies. Relay information on games as an intervention to treat the problem rather than engage in a philosophical debate over the merits of competition. For example, a confused or nontracking parent will say things such as "Competition is everywhere"; "I did it and it didn't hurt me"; "The drive to win inspires us to do our best, else we become complacent"; and my favorite, "If my child doesn't learn to fight to win he will become a loser." Rather than using the psychotherapy hour to disprove their belief systems, I acknowledge their concerns without supporting them and then carefully redirect the issue at hand. The issue is their child's problem with aggression and the forces surrounding the child that exacerbate, if not cause, the problem. Eliminating competition and violent entertainment while increasing exposure to cooperative games and win-win scenarios is a treatment intervention to remedy this problem.

Some children can be exclusively exposed to competition and never show problems with aggressive behavior. Remind the parents that this is not the case with their child. The issue of compliance is crucial, given that this treatment requires the participation of the entire family and specifically the direction of the parents. Of course, anyone working with children knows that this is usually the case anyway.

Negative behaviors are more salient than positive behaviors. Parents and teachers are more likely to notice and attend to a child that behaves aggressively than a child who shares or helps another child solve a problem. The therapeutic discussions on prosocial behaviors bring these types of behavior to the parents' awareness and attention. As you discuss prosocial behaviors with the parents, you are reinforcing the saliency of positive behaviors. The parents are now more likely to tune in to sharing, cooperating, negotiating, and joint problem solving. An encouraging cycle can begin as the children are more frequently attended to for prosocial behaviors and the parents are more encouraged and have better perspective when they are noticing a greater scope of behaviors.

Competitive structure also discourages shy children and children with failing histories from participation. Competitive games can create a more

oppressive environment, increasing aggression and decreasing cooperative, friendly, and sharing behaviors. As a result, children become more
difficult to control, require additional discipline, and decrease teacher's
instructional time. Cooperative games, on the other hand, promote easy
and efficient behavioral change. Subtly training prosocial skills to better
handle interpersonal situations while children are having fun. Cooperative games are also played by everyone in the class or family, thereby min-
imizing group disruption caused by individual treatment programs.

PUTTING IT ALL TOGETHER

Competitive activities are of the greatest concern for children who are already displaying aggressive behavior. Even if the behavior is related to
other factors, the competitive arena reinforces the child to think in an oppositional way. We are not doing these children any favors when we continue competitive exposure. The parents must be educated on the impact
of competition on their children.

Once the parents and children have been made aware of the impact of
cooperative and competitive activities, it's time to intervene. Assess the
child's usual play environments for competitive activities and reduce or
eliminate that activity. Assess for violent or aggressive activities, such as
certain video games, computer games, and favorite television shows, and
eliminate them. Work with the parents to problem-solve each eliminated
activity. Prescribing cooperative activities and cooperative games in family time, sibling play time, and other noted play sources will be extremely
beneficial. Other forms of activities can also be substituted to avoid an
overload of cooperative games; for example, individual games are fine, although they do not enhance the child's interpersonal skills.

CASE ILLUSTRATION

A 6-year-old boy, Sean, was brought into psychotherapy for problems with
aggression and difficulty getting along with his two siblings, a brother age
4 and a sister age 9. Aggressive behavior and isolation had increased over
the past six months. Problem behaviors included breaking toys, destroying
family property, hitting his little brother, not being able to "play nice" with
other children, and not making friends. After a complete intake was done
on the child and family members, the most obvious problem was addressed
first. Sean loved to play video games and played three to four hours per

day. The parents let him play these long hours because he didn't have many friends and it seemed to be the only time Sean was having fun. Many of these games were relatively violent. (This was not discovered until the older sister described the games; the parents were not aware of the violent content.) Most games were played individually, with the opponent built into the game. Some games were played with a friend or sibling and the opponent was then the other person. There were no cooperatively structured games in the entire household and the parents were unclear about the difference between games.

During the second session, the parents were educated about the role and power of children's games. A fair amount of time was spent on describing game effects and how they impact a child. The parents seemed to agree that the video games seemed to be a problem and that Sean did get more aggressive after playing them. However, their concern never evolved into any action because they feared removing his only source of joy. Like so many parents, these parents did not understand the direct impact the games made on their children. The father seemed analytical in nature but also had the attitude that competition never hurt him. It was apparent that Sean's father required more educating on the research and rationale behind cooperative versus competitive games. Once it was established that the parents were in alignment with my agenda, the first intervention was introduced. Parents were asked to remove all aggressive or violent games, video games, and television shows from the child's viewing. They had to purchase some new video games and create house rules for television and videos. In particular, Sean was given a new set of allowable video games but was limited to one hour per day of video play. Consequences for aggressive behavior were briefly discussed (i.e., using time-out consistently and for all children).

By the third session, parents reported improvement in behavior, in particular decreases in aggressive behavior. However, Sean was still not able to "play nice" with his friends or siblings. At times, there were *more* quarrels due to the increased time interacting. Remember, Sean was no longer isolating from family with video games. The intervention this session was to prescribe cooperative game play. Sean was deficient in his prosocial skills. Sharing and cooperating had always felt like a chore or punishment. A cooperative game was practiced in session for a short period until all the family members understood the rules and goals.

A discussion of the impact and experience of this game versus others the family had played was introduced. This was Sean's first experience with the family playing together while not opposing each other. Sean said the cooperative game seemed silly to him at first: There was no loser. Sean was conditioned to believe that relationships were created around a win-lose situation, just as he had experienced in so many of the games he played. He described most of his interactions in terms of somebody winning and somebody losing. He always felt like the loser in his family.

Aggression or isolation were the only forms of interpersonal contact, or lack thereof, that he understood. A discussion of everyone winning then ensued. The more the family played games (and life) in a win-win manner, the more the family might get along. Brainstorming was done with the family on their favorite games and how they might be transformed into cooperative structures. Again, a cooperative activity/game requires that all persons must participate and coordinate with each other to succeed in a shared goal. Each person was then asked to come up with one game, chore, or family activity that could be restructured to a win-win or cooperative goal.

By the fifth session, the family was upbeat and seemed to interact with each other more freely. Sean was definitely more verbal and sat closer to his parents. When asked how things went, the parents reported noticeable improvements and felt in control of what needed to be done. It was apparent to them which skills Sean was missing and how they might be practiced within the family. Sean reported that he missed some of his old games but admitted that he did seem to get upset less and his parents weren't mad at him all the time. On the whole, the children liked the new games and thought it was fun to find ways that the family could do just about anything from a win-win approach. We discussed how the win-win family approach might be introduced into other nongame situations. For example, the mother suggested that weekend chores be set up as a cooperative activity instead of an individual activity. Her idea incorporated having the children, and sometimes parents, help each other to reach a group reward. In her example, the children helped each other make their beds, put their clothes away, and dust the house. A family outing was the reward for all children. I applauded her creative thinking and added that, to prevent the oldest child from being burdened with all the work because she was more capable, it was necessary to make sure the cooperative structure was held in place; that is, that each person must participate in the shared chore to win or else they all lost. This would encourage the oldest child not to do all the work but instead encourage and assist her siblings. Although the mother seemed more excited than anyone else about her idea, the family was willing to try it.

At this point, therapy was directed toward other target play environments (i.e., certain friends and friends' houses, and school). The parents understood my tactics and felt they could carry on in other situations. At two-month follow-up, Sean and his family showed continued improvement. Sean had two new friends and played cooperative games with them at his house. The father reported that the family slacked off for a period of two weeks following a particularly stressful work situation for him. Old problem behaviors started creeping back into the family picture and the parents got the family back on track when they realized what had happened. Although the family still had some complaints, the original reason for seeking treatment, Sean's aggression and isolation, had been resolved and the family was doing better overall.

CONCLUSIONS

The motto here is: The more cooperative play, the better. Die-hard competitors need not worry: The child will still be acquiring competitive skills in myriad other situations. Cooperative games will not make a child passive and cowering. Adding skills to a child's repertoire makes him or her more effective and masterful in his or her environment. Some parents may worry their child needs competitive skills to succeed and be tough. Although the research in no way supports this notion, it is important to validate the parents' fears of their child being hurt or less competent; it is also important to help them discriminate between cooperative skills and passivity. Many of these fears are based on inadequate information and assumptions that cooperative and sharing children are passive, subassertive pushovers. Helping the parents, and sometimes the children, understand the difference between these behaviors will ease their fears.

Introduce cooperative games to siblings. Remember, rivaling siblings will need more instruction and attention when using these games initially. The more aggressive and difficult the relationship, the more likely you have a true skills deficit (not to mention other emotional problems being played out), requiring more instruction and attention to forming more appropriate skills.

If the problems are reported in school or day care environments, you may need to consult with the teachers and have the parents participate in this venture. In this scenario, you may need to educate the teachers and directors about cooperative and competitive games and activities, just as you educated the parents. Their compliance will increase once they become aware that these changes will reduce class aggressiveness on the whole, requiring less teacher discipline. One of the greatest benefits of this treatment is that it is not a specific individualized plan that singles out one child from the rest of the class or disrupts the class in anyway. Gaining teacher trust and compliance should be the therapist's primary action. Once you have that, teacher instruction is minimal and follow-up can be brief. The program sustains itself as the teacher reaps the benefits. Parents can do the follow-up and help the teacher institute new activities.

Cooperative activities and goal structures have been gaining momentum in the school system since the 1970s. This is not *new* material for many educators. Competitively structured activities, however, seem to live on despite clear negative findings from research, as does aggressive and violent content in games, television, and children's toys. Our children are what they play. Don't punish them or view them as problems; they are merely absorbing the surroundings we provide. If that environment is competitive, oppositional, aggressive and violent, then we reap what we sow. Taking games and play seriously, for the powerful influences that they are, will allow all children not only to have fun, but to learn to have fun with each other.

REFERENCES

Acton, H.M., & Zarbatany, L. (1988). Interaction and performance within cooperative groups: Effects on non-handicapped students' attitudes toward their mildly mentally retarded peers. *American Journal of Mental Retardation, 93,* 16–23.

Ames, C. (1981). Competitive versus cooperative reward structures: The influence of individual and group performance factors on achievement attributions and affect. *American Educational Research Journal, 18,* 273–287.

Bay-Hinitz, A.K., Peterson, R.F., & Quilitch, H.R. (1994). Cooperative games: A way to modify aggressive and cooperative behaviors in young children. *Journal of Applied Behavior Analysis, 27,* 435–446.

Boe, R.B. (1977). Economical procedures for the reduction of aggression in a residential setting. *Mental Retardation, 15,* 25–28.

DeVries, D.L., & Slavin, R.E. (1978). Teams-Games-Tournaments (TGT): Review of ten classroom experiments. *Journal of Research and Development in Education, 12,* 28–38.

Helmreich, R.L., Spence, J.T., Beane, W.E., Lucka, G.W., & Mathews, K.A. (1985). Making it in academic psychology: Demographic and personality correlates of attainment. *Journal of Personality and Social Psychology, 39,* 896–908.

Hoving, K.L., Wallace, J.R., & LaForme, G.L. (1979). Aggression during competition: Effects of age, sex, and amount and type of provocation. *Genetic Psychology Monographs, 99,* 251–289.

Hughes, J.D., & Hasbrouck, J.E. (1996). Television violence: Implications for violence prevention. *School Psychology Review, 25,* 134–151.

Johnson, D.W. (1975). Cooperativeness and social perspective taking. *Journal of Personality and Social Psychology, 31,* 241–244.

Johnson, D.W., & Ahlgren, L. (1976). Relationship between student attitudes about cooperation and competition and attitudes toward schooling. *Journal of Educational Psychology, 88,* 92–102.

Johnson, D.W., & Johnson, R.T. (1975). *Learning together and alone: Cooperation, competition, and individualization.* Englewood Cliffs, NJ: Prentice-Hall.

Johnson, D.W., Johnson, R.T., & Anderson, D. (1976). Effects of cooperative versus individualized instruction on student prosocial behavior, attitudes toward learning, and achievement. *Journal of Educational Psychology, 68,* 446–452.

Johnson, D.W., Johnson, R.T., & Scott, L. (1978). The effects of cooperative and individualized instruction in student attitudes and achievement. *Journal of Social Psychology, 104,* 207–216.

Johnson, D.W., Maruyama, G., Johnson, R.T., Nelson, D., & Skon, L. (1981). Effects of cooperative, competitive, and individualistic goal structures on achievement: A meta-analysis. *Psychological Bulletin, 89,* 47–62.

Kernan, J.B. (1983). On the meaning of leisure: An investigation of some determinants of the subjective experience. *Journal of Consumer Research, 9,* 381–392.

Kohn, A. (1983). *No contest: The case against competition.* Boston: Houghton Mifflin.

Madden, N.A., & Slavin, R.E. (1983). Mainstreaming students with mild handicaps: Academic social outcomes. *Review of Educational Research, 53,* 519–569.

Marcus, R.F. (1978, April 27–29). *A reinvestigation of the relationship between cooperation and empathy in young children.* Paper presented at the Biennial Southeastern conference on Human Development, Atlanta, GA.

Murphy, H.A., Hutchison, J.M., & Bailey, J.S. (1983). Behavioral school psychology goes outdoors: The effect of organized games on playground aggression. *Journal of Applied Behavior Analysis, 16,* 29–36.

Orlick, T. (1981). Positive socialization via cooperative games. *Developmental Psychology, 17,* 426–429.

Orlick, T. (1982). *The second cooperative sports and games book.* New York: Pantheon Books.

Phillips, K.M. (1981). Aggression and productiveness in emotionally disturbed children in competitive and non-competitive recreation. *Child Care Quarterly, 10,* 148–156.

Potenza, M.D., & McDougle, C.J. (1998). Potential of atypical antipsychotics in the treatment of nonpsychotic disorders. *CNS Drugs, 9,* 213–232.

Provost, P. (1981). *Immediate effects of film-medicated cooperative games on children's prosocial behavior.* Master's thesis, Ottawa, Canada.

Quanty, M.B. (1976). Aggression catharsis: Experimental investigations and implications. In R. Green & E. O'Neal (Eds.), *Perspectives on aggression* (pp. 99–127). New York: Academic Press.

Quilitch, H.R., & Risley, T.R. (1973). The effects of play materials on social play. *Journal of Applied Behavior Analysis, 6,* 573–578.

Rogers, M., Miller, N., & Hennigan, K. (1981). Cooperative games as an intervention to promote cross-racial acceptance. *American Educational Research Journal, 18,* 513–516.

Sanson, A., & Muccio, C. (1993). The influence of aggressive and neutral cartoons and toys on the behavior of preschool children. *Australian Psychologist, 28,* 93–99.

Sherif, M., Harvey, O.J., White, B.J., Hood, W.R., & Sherif, C.W. (1961). *Intergroup conflict and cooperation: The Robbers' cave experiment.* Norman, OK: University Book Exchange.

Turner, C.W., & Goldsmith, D. (1976). Effects of toy guns and airplanes on children's antisocial free play behavior. *Journal of Experimental Child Psychology, 21,* 303–315.

Wolfe, V.V., Boyd, L.A., & Wolfe, D.A. (1983). Teaching cooperative play to behavior-problem preschool children. *Education and Treatment of Children, 6,* 1–9.

Author Index

Subject Index